BRITISH AND AMERICAN PLAYWRIGHTS

1750–1920

General editors: Martin Banham and Peter Thomson

Henry Arthur Jones

OTHER VOLUMES IN THIS SERIES

To be published in 1982:

TOM ROBERTSON edited by William Tydeman
W.S. GILBERT edited by George Rowell
DAVID GARRICK and GEORGE COLMAN THE ELDER
  edited by E.R. Wood

Further volumes will include:

THOMAS MORTON and GEORGE COLMAN THE YOUNGER
  edited by Barry Sutcliffe
J.R. PLANCHÉ edited by Don Roy
A.W. PINERO edited by Martin Banham
DION BOUCICAULT edited by Peter Thomson
CHARLES READE edited by M. Hammet
TOM TAYLOR edited by Martin Banham
ARTHUR MURPHY and SAMUEL FOOTE edited by George
  Taylor
H.J. BYRON edited by J.T.L. Davis
WILLIAM GILLETTE edited by Don Wilmeth and Rosemary Cullen
AUGUSTIN DALY edited by Don Wilmeth and Rosemary Cullen

Plays by
Henry Arthur Jones

THE SILVER KING
THE CASE OF REBELLIOUS SUSAN
THE LIARS

Edited with an introduction and notes by
Russell Jackson

CAMBRIDGE UNIVERSITY PRESS

Cambridge

London   New York   New Rochelle

Melbourne   Sydney

Published by the Press Syndicate of the University of Cambridge
The Pitt Building, Trumpington Street, Cambridge CB2 1RP
32 East 57th Street, New York, NY 10022, USA
296 Beaconsfield Parade, Middle Park, Melbourne 3206, Australia

First published 1982

Printed in Great Britain at the University Press, Cambridge

Library of Congress catalogue card number: 81-18047

British Library cataloguing in publication data
Jones, Henry Arthur
Plays by Henry Arthur Jones: The silver
king, The case of rebellious Susan, The liars.
– (British and American playwrights, 1750–
1920)
I. Title II. Jackson, Russell III. Series
822'.8   PR4827
ISBN 0 521 23369 0 hard covers
ISBN 0 521 29936 5 paperback

GENERAL EDITORS' PREFACE

It is the primary aim of this series to make available to the British and American theatre plays which were effective in their own time, and which are good enough to be effective still.

Each volume assembles a number of plays, normally by a single author, scrupulously edited but sparingly annotated. Textual variations are recorded where individual editors have found them either essential or interesting. Introductions give an account of the theatrical context, and locate playwrights and plays within it. Biographical and chronological tables, brief bibliographies, and the complete listing of known plays provide information useful in itself, and which also offers guidance and incentive to further exploration.

Many of the plays published in this series have appeared in modern anthologies. Such representation is scarcely distinguishable from anonymity. We have relished the tendency of individual editors to make claims for the dramatists of whom they write. These are not plays best forgotten. They are plays best remembered. If the series is a contribution to theatre history, that is well and good. If it is a contribution to the continuing life of the theatre, that is well and better.

We have been lucky. The Cambridge University Press has supported the venture beyond our legitimate expectations. Acknowledgement is not, in this case, perfunctory. Sarah Stanton's contribution to the series has been substantial, and it has enhanced our work.

Martin Banham
Peter Thomson

CONTENTS

ILLUSTRATIONS

ACKNOWLEDGEMENTS

I am indebted to a number of libraries and museums who have given me access to unpublished material and whose curators and staff have given me invaluable and expert assistance: the Bodleian Library, the British Library, Harvard Theatre Collection, New York Public Library Theatre Collection at Lincoln Center, the Theatre Museum, and the Senate House library of the University of London. The library of the University of Chicago and the Humanities Research Center of the University of Texas have supplied me with microfilm of items in their archives. I am grateful to Mrs Dorinda Maxse for granting me permission to have copies made of her grandfather's letters in the Chicago collection, and to Mr Richard Sylvester for putting me on the track of them. Ms Wendy Warneken, of the theatre collection at the Museum of the City of New York, has been most helpful in providing copies of photographs of New York productions of the plays.

My greatest single debt is to Linda Rosenberg, who has borne patiently with my involvement with Henry Arthur Jones, accepting it as 'an average respectable case'.

Birmingham, June 1981   Russell Jackson

INTRODUCTION

The career of Henry Arthur Jones was a model Victorian success story. He rose from a lower-middle-class, provincial, nonconformist family, was to a great extent self-educated and never lost the diligence and earnestness inculcated by his upbringing. By his mid-thirties he had earned recognition as a rising star in the revival of English dramatic art. William Archer, in an appraisal of Jones published in 1882, before the success of *The Silver King*, observed that he had already done enough 'to establish for his future efforts a fair claim to respectful attention'.[1] By the turn of the century Jones was in the front rank of British dramatists.

Jones was born in 1851 at Grandesborough in Buckinghamshire, where his father was a tenant farmer. The piety, industry and rigorous discipline of the household was described in 'The Days of My Youth', an article published in 1923:

> . . . Dancing, card-playing and theatre going were vices. Lying was a sin to be promptly punished by a severe thrashing. I have never been able to tell a lie without feeling the greatest discomfort and reluctance. This has been a serious disadvantage to me in my extensive dealings with people who are not hampered by the superstitions of an outgrown moral code.[2]

After six years of formal schooling, Jones was sent at the age of twelve to earn his own living as an assistant to his uncle Thomas, a draper in Ramsgate. After three and a half years of this servitude he moved to Gravesend, where he worked for another draper, and at the age of eighteen he moved to London. These years among provincial tradespeople left him with a contempt for their narrow-mindedness that later expressed itself in dramatic caricature.

Despite the restrictions imposed by chapel-going relatives, Jones had contrived to continue his education 'by keeping up a constant and loving acquaintance with the English classics and with some of the French and German masterpieces; by a close study of social and political economy; and by extensive foragings in most of the sciences'. Herbert Spencer and Samuel Darwin particularly absorbed his attention, and he read widely in what he later described as 'the great universal fountains of wisdom and sanity'.[3] When he arrived in London Jones visited the theatre for the first time, an event which changed the direction of his literary studies:

> I left off writing a novel I was engaged upon, and gave most of my leisure to seeing plays and reading Herbert Spencer. I used to hurry from the City almost every evening at six to see the same successful play for perhaps a dozen times, till I could take its mechanism to bits.[4]

For Jones the improvement of his grasp of the playwright's art and of the theatre

1

itself became something of a mission: he later told an interviewer that the stage had a great future 'if it shows itself worthy and up to the scientific movement that began with Darwin'.[5] Meanwhile he worked hard at his trade — initially in London, then as commercial traveller for a Bradford firm — and devoted his leisure to reading, play-writing and amateur theatricals. In 1869 he became engaged and in 1875 he married and set up house in Exeter. It was there, at the Theatre Royal on 11 December 1878, that the first professional performance of a play by Jones took place: *It's Only Round the Corner* (later revised as *Harmony Restored*).

The short pieces that Jones wrote between 1879 and 1882 are conventional and uninspired reworkings of the formulas of domestic drama, with particular emphasis on one theme — the return of the prodigal. In *Hearts of Oak* (Exeter, 1879: later rewritten as *Honour Bright*) a reckless young scapegrace is forced by the effects of his improvidence to give up the family home and seek his fortune in the Queen's service. When he returns from the Colonies, where he has been busy redeeming himself, it is Christmas, and he is just in time to propose marriage to the daughter of the Prettijohns, tenants on the old estate and behind with the rent. He benefits from a change of heart experienced by the new landlord, who abandons his suit to the daughter, hands over a bag of money discovered in the hero's old home and offers to let the farm in future at a nominal rent. The familiar mixture of providence and repentance is here in double measure — both hero and villain reform. Jones managed some touching and amusing scenes of domestic affection, somewhat in the manner of Tom Robertson. *Harmony Restored* appeals to temperance enthusiasms: a blind, alcoholic church organist is about to forfeit his livelihood by sinking back into dissipation, but an appeal to the memory of his dead wife brings him round and he dashes his glass to the ground. In *A Clerical Error*, Jones's first play to be performed in London (Court Theatre, 1879), the scapegrace is Dick Capel, who left his uncle's house after being discovered forging a cheque. In *A Bed of Roses* (Globe, 1882) Charles Vellacott is a prodigal who buries his disgrace by valorous acts in Africa and returns to receive forgiveness for his errors from the heroine: 'Ah, you men don't know what a woman's heart is', she declares, ' — you don't know how we love to forgive.'

Trite and derivative as these brief domestic dramas are, they show Jones learning to please his audience. They were well suited to a theatrical market that required short, sentimental plays for private performances as well as to fill out professional bills in London and in the provinces. In *The Theatre* a reviewer praised *A Bed of Roses* as 'a simple story surrounded by a charming framework redolent of purity and sweetness'. The same journal commended *A Clerical Error*, 'the style of play that ought to win the gratitude of amateur actors, country houses, and middle-class life generally — people in fact who demand something wholesome, interesting, dramatic and pure'. Jones was following the precepts of the actor Wilson Barrett, who urged him after the success of *A Clerical Error* to produce more in the same vein:

> The public are pining for a pure English comedy — with a pure story, in which the characters shall be English, with English ideas, and English

feelings, honest, true men and tender, loving women, and from which plague, pestilence, adultery, fornication, battle, murder and sudden death shall be banished. The author who can do in three acts what you have done in 'A Clerical Error' will take as strong a stand now as Tom Robertson took years ago.[6]

Barrett was an energetic actor-manager, well-established in Leeds and on the provincial circuits, who was anxious to be accepted in London as a purveyor of worthwhile plays in handsome productions. His season at the Court Theatre in 1879–81 featured the Polish star Helena Modjeska in *Romeo and Juliet* (Barrett playing Mercutio), a version by James Mortimer of *La Dame aux Camélias* (*Heartsease*), and a new poetic tragedy, W.G. Wills's *Juana*, with dresses and decorations supervised by E.W. Godwin. It looked for a time as if he might challenge the artistic preeminence of Irving's Lyceum management.[7]

In June 1881 Barrett assumed management of the Princess's in Oxford Street — a well-appointed theatre with a large stage — and opened with a version of *Frou-Frou*, in which Modjeska starred. At the same time he continued to manage theatres in Leeds and Hull, as well as touring companies. The Princess's acquired a reputation as the home of intelligently produced and reasonably literate melodrama. Barrett assembled an efficient supporting company, commissioned scripts which gave the actor-manager his rightful prominence but at the same time allowed decent opportunities for the rest of the cast, and insisted on high standards of scene design and stage management. A eulogy in *The Theatre* in January 1883 claimed that he had 'always been actuated by the highest motives' and always had 'the well-being of the English stage' at heart. His career was presented as a triumph of self-help: 'Step by step, slowly but surely, he has carved out his career, and at last he has mounted high on the ladder of fame.'[8] By this time Barrett had benefitted from the phenomenal critical and popular success of *The Silver King*.

The Silver King was a skilful combination of traditional melodramatic effects and situations, familiar character-types and what passed in the heat of the moment for psychological insight. Wilfred Denver, a dissipated but good-hearted young man, is made to believe that he is a murderer. All the evidence points to Denver and, after disguising himself and saying goodbye to his wife, his children and his faithful old servant Jaikes, he takes to flight. Fortuitously saved from the pursuit that would undoubtedly have led to his arrest, trial and conviction, Denver finds a new life and makes his fortune in Nevada. There he becomes the Silver King, a man of prodigious wealth and power. He returns to save his wife and children from starvation, but cannot reveal his identity to them. Eventually he discovers that he is innocent and is able to bring the true murderer — the burglar Skinner — to justice. In the final moments of the play he is joined by his family and Jaikes in a prayer of thanksgiving for his deliverance. Jones claimed that the original inspiration for the play — the idea of a man who thinks himself guilty but is in fact innocent — derived from a short story he had read in *Good Words*.[9] The false accusation of the hero is a com-

1 Wilson Barrett as Wilfred Denver in *The Silver King*

mon plot-device in melodrama, and Sims's *The Lights of London*, produced by
Barrett in October 1881, had recently furnished a good example of its use – Sims's
hero is a 'prodigal son' who is falsely convicted of a bank robbery. Tom Taylor's
The Ticket of Leave Man (1863) was a famous and popular variation on the same
theme and some commentators thought that *The Silver King* reminded them of
Fitzball's *Jonathan Bradford* (1833). Jones was working in a tradition with well-
established modes of characterisation and using a plot that had the satisfying
pattern of a myth – man's discovery of innocence and awakening to his own
potential and real virtues. Although he was collaborating with Barrett and with a
co-author, Henry Herman (who later disputed his part in the undertaking), Jones
appears to have been responsible for the overall treatment of the story, as well as
for most of the actual writing.[10] The theme was congenial with his own attitudes to
the evolution of the superior being, expressed directly in the epigraph he chose
from Tennyson's *In Memoriam*: 'That men may rise on stepping-stones/Of their
dead selves to higher things.'

The new melodrama was remarkable for lively and unforced dialogue and honest
character-drawing (albeit along familiar lines), but it was also notable for the
absence of certain features that had begun to worry critics by their domination of
contemporary melodrama. There was no spectacular scenery, no sensational special
effects such as were proving wearisome in the plays seen recently at the Adelphi
and Drury Lane. The nadir (it was hoped) had been reached in *Pluck; a Story of
£50,000* by Augustus Harris and Henry Pettit, produced at Drury Lane in August
1882. The incidents of *Pluck* included a double train-crash, the interruption of a
wedding-breakfast (with the arrest of the bridegroom), the placing of the corpse of
a murdered banker inside a Chatwood safe, the chance appearance of most of the
surviving characters outside the Criterion Restaurant during a snowstorm at dead of
night and the reunion in the same place and at the same time of a father and his
long-lost child. The villain was killed in a spectacular conflagration which destroyed
a three-storey slum dwelling. 'What next?' asked the critic of *Vanity Fair*, 'Shall we
dramatise the deluge or the apocalypse?' No expense or exertion had been spared in
the staging, but 'In the mad hunger after "effect" the authors . . . have crushed all
semblance of humanity out of their puppets.'[11] *Pluck* was one of many such spectacles – often with similarly arresting one-word titles – in which consistency and
probability had been abandoned in a manner so gross as to break even the flexible
rules of melodrama. Every year's crop of pantomimes brought similar complaints
from reviewers that spectacle and exciting visual effects were taking over from the
human interest that was the proper source of fun, sentiment and suspense.

The veteran critic George Augustus Sala announced when *The Silver King*
appeared that deliverance was at hand: 'There is a rift in the clouds, a break of blue
in the dramatic heavens, and it seems as if we were [sic] fairly at the end of the
unlovely.' In *The Theatre* an anonymous reviewer insisted that the play was 'pitched
in a much higher key than the ordinary melodramas of the day, and, in truth . . .
must not be confused with the sensational panoramas which nowadays so often

pass for plays'. *The Silver King* was 'thoroughly honest in purpose, dramatic, full of human nature, and, withal, an original drama of English life, sentiment, and feeling'.[12] For Jones the most satisfying notice must have been Matthew Arnold's in *The Pall Mall Gazette*. Arnold's praise of the dialogue was a marvellous compliment from a critic who had held up the French theatre and its dramatists as an example to be followed by the disorganised, inartistic British theatre: ' . . . In general throughout the piece the diction and sentiments are natural, they have sobriety and propriety, they are literature.' He hailed Jones's effort as 'an excellent and hopeful sign' and described Barrett's production as a model of professionalism and artistic integrity:

> Instead of a company with a single powerful and intelligent performer, with two or three middling ones, and the rest moping and mowing in what was not to be called English but rather stagese, here was a whole company of actors, able to speak English, playing intelligently and supporting one another effectively.[13]

Barrett was able to claim on the hundredth night of the run that he had laboured 'to raise what for want of a better word was called melodrama into the region of literature and poetry, and natural tragedy' and to have attempted 'to produce on the melodramatic stage work which would have a more than ephemeral existence.'[14]

The surviving manuscript drafts for the play illustrate Jones's efforts − guided by Barrett − to simplify its narrative and make the high points of the protagonist's career more telling. It seems likely that the text performed at the Princess's in 1882 contained more conventional piety than that prepared by the author for publication some twenty years later, and that considerable modifications had been made before the New York première in 1883. Some discussion of these matters will be found in the appendix (p. 220 below) together with the New York text of a scene omitted from the published version. Jones's anxiety to avoid sensationalism for its own sake is beyond doubt. He drafted but rejected a number of more picturesque and violent dénouements, including one in which Skinner went after Denver with an air-pistol and fought hand-to-hand with him. Instead he settled for the simple irony − reminiscent of *Le Tartuffe* − with which the villain instructs the detective to arrest the murderer of Geoffrey Ware. Although the action hinges on a train-crash no train is seen on stage, and the temptation was resisted of showing any striking and spectacular representation of the well-known sights of London. The underworld 'colour' is amusing and unelaborate, and the villain chooses to live in respectable, quiet Bromley, rather than in the midst of the high society he robs for a living. The attempts to show how the 'upper ten thousand' pass their time that had made 'Adelphi guests' a by-word for the unconvincing assumption of sophistication did not appeal to Jones and Barrett. The rural scenes are simple and amusing, without any heavy emphasis on the traditional opposition of virtuous country and vicious town. One effect of this restraint is to throw into greater relief the principal character, Denver. Apart from Skinner's striking scene at the beginning of act III, when he is seen at his villa, it is Denver who has the best moments: his discovery of the corpse in act I; his soliloquy after the escape from the wrecked train in act II; his return from exile in act III (Barrett suggested the tableau of Denver standing in the snow listening to the hymn); his disguise as Dicky and his description of the nightmare in act IV. Denver's major speeches — inspirational, visionary, pathetic — form the 'sensations' of the play and although to some critics, including Arnold, the descriptions of Denver's escape and his nightmare seemed excessively rhetorical and forced, there is no question that the focus is on character and feeling rather than scenic display.

It must be admitted that a good deal of the characterisation in *The Silver King* is rudimentary. Jaikes is a tiresome repetition of a type familiar on the English stage since old Adam offered Orlando his life-savings in *As You Like It*. Both he and Nelly Denver, a standard victim-heroine, illustrate the precision of Jerome K. Jerome's satire in *Stage-land*, where the good old man and the heroine (pushed out into the snow with her children) are lovingly anatomised.[15] Baxter, the detective, is notable chiefly for his ability to arrive just too late to prevent things happening, despite his air of knowing ubiquity. More adroit is the use made of stock characterisation in Corkett, the cockney who progresses from gambling to theft and prison, and Selwyn, the secretary who passes a forged cheque but is rescued from ruin by his kind and wise employer. Both reflect Denver's career as a redeemed sinner. With Ware, Jones skilfully plays on the audience's expectations by setting up a potential villain of a conventional kind (the man who wanted to marry the heroine and bears a grudge) and killing him off at the end of the first act. With the death of Ware the disengaged professional criminal Skinner, 'the Spider', takes over.

Skinner is for the modern reader the play's most interesting character, not least by virtue of his sophistication and sardonic detachment in a dramatic world where moral virtues and the proper degree of commitment to them are of paramount importance. His motives for cruelty to Nelly Denver and her family and his wish to see Denver caught and convicted are not personal in accordance with the traditional formulas of villainy. There is nothing mysteriously evil about 'the Spider', he simply needs to save his own skin. At the same time a peculiar abstract distaste for the poor informs his reasons to Olive for turning Nelly off the estate (in act III, scene 1) even before he knows whose widow she is. Details of the stagecraft reinforce the impact he makes as a sinister figure. As he prepares for the burglary in act I the stage is darkened and his white shirt-front and sleeves are picked out by the lime-light. The blazing fire in his Bromley villa is a contrast with the meagre fire kindled by Jaikes in the cottage — when Coombe comes to take possession he first takes up a commanding position in front of the fire. When the family group has reassembled around the garden seat in act V (p. 100) Skinner looms up behind them, a visible expression of the threat to the Denvers's peace and security. His manners and self-possession distinguish Skinner from the men he has to employ: Corkett's later assumption of a 'swell's' nonchalance and his loud clothes serve to emphasise Skinner's real elegance. E.S. Willard, who appeared as Skinner at the

Princess's, gave a powerful and convincing account of the character and (noted *The Era*) 'was occasionally hissed, but the hisses were compliments to his accomplished acting'. Clement Scott singled out as particularly effective Skinner's reaction to the revelation that turns the tables on him in the final scene: 'Then came the white face and the quivering lip, the ashen expression of a desperate man at bay.'[16]

The Silver King was a turning point in Jones's career and a great asset to Barrett, who kept it in his repertoire for many years. But to all intents and purposes melodrama was a dead end for the dramatist. Jones was at least working on a larger scale than that of his Robertsonian domestic dramas, but there is little to distinguish his subsequent work for Barrett from the efforts of popular hacks like Sims, Pettit, Merritt and Augustus Harris. In *Hoodman Blind* (1885) and *The Lord Harry* (1886) Jones seemed to have taken a step backward. Mark Lezzard, villain of *Hoodman Blind*, is sad stuff after the urbane Skinner: 'Oh if I could torture you and him − if I could but once stick my teeth into your two hearts (*Gnaws stick which he carries.*) − and gnaw them bit by bit, and then − go straight to hell for it!'[17] *The Noble Vagabond* (1886), *Hard Hit* (1887) and *Heart of Hearts* (1887) were more or less efficient reworkings of hackneyed material but they served their immediate purpose of keeping Jones's name before the public as author of marketable plays for the popular theatre. He firmly believed that the theatre should be improved from within. 'No sympathy', he wrote in 1915, 'should be given to dramatists, however lofty their aims, who will not study to please the general body of playgoers of their age.'[18] Jones had great faith in the public's judgement, but in the course of his career this faith was tried on a number of occasions when he made a move to break out of the confinement imposed by popular taste and prejudice.

   One such occasion was the production of *Saints and Sinners* in 1884. Jones attempted to bring out something superior to 'the cheaper and coarser art of melodrama', but he relied on a frankly melodramatic plot, in which a dissenting minister's daughter runs away with an unscrupulous philanderer, bringing disgrace and ruin to herself and her father. The original ending of the play − reinstated in the published text − was unhappy, but Jones was persuaded to save the minister's daughter from the death he proposed for her, and to give her a new lease of life with a sweetheart providentially brought back from the Colonies. The serious burden of the piece consisted in the representation of the minister as a man of principle defeated and brought down by hard-hearted, sanctimonious and hypocritical members of his congregation, one of whom − the villainous Hoggard − absconds with the 'Penny Bank' and is saved by his victim from the pursuit of an angry mob. *Saints and Sinners* was a commercial success, but to Jones's dismay the opening night was disrupted by the audience's objections to the use of scriptural expressions by unsympathetic characters − a painful instance of the pious triviality of mind he had grown up with and had satirised in the play. In the January 1885 issue of *The Nineteenth Century* Jones defended the dramatist's right to deal with religion and its professors, insisting that he should be allowed to discuss and depict the whole of human life, with 'perfect freedom of choice of subject, persons, place, and mode of treatment'.[19]

In *The Middleman* (Shaftesbury Theatre, 1889) Jones moved into another area of potential controversy, the relations between capital and labour. Willard played Cyrus Blenkarn, a brilliantly inventive potter who is exploited by his snobbish, vulgar and ambitious employer. The climax of the play is provided by Blenkarn's struggle to achieve an elusive glaze whose secret has been lost for centuries but the rediscovery of which will make the manufacturer's fortune and save him from bankruptcy. Possession of the successful formula enables Blenkarn to take over the enterprise and dictate the terms of a happy ending. Jones gives an amusing satirical picture of the electioneering process and there is a romantic subplot in which the capitalist's son hopes to marry the potter's daughter but is expected by his father to make a politically and socially advantageous match with one of the local nobility.

The Middleman is vigorous, often amusing and generally well-constructed, with a substantial character part at its centre and plenty of good roles for the rest of a company. It represents an advance from *The Silver King* in so far as conflict and tension now arise ostensibly from the social and economic situation of the characters — the threats to the livelihood of the hero and his family are identifiable as similar to the problems of everyday life. Denver's years of work and his transformation into the wealthy, venerable and justice-dispensing 'Silver King' of Nevada are not as vividly presented as Blenkarn's on-stage struggle for the glaze (although Denver's account of his nightmare helps to give him a heroic, quasi-mythical status). Blenkarn's faith is in his prowess as a technician, Denver's is a more conventional faith in God's providence. Compared with Galsworthy's *Strife* and Granville-Barker's *The Madras House*, Jones's analysis of economic and social life seems timid and lacking in penetration. The conflict between industrial and aristocratic, land-derived wealth is not treated with any fresh insight and represents no great advance on Tom Taylor's *New Men and Old Acres* (1869). A.B. Walkley detected an element of *réclame* in Jones's adoption of the subject, 'at a time when sociology is being brought home to all our doors, and economics are served up hot with the morning muffin'.[20] Nevertheless *The Middleman* shows Jones engaged in the business of reconciling serious issues with what could 'go' on stage. It also shows him evolving the formula that was to serve him well for a good many years (if not with such spectacular results as Blenkarn's glaze achieves): the life-struggles of the man of principle.

It seems reasonable to suggest that this theme — in which a man of principle fights for his integrity against the blandishments and threats of a self-seeking, cynical world — bore direct relation to his own career as a dramatic author. The sense of personal spiritual responsibility and guilt (a sense fostered by his religious upbringing), anger at the stupidity and narrowness of provincial life, sympathy for the prophet who is ignored and persecuted in his own country — these themes dominate many of Jones's plays. His men of principle are often religious by profession (*Judah*, *Michael and his Lost Angel*, *Saints and Sinners*, *The Hypocrites*) or possessed by some other unworldly faith. They are put to the test by their fellow-men, who do not understand their motives or their high-minded concern with moral absolutes. Sometimes – as with the 'philistines' of *The Triumph of the Philistines* (St James's, 1895) – their opposition to the hero is a combination of misguided religious and social principle with envy of the idealist's freedom of spirit.

Usually there is a woman in the case, as a focus for the animosity of the hero's adversaries and as a threat in herself. Women stir up the baser instincts of the finest beings. Thus Drusilla Ives in *The Dancing Girl* (Haymarket, 1891), 'two-thirds delightful Quaker innocence, one-third the devil's own wit and mischief', having forsaken her sternly puritan home village, becomes a skirt-dancer and is taken up by the Duke of Guisebury. Guisebury, as it happens, owns the village but spends too much time on a life of debauchery in London to bother with essential maintenance and repairs. Drusilla's attractions tempt John Christianson, one of the stern puritans, who defends himself appropriately: ' . . . Set any price upon yourself! I'll pay it! I'll give you all – all – save only my word, my faith, my soul! I will not pay them for you! Not them! Not them! No! No! No!'[21] The connection between Guisebury and Drusilla is a means of involving the career of the temptress and her victim with the livelihood of a community, but Jones makes the point unskilfully: because of Guisebury's failure to build a breakwater, the men of the village give up the attempt to make a living out of the sea and enlist *en masse* for a polar expedition.

Better handled, but still within the melodramatic tradition, is the story of David Remon in *The Masqueraders*, produced by George Alexander at the St James's in 1894. Remon is an unworldly – indeed, other-worldly – astronomer who falls in love with Dulcie Larondie, a well-born girl who has been obliged by a fall in the family fortunes to take a job as barmaid in a local inn. She longs for London ('I was made for society! Oh, for London! Oh, for pleasure!') and her wishes are granted when, at a charity ball, one of her kisses is auctioned to the raffish Lord Skene. Remon bids recklessly against the rake, but to no avail. When in due course Dulcie marries Skene she becomes a leader of society. But Skene is a brutal, stupid spendthrift. Remon attends one of her brilliant receptions and the falsity of her position is patent to him. He admonishes Dulcie:

> Your trouble isn't real. This society world of yours isn't the real world. There's one little star in Andromeda where everything is real. You've wandered amongst these shadows when you should have stayed at home . . . They are only masquerading. Good God, I think we are all masquerading!

By the final act Remon has won possession of Dulcie and her child by drawing cards with Skene, but her sister persuades him not to live with his prize: 'Make this one sacrifice. Keep her pure for her child. I know the woman who gives herself to another man while her husband is still alive betrays her sex, and is a bad woman . . . '[22] Remon sets off to Africa on an expedition whose rigours may well be the death of him. If he comes back alive, and if Skene obliges by dying in the meantime, he will be reunited with Dulcie. If things do not fall out, they will certainly meet 'In that little star in Andromeda', and the play ends with a tableau of Remon setting off through the snow, while Dulcie watches through the window.

More miserable is the fate that Jones reserves for the title character of *Michael and his Lost Angel* (Lyceum, 1896) in which Johnston Forbes-Robertson played an ascetic high-church priest who sacrifices his calling and his chastity to his passion for Audrie Lesden, a worldly, charming and magically sensual woman. By the logic of his integrity Michael, who at the beginning of the play extracted a public confession from the erring daughter of a parishioner, feels that he must make a similar avowal. He does so at the ceremony that is to celebrate extensive renovations which have been carried out in his church — renovations paid for in part by his temptress. She is to be the 'angel' in his life, replacing his dead mother in that office, but Michael is obliged by his guilty conscience to give up his mission (which, it seems, would involve the spiritual cleansing of the nation). They die in exile but not happily united. The failure of this play angered and saddened Jones. There had been disagreement between him and his interpreters from the beginning of rehearsals. Mrs Patrick Campbell resigned the role of Audrie a few days before the first night, after Jones had refused to make alterations in her part. Forbes-Robertson had tried to persuade the author to change his title ('lost angel' had been for many years 'a term for a lady of pleasure') and appears to have lost faith in the play. The controversy that *Michael and his Lost Angel* aroused might have kept it in good business for some time, and Jones felt betrayed by its withdrawal after ten nights.[23]

The failure of *Michael and his Lost Angel* was another shock to Jones's belief that the commercial theatre could do justice to the work of a serious playwright. Five years earlier with *The Crusaders* he had gone into management on his own account, taking the Avenue Theatre and decorating the stage in accordance with the principles of one of the sages he most admired:

> I gave William Morris *carte blanche* for the scenery and furniture, and he advised me on the whole production. I engaged the best possible cast, filling even the small parts with actors of great ability. It was hooted and booed, and again I met with the general condemnation of the London press. I lost four thousand pounds, and had to go out and collect the general public around me again.[24]

The plot of *The Crusaders* has a man of principle — this time his higher purpose is social reform — in love with a woman but renouncing her in order to protect her reputation and allow her the prospect of marriage to another man. Jones treats his hero with a mixture of respect and suspicion, and loads the dice against social reformers in general by printing a quotation from Emerson in the programme: 'Rely on the laws of gravity. Every stone will fall where it is due. The good globe is faithful and carries us securely through celestial spaces. We need not assist the administration of the universe.'[25] The presence in the play of Mr Burge Jawle, the

Great Pessimist Philosopher, and Mr Palsam, Vice-President of the London Reformation League — respectively a gross and a lesser humbug — makes it hard to believe that the shining vision of the hero's mission has any chance of becoming reality. Irony and caricature support the argument for *laissez-faire*, while the language of inspiration and dedication are left to uphold the hero's dignity and our sympathy for him.

Jones remained convinced that a popular drama of ideals was both essential to the well-being of the British theatre and an eminent practical possibility. The drama of ideas appealed to him less. In 1919 he wrote that 'the Theatre does not, cannot and ought not to teach directly, and with obtrusive malice aforethought', summing up an opinion he had held for many years and which had figured among the lessons taught him by Barrett.[26] He had an autodidact's admiration for the authority of the 'great universal fountains of wisdom and sanity' and visitors remarked on the fact that his library shelves were well-stocked with the standard authors: an interviewer in 1894 noticed two shelves devoted to Ruskin and Matthew Arnold, another two filled by Huxley, Darwin, Herbert Spencer and Ibsen, and the balance consisting of the English and foreign classics. Arnold was always a major source of support and inspiration: 'Arnold consistently sends out the loftiest and most invigorating religious strains and impulses. We can lean upon him and face the darkness with him.' It was Arnold, Jones claimed in 1923, 'who chiefly propped my mind and steered my course'.[27] Although he came to admire Ibsen as 'a tense and shattering genius', thought him 'a frowning landmark in the domain of drama', and was temperamentally inclined to feel that his earnestness and idealism demanded respect and study, Jones sided at first with the critics who found his work 'parochial' and unpleasant. In the prologue to his verse-drama *The Tempter* (Haymarket, 1893) Jones urged his audience not to follow

> the bleak Norwegian's barren quest
> For deathless beauty's self and holy zest
> Of rapturous martyrdom in some base strife
> Of petty dullards, soused in native filth.[28]

Jones often spoke and wrote of the need for reform in theatrical censorship, but he made it clear that the right he demanded for the playwright was that of dealing with the passions of men and women 'in the broad, wise, searching morality of the Bible and Shakespeare'.[29] His preference for ideals over ideas sometimes led him into know-nothing philistinism, particularly in the later phase of his career when he saw himself as champion of the British spirit against the forces of scepticism and anarchy. In a reply to William Poel's criticism of his pamphlet *Patriotism and Popular Education* he exclaimed: 'How thankful we may be that "ideas" were not invented in Shakespeare's time!'[30]

From the mid-1880s Jones's ideals and aspirations became familiar to the public through a stream of letters to the press, articles, pamphlets, speeches and interviews, some of which were collected in *The Renascence of the English Drama* (1895) and

The Foundations of a National Drama (1913). In a letter to the critic, Moy Thomas, Jones attempted to make clear his position as a polemicist: his article 'A Dramatic Renascence', published in 1884, was written 'with no presumptuous intention of setting the dramatic world in order, and with no thought of dictating to the many better and cleverer writers for the stage than myself, but rather with a view of putting my own house in order, of keeping myself on the right path, and of publicly marking out a course that I may not be hereafter tempted to depart from'.[31] Jones suggested in 'The Dramatic Outlook' that well-wishers of the drama should keep themselves in 'a state of wholesome, watchful discontent', a phrase which reflects his religious background.[32] The critical writings may be seen as a Whole Theatrical Duty of Man, in which Jones treats his own career as a witness or testimony to something greater than himself. In the preface to *The Theatre of Ideas* Jones appears as a representative dramatist, doing battle with the forces of philistinism and the market-place but hoping to come to some arrangement with them. His support of the scheme for a National Theatre and advocacy of municipal theatres show how far he was prepared to go in abandoning his cherished belief in *laissez-faire* for the sake of the art he loved. On the other hand, plays like *Carnac Sahib* — a feeble military melodrama produced by Tree in 1899 — show how far he was willing to compromise with the commercial theatre. Although he supported the Stage Society and the Independent Theatre, Jones was suspicious of 'advanced' literary and theatrical coteries, and of any withdrawal from the wider theatrical world. That world had to be met and conquered on its own terms.

In the account of his progress which prefaces *The Theatre of Ideas* Jones recalled his collaboration with Sir Charles Wyndham and Mary Moore as a piece of great good fortune, marking a decisive point in his career. From Wyndham he was able to get 'a very finished performance of my comedies' which were in consequence 'uniformly and universally successful'.[33] Working for Barrett had taught Jones how to write full-length plays with 'strong' situations for a good melodramatic actor and using big casts on a large stage. Wyndham was an intimate actor, firmly established as an intelligent, charming and skilful representative of roles high on the social scale. The Criterion and Wyndham's (which opened in 1899) were both intimate theatres where finesse was called for from playwright and actor. The parts that Jones created for Wyndham were older, experienced, sympathetic men-of-the-world with a touch of pathos and a hint of courage. Wyndham was able to irradiate them with charm and youthfulness, giving them powerful romantic appeal. Irene Vanbrugh gives a vivid picture of him in the 1890s:

> Rather a rough-hewn face, capable of being transformed into any character. A somewhat nasal voice, graceful figure, expressive hands and swift, definite movements. Each step in accord with the thought in his mind. He was unerring in his timing and every look and tone in his voice created an illusion round the woman he was in love with in the play and marked her as his goddess.

She listened many times to his delivery of Deering's long speech in the final act of *The Liars*: ' . . . Nothing has ever taught me more than listening to him night after night; the variations, the sincerity and the polish were a revelation to me.'[34]

The best of the characters Jones wrote for Wyndham were Sir Richard Kato in *The Case of Rebellious Susan* (1894), Colonel Sir Christopher Deering in *The Liars* (1897) and Sir Daniel Carteret in *Mrs Dane's Defence* (1900). All are supposed to possess authority in the world as confirmation of their function as *raisonneur* in the play: Kato and Carteret are lawyers, Deering a military man. It is their experience and wisdom, rather than any special idealism, that has entitled them to this authority and to the audience's respect. They speak frequently for the modification of ideal standards of conduct in the light of the practical possibilities of life, and they advocate the accommodation of the desire for personal fulfilment to the limitations imposed by society. They are not perfect themselves, nor are they immune to heart-stirrings. They are in every sense 'men of the world'. Although Jones was capable of a return to the earlier patterns of melodrama (as in *Carnac Sahib*) or man-of-principle plays (including *The Physician*, produced by Wyndham in 1897) after the success of *The Case of Rebellious Susan* most of his energy was channelled into social comedies with an upper-class setting and a subtler, more consistently realistic method. In these plays recognisable and imperfect men and women cope with problems less exalted than Remon's little star in Andromeda or Michael's pursuit of truth and spirituality. One consequence of this change of direction was the necessity of showing marriage and the contemporary married woman on stage.

Jones's idealists had been accompanied by the appropriate women, cast in the traditional moulds as saints or temptresses or, on occasion, an intriguing combination of the two. Even when his women are granted the needs and desires that contemporary social mores deemed acceptable only in men, Jones makes them undergo the redemption-through-misery that convention demanded. Pinero's heroine in *The Notorious Mrs Ebbsmith* (1895) and Herminia Barton in Grant Allen's novel *The Woman who Did* (1895) both suffer wretched defeat as a reward for their courage in making it a matter of principle to live with a man out of wedlock. Jones, in his society comedies, does not raise the odds this high: his heroines feel frustration as a result of the moral code that binds them to an uncongenial husband or fetters them to the consequences of a past mistake, but they do not generalise their situation into a reforming campaign against the institutions of civilised life. There is often a sense that this might be the next step — and in Jones's favour it might be argued that he intends the audience to feel this possibility — but the step is not taken. Lady Susan and Lady Jessica are campaigning for nothing more than their right to be loved and understood, 'Mrs Dane' — more pathetically — for her right to a place in society. Current anxieties and jokes about the 'New Woman' and the debate about divorce-law reform have a bearing on the response of audiences to the plays at the time of their first production, but they are not the true subject of the society comedies.

The Case of Rebellious Susan has a simple plot. Lady Susan, exasperated by the habitual infidelity of her dull husband, decides to pay him back in his own coin and separates from him. In Cairo she becomes involved with a young man whom she meets at her hotel, but the extent of this involvement is not made clear. Sir Richard Kato, a QC and an old family friend, dissuades her from going too far. She renounces her love for the young man and agrees to a reconciliation with her husband. Jones intended to make things more difficult for his characters and for the audience by implying that Lady Susan's behaviour in Cairo had gone a step beyond flirtation. Wyndham persuaded him that the imputation of unchastity would be unacceptable, insisting that it was also improper in a playwright:

> I stand as bewildered today as ever at finding an author, a clean-living, clear-minded man, hoping to extract laughter from an audience on the score of a woman's impurity. I can realise the picture of a bad woman and her natural and desirable end being portrayed, but that amusement pure and simple should be expected from the sacrifice of that one indispensable quality in respect for womanhood astounds me.[35]

Wyndham argued that Jones appeared at first to be setting out that, in Kato's words in act I, there is no 'gander sauce' but had ended by suggesting that there was indeed such a commodity:

> No man, to my mind, who has daughters of his own can advance such a theory as you wish in this piece — that a weak woman often goes to these extremes and then when there is no other refuge left, sneaks back to her husband's bed. I am not speaking as a moralist, I am simply voicing the public instinct.[36]

In the event, after Jones had made Lady Susan's account of what happened in Cairo equivocal, audiences appear to have been happy to accept that the character was too sympathetic to allow of anything other than an innocent interpretation. William Archer, for one, came away from the theatre with a strange feeling that he had heard one thing and understood another.[37]

It may well be that *The Case of Rebellious Susan* in its original state would have been only superficially more adventurous. Jones could not have come to a truly radical conclusion, endorsing Lady Susan's rebellion, and the present version, in which hers is 'an average respectable case', is the more effective for showing just that. We are given a sense of how the world seemed in the 1890s to a rich, bored young woman at once livelier in spirit and more circumscribed in her life than her ineffectual but actively unfaithful partner. Harabin is a stupid man, and there is real pathos in Lady Susan's acquiescence in the final scene as her friends reiterate the 'worldly wisdom' on marriage and men:

> LADY DARBY: You see, dear, we poor women cannot retaliate.
> LADY SUSAN: I see.
> LADY DARBY: We must be patient.

> INEZ: And forgive the wretches till they learn constancy.
> LADY SUSAN: I see.
> LADY DARBY: And, dear, yours is a respectable average case after all.
> LADY SUSAN: Yes, a respectable average case after all.

Harabin offers a villa at Cannes and jewellery as part of the settlement. It is clear that having his wife back is largely a matter of healing his wounded self-respect, and he never displays any real understanding or feeling (although he is allowed to be miserable as a result of the separation). His promises of future affection are not necessarily hypocritical, merely demonstrative of his failure to perceive what is at stake for Lady Susan:

> HARABIN: . . . How well you look, Sue! I'll take you down Bond Street
>   tomorrow morning and buy you — the whole street! I have never
>   loved you so much as I do at this moment.
> LADY SUSAN: How long will your love last? For three weeks?
> HARABIN: For three weeks? For life!
> LADY SUSAN: Are you sure? Love me, Jim! I want to be loved!

A reviewer in *The Theatre* found the play's conclusion very near to tragedy: ' . . . There can never be any true happiness in such a reunion, for Lady Susan has an aching void in her heart which can never be filled . . . so that the woman suffers, and the man goes unscathed.' But the effect was softened by the tone of the play, its 'bright and sparkling dialogue'.[38]

Jones does not make explicit the consequences of a separation from her husband and an affair with Lucien Edensor, but they would have been perfectly intelligible to an audience in 1894. Lady Susan and her lover would have been social outcasts, isolated and drifting in the kind of life described by Deering in his long speech towards the conclusion of *The Liars* (pp. 215–16 below). A contemporary audience might also have inferred that Edensor — who may nowadays seem excessively boyish and submissive — had to be 'saved' from the ruin of his career, much as it is the business of Sir Daniel Carteret in *Mrs Dane's Defence* to 'save' young Lionel from the woman with a past. Kato is labouring for the sake of the future, as represented in the young man. The urgent dispatch of Edensor to New Zealand is somewhat melodramatic, but Jacomb's account of his engagement and marriage has a comic touch that enables us to view the young lover with some detachment, as part of a brisk, practical, masculine world from which Lady Susan is excluded. Given the choice between a young man's career and a woman's happiness it seems that we are expected to opt for the former. In *The Liars* there is a stronger sense of this: men are the providers in society and the maintainers of civilisation, a national investment that must not be sacrificed to a woman's affections.

Three couples are present to set beside Lady Susan and her husband. Two of them — the Admiral and his wife, Kato and Inez — exemplify the reward of worldly wisdom qualified by sentiment and sensitivity. The third, Elaine Shrimpton and

Fergusson Pybus, are caricature radicals. Elaine has features familiar in anti-feminist humour of the period: she is severe, arrogant, mannish, argumentative and graceless. *Punch* was full of the type and Sydney Grundy had put a squadron of the harridans on stage in *The New Woman* (Comedy Theatre, 1894). Pinero's Agnes Ebbsmith, whom he treats with sympathy, is described in a stage direction as wearing a dress 'plain to the verge of coarseness', with little colour in a face which is 'at the first glance almost wholly unattractive'. When Agnes (formerly known as 'Mad Agnes') harangues the Duke of St Olpherts, it is 'With changed manner, flashing eyes, harsh voice and violent gestures'.[39] The introduction by Jones of a 'New Woman' of this kind highlights the elegance and poise of Lady Susan. Pybus, with his combination of fawning and self-obsession, may even create some fellow-feeling for Harabin. The couple's presence also allows Kato to adopt in his dealings with them a tone that would not be appropriate to his diplomatic handling of Lady Susan's problem:

> While you ladies without passions — or with distorted and defeated passions — are raving and trumpeting all over the country, that wise, grim, old grandmother of us all, Dame Nature, is simply laughing up her sleeve and snapping her fingers at you and your new epochs and new movements. Go home! Be sure that old Dame Nature will choose her own darlings to carry on her schemes. Go home! Go home! Nature's darling woman is a stay-at-home woman, a woman who wants to be a good wife and a good mother, and cares very little for anything else . . .

This, rather than the 'gander sauce' speech, is the ideological centre of the play. Lady Susan's case is dealt with on the level of what is permissible in society, but Elaine is treated to a sermon on the future of the race — a sermon that derives from Jones's interest in evolution, social and biological, and which is not far removed from the tone of other conservative male perspectives on the women's movement in the 1890s. A columnist in *The Spectator* had argued in these terms in April 1894 in a consideration of 'The "Claims" of Women', affirming 'the perma-nent faith that is in us — *viz*, that the laws of Nature will not be upset because a few scores of clever women, sometimes eloquent and not unfrequently pretty, are receiving from a languidly amused public permission to protest that their sex, [in] default of women's political and social rights, is hideously oppressed'. The writer concedes that just now society is in an easy-going, liberal mood but he looks for-ward to a change:

> The wave of pity is at flood now; by 1925 it will have receded, leaving behind it, we hope, many inestimable treasures, but also, we feel certain, leaving many gaps; and among them that placid content of women with their unalterable destiny, which in so many countries has been one secret of their power.[40]

Kato's rhetoric — distasteful as it may be — is unusual rather by its energy than its sentiments. The comic form taken by Elaine's agitation — mobilising the Clapham telegraphists — was not as fantastic as it may now appear. In 1895 the Women's Protective League backed a strike at a weaving mill in Glasgow, which involved (wrote an adversary) 'the girls going about begging at football matches and other public places, rioting, boycotting, and being demoralized in various ways'.[41] Kato's 'Go home!' and the Admiral's kindly injunction to 'Shake down!' are pleas for the acceptance of the *status quo* — in the one case as natural law, in the other as good sense if you want a tolerable life. In order to add to our feeling that Lady Susan's opposition to the 'double standard' of morality is comprehensible but unwise, we are given the comic and sentimental exchanges in which Kato and Inez agree that the ludicrously exhaustive lists of their past loves cancel each other out — reassurance that loving relationships are formed by sensible, worldly, tolerant men and women.

Elaine's insistence on marrying before she is mistress of her inheritance obliges her to live in Clapham. This provides what is clearly meant as a comically appropriate setting for her social activism. She has a mission to Clapham and at the same time she is dramatising the oppression which she and womankind suffer — forced into the dreariest suburbs. But it represents the play's only acknowledgement of a world outside the privileged West End (or its colonial outpost in Cairo). There is no sense of commerce or work in the play apart from the references to Kato's business as a lawyer and the Admiral's absences at sea. This is the rarefied atmosphere in which women have little to do except fulfil social engagements. Lady Susan does not have any children (would this have suggested the extent of her estrangement from Harabin?) and no function in life. In *The Liars* the sense of futility is more pronounced, and there is a strong feeling that Falkner must be rescued not only from a potentially disastrous emotional tangle but from an enervating environment. He must remain a man of action and in his case we are expected to believe that the nation waits anxiously for his decision — only he can deal with the native chiefs and bring off the struggle against slavery. As in *The Case of Rebellious Susan*, the task of the *raisonneur* is to prevent a flirtation turning into an affair. Again, the husband is an unprepossessing figure — although this time his behaviour might well turn an innocent encounter between his wife and another man into the basis for something more serious. Once more Jones offers parallels for the principal married couple — Freddie Tatton and Lady Rosamund, Archibald and Dolly Coke — and the Wyndham character is paired off with a warm, intelligent woman. Before Beatrice Ebernoe sets foot on stage she is heard playing the piano. Archer remarked that Wyndham's 'Yes' in reply to the question, 'Is that not Mrs Ebernoe?' conveyed the fact that Deering is 'devotedly, chivalrously, adoringly in love with this Mrs Ebernoe who, be it observed, we have not seen and of whom we know nothing'. Wyndham's 'Yes' deserved 'to rank with Lord Burleigh's nod in point of conversation'.[42]

Deering is engaged in two intrigues: a serious campaign to steer Lady Jessica and Falkner away from a *liaison* that would ruin them and a comic plot devised to keep the Nepean brothers from discovering the truth about a *rendez-vous* arranged by the lovers. Jones gets a good deal of fun out of the dinner in act II, which is discussed throughout the act but served, with comic urgency, only in the last moments. In the third act character after character has to be included in the intrigue, until the deception begins to collapse under the strain (which is augmented by the dilemma of a man who finds it difficult to tell a lie). Then the atmosphere changes in the final sequence of the act, surprising the characters and the audience with Falkner's sincere declaration of love. It was this act that Jones claimed came to him 'not as a sequence of situations, but at one glance, as one sees a landscape, foreground and middle distance and background all at once'.[43] The change brought about by Falkner's announcement leaves the audience in suspense during the interval and demands a change in Deering's function. He now has to redouble his efforts to part the lovers, to persuade Falkner that duty calls, and at the same time convince Nepean that nothing serious has happened. Deering becomes the stage manager of his own apartment-sized theatre, with a handy concealment space at his disposal and a compelling reason for his actors and actresses to keep up a brisk pace — Deering must pack for the expedition. Beatrice Ebernoe has to make up her mind to marry him, Lady Jessica and Falkner must be brought to their senses, Nepean must be persuaded he has grounds for reconciliation. Jones has set himself and Deering an agenda that many dramatists would spend four acts on. The business of packing and the frequent glances at his watch maintain the act's momentum and sense of comedy. If it is accepted that the long speech in which Deering describes to the lovers the consequences of their affair was in Wyndham's performance a compelling and brilliant passage Jones's technical achievement in this act can be acknowledged.

It is made clear in the course of the act that Lady Jessica is excluded from the world inhabited by Falkner, not merely by the social conventions that will outlaw her if she runs off with him, but by the fact that her temperament and way of life do not suit her to the life he must lead. Beatrice Ebernoe has the proper qualifications for whatever 'women's work' awaits her with the expeditionary force: Lady Jessica does not, and is reclaimed in a manner that is awkward and sad. Nepean must give Deering a 'message' to his wife, who is in fact overhearing them from behind the curtain.

> SIR CHRISTOPHER: Will you let me take a message to her? May I tell her that for the future you will treat her with every kindness and consideration?
> GILBERT: Yes — yes. Say — oh — tell her what you please. Say I know I've behaved like a bear. Tell her I'm sorry, and if she'll come home I'll do my best to make her happy in future.
> SIR CHRISTOPHER: And (*taking out watch*) it's rather too late for dinner, may I suggest an invitation to supper?
> GILBERT: Yes — yes.

As they leave for their supper at the Savoy, Jones brings Falkner forward 'in great despair'. Lady Jessica returns to the wealth, ease and boredom she hoped to escape from. She must accept that her idea of Falkner was only a 'fancy picture' of him, a lie in itself. The hazardous expedition unites Deering, Falkner and Beatrice and the final curtain falls on the picture of Deering with 'one arm round each affectionately':

Tomorrow! My wife! My friend! My two comrades!

They have been liberated to a life of strenuous idealism.

It is surprising to find some contemporary critics taking Jones to task for cynicism or unpleasantness. *The Era*'s description of *The Case of Rebellious Susan* shows how daring that play could appear even in its altered state:

> The note of loose morality so subtly and cleverly struck; the caustic wit of many of the lines; the sensuous sexuality of the wife-and-lover scene in the second act; the deliberate cynicism of the intention; the attacks on the New Woman and the jaunty handling of the everlasting adultery difficulty combine to create this result; and we have little doubt that Mr Wyndham's fashionable following, and the sets and sub-sets who follow *them*, will crowd the stalls and boxes of the Criterion Theatre for many weeks to come.[44]

Moy Thomas, reviewing *The Liars* in *The Graphic*, complained of the 'needlessly harsh flavour' that was 'not confined to the title of this brilliant and original production': 'The crude, bitter taste of the sloe recurs rather frequently in the dialogue of its first two acts, and surely the defects in its leading personages are drawn with too uncompromising a hand.' Lady Jessica was an 'insolent, selfish, self-willed and provoking personage' and Falkner's infatuation with her made him 'cut a contemptible figure'. The return of Lady Jessica to Nepean was a sufficient punishment for her 'faults' and it was a tribute to Mary Moore's skill 'that the spectators were not allowed to lose interest in her proceedings'.[45] *Punch*'s critic wrote that it was a mistake to allow Lady Jessica ('that irritating, flirty flighty little person, the liar-in-chief') to look back at Falkner, which he construed as 'just one attempt at winning the sympathy of the audience':

> This is most decidedly a mistake; there should have been no secret parting with her devoted lover, leaving the audience in doubt as to what really took place at that final meeting; and if the husband . . . is compelled by the author to propose an enjoyable supper-party, we ought to see at a glance how, in another second, she will be all smiles and enthusiasm over a delicious pâté and inspiring champagne.[46]

Perhaps, it was suggested, Mary Moore had persuaded Jones to treat Lady Jessica more leniently than she deserved. These criticisms of Jones's handling of his theme and the personality of his characters amply illustrate the conservatism of playgoers in the decades before the Great War — evidence more telling than the celebrated attacks of Clement Scott on Ibsen. They also support Shaw's contention that Jones habitually flattered his characters by transferring to them his own qualities of mind: in *The Physician* Lady Val was 'very carefully studied' from life but departed from it 'in respect of a certain energy of vision and conscience that belong to Mr Jones and not in the least to herself'.[47]

Elsewhere Shaw wrote that his own plays had as their 'one overwhelming characteristic' the friction between people on 'different planes of thought, of character, of civilization & of class prejudice', but the 'ordinary Pinero—Jones—Grundy play' presented characters who were on the same plane in these respects, and imposed on them a conflict that was 'purely external and artificial'.[48] In the third phase of his career — between the middle of the 1890s and the outbreak of the Great War — Jones sometimes came near to achieving a drama where conflict arises from the sources nominated by Shaw. In *The Lackey's Carnival* (Duke of York's, 1900) Max Beerbohm recognised a praiseworthy attempt to avoid the usual clichés and see the phenomenon of domestic service from the employee's perspective. Unfortunately the principal character — a valet whose knowledge of the family secrets gives him power over his masters — was too stagey and glamorous and the plotting of his defeat too conventional.[49] *The Heroic Stubbs* (Terry's, 1906) begins promisingly, with a bootmaker's infatuation with one of his aristocratic clients, but soon turns into well-travelled paths as he pursues her to the seaside, rescues her from the attentions of a notorious seducer and delivers her, her reputation and virtue intact, to the husband she was bored with. The servility expected of Edwardian shop-keepers and their staff and the pathetic sentimentality of Stubbs's love for his customer complement each other in an amusing way, and there is a suggestion that the class he serves is unworthy of his respect. Unfortunately, Stubbs has none of the dynamism and energy that Wells or Bennett might give such a character: Jones seems to be inviting his audience to patronise him.

In this phase of his career Jones returned to themes and situations he had treated earlier, looking at them in a fresh light and sometimes feeling able to be more explicit about the sins and errors that give impetus to the dramatic situation. In *The Hypocrites* (first London performance 1907) one of the issues that confront the ascetic, idealistic curate is the paternity of an illegitimate child, along with the political and commercial leverage of a brewery in his small provincial parish and the arguments of a man of the world who for once is on the wrong side. The sinister advantages of not telling the truth and the existence of an illegitimate child (passed off as hers by her unscrupulous sister) combine to strip the heroine of *The Lie* of reputation, marriage prospects and any joy in life. First performed in New York in 1914 *The Lie* was revived in 1923 by Sybil Thorndike and Lewis Casson and gave Jones a temporary post-war currency as author of a compelling, unpretentious 'shocker' with a star part for a fine tragic actress. The nerve that is touched in *The Case of Rebellious Susan* when Harabin complains that he has been betrayed on all sides — 'My servants, my tradesmen and confounded womankind' — is probed again in *Joseph Entangled* (Haymarket, 1904) where Jones gives the rejected husband a scene reminiscent of Strindberg's hunted males:

You have thrown dust in my eyes! you are all of you in a league against
me! You and your friends and your servants! They come to me with lies so
palpable, so thick, they can't swallow them. I see, I feel, I know, I've been
deceived. I, good heavens, my servants pity me! I see it in their faces.
(*going to her and losing all self-control*) I say you have deceived me with
this man! If you haven't, satisfy me . . . [50]

As well as these somewhat sombre plays of deceit and sexual relations Jones produced treatments in a lighter mood: *Dolly Reforming Herself* (Haymarket, 1908),
The Manoeuvres of Jane (Haymarket, 1898) and *Whitewashing Julia* (Garrick,
1903). Dolly's self-reform is an attempt to cut down the amount by which she
exceeds her dress allowance, Jane's manoeuvres are innocent and only superficially
dangerous to her health and reputation, and Julia's 'past', although doubtful, does
not offer as much of a threat as that unearthed by interrogation in *Mrs Dane's
Defence.*

The last two decades of Jones's life were darkened by poor health and an oppressive
sense that the intellectual world had left him behind. He engaged in bitter and shrill
polemics against Shaw and Wells, whose attitude to the war he interpreted as that
of virtual fifth columnists and agents for Bolshevism. *My Dears Wells: a Manual for
Haters of England* (1921) and the pamphlet *Mr Mayor of Shakespeare's Town*
(privately printed in 1926) make sad reading. In the latter Jones attacked the invitation to Shaw as proposer of the toast to Shakespeare's memory at the 1925
celebration of the poet's birthday. Gaunt's description of England — 'this other
Eden, demi-paradise' — is contrasted with Shaw's allegedly subversive and anti-
English pronouncements. Shakespeare had figured before in Jones's attacks on
intellectuals who did not wholeheartedly support the war against Germany. In
Shakespeare and Germany (1916) he responded to the enemy's claim that
Shakespeare would have taken their side:

> [Shakespeare] would be congenially employed in hounding and routing all
> the legion tribes of cranks, freaks, windbags, wordsters, and impossibilists
> that infect our island; all the crazy pacifists, whose mewlings and pukings
> have brought about this war; all the slugabeds and time-servers and
> pleasure-seekers, that have lulled themselves with the sleepy drench of that
> lake of forgetfulness and sloth, wherein England has lain sprawling for the
> last generation.[51]

In the prose satire *The Theatre of Ideas* (1915) Shaw appeared under the guise of
the 'polyfadistic impossibilist' and the 'cranks, freaks, windbags and wordsters'
appeared as the eponymous subject of *The Pacifists* (St James's, 1917). In the crude
one-act propaganda sketch *Fall In, Rookies!* (Alhambra, 1910) Jones had demon-
strated the capacity of military training for turning a village drunkard into a worthwhile human being, and had shown his hero defying the cringing, whining and

comic cranks campaigning for pacifism. Although the energy and freedom from 'forgetfulness and sloth' that he found in America led him to bring out a number of his plays there, Jones was deeply patriotic and was genuinely appalled by the sacrifice of national defence to liberal ideology.

The bitterness of Jones's declining years was recalled by St-John Ervine when he reviewed Doris Arthur Jones's *Life and Letters* in 1930. Jones once told him of the severity of his illness and the continual pain and discomfort that it caused: ' "That's why I wrote all those bad plays!" he added, with a pathetic look of regret on his kindly face.'[52] After a visit to Ellen Terry in 1924 he found he was at once cheered and saddened by the contrast of her 'inexhaustible gaiety of heart' and 'abiding charm' with his own state of mind:

> . . . I am still in peevish rebellion against old age, the condition of the drama, the impending dangers to the British Empire, the clumsy structure of the prostate gland, and other evils that magnify themselves by reason of my enforced leisure . . . All my life I have alternated between extravagant good spirits and these black months with giant despair.[53]

The attentions of his family supported Jones through the disappointments and suffering of his last decade. He died peacefully on 7 January 1929.

Jones's last message to his public, conveyed in his will, was characteristically modest and dignified. His successes had been great but there had been failures – 'several occasions when I have felt encouraged to offer the Public my best work, regardless of popular success'. He had tried to capture 'that wide and popular approbation without which no dramatist can hope for influence and authority'. He had done his best to elevate drama to the level of literature, by encouraging the reading and study of modern plays and by personal efforts 'to draw English men of letters to the Theatre'. He was conscious of having 'largely failed' in this:

> It is with some hope that the causes I have advocated may yet succeed that I ask English men of letters and English playgoers to accept from me, in a spirit of forbearance and friendliness, this legacy of a last few words.[54]

The obituaries were for the most part respectful but restrained. H.M. Walbrook wrote in *The Observer* that Jones's best works – *The Case of Rebellious Susan* and *The Liars* – were 'little more than storms in tea-cups, but managed with an art, observation and humour of the finest and most delicate'. When Doris Arthur Jones's *Life and Letters* appeared in 1930 a reviewer in *The Times* dismissed Jones's plays as not being 'original in the richest sense', but admitted that he had at least given the public what it wanted 'in a quality which had not been provided for a century'.[55] In 1932 Richard A. Cordell's book-length study, *Henry Arthur Jones and the Modern Drama*, concluded with the assertion that even if Jones was not 'a first-rate dramatist' he was due a 'generous share' of the credit 'for restoring the drama in England to its rightful position as a civilized and civilizing art'.[56]

Measured by one of the standards Jones set himself — the need for plays 'of great passion or serious intellectual import' — he seems to have achieved no more than an honourable defeat, a demonstration of the restrictions imposed upon a playwright by the conservative theatregoing public of the period. On a number of occasions Jones confronted this powerful force and lost, at other times he made what now appear shameful peace treaties. His early adaptation (with Herman) of *A Doll's House* has Flossie (Nora) decide to continue living with her husband ('Nothing has happened,' we are told in the final line, 'except that Flossie was a child yesterday: today she is a woman.')[57] Several of his plays in the 1880s were written to a formula he no longer believed in, gave him little other than financial satisfaction at the time and occasioned considerable regret when he came to look back on them. Even conscientious and fair-minded actor-managers like Wyndham could take their public only a little way towards accepting certain issues as the province of dramatic art. The rules were simple: plays should have a love-interest; they should present a satisfying resolution with no practical or ethical ambiguities; there should be little or no irony or cynicism in the author's approach to those characters with whom he expected the audience to sympathise, and the characters in question should have unimpeachable moral credentials; plays should be optimistic in outlook; anything unpleasantly specific about birth, death, sexuality, drunkenness or disease should be avoided. Some of these rules were enforced informally by the public itself, some were implemented by its legally appointed guardians, the Lord Chamberlain and his readers. It was a remarkable achievement on Jones's part that he managed despite these by-laws to produce popular plays that were on the whole intelligent, to create believable characters speaking interesting and credible dialogue and to raise important moral issues. The Shavian or Wildean strategy — of mocking the conventions while insisting on taking them *au pied de la lettre* — did not appeal to Jones's temperament. Perhaps that lifelong fear of deceit held him back from the imaginative leap that turned the traditions of farce into *The Importance of Being Earnest* or romantic military drama into *Arms and the Man*. When Shaw's critics complained that his Bluntschli did not behave like a real soldier, he answered as 'A Dramatic Realist' that his character was based on the truth about military life. When Jones was reproved for alleged inaccuracies in *The Bauble Shop* (Criterion, 1893) he was genuinely annoyed and depressed by the criticism: had he not taken great pains to verify every detail of Parliamentary procedure?

In the history of British nineteenth-century drama, Jones exemplifies what could be done by a skilful, honest writer without breaking through the accepted conventions of public taste. He had begun his career by writing in the manner of Tom Robertson, he achieved one of the best melodramas ever written, he managed to some degree to turn the methods he had learned to the service of a serious drama, and he created society comedies with an edge of scepticism. The direction taken by Jones's literary ambitions may have been altered by that first experience of the live theatre — *Leah* with Miss Bateman — but there was a sense in which they remained constant. The great task he was labouring at was the creation of a drama that would rank on an equal footing with other literature, that would be read, discussed and performed with intelligence and skill, and which would hasten the evolution of an audience capable of still higher things. Literary ambition was in itself a powerful force in the development of the Victorian theatre. In the notes for a final chapter to his unfinished book on Henry Irving Jones pondered the difference between 'theatre' and 'drama'. One of the conclusions he reached is imbued with the bitterness that came of his years striving to assert the playwright's claims against the rival authorities of the actor's own temperament, financial responsibilities and ambitions:

> Now the drama always implies, always has to contain theatrical entertainment. But theatrical entertainment does not mean drama. You cannot have good drama without also having good theatrical entertainment. But you may have theatrical entertainment that is the very curse and bane and hangman's rope to drama.[58]

The three plays in this collection have been chosen with a view to representing Jones by his best work in both the popular melodramatic tradition (*The Silver King*) and the more sophisticated mode of the Society Comedy (*The Liars*). *The Case of Rebellious Susan* has been included as a commercially successful play which illustrates the difficulty for a dramatist of Jones's generation of writing with comic detachment about a controversial moral and social issue. It has been preferred to *Michael and his Lost Angel* (which the author inclined to regard as his best work) on the ground that it shows what the commercial theatre could accept rather than what it could not. The principal characters of *The Case of Rebellious Susan* convince as a picture of contemporary motivation, feeling and opinion, although the modern reader may be alienated by the play's wistfully reactionary tone and unsatisfied by its resolution. All three plays show Jones as William Archer described him in *The Old Drama and the New*, 'a born playwright, an irrepressible practitioner of the dramatic form'.[59]

NOTES

1   William Archer, *English Dramatists of Today* (1882), p. 225.
2   Quoted by Richard A. Cordell, *Henry Arthur Jones and the Modern Drama* (New York, 1932), p. 21.
3   Doris Arthur Jones, *The Life and Letters of Henry Arthur Jones* (1930), p. 31 (referred to subsequently as *Life and Letters*). Letter from HAJ quoted by Aubrey Ward Goodenough, 'Henry Arthur Jones: A Study in Dramatic Compromise', (unpublished PhD thesis, Iowa, 1920).
4   *Life and Letters*, p. 34.
5   Quoted by Goodenough, 'Henry Arthur Jones', p. 84.
6   Reviews in *The Theatre*, n.s. V (March 1882), 176; n.s. II (December 1880), 369. Barrett's advice in a letter to HAJ, 30 October 1881, in the Brotherton Collection, University of Leeds. See Marjorie Thompson, 'Henry Arthur Jones and Wilson Barrett, Some Correspondence, 1879–1904', *Theatre Notebook*, XI (1957), 42–50; p. 44.

7   Despite his early promise as a London manager, Barrett suffered a number of disappointments in his career, and relinquished his management of the Princess's in 1886. In addition to *The Silver King* his name was particularly associated with his own religious melodrama, *The Sign of the Cross*. He died in 1904. For a useful account of his work at the Princess's, see Raymond Mander and Joe Mitchenson, *The Lost Theatres of London* (2nd edn, 1976), pp. 41–3.

8   Austin Brereton, 'Wilson Barrett', *The Theatre*, n.s. VII (January 1883), 33–41; p. 33.

9   The story, 'Dead in the Desert', by H.C. Pauling, appeared in *Good Words* (1863), pp. 810–13. Denver's rise to wealth may be compared to that of the 'Bonanza Kings' of Virginia City, Nevada: their mines brought in $150 million in twenty-two years.

10   See appendix, pp. 220–4 below.

11   *Vanity Fair*, 12 August 1882.

12   Sala, review in *Illustrated London News*, 25 November 1882; anonymous notice in *The Theatre*, n.s. VI (December 1882), 357–60.

13   Brander Matthews, ed., Matthew Arnold, *Letters of an Old Playgoer* (*Publications of the Dramatic Museum of Columbia University*, series 4, number 4, New York, 1919), pp. 23–8.

14   Reported in *The Times*, 19 March 1883.

15   'After her husband has been found guilty of murder, which is about the least thing that can ever happen to him . . . and the home of her childhood has been sold up, then her infant goes and contracts a lingering fever.' (*Stage-Land: Curious Habits and Customs of its Inhabitants*, 1889, p. 15). George Barrett was successful in the part of Jaikes, but Mary Eastlake as Nelly Denver was too lachrymose for most of the critics.

16   *The Era*, 18 October 1882; *Illustrated London News*, 25 November 1882. In Barrett's *Hamlet* (1884) Willard played an unconventionally plausible and attractive Claudius. He later went into management on his own account.

17   *Hoodman Blind*, licensing copy in the Lord Chamberlain's Collection of Plays, British Library, MS. Add. 53341 (I).

18   Preface to *The Theatre of Ideas* (1915), p. 9.

19   'Religion and the Stage', in *The Renascence of the English Drama* (1895) pp. 26–55; p. 28.

20   A.B. Walkley, *Playhouse Impressions* (1892), p. 116.

21   *The Dancing Girl* (French's edn, 1907), p. 71.

22   *The Masqueraders* (Macmillan's edn, 1899), pp. 56–7; *ibid.*, p. 111.

23   See *Life and Letters*, pp. 172–80.

24   Preface to *The Theatre of Ideas*, p. 12.

25   *The Crusaders* (Macmillan's edn, 1892), p. xiii. HAJ reported to the American impresario H.M. Palmer that despite an 'awful' first night ('in fact a number of people were sent in to hiss the piece') and bad notices, the play was doing well in its first week, with 'every prospect of a long run' (letter dated 4 November 1891, Harvard Theatre Collection). The play closed on 30 January 1892, and was replaced by a revival of *Judah*.

26   Letter, 'Reconstruction of the Theatre', *The Morning Post*, 9 April 1910.

27   HAJ's library described by J. Angus Hamilton, 'Henry Arthur Jones', *Munsey's Magazine*, XI (New York, 1894), 174–8. HAJ's article, 'My Religion', *Daily Express*, 24 September 1923.

28   *The Tempter* (Macmillan's edn, 1898), Prologue (unnumbered page).
29   'The Corner Stones of Modern Drama', lecture delivered at Harvard, 31 October 1906, in *The Foundations of a National Drama* (1913), pp. 20–43; p. 37.
30   Letter dated 10 April 1919, Henry Arthur Jones Collection, University of London Library, Senate House.
31   'The Dramatic Outlook', *The Renascence of the English Drama*, pp. 153–93; p. 156.
32   Letter dated 11 July 1884, University of Chicago Library.
33   Preface to *The Theatre of Ideas*, p. 13. Recent accounts of Wyndham's life and work by George Rowell and Wendy Trewin are listed in the bibliography, p. 227 below.
34   Dame Irene Vanbrugh, *To Tell My Story* (1948), pp. 37, 38.
35   Quoted in *Life and Letters*, pp. 164–5.
36   *Ibid.*, p. 166.
37   William Archer, *The Theatrical 'World' of 1894* (1895), p. 269.
38   *The Theatre*, n.s. XXII (November 1894), 249–51. The possibility of tragedy is raised in the play itself (p. 126 below) and in the postscript of Jones's letter of dedication (p. 107 below).
39   Arthur Wing Pinero, *The Notorious Mrs Ebbsmith* (1895), pp. 14, 89. For a discussion of the 'New Woman' stereotype see Gail Cunningham, *The New Woman and the Victorian Novel* (1978).
40   *The Spectator*, 7 April 1894.
41   Reported in *The Englishwoman's Journal*, 15 January 1895, from a letter published by *The Morning Post*, a leading conservative newspaper.
42   William Archer, *The Theatrical 'World' of 1897* (1898), p. 283.
43   From HAJ's reply to a questionnaire sent to him in 1923, reprinted in *Life and Letters*, pp. 433–7; p. 433.
44   *The Era*, 6 October 1894. Compare Kate Terry Gielgud's opinion of Lady Susan as a 'silly, petulant, spoiled child'. (*An Autobiography* (1953) p. 170.)
45   *The Graphic*, 16 October 1897.
46   *Punch*, 23 October 1897. French's edition omits the final look of farewell: see note to p. 218 below.
47   Shaw, *Our Theatres in the Nineties* (3 vols, 1932), III, 93.
48   Shaw, letter to William Archer, dated 30 August 1904, in Dan H. Laurence (ed.), *Collected Letters . . . 1874–1897* (1965), p. 450.
49   Max Beerbohm, *Around Theatres* (1953), pp. 104–5: 'Hitherto, the dramatist had been content to use servants as a means of unfolding the past of their betters at the beginning of the first act, after which they were allowed to subside into fitful and bald announcements that dinner was served or the carriage waiting.'
50   *Joseph Entangled* (French's edn, 1906), p. 122.
51   *Shakespeare and Germany* (1916), pp. 111–12.
52   *The Observer*, 18 February 1930.
53   Letter to Brander Matthews, 9 July 1924, quoted in *Life and Letters*, pp. 368–9.
54   *Life and Letters*, p. 408.
55   *The Observer*, 13 January 1929; *The Times*, 13 May 1930.
56   Cordell, *Henry Arthur Jones and the Modern Drama*, pp. 252–3.
57   Henry Arthur Jones and Henry Herman, *Breaking a Butterfly* (privately

printed, 1884), p. 76. Jones later 'repented' of the violence he had done to Ibsen, but he denied that his own work had been influenced by the Norwegian's. Resemblances between his 'man of principle' plots and similar patterns in Ibsen were, he insisted, coincidental. See, for example, *Life and Letters*, pp. 87–8.

58   *The Shadow of Henry Irving* (1931), p. 108.
59   William Archer, *The Old Drama and the New: An Essay in Re-valuation* (1923), p. 293.

BIOGRAPHICAL RECORD

20 September 1851	Henry Arthur Jones born at Grandesborough, Buckinghamshire, eldest son of Silvanus and Elizabeth Jones, tenant farmers and nonconformists. HAJ educated locally until age of 12, when he is sent to work for his father's brother, a draper in Ramsgate. His self-education continues. After three and a half years he moves to another draper in Gravesend. Writes first play at age of 16.
1869	HAJ moves to London, where he visits a theatre for the first time (Kate Bateman in *Leah* at the Haymarket) and resolves to be a dramatist. Becomes engaged to Jane Eliza Seeley, daughter of Richard Seeley, manufacturer of artificial flowers.
1870–8	Works as commercial traveller for drapery firms in London, Bradford, Exeter. Spends his spare time writing and appearing in amateur theatricals (début as second gravedigger in *Hamlet*, 1871). Plays include *The Golden Calf*, unperformed, unpublished and derived from Lytton's *Money*.
2 September 1875	HAJ and Jane Seeley married. Three-volume novel about clergyman who commits murder refused by Kegan Paul. Takes house in Exeter, where they live for six years.
1877	First child, stillborn.
11 December 1878	First performance of a play by HAJ, *It's Only Round the Corner* (later retitled *Harmony Restored*) at Theatre Royal, Exeter, by Wybert Rousby's company. Jones subsidises performance by agreeing to take half of dress-circle.
1879	Second child, Philip (d. 1896).
13 August 1879	Wilson Barrett produces *Harmony Restored* at Grand, Leeds.
13 October 1879	Barrett produces *A Clerical Error* at Court, London. Success of this (the first performance of one of his plays in London) decides HAJ to give up trade and devote himself to playwriting.
1880	Third child, Winifred.
6 November 1880	Barrett produces *An Old Master* as curtain-raiser to Edwin Booth's *Hamlet*. HAJ moves to Hampton Wick.
16 April 1881	*His Wife*, HAJ's first full-length play to reach performance, staged at Sadler's Wells: based on novel, *A Prodigal Daughter*, by Mark Hope.
26 January 1882	One-act comedy, *A Bed of Roses*, produced at Globe.

16 November 1882	Success of *The Silver King* (collaboration with Henry Herman) at Princess's brings HAJ financial security and critical acclaim. Cast includes Wilson Barrett, E.S. Willard and Mary Eastlake.
1883–5	HAJ writes a number of plays that are not taken up by managements or published (*Rex, Vladimir, The Jolly Waterman, The Wedding Guest*) and publishes his first important article, 'The Theatre and the Mob'. Third child, Ethelwyn, born in 1883.
3 March 1884	*Breaking a Butterfly*, adaptation (with Herman) of *A Doll's House*, produced at Prince's: cast includes Tree, Kyrle Bellew, Miss Lingard.
1884	Fourth child, Gertrude.
22 May 1884	*Chatterton* (again with Herman) produced by Barrett at Princess's: one-act drama, notable for monologue – 'What's the use of poetry!' – and 'realization' of Wallis's painting, *The Death of Chatterton*.
25 September 1884	Thorne produces *Saints and Sinners* at Vaudeville, after performances at Greenwich and Margate, with E.S. Willard in principal role. HAJ upset by Thorne's insistence on a revised, 'happy' ending and public's objection to use of scriptural quotations by unsympathetic characters.
7 October 1884	HAJ's first public speech, 'The Dramatic Outlook', at Playgoers' Club.
1885	First visit to United States.
18 August 1885	*Hoodman Blind* (collaboration with Barrett) at Princess's. One of a series of melodramas for Barrett and other managers written with a growing sense of dissatisfaction with the genre: *The Lord Harry* (Barrett, Princess's 1886), *The Noble Vagabond* (Princess's, 1886), *Hard Hit* (Tree, Haymarket, 1887), *Heart of Hearts* (Vaudeville, 1887). Meanwhile a comedy, *Welcome, Little Stranger*, is refused a licence by the Lord Chamberlain's office on account of its suggestion that a childbirth is taking place off stage.
1888	Fifth child, Jenny.
27 April 1889	Tree produces *Wealth* at Haymarket.
27 August 1889	*The Middleman* produced at Shaftesbury, with Willard as Cyrus Blenkarn. First notable success since *The Silver King*.
16 November 1889	HAJ publishes letter on the performance of plays in music-halls in the *Daily Telegraph*: first of a series of contributions to the debate on the contradictions of the censorship system.
21 May 1890	*Judah* produced by Willard at Shaftesbury.

27 August 1890	Willard appears in one-act comedy *The Deacon* at Shaftesbury.
1891	After change in American copyright laws makes it possible to publish plays without risk of piracy in United States, HAJ publishes *Saints and Sinners.*
15 January 1891	Tree produces *The Dancing Girl* at Haymarket, with Julia Neilson as Drusilla Ives.
2 November 1891	HAJ goes into management on his own account to produce *The Crusaders* at Avenue: sets from designs by William Morris, innovation of free programmes. Play's failure entails loss to HAJ of more than £4000.
1891	On visit to New York HAJ meets Brander Matthews, who becomes one of his closest friends and supporters in America. Quarrel with Willard over actor's changes to ending of *Wealth* during American tour.
1893	Sixth child, Lucien.
26 January 1893	*The Bauble Shop* at Criterion marks beginning of HAJ's successful collaboration with Charles Wyndham.
20 September 1893	Despite Tree's lavish production and energetic performance of the title role (the Devil) HAJ's verse-tragedy *The Tempter* fails at Haymarket.
28 April 1894	First work for George Alexander, *The Masqueraders*, produced at St James's, with Mrs Patrick Campbell.
3 October 1894	Success of *The Case of Rebellious Susan* at Criterion (Wyndham and Mary Moore).
1895	Publishes collection of articles, speeches and other writings on the theatre, *The Renascence of the English Drama.*
11 May 1895	Alexander produces *The Triumph of the Philistines, and how Mr Jorgan Preserved the Morals of Market Pewbury under Very Trying Circumstances.* (Closes after only 44 performances at St James's.)
15 January 1896	Johnston Forbes-Robertson produces *Michael and his Lost Angel* at Lyceum: Mrs Patrick Campbell withdraws at late stage in rehearsals after disagreements with HAJ. Marion Terry takes over. Forbes-Robertson decides to close after 10 performances.
21 April 1896	*The Rogue's Comedy* (with Willard) at Garrick: HAJ called on stage and 'booed for 25 minutes' on first night.
1897	Wyndham produces two plays by HAJ at Criterion: *The Physician* (25 March) and *The Liars* (6 October). HAJ writes *The Goal*, with Irving in mind (acted in United States in 1914; first performed in London at Palace Theatre in 1919)

	and *Grace Mary*, one-act tragedy in Cornish dialect (unperformed).
29 October 1898	*The Manoeuvres of Jane* produced at Haymarket, with Cyril Maude and Winifred Emery; successful (281 performances) despite a poor reception in the press.
12 April 1899	*Carnac Sahib* produced by Tree at Her Majesty's.
26 September 1900	Allen Aynesworth appears in *The Lackey's Carnival* at Duke of York's.
9 October 1900	*Mrs Dane's Defence* successful at Wyndham's (Charles Wyndham, Lena Ashwell, Mary Moore): runs 209 performances.
11 March 1902	*The Princess's Nose* produced at Duke of York's, with H.B. Irving and Irene Vanbrugh: unsuccessful.
9 September 1902	*Chance, the Idol* produced at Wyndham's, with Lena Ashwell and H.V. Esmond.
2 March 1903	*Whitewashing Julia* successful at Garrick (Arthur Bourchier, Violet Vanbrugh), but the decision to bar Walkley, the *Times* critic, from attending the first performance causes controversy.
19 January 1904	*Joseph Entangled* produced at Haymarket, with Cyril Maude.
18 March 1904	HAJ lectures at the Royal Institution on 'The Foundations of a National Drama'. Continues his support for censorship reform and the establishment of an endowed theatre.
27 August 1904	*The Chevaleer* produced by Bourchier at Garrick: withdrawn at end of October.
1905	Writes *The Sword of Gideon* (unacted).
24 January 1906	*The Heroic Stubbs* (Terry's Theatre).
30 August 1906	*The Hypocrites* given copyright performance in Hull and American première at Hudson Theatre, New York.
31 October 1906	HAJ lectures at Harvard on 'The Corner Stones of Modern Drama'.
June 1907	Returns to Harvard to receive honorary degree.
27 August 1907	London première of *The Hypocrites* at Hicks's Theatre, produced by Charles Frohman in partnership with HAJ.
September 1907	Performances of *The Evangelist* at Knickerbocker Theatre, New York on 30 September and (as *The Galilean's Victory*) at Stockport on 25 September.
3 November 1908	*Dolly Reforming Herself* (Haymarket, with Robert Loraine and Ethel Irving) gives HAJ his first London success for some time.
20 December 1909	Sketch, *The Knife*, produced at Palace, with Bourchier and Violet Vanbrugh.
24 October 1910	Sketch, *Fall in, Rookies!*, performed at Alhambra, extols virtues of military training for working class.

31 December 1910	*We Can't be as Bad as All That* produced at Nazimova's Theatre, New York (first British performance 1916).
11 September 1911	Alexander produces *The Ogre* at St James's.
1 February 1912	Margaret Anglin appears in *Lydia Gilmore* at Lyceum Theatre, New York.
April–May 1912	HAJ writing *The Divine Gift.*
June 1912	HAJ suffers physical and nervous breakdown on return from United States. Cancer diagnosed. Undergoes major surgery (colotomy) which leaves him a semi-invalid.
1913	Publication of *The Divine Gift*, with dedication to Gilbert Murray. Collection of essays, *The Foundations of a National Drama.*
18 September 1913	*Mary Goes First* produced at Playhouse.
26 October 1914	*The Goal* produced at Princess's Theatre, New York.
24 December 1914	*The Lie* produced at Harris's Theatre, New York.
1915	Jones quarrels with Shaw, outraged by what he considers treacherous public comments on the war with Germany.
27 December 1915	*Cock o' the Walk* produced at Cohan Theatre, New York.
1916	*Shakespeare and Germany*, pamphlet, written during Battle of Verdun.
4 September 1917	*The Pacifists*, 'parable in farce', produced at St James's. HAJ's last play to be staged.
1919	*Patriotism and Popular Education* published.
20 May 1919	London première of *The Goal* at Palace.
1921	Attacks on H.G. Wells published together as *My Dear Wells: A Manual for Haters of England.*
1923	Six chapters of projected book, *Bernard Shaw as Thinker*, appear in *English Review.*
13 October 1923	London première of *The Lie* at New Theatre, a success (Sybil Thorndike, Lewis Casson).
1925	More chapters on Shaw appear as *What is Capital?* Attack on choice of Shaw to speak at Shakespeare's birthday celebration, *Mr Mayor of Shakespeare's Town*, withdrawn by printer for fear of libel action. *Angina pectoris* further weakens HAJ's health.
1925	*Representative Plays* in four volumes, edited by Clayton Hamilton, appears in United States. HAJ increasingly reliant on alcohol to keep going: kidneys begin to fail.
1926	Two major operations: supra-pubic cystotomy and removal of prostate. *Representative Plays* published in Britain.
7 January 1929	Death.

NOTE ON THE TEXTS

Like Pinero and Shaw, Henry Arthur Jones took pains to see that his plays were performed in accordance with his intentions and were made available to the reader in well-printed texts, free from the clutter of stage directions that disfigured 'acting editions'. When he was established as a dramatist he prided himself on his ability to deliver to managers a printed copy of the play before rehearsals began, and he liked to have an active part in the preparation of the performance — although circumstances and temperaments did not always make this easy. These texts, printed privately by the Chiswick Press, were used in the theatre, were submitted to the Lord Chamberlain's office for licensing purposes and found their way into the hands of friends and reviewers before the first night. They seem, with emendations, to have furnished copy for the published editions that appeared after 1891 when American copyright law was changed. Macmillan's editions of Jones's plays appeared regularly on both sides of the Atlantic, and gave him the opportunity to present his work in the form he preferred and with prefaces and supplementary material by himself and others. The first, *Saints and Sinners*, had a preface by Joseph Knight and included as an appendix the dramatist's own article, 'Religion and the Modern Stage'.

Beginning in 1903, a series of twenty-four of Jones's plays was published by Samuel French Ltd. These were in a larger format than the Macmillan volumes (demy 8vo as against 8vo) and, in accordance with French's usual practice, included detailed stage directions indicating move by move the position of the characters on stage. In order to maintain the policy of printing his work without obtrusive technical directions, Jones adopted a system whereby only those essential to the reader's understanding of the play remained in the body of the text and the remainder were relegated to a margin on the right or left of the page. A pamphlet, *On Reading Modern Plays*, setting out his views on the study of dramatic texts and explaining the method used in these editions, was published by French's in 1906. Some of the plays in French's series had already appeared with Macmillan, others — including *The Silver King* and *The Middleman* — received their first publication in this format. Because the standard of printing and proof-reading in the French's editions is not as good as that achieved in Macmillan's, the latter have been adopted as copy-texts for *The Case of Rebellious Susan* and *The Liars* in the present volume.

In 1925 a four-volume edition of seventeen plays, *Representative Plays*, edited with introductions to each volume by Clayton Hamilton, was published in the United States by Little, Brown. An English edition was issued by Macmillan in the following year. The texts were based on those prepared under Jones's supervision, but have no independent authority.

The present edition of *The Silver King* is based on that published by French's in

1907. The dialogue is printed as it appears there and marginal stage directions that indicate business, music cues and lighting have been incorporated in the body of the text, but most of the detailed notations for 'blocking' has been omitted. The 1907 edition appears to have been prepared by Jones from a text similar to that used by Osmond Tearle in the 1883 New York première, a manuscript promptbook of which is now in New York Public Library's Theatre Research Collection at Lincoln Center. Some minor inconsistencies in French's edition have been rectified by reference to this promptbook. The relationship between Tearle's, the other unpublished versions and French's edition is discussed in the appendix (pp. 220–4 below), which also contains the text of a scene omitted in the published play.

Proofs of the privately printed issue of *The Case of Rebellious Susan* (1894) served as the licensing copy. The private edition itself incorporates some minor alterations, and further variants appear in Macmillan's edition (1897). French's edition (undated) includes additional stage directions, and differs in some particulars from Macmillan's. The present text is that published in 1897, significant variants being recorded in footnotes. The most important of these are the alterations made in act II to avoid any suggestion of impropriety in Lady Susan's relationship with Lucien Edensor (p. 129 below). A promptbook used by James Neill's stock company is now in New York Public Library's Theatre Research Collection but it appears to have been based on the published text of the play. Two manuscript drafts of the dedication are now in the Theatre Museum (the longer, which differs substantially from that published, is signed 'Yours with my tongue in my cheek').

The licensing copy of *The Liars* — like that of *The Case of Rebellious Susan* — consists of proofs of the privately printed text. Macmillan's 1901 edition, published in New York, incorporates a few alterations: the second edition of 1904 offers no significant variants, but bears a British imprint and was published in London. French's edition (1909) contains some additional lines and stage directions which may reflect theatrical practice. A promptbook in the Henry Arthur Jones Collection in the library of the University of London (Senate House) is made up from an imperfect copy of the proofs of the private issue, but appears to have been compiled after the publication of French's edition. Another promptbook, in the Theatre Museum, is based on a copy of the 1901 edition of the play, disbound and interleaved in an exercise book. It was once the property of Samuel French Ltd and may have been made up in preparation for their 1909 edition: there is no sign of wear and tear that might indicate its having been used in a theatre. A copy of the 1901 Macmillan edition in New York Public Library's Theatre Research Collection is marked for performance and may derive from the 1915 New York revival. The present edition follows Macmillan's 1901 version, with some variants from French's recorded in footnotes.

Spelling and punctuation have been made consistent with modern British practice.

III *The Silver King*, Wallack's Theatre, New York, 1883. Osmond Tearle and Rose Coghlan as Wilfred and Nelly Denver, with Jaikes (John Gilbert) and the children (Carrie Eberts and May Germon)

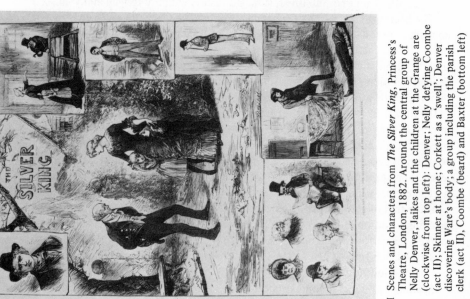

II Scenes and characters from *The Silver King*, Princess's Theatre, London, 1882. Around the central group of Nelly Denver, Jaikes and the children at the Grange are (clockwise from top left): Denver; Nelly defying Coombe (act II); Skinner at home; Corkett as a 'swell'; Denver discovering Ware's body; a group including the parish clerk (act II), Coombe (beard) and Baxter (bottom left)

THE SILVER KING

A drama in five acts

by HENRY ARTHUR JONES and HENRY HERMAN

I held it truth with him who sings
    To one clear harp in divers tones,
That men may rise on stepping-stones
    Of their dead selves to higher things.

But who shall so forecast the years
    And find in loss a gain to match?
Or reach a hand thro' time to catch
    The far-off interest of tears?
               Tennyson, *In Memoriam*

First performed at the Princess's Theatre, London, on 16 November 1882, with the following cast:

WILFRED DENVER	Wilson Barrett
NELLY DENVER, *his wife*	Miss Eastlake
CISSY and NED, *their children*	Misses C. Clitherow and C. Burton
DANIEL JAIKES, *their servant*	George Barrett
FRANK SELWYN, *private secretary to Mr John Franklin*	Neville Doone
GEOFFREY WARE, *an engineer*	Brian Darnley
SAMUEL BAXTER, *a detective*	Walter Speakman
CAPTAIN HERBERT SKINNER, *also known as* 'the Spider'	E.S. Willard
HENRY CORKETT, *Ware's clerk*	Chas. Coote
ELIAH COOMBE, *a receiver of stolen goods*	Clifford Cooper
CRIPPS, *a locksmith*	Frank Huntley
MR PARKYN, *parish clerk of Gaddesden*	J. Beauchamp
MESSRS BINKS and BROWNSON, *tradesmen*	H. Deane, Chalford
BILCHER and TEDDY, *betting men*	Warin, C. Gurth
TUBBS, *landlord of the Wheatsheaf*	H. de Salla
GAFFER POTTLE	J.B. Johnstone
LEAKER, *Ware's porter*	W.A. Elliott

[TIPSY PASSENGER]
[INSPECTOR, *at Euston Station*]
PORTER   Carson
NEWSBOY   Besley
DETECTIVES   Polhill, Bland
SERVANTS   C. Crofton, Coles

OLIVE SKINNER, *Captain Skinner's*   Miss Dora Vivian
   wife
TABITHA DURDEN   Mrs Huntley
SUSY, *waitress at the Chequers*   Miss Woodworth
MRS GAMMAGE   Mrs Beckett
LADY PASSENGER   Miss Nellie Palmer
SCHOOLGIRLS   Misses J. and F. Beckett
[DRINKERS, *at the Wheatsheaf*]
RAILWAY OFFICIALS, CLERKS, PASSENGERS

ACT I

SCENE 1.   *The skittle alley at the Wheatsheaf, Clerkenwell. Music*
takes curtain up. Discover TUBBS, TEDDY, BILCHER *and drinkers.* BILCHER *is*
in the midst of an excited narrative, the others are grouped round him at bar.

BILCHER: And they kept like that, neck and neck the three of 'em till just as they
were turning the corner drawing in home, and then Marcher put on a bit of a
spurt, and by Jove, Blue Ribbon shot ahead like a flash of greased lightning
and won by a short head. Never saw such a pretty finish in my life!

(*Enter* WARE.)

WARE: (*to* BILCHER) Well, what about Denver?

BILCHER: (*to* WARE) Doubled up this time and no mistake. Went a smasher on
Patacake and lost everything — owes me a hundred and fifty pounds besides.

WARE: Ah! (*aside*) It has come at last then. (*to* BILCHER) You're sure you've
cleaned him out?

BILCHER: Oh yes, me and Braggins between us. Much obliged to you for introducing him to us.

WARE: How did he take it?

BILCHER: Oh, tried to laugh and joke it off. He's as drunk as a fiddler; he was
pretty mellow when we started this morning, and we've kept him well doc-
tored up all day.

WARE: That's right. Keep him at it. Where is he?

BILCHER: We left him drinking at the bar at Waterloo Station; but he's promised
to turn up here.

WARE: I'll run in and have a look at him by and by. (BILCHER *returns to bar.*
WARE, *going, speaks in an aside.*) Ruined! Now, Nellie Hathaway, I think I'll
show you that you made a slight mistake when you threw me over and
married Wilfred Denver. (*Exit.*)

TUBBS: (*behind bar*) So poor young Denver came a cropper today?

BILCHER: Yes.

TUBBS: Poor fellow! I'm sorry for him. He's a downright good-hearted, jolly young
fellow, Mr Denver is.

TEDDY: So he is, Tubbs, when he's sober.

BILCHER: And that ain't been the last six months — (*Music cue.*) Tubbs takes care
of that.

(*Enter* JAIKES, *as if looking round for somebody.*)

TUBBS: (*in a low voice to drinkers at bar*) Look! There's Mr Denver's old servant —
he's come to look after his master.

JAIKES: What cheer, Mr Tubbs?

(TEDDY *hands* JAIKES *stool, which* JAIKES *sits upon, centre.*)

TUBBS: You must give him a little extry time tonight. There's a good many public
houses between Epsom and here.

Clerkenwell: jewellers' and watchmakers' quarter in north-west London, within walking distance of Gray's Inn Road and Hatton Garden.
Epsom: the Derby is raced annually over a course on Epsom Downs: Derby Day is a Wednesday
at the end of May or beginning of June.

JAIKES: Ah, but he'll be home early tonight; he promised the missus he would; and I want to ketch him and pop him off to bed quiet afore she sets eyes on him, d'ye see?

TUBBS: Ah, I shouldn't wonder if he's a bit fresh, eh?

JAIKES: Anybody might happen to get a bit fresh on Derby Day, you know.

TUBBS: He's been going it a pretty pace lately, ain't he?

JAIKES: Well, he's a bit wild, but there ain't no harm in him. Bless you, it's the blood; he's got too much nature in him, that's where it is. His father was just like him when he was a young man. Larking, hunting, drinking, fighting, steeple-chasing — any mortal spree under the sun, out all night, and as fresh as a daisy in the morning! And his grandfather, old Squire Denver, just such another. There was a man for you if you like. The last ten years of his life he never went to bed sober one night. Yes, he did one night, when the groom locked him in the stable by mistake, and then he was ill for months afterwards. (*All laugh.*)

TEDDY: Oh, he could take his lotion pretty reg'lar, eh?

JAIKES: I believe you. Well, when I was a dozen years younger, I could take my whack, and a tidy whack it was too, but bless you, I wasn't in it with old Squire Denver, and Master Will's a chip of the old block. He'll make a man yet. (*Music cue.*)

BILCHER: He'll make a madman if he doesn't leave off drinking.

JAIKES: You let him be! He's all right — Master Will's all right!

(DENVER *rolls in at gate.*)

DENVER: (*very drunk*) Yes, I'm all right — I'm all right! I'm 's drunk as a fool, and I've lost every cursed ha'penny I've got in the world. I'm all right! (*Goes to table.*)

TUBBS: What, backed the wrong horse, Mr Denver?

DENVER: No, Tubbs, no, I backed the right horse, and then the wrong horse went and won. (*Sits.*)

TEDDY: That's a pity!

DENVER: Not a bit of it. I've lost, you've won — if there were no fools like me in the world, what would become of the poor rogues?

BILCHER: Well, you seem pretty merry over it.

DENVER: Yes, Bilcher, I've lost my money today and tomorrow I shall lose your acquaintance. I'm quite satisfied with the bargain.

JAIKES: What, bad luck again, Master Will? (*Goes to* DENVER.)

DENVER: The devil's own luck, Jaikes. I put everything on Patacake, and I'm ruined, Jaikes.

JAIKES: No, Master Will, don't say that!

DENVER: Well, say stumped, cleaned out, licked into a cocked hat. Bilcher, I owe you a hundred and fifty pounds.

BILCHER: Yes, and I should like to know how I'm to be paid.

DENVER: So should I, Bilcher!

---

steeple-chasing: here used in its original sense of cross-country horse-racing.

BILCHER: Why didn't you take my advice? I told you that blackguard Braggins was doing you.

DENVER: Yes, and Braggins told me the same about you. Come, Bilcher, don't be greedy — (*rising and going centre*) You've had a good picking out of me, let the other blackguards have their turn.

BILCHER: I wash my hands of you.

DENVER: Very well, Bilcher, they won't be any the worse for a good wash. (*Returns to table.*)

JAIKES: Come Master Will, you'd better come home.

DENVER: Home! What should I go home for? To show my poor wife what a drunken brute she's got for a husband? To show my innocent children what an object they've got for a father? No, I won't go home, I've got no home. I've drunk it up.

JAIKES: For mercy's sake, Master Will, don't talk like that!

DENVER: (*furiously*) Get home with you!

JAIKES: Yes, I'll go home!

DENVER: (*Drops his voice.*) Jaikes, don't let her come here and find me like this — tell her I haven't come back — tell her I'm not to be found — tell her any lie that comes handiest, but don't let her see me. Be off now, be off!
(*Enter* BAXTER.)

JAIKES: (*going*) Poor Master Will! Ruined! What'll become of poor missus and the dear little 'uns? (*Exit.*)
(COOMBE *enters, looking about — goes to bar and gets drink in a pewter pot.*)

DENVER: (*Seated at table, takes out revolver.*) There's always one way out of it. If it wasn't such a coward's trick I'd do it.

BAXTER: (*in a low voice, to* DENVER) If you don't know what to do with that, I'll take care of it for you.

DENVER: (*putting revolver in pocket again*) Thank you, I do know what to do with it, much obliged for your advice. (*aside*) I may want it, tonight. (*Goes to counter.*)
(BAXTER *looks after him, shrugs his shoulders, goes to table and picks up newspaper.* COOMBE *has moved to a table. Enter* HENRY CORKETT, *a young cockney clerk, flushed, swaggering, cigar in mouth, hat on one side. He goes straight to bar.*)

CORKETT: (*with a patronising wave of hand to* TUBBS) Ha, Tubbs, how do?

TUBBS: How do, 'Arry?

CORKETT: 'Enery Corkett, Esquire, from you, Tubbs, if you please. What do you think of that, Tubbs, eh? (*flourishing a roll of banknotes*) Backed Blue Ribbon for a win and and place, and landed five hundred pounds. Look there! (*flourishing notes*)

DENVER: Biggest fools, best luck!

CORKETT: (*turning round angrily*) What did you say?

'*Arry*: the generic name (in comic writing) for a self-assertive but unrefined cockney.

DENVER: I said I wished I'd got no brains, because then I could make money at horse-racing.

CORKETT: Oh it's you, is it, Mr Denver? I've seen you at my guv'nor's place in Hatton Garden. You know me. My name's Corkett — I'm Mr Ware's clerk.

COOMBE: (*aside*) Mr Ware's clerk!

DENVER: (*after staring at* CORKETT *for a moment*) No, beg pardon, but I don't know you.

BAXTER: (*aside, seeing* COOMBE) Mr Eliah Coombe! Any little game on tonight, I wonder? (*to* TUBBS) A glass of bitter.

CORKETT: (*at bar*) Bitter be blowed! Have some champagne. Tubbs, it's my shout. Champagne for everybody.

COOMBE: (*aside, watching* CORKETT) Mr Ware's clerk. If I could get hold of him it would make our little job easy tonight. (*Rises and goes up to skittle alley with drink.*)

CORKETT: Come, gentlemen all, drink my health!

DENVER: Certainly! (*raising his glass*) Here's to the health of the beggars that win — put them on horseback and let them ride to the devil! (*Goes to table and sits.* CORKETT *goes towards him but is held back by others.*)

TUBBS: (*to* CORKETT) Don't take any notice of him. He's been hard hit at the Derby today.

CORKETT: Look here, gentlemen, I'm fly! Hang the expense! (*Returns to bar.*)

BAXTER: You young ass, put those notes in your pocket and go home to bed. (*Goes to a table and sits.*)

CORKETT: (*Turns sharply round.*) Shan't! Who are you? (*Goes to head of table.*) Can you show as much money as that? No! Then you shut up and take a back seat. I've won my money fair and honest and I shall spend it how I like. Hang it, I shall light my pipe with it if I like. Give me a cigar, Tubbs. (TUBBS *gives him a cigar.* CORKETT *strikes match, takes out banknote and turns to* BAXTER.) There! That's a five-pound note. (*Lights the note with match and then lights cigar with note.*) There, that'll show you what I'm made of! I'm a gentleman, I am. Money ain't no object to me. (*Returns to bar.*)

DENVER: (*aside*) That fool with five hundred pounds, and tomorrow my wife and children will be starving. (*to* CORKETT) Look here, you! You've got more money than you know what to do with, I'll have you at any game you like — for any stake.

CORKETT: I don't want your money.

DENVER: But I want yours! If you've got the pluck of a rabbit, stake it, win or lose.

CORKETT: Very well, what shall it be?

DENVER: (*Rises and goes centre.*) Cards — billiards, I don't care.

CORKETT: Fifty up then — I'm ready!

---

it's my shout: 'I'm buying the drinks.'
put them on horseback: proverbial: 'Put a beggar on horseback and he'll ride to the devil'.
I'm fly!: 'I'm game!'
Fifty up: in billiards, a relatively short game, the winner being the first player to reach a score of fifty.

DENVER: Come on, then. Hang it all, my luck must change! It shall change! I will win or the devil's in it! (*Exit. Music cue.*)

CORKETT: Come on, gentlemen, and see the fun! (*Exit, followed by several of the drinkers, leaving only one or two at the bar.*)

COOMBE: (*aside*) The Spider at last! (*Music cue.*)

 (*Enter* SKINNER, *very well dressed: light summer overcoat and faultless evening dress.*)

BAXTER: (*aside*) The Spider and Coombe. There's some big game on tonight.

SKINNER: (*glancing round*) Baxter the detective! The deuce! (*Goes to* BAXTER*'s table and sits.*) Anything fresh in the paper?

BAXTER: Blue Ribbon pulled it off today.

SKINNER: Ah, I don't bet.

BAXTER: They've caught the man who committed the jewel robbery at Lady Fairford's. (*giving him paper and indicating paragraph*) It may interest you, it seems he was quite a swell, as well dressed as you are!

SKINNER: Was he? The cheek of these fellows!

BAXTER: You're right — they are cheeky! (*Looks straight at* SKINNER *for some moments.* SKINNER*'s face remains perfectly impassive.* BAXTER *speaks aside.*) A cucumber isn't in it with him. (*Rises and goes to bar.*)

COOMBE: (*Has crept down to* SKINNER.) My dear boy, I'm so glad you've come.

SKINNER: (*in a low voice, without taking his eyes off the paper*) If you accost me again in a public place, I'll wring your neck for you, you old weasel!

COOMBE: (*Crosses in front of* SKINNER *and sits at table.*) My dear boy, business is business, and it's a big fortune for us all — a sackful of diamonds in Hatton Garden — no risk — no danger, all as safe and easy as saying your prayers.

SKINNER: How do we get in?

COOMBE: Cut through the wall of the next house. There's a young chap playing billiards inside —

SKINNER: Will you hold your infernal cackle? Don't you see that man watching us? (BAXTER *has seated himself at a table.*) It's Baxter the detective.

COOMBE: (*alarmed*) Baxter the detective?

SKINNER: Yes, you fool, don't look at him. He means to follow me up. I'll throw him off the scent directly.

 (*Re-enter* CORKETT, *followed by drinkers, and goes up to bar.*)

CORKETT: (*elated*) Landed him proper, didn't I? Ha, Tubbs, pulled it off again, my boy!

TUBBS: What — have you won, 'Arry?

CORKETT: Rather! Why, he wasn't in it.

COOMBE: (*aside to* SKINNER) See that young sprig there — he sleeps in the house we want to get into — if we could get hold of him —

SKINNER: Will you shut up?

CORKETT: Now, gentlemen, let's be merry! Drink up! Look here, I've made my money like a gentleman and I'll spend it like a gentleman.

Hatton Garden: street running north from Holborn Circus to Clerkenwell Street, associated with jewellery (esp. diamond) trade.

SKINNER: Just relieve him of those notes while I draw off Baxter's attention. You'll be able to get hold of him when he's cleaned out.

COOMBE: You'll be there as soon as it's dusk — a hundred and fourteen, Hatton Garden.

SKINNER: Where's the Ancient Briton?

COOMBE: He'll be on the spot. (*Goes up to counter.*)

SKINNER: Right! So you want to have a finger in our pie, do you, Sam Baxter? (*Goes up stage towards exit, then comes back to table to get his stick. Crosses towards gate, sees that BAXTER is cautiously following him.*) That's right! Follow me up! I'll lead you a pretty dance tonight! (*At gate, shouts off.*) Hi! Boy! Get me a Hansom! (*Exeunt SKINNER and BAXTER.*)

(COOMBE *has in the meantime picked* CORKETT's *pocket.*)

CORKETT: Now, gentlemen, I'm blowed if I don't stand you another bottle of champagne. I've got money enough — (*Stops suddenly.*) Here, somebody's stole my money (*coming centre*).

TUBBS: What? Nonsense! 'Enery, there ain't no thieves here. Feel again (*coming from behind bar*).

CORKETT: (*feeling desperately in his pockets*) Yes, it's gone. It's gone. My money — I'm robbed, I'm ruined! I'm ruined! Give me my money, do you hear — give me my money or I'll — (*Seizes* BILCHER, *who happens to stand next to him, by the throat.*)

BILCHER: (*shaking him off roughly*) You hold off, youngster, or I'll smash you. I haven't got your money.

CORKETT: Somebody's got it! Somebody must have it!

COOMBE: Come, gentlemen, no larks with the poor young fellow. If you've got his money give it back to him!

CORKETT: (*crying piteously*) I'm ruined, you know, I'm ruined!

COOMBE: (*suddenly*) Why, of course, that man must have it.

CORKETT: Which? (*Runs to* COOMBE.)

COOMBE: Why, the man with the billy-cock hat and check trousers! (*describing* BAXTER) I saw him sneaking round your elbow — he's got it.

CORKETT: Which way did he go?

COOMBE: This way — come on! I'll help you catch him — I shall know the rascal again when I see him — come on!

CORKETT: Come on, gentlemen, and help me find him. I'm ruined. I'm ruined (*crying piteously*).

(*Exit* COOMBE, *followed by* CORKETT. *Enter* DENVER.)

DENVER: There's another man ruined. Cheer up! We'll go to the dogs together. Tubbs, give me some brandy! (*Goes to bar.*)

TUBBS: (*now back behind bar*) You've had enough, Mr Denver.

DENVER: I'm the best judge of that — it's a free country — anybody can drink himself to death that likes — I will have it, I will. (*Sits at table.*)

(*Enter* GEOFFREY WARE.)

WARE: (*watching* DENVER) Ah, there you are, my fine fellow. I think my plan is

---

billy-cock hat: popular style of hard felt hat, bowler-shaped and with a curled-up, narrow rim.

working pretty well. I think Nelly had better have married me after all. Stick to it, I'll bring you to the gutter, I'll see you in the workhouse yet before I've done with you. (*Comes up to* DENVER, *slaps him on the back cordially.*) Well, Will, how are you?

DENVER: I'm three parts drunk and the rest mad, so keep out of my way, Geoffrey Ware.

WARE: Nonsense, Will, I never saw you looking so bright and sober. I'm very glad for Nelly's sake.

DENVER: (*fiercely rising*) Whose sake?

WARE: Mrs Denver — excuse the slip of the tongue. She was once engaged to me, you know.

DENVER: She knew better than to marry you, didn't she?

WARE: It seems she did, for she married you.

DENVER: Yes, and she'll stick to me through thick and thin. Why, you sneaking cur, do you think my wife can't see through you? Do you think I don't know why you're always creeping and skulking about my house under pretence of being my friend? Now listen to me, I'm going to the dogs (*rising*) — I'm drinking myself to death as fast as I can. I shall be dead in no time, but she won't marry you, Geoffrey Ware. She'll marry a sweep sooner — you know, a sweep of the other sort, I mean. Now you've got it straight, go and chew the cud of that, and then buy a rope and hang yourself. (*Takes up his glass and sits at other side of table.*)

WARE: Come, Will, I don't bear you any grudge for taking away my sweetheart, I'm only glad to see what a nice, kind, sober husband she's got.

DENVER: I've warned you once. Take a fool's advice and keep out of my way. The devil's in me tonight, and he'll break out directly.

WARE: Ah, well, take care of yourself, dear boy, for my sake. Give my kindest regards to Nelly.

(DENVER, *rising, dashes the contents of his glass in* WARE's *face.* TUBBS *and* BILCHER *come down and seize* DENVER. TEDDY *gets* WARE *away.*)

DENVER: (*held by* TUBBS *and* BILCHER) Take that man away! Take him away before I kill him.

WARE: Ta, ta, Will, don't forget my message to your better half. (*Exit.*)

TUBBS: Now, Mr Denver, you'd better go home, you know.

DENVER: (*seated*) No, no, let me stay here, Tubbs! Oh, my head! (*Lets his head fall on table.*)

TUBBS: Come away, Mr Bilcher, perhaps he'll drop off to sleep and then we can carry him home. (*Goes back into bar.*)

DENVER: Yes, carry me home, Tubbs, and sing 'Here the conquering hero comes!' and then bury me and play the Dead March in Saul. (*Music cue.*)

---

the slip of the tongue: i.e. the insultingly familiar use of Mrs Denver's first name.
sweep of another sort: i.e. thief (although Denver may mean that Ware is a thief, and Nelly would rather marry a chimney-sweep).
'Here the conquering hero comes!': misquoting the popular chorus from Handel's oratorio *Joshua*: 'See the conquering hero comes:/Sound the trumpets, beat the drums!'
the Dead March in Saul: Handel's oratorio, first performed in 1739.

(TUBBS *has beckoned all off.* DENVER *is alone.* NELLY *enters at gate and comes down behind him very timidly. He starts, turns around and sees her.*)

DENVER: Nelly, you here! You in this place?

NELLY: Yes, isn't a wife's place by her husband's side?

DENVER: Not when he's such a husband as I am. You go home, my darling; you go home, I'll come by and by.

NELLY: No, my poor Will, come now!

DENVER: I've ruined you, Nell, I've lost every sixpence I've got in the world. Tomorrow you and the chicks will be starving. Ah, Nell, my bonnie, bonnie girl, look at me — what made you marry me, a drunken brute like me?

NELLY: Because I loved you — I love you still. Never mind the past, dear, come home and make a fresh start tomorrow.

DENVER: I can't. I must go on. I can't stop. I'm going down, down as fast as I can go — I don't know where!

NELLY: (*throwing her arms around him*) Oh, don't say that, dear. You must stop yourself for my sake — for your Nell's sake.

DENVER: (*stroking her face*) The sweetest and truest wife a man ever had, and married to such a wretch as I am. (*changing his tone*) Don't you come here! You only make me think what a brute I've been to you.

NELLY: Oh, Will, I have just put our little Cissy and Ned to bed and they have said 'God bless our dear father!'

(WARE *enters behind unperceived.*)

DENVER: (*starting up maddened*) Ah! Don't teach them that! Don't teach them to pray for me. Teach them to curse and hate me. Go away, Nell, — don't you see the people all staring at us? Go home, my girl! I'll come home when I'm sober. Go home, my girl, go home! (*Rushes to her.*) Tubbs, give me some brandy, don't keep me waiting!

(NELLY *goes a step after him and then sinks into a chair, crying.*)

WARE: (*in a low voice, coming down behind* NELLY) Have you suffered enough?

NELLY: (*rising, hiding her tears*) Geoffrey Ware! (*aside*) That he should see me here!

WARE: Has he dragged you deep enough into the mire or will you go deeper still, to rags, to the gutter, to starvation? Nelly, you once promised to be my wife.

NELLY: Yes, and I repented even before I promised. I never loved you and you know it. You worried me into a consent, and when I found out my mistake, I told you of it and married a better man!

DENVER: (*whose back is turned towards them*) That hound back again, and talking to my wife.

WARE: Ah, there stands the better man! Look at him. A pattern husband — a pattern father, prosperous, happy, respectable, sober!

NELLY: Oh, this is manly of you. What harm have I ever done to you?

WARE: You married him. I swore that day I'd ruin him, and I kept my word. Good evening, Mrs Denver. (*Crosses towards exit.*)

DENVER: (*turning*) Stop, you cur, and answer to me (*flourishing revolver*).

WARE: (*coolly*) My dear fellow, you're drunk, you know. (*Exit, laughing at* DENVER. DENVER *rushes at him.* NELLY *stops him.*)

NELLY: Ah, Will, he's not worth it.

> (TUBBS *and others enter from house.* JAIKES *enters from gate.*
> *Both* NELLY *and* JAIKES *hold* DENVER.)

DENVER: Let me get at him! Let me go!

JAIKES: Master Will! Master Will!

NELLY: No, no! Will, he's not worth it.

JAIKES: What are you going to do, Master Will?

DENVER: I'm going to kill that man! I'll shoot him like a dog! (*Breaks from them and rushes off.*)

NELLY: (*calling after him*) Will! Will! Stop! Ah, will nobody stop him? (*Music:* JAIKES *and* NELLY *follow* DENVER *off.*)

> *Scene changes.*

> SCENE 2.   *A street in Clerkenwell. Lights three-quarters down. Enter*
CORKETT, *running, followed by* COOMBE, *out of breath.*

COOMBE: You say you don't know the numbers of the notes?

CORKETT: No, I only took 'em off the bookmaker this afternoon and I never took the numbers.

COOMBE: (*aside*) That's lucky! (*aloud*) Well, you see the man got off with them.

CORKETT: Yes, and I say, you won't split on me, will yer? I'd borrowed that money to put it on Blue Ribbon.

COOMBE: Borrowed the money?

CORKETT: Yes, eighty pounds off my guv'nor, Mr Ware.

COOMBE: Oh, I see, without his knowing, that's awkward — that's very awkward.

CORKETT: I'd got the straight tip — I knew Blue Ribbon was a moral, and I meant to put the money back, honour bright I did.

COOMBE: Of course you did. You was actuated by very honourable intentions.

CORKETT: And now I shall be found out tomorrow and have to go to quod.

COOMBE: Ah, that's a pity, and the worst of it is the judges are so unfeeling to parties as borrow their guv'nor's money without mentioning it to their guv'nors.

CORKETT: Are they?

COOMBE: Oh, brutal, especially to young men as borrow their guv'nor's money to put it on horses.

CORKETT: You don't say so. I say — how long do you think I shall get?

COOMBE: Well, if you happen to get a nice, kind, feeling judge with his stomick in good working order, you may get off with say — seven years.

CORKETT: Seven years?

COOMBE: Yes, but don't reckon on that. There was a young fellow tried at the Old Bailey a week or two since, for borrowing money as you've done, a handsome, pleasant young man he seemed to be, just like you.

CORKETT: Yes, and what did he get?

COOMBE: Fourteen years.

---

the straight tip: reliable (probably, inside) information.
a moral: a (moral) certainty.
quod: prison.

CORKETT: (*Collapses, falling on* COOMBE*'s shoulder.*) Fourteen years!

COOMBE: Yes, I felt quite sorry for him.

CORKETT: I say, what's it like in —

COOMBE: Speaking from hearsay, it ain't likely to suit a young man of your constitution. It'll bottle you up in less than three months.

CORKETT: Think so?

COOMBE: Sure of it. Skilly won't relish much after champagne, will it? And as for the treadmill, though it's a prime *exercise*, as a *game* it ain't to be compared to billiards.

CORKETT: What can I do?

COOMBE: Well, I've took a bit of a fancy to you, and I'll tell you what I'll do. I'll lend you the eighty pounds.

CORKETT: (*seizing his hand eagerly*) You will? You're a brick!

COOMBE: Yes, providing you'll oblige me in a little matter.

CORKETT: I'll do anything for you. You're a jolly kind old man and no mistake.

COOMBE: You live at a hundred and fourteen Hatton Garden, don't you?

CORKETT: Yes.

COOMBE: Who sleeps in the house beside you?

CORKETT: Only my guv'nor and the old porter.

COOMBE: Your guv'nor spends his evenings out, don't he?

CORKETT: Comes in about twelve as a rule.

COOMBE: Well, a friend of mine wants to spend half an hour in your guv'nor's sitting-room tonight — he's a photographer and he's taking views of London. Could you let us into the house and keep the old porter out of the way?

CORKETT: I say, what's up?

COOMBE: Never mind. Will you help us or will you go to quod tomorrow?

CORKETT: I'll help you.

COOMBE: There's a sensible young man.

(*Enter* JAIKES, *excited.*)

JAIKES: (*crossing*) I've lost my way in these courts and alleys and goodness knows what mischief's happening. (*seeing* CORKETT) Ah, you're Mr Ware's clerk, aren't you?

CORKETT: Yes. Why, it's Mr Denver's servant, ain't it?

JAIKES: Yes, come on with me to Mr Ware's in Hatton Garden. Come on quick.

COOMBE: (*aside*) Hillo, I must stop this.

CORKETT: (*exchanging a glance with* COOMBE) What's the matter?

JAIKES: Murder'll be the matter if we don't stop it. My poor master's got the drink inside of him. He's beside himself. He's threatened to kill Mr Ware. Come and help me get him away.

COOMBE: (*coming between them*) I beg your pardon, are you looking for the young gentleman as was drinking in the Wheatsheaf just now?

---

skilly: thin gruel or stew, a staple of prison diet.

the treadmill: this form of punishment remained in use until it was abolished by Act of Parliament in 1898.

views of London: Tearle's promptbook makes the excuse more plausible: '. . . he's taking night views of London by a new patent process'.

JAIKES: Yes, have you seen anything of him?

COOMBE: Yes, he came out of that public house not two minutes ago, and he took a cab and told the driver to go to Charing Cross Station, didn't he? (*to* CORKETT)

CORKETT: Yes, 'ansom.

JAIKES: Are you sure it was my master?

COOMBE: Oh, quite sure. (*to* CORKETT) You're sure it was Mr Denver, ain't you?

CORKETT: Oh yes, I'll take my oath of it.

COOMBE: It's very lucky you met us. You'll find your master at Charing Cross railway station. Make haste.

JAIKES: Thank you, mate, thank you, I'll go there straight! (*Exit.*)

COOMBE: Yes, do, you old fool, and you won't find him. We shall have to look out and keep that tipsy fellow out of the way. (*to* CORKETT) Now, my dear boy, you stroll on just in front of me. Don't get out of my sight – that's it!

CORKETT: No, and if I once get out of this mess I'll never get into another. (*Exit.*)

COOMBE: That's done neat and clean. Now if the Ancient Briton can't work in off the leads, this young gentleman will open the front door for us, and all we've got to do is walk upstairs. (*Music cue. Exit.*)

       Scene changes.

    SCENE 3.   GEOFFREY WARE's *sitting-room in Hatton Garden.*
Lights half up. Window right. Table with cloth centre, sideboard against right wall.
Door at back. Discover WARE *standing by table with hat on, buttoning his gloves,*
also LEAKER, *an old porter, at door.*

WARE: Leaker, I'm going out. Leave the door on the latch.

LEAKER: Yes, sir. Shall I wait up for you sir?

WARE: No. I don't know what time I shall be back. I may come in in half an hour, or I may not come in at all. You can go to bed when you like. (*going out at door*) Good night.

LEAKER: Good night, sir. (*Music cue.*)

       (*Exit* WARE *at back.* LEAKER *takes out light and exit after him.*
       Lights check to quarter. A pause. Stage dark. CRIPPS *is seen at*
       window, he lifts window noiselessly and enters very softly, with
       dark lantern in his hand.)

CRIPPS: Coast clear, that's all right! (*Crosses to sideboard and moves it away from wall.*) This must be the spot. (*Listens – a short, faint, peculiar whistle is heard off.* CRIPPS *returns it and goes on lifting sideboard. Enter* SKINNER *at back.*)

SKINNER: All clear?

CRIPPS: Yes, Captain!

SKINNER: Light!

       (CRIPPS *turns lantern on* SKINNER, *helps him off with coat,*

Charing Cross: conveniently far away at the west end of the Strand.
the leads: the roof.
(s.d.) check: i.e. 'dim'.

discovers faultless evening dress-suit. SKINNER, at head of table, centre, turns up his sleeves.)

SKINNER: Give me my tools. You'll find them in that pocket.

(CRIPPS *takes case out of pocket, hands it to SKINNER, then puts coat on front of table. SKINNER opens case and looks at tools.)*

CRIPPS: Beauties, ain't they? I was a week making them jemmies.

SKINNER: Well, it was time well spent. What the plague did you want me for tonight? I was just starting for Lady Blanche Wynter's dinner party.

CRIPPS: *(measuring along wall)* What the blazes has that got to do with me? If you're above your business, say so, and I'll crack the crib myself.

SKINNER: *(Takes a tool from neat mahogany case and lays it on table.)* Give me the plan! (CRIPPS *gives him the plan — he studies it.)*

CRIPPS: The safe's just the other side of this wall here. Thinks I when I was a-fixing up that there safe, 'this'll be a splendid plant for us'; and the gents next door was extry particular about having it made strong. 'Cause', says they, 'there'll often be fifty pounds' worth of diamonds in that there safe.'

SKINNER: *(who has been studying plan and not listening to CRIPPS)* Shut up! Not so much cackle. Now, Cripps, look alive, because I must be at Lady Blanche's dance at twelve.

CRIPPS: Blow Lady Blanche!

(SKINNER *takes up instrument, comes to wall, is about to pierce it when noise of knocking and ringing is heard downstairs.)*

SKINNER: What's that row?

(Enter COOMBE in great trouble.)

COOMBE: My dear boy, here's that tipsy fellow down at the door, playing deuce and tommy, swears he'll pull the house down if we don't let him come up. *(Knocking and ringing continue.)*

SKINNER: What's he want?

COOMBE: Mr Ware. He won't take our word he's out. What can we do?

SKINNER: Send him up here.

COOMBE: What, here?

SKINNER: Yes, tell him Mr Ware's at home and send him up. *(Exit COOMBE.)* Where's my chloroform pad? *(Gets pad from pocket.)* Oh, here it is. *(Pours chloroform onto pad.)* I'll soon quiet him. Cripps, out with that light. Stand there! *(Music cue. Stage dark. They stand behind door.)*

COOMBE: *(outside)* There he is — you'll find Mr Ware in that room.

(Enter DENVER with revolver, followed by COOMBE.)

DENVER: Now, you hound, come out and settle accounts with me. Come out and show your face. Where are you?

(SKINNER *leaps out on him, and puts chloroform pad over DENVER's nose. CRIPPS helps him. DENVER struggles but is overpowered; they lay him on rug by fireplace.)*

SKINNER: That revolver! Take it away from him, put it on the table. (CRIPPS

---

crib: safe.

plant: the object of a robbery (the word can also mean 'hiding place for stolen goods').

playing deuce and tommy: causing a disturbance.

takes revolver.) Lie there, you brute! You won't trouble us any more.
(CRIPPS *is examining revolver as* SKINNER *crosses.*) Put that revolver down,
Cripps, anywhere on the table. Look alive! Show me a light (*getting to wall
again*).

    (*Enter* CORKETT *suddenly.*)

CORKETT: (*in a frightened whisper*) Here, where are you? I say, clear out of this
all of you. Here's my guv'nor coming back — he's left something. Oh, crimes,
here he is.

    (*Enter* WARE. *He stands a moment in doorway — strikes match.*
    CORKETT *tries to dodge by him.*)

WARE: (*Sees him.*) Hillo? What are you doing here? Who are these men? What
business have you here?

SKINNER: We are friends of your clerk — we met him at the Derby, and he insisted
on our coming here to spend the evening with him, and so naturally as a
matter of course — (*coolly putting tools in box*) — excuse me, I have an
appointment!

WARE: Wait a bit, I want this cleared up! (*Sees tools on table.*) Ah! These are
burglars' tools! A revolver! Help! Murder! Thieves!

SKINNER: (*snatching up revolver and shooting* WARE) Take that, you fool, since
you won't be quiet!

    (WARE *falls in front of table — a pause.*)

COOMBE: My dear boy, this is terrible.

CORKETT: He's killed him, he's killed him!

SKINNER: Cripps, back with the case sharp! Everybody off.

    (*They put back bookcase, quickly.*)

CORKETT: We shall all swing for this. (*Shows great fright.*)

SKINNER: You will, if you don't keep your mouth shut.

CRIPPS: We must risk the leads — come on — we mustn't be seen coming out of the
door. (*Gets out at window.*)

SKINNER: (*putting on coat and coolly pocketing tools*) Look alive, Coombe!
Shake up that idiot! (*indicating* CORKETT, *who is paralysed with fright*)

COOMBE: (*shaking* CORKETT) Come on, or else they'll collar you for this.

    (*Hurries him out of window and gets out himself.* SKINNER *is about to
    place revolver in his pocket when he sees* DENVER *and places it on table
    instead.*)

SKINNER: (*looking at* WARE) I've gone a step too far this time. The fool! Why
wouldn't he let me pass? (*Gets out of window and closes it down.*)

    (*Stage dark. A pause. Enter* LEAKER *with candle, rubbing his eyes
    and yawning as if just awakened from sleep.*)

LEAKER: (*yawning*) I thought I heard a noise like a shot. I must have been dreaming. I wonder how long I've been asleep? Mr Ware not come yet. (*going a step
or two and stumbling over* DENVER) Hillo! Who's this? (*Stoops and looks
down.*) Why, it's Mr Denver! How did he get in here? (*Puts candle on shelf,
kneels down and shouts at and shakes* DENVER.) Mr Denver! Wake up, wake
up! (DENVER *mutters something and stirs.*) Don't lay there, sir. Let me
assist you into this chair. (*Shakes him.*) Drunk again. D'ye hear, Mr Denver,
wake up! (*Shakes him and gets him into armchair.*)

DENVER: (*rousing himself and opening his eyes*) All right! Don't be in a hurry. Where am I?

LEAKER: You're in Mr Ware's room at Hatton Garden, sir.

DENVER: (*in chair*) Of course I am. (*Passing his hand over his head, drops back into chair.*)

LEAKER: Shall I light you downstairs?

DENVER: No, I'll go soon. Who is it — Leaker?

LEAKER: Yes, it's Leaker.

DENVER: You know me, Leaker?

LEAKER: Yes, I know you, sir. (*aside*) I'd better let him stay, he won't do any harm. (*to* DENVER) I'll leave you the candle, sir, and you can go home when you've quite woke up. Well, good night, sir, I'm going to bed. Mind you latch the street door when you go out. Good night, sir.

DENVER: Latch street door — all right, Leaker. (*Exit* LEAKER. DENVER *sits up and stares round him, tries to collect himself.*) What's up? What's the matter? (*Shakes himself.*) What am I doing here? This won't do! Get home! Get home you drunken scoundrel! Aren't you ashamed of yourself, Will Denver? Keeping your poor wife sitting up half the night for you — get home, d'ye hear, get home. (*Raises himself with difficulty and stares round and staggers.*) What's the matter with my head? I can't recollect! What place is this? (*with a sudden flash of recollection*) Ah! Geoffrey Ware's room, I remember — yes, yes, I said I'd kill him and — Oh, my head, I'd better get home. Where's my hat? (*Gets up, takes candle, staggers, steadies himself, comes round table, sees* WARE.) What's that? It's Geoffrey Ware! What's he doing here? Get up, will you? (*Kneels down.*) Ah, what's this? Blood! He's shot! My God, I've murdered him. No! No! Let me think. What happened? Ah yes, I remember now — I came in at that door, he sprang at me and then we struggled. (*looking at revolver*) My revolver — one barrel fired — I've murdered him. No, he's not dead. Geoffrey Ware! Is he dead? (*eagerly feeling* WARE's *pulse*) No, it doesn't beat. (*Tears down* WARE's *waistcoat and shirt, puts his ear over* WARE's *heart.*) No, no, quite still, quite still. He's dead! Dead! Dead! Oh, I've killed him — I've killed him. (*Rising frantically, takes up revolver and puts it in his pocket.*) What can I do? (*with a great cry*) Don't stare at me like that! (*snatching off table cover and throwing it over body, his eyes fixed and staring at it, unable to take off his glance*) Close those eyes, Geoffrey, close them. Ah, yes, I murdered him — I've done it — I've done it — murdered him! (*Exit, his lips mechanically jabbering.*) I've done it! I've done it! I've done it! I've done it! I've done it! (*Music. Exit.*)

　　　　　　End of act I
(*A night passes between act I and act II.*)

ACT II

　　　　SCENE 1.　　　　*Interior of* DENVER's *house. Window at back. Doors right and left. Small table centre of stage. Chairs right and left. Music to open. The clock strikes six. Lights full up.* NELLY *discovered at window looking anxiously off.*

NELLY: Six o'clock! Will he never come? (*Enter* JAIKES.) Well, Jaikes?

JAIKES: I can't see nothing of him, missus!

NELLY: You don't think he has carried out his threat?

JAIKES: Not he, missus, don't you fear. Mr Will won't do no harm. Now don't you sit up any longer, missus.

NELLY: I'm used to it, Jaikes, I'm used to it.

JAIKES: This sitting up o'nights is making you quite pale and thin, and such bonny rosy cheeks you used to have in the old days.

NELLY: Ah, the old days — the dear old Grange. The happy, happy times that will never come again.

JAIKES: Yes, it will, missus. I don't know how, but some'ut inside me prophesies as it will.

NELLY: Bless you, Jaikes, I don't know how I shall bear my troubles when you are gone.

JAIKES: When I'm what, missus?

NELLY: Gone — yes, we're ruined; we can't pay you the wages we owe you.

JAIKES: There'll be time enough for that when I asks you.

NELLY: Ah, but we can't afford to keep a servant any longer — you have clung to us all through, my old friend, but we shall have to part from you now.

JAIKES: Will you, though? You won't find me so easy to get rid of.

NELLY: Ah, Jaikes, we're a sinking ship, you'd better leave us before we go down.

JAIKES: No, missus, my voyage is pretty well over, and if you go down, I'll go down with you. I stuck to you in your prosperity — I took your wages when your purse was full, and your hand was free, and I ain't going to leave you now adversity's come and the cupboard's empty. No! No!

NELLY: Dear, kind Jaikes, but you know you could go back to the Grange; they want a butler, and would be glad to have you.

JAIKES: I daresay they would, but they won't get me — I know when I'm well off.

NELLY: But I am forgetting, Jaikes, you must be very tired. Go and get some sleep.

JAIKES: I'd rather wait with you, missus.

NELLY: I'll call you, Jaikes, if I want any help. Go, Jaikes, go just to please me.

JAIKES: Very well, missus, if you wish it.

NELLY: There's a good Jaikes. Good night.

JAIKES: Not 'good night', missus, it's 'good morning'. (*Music. Exit.*)

NELLY: (*Goes to window.*) Ah! if it were the dawn of a new and happy life! (*Enter* DENVER.) Will!

DENVER: Don't touch me! You don't know what I am! Keep away from me!

NELLY: (*after a momentary look of bewilderment*) Ah, Will! Not that — not that! For mercy's sake, say it's not true!

DENVER: Ah, if I could! Yes, it's true! I've killed him! Oh, if I could wipe it out! If I could bring back the past few hours! Fool! Fool! Fool!

NELLY: How did it happen?

DENVER: I don't know! I was mad — dazed. I went to his rooms, it was dark — I called out for him — he sprang upon me from behind the door — we struggled — I suppose my revolver must have gone off — and then — I — I — I don't know what happened. The next thing I remember was Leaker, the porter, woke me and left me — and I looked round the room — and — and — (*picturing the scene*) there he was — dead — dead — shot by me! (*Retreats to wall.*)

Look! Look! He's staring at me. Look! Look! He'll stare at me for ever. There! Don't you see him? (*pointing to the floor*) Hide him — hide him from me!

NELLY: (*With a great cry of pity goes to him and covers his face with her hands.*) Oh, my poor Will!

DENVER: Don't touch me, I say! There's blood on my hands. (*Sinks on chair.*) Oh, my poor girl! Have I brought you to this?

NELLY: (*coming to him*) Don't think of me — think of yourself — you must hide!

DENVER: Hide! No! let them come and take me, you will be well rid of me. (NELLY *puts her arms round his neck.*) Don't pity me. If there is a spark of love left in your breast for me, crush it out. Oh, I've been the maddest fool that was ever sent upon this earth to work mischief.

NELLY: What time was it when it happened?

DENVER: I don't know — a little before twelve, I think. I've been rushing about the streets ever since trying to get away from him and from myself.

NELLY: You mustn't stay here! This will be the first place they will search. You must go to one of the big railway stations and take a ticket for a long distance — do you see — make it appear you are trying to leave the country, and then you must leave the train at the first station, and so throw them off the scent. (*Puts her arms round* DENVER*'s neck from behind.*) You'll do as I tell you, won't you, Will?

DENVER: Oh, my wife! Why don't you hate me? Why don't you curse me?

NELLY: Because you never had so much need of my love and of my prayers as you have now. We're wasting time. What money have you?

(DENVER *feels in his pocket, takes out revolver.*)

DENVER: Ah! this cursed thing! Take it away before I do any more mischief with it. (NELLY *takes it from him.*)

NELLY: Never mind that now. I'll get rid of it when you are gone. (*Puts revolver on table.*) What money have you?

DENVER: Not a shilling in the world.

NELLY: Nor I. Ah, you will be lost and all for the want of a few pounds.

(JAIKES *has entered during the last speech.*)

JAIKES: No, missus, he shan't. I've saved up a little money against a rainy day, and Master Will's as welcome to it as if it was his own. But what has happened?

NELLY: Oh, the worst! Out of pity don't ask. Only help us.

JAIKES: Aye, that I will. What can I do?

NELLY: Quick, get the money. Wait! Your master must have some disguise. Think what he can have.

JAIKES: Yes, missus. There's my poor brother Frank's things. They sent 'em to me when he died. How will they do?

NELLY: Sailor's clothes! They'll do. Quick! Get them and put them into the portmanteau — and, Jaikes, his topcoat and hat. Hurry, it's life or death! (*Exit* JAIKES. NELLY *goes to* DENVER *and puts her arms round his neck.*) Oh, Will, you must save yourself for my sake.

DENVER: I shan't escape — they'll soon run me down, Nell.

NELLY: Ah! no, no, no, you must escape! You shall! Oh, how I will pray for it this night. And you will do your utmost for my sake? You will find means of letting me know where you are?

DENVER: Yes, and the children — my little Ned and Cissy — dare I kiss them before I go?

NELLY: Yes — come, they are asleep. (*She leads him towards door. He pauses, and retreats to front of table.*)

DENVER: No! No! I'm not fit to kiss them! Oh, Nelly, when they grow up and ask for their father, what will you say? (*Bursts into tears. Enter JAIKES with overcoat, hat, portmanteau and purse.*)

JAIKES: Here you are, Master Will. You'll find poor Frank's clothes inside — he was about your figure. Here's the money — there's nearly forty pounds. (NELLY *helps* DENVER *on with his overcoat.*)

DENVER: I can't take your savings, Jaikes.

JAIKES: Don't say mine, Master Will. It all came from you — and if the last drop of blood in my old heart could save you, you should have that as well.

NELLY: Quick, dear! You must take it.

DENVER: Give me a few pounds and then I'll shift for myself. (*Takes money from purse.*) Here, you keep the rest — for her. You'll take care of her, won't you, Jaikes?

JAIKES: You needn't ask me that, Master Will.

NELLY: (*throwing her arms round* DENVER) Oh, Will! that ever we should part like this! (*loud knock at door*) What's that?

DENVER: They have come for me.

JAIKES: (*Goes to window and looks off.*) A chap with a billy-cock hat and check trousers. (*Describes* BAXTER.)

DENVER: It must be a detective. What shall I do?

NELLY: This way — quick, we'll try to keep him (*getting him towards the other door*).

DENVER: Goodbye! Oh, my wife, forgive me! Forgive me! (*Kisses* NELLY.)

NELLY: Go for your life! (*Hurries* DENVER *off, then turns to* JAIKES.) Jaikes, quick to your room. Look out of the window. Ask the man to wait a few minutes. Keep him as long as you can. (*Music cue. Hurries* JAIKES *off. Sinks exhausted into chair.*) Oh, my husband! my husband! (BAXTER *enters through window, and comes down stage.* NELLY *hears him and turns with a shriek. Rises and stands in front of table.*) Ah, what do you want?

BAXTER: Mr Wilfred Denver — is he at home?

NELLY: (*making a desperate effort to appear calm*) Yes — of course he is — he is upstairs in bed. What do you want him for?

BAXTER: (*looking at her keenly*) I think you know; but if you don't I'd rather not tell you. I must see him at once.

NELLY: Yes, on what business? Can't you tell me? I am his wife.

BAXTER: God help you then!

NELLY: Why — why? Tell me your business — I must — I will know.

BAXTER: Since you will know, I want him on a charge of murder.

NELLY: Murder! Oh, he is innocent, he'll be able to explain.

BAXTER: No doubt! I must see him at once.

NELLY: I'll tell him. Will you kindly sit down and wait a few minutes till he is dressed?

BAXTER: Mrs Denver, forgive me, you are not telling me the truth — your husband is not in this house.

NELLY: Yes – yes, wait a few moments. What makes you think I am deceiving
you? Wait – sit down, I will fetch him. (*Goes towards door, but* SECOND
DETECTIVE *rushes in through it.*)
SECOND DETECTIVE: Here, Sam! Look alive! Our man's got away in a cab.
Quick, we'll catch him! (*Exit.*)
>   (NELLY *throws up her arms in despair.* BAXTER *is going, sees
>   revolver on table, picks it up.*)
BAXTER: Revolver! One barrel fired! We'll see if the bullet'll fit it.
NELLY: (*at door, clinging to* BAXTER) No, no, you shan't go!
BAXTER: I must do my duty! Stand aside, Mrs Denver, I must do my duty. (*Exit,*
NELLY *clinging to him and trying to stop him.*)
>   *Scene changes.*

>   SCENE 2.   *A London railway station. Music to open: lights full up.*
Folding doors on right giving access to platform. INSPECTOR *opens doors. During
scene, passengers of all classes enter from left and pass off through doors at back.
Enter* DENVER *hurriedly with portmanteau; he glances behind him, looks furtively
around.*
DENVER: They're after me. Will they reach the station before the train starts? It's
my last chance!
>   (NEWSPAPER BOY *comes through door.*)
BOY: Paper, sir?
DENVER: No!
BOY: Winner of the Derby, sir! Murder in Hatton Garden last night.
DENVER: (*starting slightly*) Yes, give me one – any one will do. (*Gives coin to*
BOY *and takes paper.*)
INSPECTOR: (*coming through doors*) Now, sir, quick if you're going by this train.
Your ticket? (DENVER *shows ticket;* INSPECTOR *looks at it.*) Liverpool –
front carriage next the engine. Make haste! (DENVER *exit hurriedly through
folding doors. Whistle heard off – a second whistle heard in reply at a little
distance off.*)
BOY: That cove's in a big hurry. Give me a tanner – penny for the paper, fivepence
for the boy. (*Exit.*)
>   (*Enter a* TIPSY PASSENGER.)
TIPSY PASSENGER: (*going up to* INSPECTOR) Excuse me, sir, I want to ask you
a simple question.   '
INSPECTOR: Well, what is it?
TIPSY PASSENGER: I've got a third-class ticket for Glasgow, guv'nor. (*Produces
ticket.*) Look there, you can see it's all square – what I wish to know is
simply this – does that include refreshments on the road?
INSPECTOR: (*angrily*) No, it don't!
TIPSY PASSENGER: All right, guv'nor, no 'fence, I hope – merely a suggestion on
my part – Railway Companies pr'vide r'freshments on the road. Splendid

---

A London railway station: Euston.
cove: fellow.
tanner: sixpence.

idea, old f'low! Bring you in lots of traffic. (INSPECTOR *throws* TIPSY
PASSENGER *to one side. Enter a well-dressed* LADY. INSPECTOR *leaves*
TIPSY PASSENGER *and goes up to her, touches his cap very respectfully.*)
INSPECTOR: (*very servilely*) Can I find you a carriage, madam?
LADY: Yes. First-class to Manchester.
INSPECTOR: Yes, madam. Allow me to take your rugs and umbrella. (LADY *gives
up things to* INSPECTOR.) Thank you — this way, madam. (*Bows her off
very respectfully, and exit.*)
TIPSY PASSENGER: That's because she's a first-classer. They don't show me to
my carriage.
PORTER: (*Coming to door at back, rings bell.*) This way for Rugby, Stafford,
Crewe, Manchester, Liverpool and the North. (*Goes off again. Re-enter*
INSPECTOR.)
TIPSY PASSENGER: (*with much tipsy dignity*) Will you kindly conduct me to a
third-class smoking carriage?
INSPECTOR: Third-class smoking — at end of the train.
TIPSY PASSENGER: Kindly conduct me to my carriage and open the door for me.
INSPECTOR: Get out! Go and find your carriage.
TIPSY PASSENGER: No, I will not find my carriage. I will be escorted to my
carriage. (INSPECTOR *takes him by the scruff of the neck and runs him off.*
BAXTER *rushes on.*)
BAXTER: Express gone?
INSPECTOR: Yes, three minutes ago.
BAXTER: Just my luck again. I missed the Spider last night, and now this man's
missed me. (*to* INSPECTOR) Did you happen to notice a gentleman in a
brown overcoat, brown hat, with a portmanteau?
INSPECTOR: Rather dark, with small beard and moustache?
BAXTER: Yes.
INSPECTOR: The very man. Came through this door about three minutes ago — he
caught the express. He's got a first-class ticket for Liverpool. He's in the front
carriage of the train.
BAXTER: Where does the train stop — the first place?
INSPECTOR: Rugby — nine thirty-five. (*Exit.*)
BAXTER: (*Takes out pocketbook and writes hurriedly.*) 'From Sam Baxter,
Scotland Yard. To Police Station, Rugby. Meet nine thirty-five down express,
detain Wilfred Denver — front carriage of train — about thirty, dark, small
beard and moustache, brown hat, brown overcoat. Wanted for murder.' I'll
just nip across to the Telegraph Office, then to Scotland Yard. We shall nab
him at Rugby. (*Music. Exit.*)
　　　　　Scene changes.

　　SCENE 3.　　*The exterior of the Chequers, a wayside inn with a deeply
recessed porch towards right. Lights full up. Discovered seated in the porch drinking*

---

down express: trains run 'up' to London and 'down' to other parts of the country.
Scene 3: see appendix (p. 224 below) for the 'country lane' scene which preceded this scene in
versions before French's.

and smoking are BINKS *and* BROWNSON, *two tradesmen, and* PARKYN, *the parish clerk.* PARKYN *is reading the 'Daily Telegraph'.*

BINKS: (*politely*) When you've quite finished with that paper, Mr Parkyn.

PARKYN: When I've quite finished with it, Mr Binks, I'll hand it over to you.

BROWNSON: Yes, Parkyn, don't be greedy. Let's all have benefit of the news.

PARKYN: I'm reading about a murder as was committed in Hatton Garden, London, last night.

BROWNSON: Ah, I like a good murder; it's very pretty reading.

BINKS: Ah! It's wonderful how tastes differ. Now my wife, she's all for divorce and breach of promise cases.

BROWNSON: So's my missus. It's my belief that women never look at a newspaper for anything except these spicy little bits.

BINKS: Well, a divorce is all very well in its way, but I say, give me a jolly good murder, one as ain't found out for a month or two, and puzzles judge and jury and everybody. That's what I like.

BROWNSON: Ah! and where you ain't quite certain it's the right man till after he's hung, eh? (*regretfully*) Ah! we don't get such murders nowadays.

BINKS: Have they found out who done the murder as you're reading about, Mr Parkyn?

PARKYN: Oh, yes, a party by the name of Denver. There ain't no doubt about that.

BROWNSON: Ah, that's a pity. It takes away all the interest and excitement.

BINKS: I don't wish to hurry you, Mr Parkyn, but when you've *quite* finished with the paper. Excuse me.

PARKYN: Don't mention it, Mr Binks.

BINKS: (*aside to* BROWNSON) Parkyn gets more hoggish over the paper every day.

BROWNSON: Read it out loud, Parkyn, and then we can all hear it.

PARKYN: Very well, gentlemen, if it's the wish of the company.

BINKS: I think it's my turn to read out loud tonight, Mr Parkyn. You read out the 'Horrible affair at Camberwell' last night, and the 'Revolting Tragedy' the night before.

PARKYN: Well, Mr Binks, and if I did, am I not the clerk of this parish?

BINKS: Yes, Mr Parkyn, but because we're obliged to listen to you on Sundays when you've got us in church and we can't help ourselves, is no reason why you should bullyrag us a-weekdays when we've got the right of reply.

PARKYN: Perhaps you are not aware, Mr Binks, that the Lord Bishop of this diocese has particularly admired my reading of the psalms.

BINKS: Very likely, Mr Parkyn, but then the psalms is one thing and the *Daily Telegraph* another.

PARKYN: Gentlemen, I'm in your hands.

BROWNSON: Go on, Mr Parkyn, read out — let's hear all about this murder.

PARKYN: Mr Binks, you are in a minority. (PARKYN *puts paper under his left arm.* BINKS *and* BROWNSON *read it furtively,* PARKYN *sees them and*

---

clerk of this parish: in addition to administrative duties, the parish clerk assisted the clergyman at services.

bullyrag: harangue, domineer.

snatches paper away. Coughs, adjusts his spectacles, looks severely at BINKS
and begins.) 'A Downward Career'.
BROWNSON: Wait a bit, let's fill up our glasses and then we can start comfortable.
(*Calls.*) Susy! Susy, my dear!
    (*Enter* SUSY *from house.*)
SUSY: (*Goes to* BINKS) Did you call, sir?
BROWNSON: (*giving her his glass*) As per usual, my dear.
    (SUSY *takes glass, chucks* BINKS *under chin, then* PARKYN, *who*
    rustles paper at her as she leaves. BINKS *and* BROWNSON *cough.*)
PARKYN: (*reading*) 'A Downward Career. Last night a shocking murder was com-
mitted at 114 Hatton Garden. The victim was a young engineer named
Geoffrey Ware, who occupied the first and second floors of the house in
question. It appears that a few minutes before eleven last night, James Leaker,
the porter, and the housekeeper of the premises, went into Mr Ware's room,
and found there an acquaintance of the deceased, by name Wilfred Denver.'
(*Music.*)
    (*Enter* SUSY *with glass of grog which she places in front of*
    BROWNSON.)
SUSY: Hot or cold, Mr Brownson?
PARKYN: If you interrupt, Susy, it's impossible for me to read. (*Stops and waits*
for BROWNSON's *grog to be mixed. Meanwhile* DENVER *limps on in travel-*
stained sailor's dress, haggard and lame — he is clean shaven and appears
utterly prostrate and exhausted.)
DENVER: (*aside*) I can't drag a step further. Let them come and take me and end
it. (*Gets to porch and sinks on seat.* SUSY, *who has been mixing grog, now*
goes into inn.)
PARKYN: (*resuming*) 'And found there an acquaintance of the deceased, by name
Wilfred Denver.'
    (DENVER *starts up as if shot, glances fiercely round at all of them.*)
DENVER: Well! (*They all stare round at him.*)
BROWNSON: What's the matter, mate?
DENVER: (*recovering himself*) Nothing — I beg pardon, gentlemen — I was think-
ing of something else. Don't take any notice of me. (*Sits.*)
BROWNSON: Go on, Mr Parkyn.
PARKYN: (*resuming*) 'Wilfred Denver, a young fellow of good connections, who
has lately been leading a life of gambling and dissipation and who had
returned from the Derby in a drunken frenzy, aggravated it is said by heavy
betting losses.'
DENVER: (*starting up fiercely and calling*) Waiter! Waiter!
PARKYN: (*looking at him severely over his spectacles*) I really cannot read, sir, if
you interrupt.
DENVER: Who asked you to read? Keep your tongue quiet for a few minutes,
can't you?

Hot or cold, Mr Brownson?: the business of mixing the grog (here given as specified by Tearle's
promptbook) affords some moments of silence for Denver's entrance and the music which
accompanies it.

(PARKYN *puts down paper in disgust.* BINKS *and* BROWNSON *snatch it up and read. Enter* SUSY *from inn.* BROWNSON *snatches paper from ground.* BINKS *snatches it from* BROWNSON. PARKYN *feels on ground for paper and is visibly annoyed when he finds* BINKS *has it.*)

SUSY: Did you call, sir?

DENVER: Yes, something to eat. Anything there is in the house. Lay it in a private room.

SUSY: Yes, sir. (*Exit into house.*)

BROWNSON: Have they caught the man? (DENVER *listens attentively.*)

BINKS: No, but the police are after him. Here's a description of him. 'About thirty, medium height, well built, clean cut features, with dissipated look, a small beard and moustache.'

PARKYN: Poor fellow, I wonder how he feels tonight.

BROWNSON: Ah! I shouldn't like to be in his shoes.

DENVER: Are you talking about the Hatton Garden murder?

PARKYN: Yes, sir, we are!

DENVER: Ah! I know Hatton Garden very well. Have they discovered anything fresh?

BINKS: No, that's only the morning paper. The evening paper ain't come yet.

DENVER: It is to be hoped they'll catch the man before long.

PARKYN: Oh, I expect they'll soon run him down.

DENVER: Yes, I expect so. (*aside*) I shall betray myself in another moment.

BINKS: (*to* DENVER) Stranger in these parts, mate?

DENVER: Yes — no — I know them a little.

BINKS: Sailor, eh? (*noticing* DENVER's *clothes*)

DENVER: Yes.

PARKYN: Where might you be making for, sir?

DENVER: I'm going to join my ship.

BROWNSON: And where might that be, mate?

DENVER: She's at — at — at — (*starting up furiously*) What the devil's that got to do with you? (*Shouts.*) Waiter! Waiter! (*Enter* SUSY *from inn.*) Show me to a private room where these men can't pester me. (*Exeunt* DENVER *and* SUSY *into house.*)

PARKYN: (*rises*) Pester him! Why, what's the matter with the man?

BINKS: (*rising*) Pester him indeed! I wonder who he is? (*crossing and looking after him*)

PARKYN: He's a madman, that's what he is. Did you notice how he stared at us?

BROWNSON: Perhaps he has escaped from somewhere.

BINKS: Let's go in and put Mrs Buddens on her guard. He's a dangerous character to have about the house. (*Exit through porch.*)

BROWNSON: Yes, come on, Mr Parkyn, we may find out something more about him. (*Music. Exeunt into inn.*)

Rapid change to interior.

SCENE 4.　　*Room in the Chequers. Discover* DENVER *hanging cap on peg,* SUSY *at table laying cloth. Music to begin.*

SUSY: You look tired.

DENVER: Yes, my girl, I am.

SUSY: What's the matter with your foot?

DENVER: Nothing.

SUSY: That's a fib — you're quite lame.

DENVER: No, no, I've walked a good bit today and I'm dead beat. (*Sits.*)

SUSY: Never mind, you'll be better tomorrow.

DENVER: Yes, I shall be better tomorrow. Bring me some water, will you?

SUSY: Yes — anything else?

DENVER: You get the evening paper here?

SUSY: Yes; it generally comes about this time.

DENVER: Let me have it the moment it comes. (*aside*) I can't help what they
    suspect, I must know. (SUSY *is looking compassionately at him.*) Don't look
    at me, there's a good girl, go out — shut the door, and don't let me be dis-
    turbed.

SUSY: (*going out, aside*) Poor fellow, I wonder who he is? (*Exit, leaving door
    open.*)

DENVER: How long will it last? I wonder if anyone saw me jump from the train?
    What a fearful jump! What a mercy I wasn't dashed to pieces. I wonder what
    time it is. It must be about a quarter past eight. A quarter past eight. And
    yesterday at this time I was innocent! Yesterday he was alive — and I could
    laugh and play the fool, and now! Oh God! put back Thy universe and give
    me yesterday! Too late! Too late! Ah, my wife, how thoughtful she was.
    Shall I ever see her again — and my children? Ah, Heaven, work out some
    way of escape for me — not for my own sake, not to shield me from the just
    consequences of my crime, but for the sake of my dear wife and innocent
    children who have never done any wrong. Spare me till I have made atone-
    ment for the evil I have done. (*Looks round.*) I wonder where I am? I must
    have dragged at least twenty miles today. (*Sees railway timetable.*) Ah, a
    railway timetable, then there is a station somewhere near. (*Crosses, gets time-
    table, returns to table and sits. Enter* SUSY *with water.*)

SUSY: (*pouring out water*) There you are!

DENVER: Thank you, my girl. (*Drinks.*)

SUSY: (*polishing tray*) You ain't a bit like a sailor.

DENVER: Why not? What makes you think that?

SUSY: Sailors are always hearty and jolly, and want to kiss me. (*Polishing tray
    furiously; pauses.*) I know you've hurt your foot — I wish you'd let John the
    ostler see it — he's as good as a doctor for sprains, and he'll tell you what to
    bathe it with.

DENVER: No — no — let me alone, that's all I want, and don't forget the evening
    paper.

SUSY: Very well, you shall have it the moment it comes. (*Exit, leaving door open.*)

DENVER: I can't eat, and yet I must — I must put some strength into me. I can't

---

How long will it last? . . . : see appendix (p. 224 below) for a version of this speech to be used
in conjunction with the 'country lane' scene.

last out another day like this. (PARKYN *and* BROWNSON *talk outside.*
DENVER *sees the door open, limps up to it and is about to shut it when his*
attention is arrested.) Hark! What are they talking about in there?

PARKYN: (*voice heard outside*) I never heard sentence of death passed but once,
and that was when I was a boy, but I shall never forget it.

BINKS: (*outside*) Tell us all about it, Mr Parkyn.

PARKYN: (*outside*) Well! It was on James Beecroft, the Aylesbury murderer; and
the jury had been over two hours deliberating and it was late at night and the
court was lighted with candles in them days. And one of the candles was
burnt down to the socket and kept on drip, drip, drip, on my shoulder; and I
couldn't stir, for we was packed as tight as herrings in a barrel; and the jury
came out and everybody was as quiet as death; and the foreman of the jury
gave in the verdict, and that candle went out the very moment as he said
'Guilty'. And the man's wife was in court and she screamed out to the judge
to save her husband, and they had to drag her out of court, and she was
carried out shrieking like a mad thing. And the judge was sobbing like a baby
and when the court had got quiet again, the judge took out the Black Cap —
(DENVER *slams the door furiously.*)

DENVER: God! I can bear it no longer. Have mercy upon me, and end it now.
(*Comes down centre. Enter* SUSY *with paper. He stares at her.*) Well?

SUSY: Paper, sir.

>(DENVER *takes paper from her mechanically and watches her out*
>*of room. She delays her exit a moment, looking at him. The moment*
>*she has gone, he opens the paper and with feverish haste looks up*
>*and down it.*)

DENVER: (*Sits at table.*) What's this? 'Terrible railway calamity. Seven thirty-five
express from Euston — ' That's the train I was in. (*reading breathlessly*)
'ascending an incline came into collision with some detached wagons of a
goods train descending the incline on the same line of rail — one of the
wagons was loaded with petroleum — the barrels burst with the shock, the
vapour of the oil came in contact with the engine fire and in a moment the
front part of the train was wrapped in fierce and inextinguishable flames. The
three front carriages, with all their occupants, were burning for upwards of an
hour, and were unapproachable on account of the intense heat. Nothing was
left of them but cinders. Amongst the ill-fated passengers was Wilfred Denver'
— 'who committed the murder in Hatton Garden last night' — What's this? —
'and who has thus paid the last penalty of his crime in the very act of flying
from justice.' (*Reads again.*) 'Amongst the ill-fated passengers was Wilfred
Denver — ' Yes, it is here! — 'paid the last penalty of his crime.' Then I am
dead — dead to all the world. (*Rises.*) Dead! Yes, dead! (*Music.* DENVER
kneels.) Merciful Father, Thou hast heard my prayer and given me life. I take
it to give it back to Thee. My wife! She will see this and think me dead. Ah!
better so than to be tied to a murderer! (*Rises.*) Yes, my darling, I have done

---

the Black Cap: square of black cloth donned by the judge when the death sentence is passed.

you harm enough! Now I will set you free. (*Enter* SUSY.) How far is it to the
station?

SUSY: A mile, sir.

DENVER: There is a late train down to Bristol, is there not?

SUSY: Yes, sir, the down night mail.

DENVER: Order a horse and conveyance to meet it at once.

SUSY: Yes, sir. (*Exit.*)

DENVER: I shall reach Bristol tonight — Wilfred Denver is dead! Tomorrow I begin
a new life! (*Music forte for curtain.*)

        End of act II.

(*Three years and a half elapse between acts II and III.*)

    ACT III

    SCENE 1.   SKINNER*'s villa at Bromley. A very luxuriously furnished
apartment. Doors left and right. Window at back showing a snowy landscape outside. Fireplace right, with large comfortable fire burning. Lights full up. Music to
open. Discover* OLIVE SKINNER *at window looking out.* SKINNER *is seated in a
luxurious armchair near fire. He is reading a French novel.*

OLIVE: (*by window*) More snow! (*coming down to* SKINNER) Herbert, you don't
really mean to turn that poor woman and her children out of that wretched
cottage?

SKINNER: Yes I do!

OLIVE: Why?

SKINNER: They are starving, one of the children is dying. I object to people
starving and dying on my property.

OLIVE: But what will they do? Where will they go?

SKINNER: There's a nice comfortable workhouse about two miles off.

OLIVE: (*Puts her arm on the back of his chair.*) But surely, Herbert —

SKINNER: Now don't argue, Olive, the woman can't pay her rent — she must go!

OLIVE: But it isn't her fault she is poor. (*pause*)

SKINNER: Fault! It's no fault in England to be poor. It's a crime. That's the reason
I'm rich.

OLIVE: Rich? When I think how our money is got, I grudge the poorest labourer's
wife her crust of bread and drink of water. (*pause*)

SKINNER: Ah, that's foolish. My dear Olive, all living creatures prey upon one
another. The duck gobbles up the worm, the man gobbles up the duck and
then the worm gobbles up the man again. It's the great law of nature. My profession is just as good as any other, till I'm found out.

OLIVE: (*Rises, goes to him.*) When you talk like that I hate you. Your profession
indeed! Burglary — burglary and — (*in a whisper*) — murder!

---

down night mail: cf. footnote to p. 57 above.

(s.d.) Bromley: suburb to the south-east of London, 'in much favour with City merchants, for
whom comfortable villas have been, or are building, on every available site'. Bromley had 'a
quiet air of conscious respectability' (Thorne's *Handbook to the Environs of London*, 1876).

(s.d.) French novel: recognisable as such by its yellow paper covers.

SKINNER: (*Starts up with a frightened look and seizes her by the wrist.*) If you remind me of that cursed affair again I'll — I'll — (*dropping her hand*) There, don't be a fool, Olive, don't do it again, there's a good girl. (*Sinks into a chair, deadly quiet, and stares in front of him.*)

OLIVE: You're not quite deaf to the voice of conscience, it seems.

SKINNER: I wish to goodness I could be deaf to your voice occasionally.

OLIVE: (*Sits.*) Herbert, can't you make some reparation, can you not do something to wipe the stain off that man's memory?

SKINNER: No, I can't! (*rising and putting his arm on the mantelpiece*) Shut up! What a fool I was to tell you.

OLIVE: Do you think I would have let you tell me if I had guessed what your secret was? I've not had one peaceful moment since.

SKINNER: (*turning to her*) No, and what's more, you haven't let me have one either. For heaven's sake, Olive, don't look like that, or you'll be old and ugly in no time. Let's forget the cursed thing. (*Enter* SERVANT. SKINNER *turns to him, his manner entirely changed.*) They've come?

SERVANT: Yes, sir.

SKINNER: Send them up. (*Exit* SERVANT. OLIVE *rises and is going out.*) You'd better stay — one must be polite to one's business acquaintances.

(*Enter* SERVANT, *showing in* COOMBE *and* CRIPPS, *then exit.*)

COOMBE: (*advancing to* SKINNER) My dear boy! (*crossing to* OLIVE) How d'ye do, ma'am? (*He holds out his hand to her, she shrinks from taking it.* SKINNER *throws her a look of command: she then shakes with* COOMBE.)

CRIPPS: (*Is smoking a short pipe, does not take off his hat: nods familiarly to* OLIVE.) My respects, ma'am. (*Looks round the room.*) Spider, this is a blazing snug crib you have got here.

SKINNER: Yes, pretty well. By the way, Cripps, I wish you'd be a little more careful in your selection of adjectives.

CRIPPS: (*Sits in chair.*) What's the matter with my adjectives? Them as don't like my company can leave it.

OLIVE: (*crossing to door*) There's no occasion for me to stay, I think.

CRIPPS: (*seated in easy-chair, stretching out his legs and smoking pipe*) Not a bit, ma'am. No offence to you, but I hates a parcel of womenfolk poking their noses in where they ain't wanted. (*Exit* OLIVE. SKINNER *opens door for her.* COOMBE *has seated himself in an armchair.*) There! That's what I call business. There ain't no nonsense about me.

SKINNER: (*coming down centre, between the two men*) No, nor any superfluous politeness.

CRIPPS: I hates politeness. I hates folks as are civil and stuck up.

SKINNER: My dear fellow, consider the dignity of our profession. There's no reason why we shouldn't be gentlemen.

CRIPPS: Gentlemen! There's nothing of the gentleman about me.

SKINNER: Hush, don't tell us so, or we shall begin to believe it by and by.

---

crib: here, and subsequently, a hideout.

your selection of adjectives: i.e. 'blazing', itself a conventional substitute for stronger language.

COOMBE: Now, my dear boys, let's get to business.

SKINNER: Fire away, Father Christmas! (*Leans against the arm of* COOMBE'*s chair.*) I'm all attention, but before we set out for fresh woods and pastures new, let's square Lady Blanche's diamonds. Where are they?

COOMBE: Down at my wharf by the river along with the other swag.

SKINNER: Who looks after that place now?

COOMBE: It's locked up at present.

SKINNER: That won't do, you know — you must keep somebody there — somebody you know.

COOMBE: You can't spare one of your people, I suppose?

SKINNER: No, I'm very comfortably suited just now. My coachman has just done eighteen months; my cook's a jewel — she's the one that stole Lord Farthinghoe's silver — I always like to encourage enterprise. My housemaid was born in Durham jail, and my footman I took out of charity when his father went to do his fourteen years. In fact, I haven't a soul about the place that I can't trust.

(*Enter* SERVANT.)

SERVANT: The Duke of New York's below, sir.

SKINNER: That fellow! Give him a bit of dinner and kick him out of the place.

SERVANT: He says he must see you, sir.

SKINNER: (*Shrugs his shoulders.*) Send him up.

SERVANT: (*looking off*) Here he is, sir.

(*Enter* CORKETT: *seedy, half-starved, dirty, shivering, unshorn, ragged, his hair cropped as if just out of prison. Exit* SERVANT.)

COOMBE: (*Rises.*) Dear me! Why, it's our dear old friend, Mr 'Enery Corkett.

CORKETT: (*between* COOMBE *and* CRIPPS) Your old friend. A pretty hole you let your old friends into.

COOMBE: My dear boy, what was we to do? Why, it might have happened to any of us.

CORKETT: All my eye, Father Christmas. You were wide, oh, you three, and you meant to let me in. There's Spider there. (*Goes to* SKINNER.) Now then, Mr Spider, can't you speak to an old pal?

SKINNER: (*seated in armchair*) So! you're out again, are you?

CORKETT: Yes, I've just done the twelve months as you ought to have done.

SKINNER: (COOMBE *has seated himself again.*) Very well, don't brag about it, and perhaps you'll get another twelve months.

CORKETT: Oh no, I shan't, I'm going to turn honest.

SKINNER: Very well — you make an infernally bad rogue, Corkett — I don't know how you'll answer in the other line. My private opinion is you won't be a credit to either.

CORKETT: I ain't going to be your tool and cat's-paw any longer.

SKINNER: Very well.

---

fresh woods and pastures new: cf. the final line of Milton's *Lycidas.*
The Duke of New York: earlier versions give Corkett's nickname as 'The Duke of York'.
wide: crafty, in the know.

CORKETT: Here you are living in bang-up style, surrounded by every luxury.

SKINNER: The fruits of years of honourable industry.

CORKETT: While I ain't got the price of a glass of bitter.

SKINNER: Try a few bitter reflections.

CORKETT: No, I shan't! I shall try honesty.

SKINNER: Do — it's always the last resource of people who fail as rogues.

CORKETT: And mind you, Spider, once I do turn honest, I shall turn damned honest, and make it jolly hot for all of you.

COOMBE: (*Comes to* CORKETT *and gets him centre.*) Come, come, you know what the Spider is, you must brush him the right way of the wool. (CORKETT *goes up to cabinet at back.*) Now we've got a splendid plant on, ain't we, Spider, and he shall stand in.

SKINNER: No, I'm d----d if he shall.

COOMBE: (*aside to* SKINNER) My dear boy, we must keep his mouth shut or else he'll go and blab about that Hatton Garden affair.

SKINNER: Corkett! Corkett! (CORKETT *goes to him.*) I'm not to be bullied, but if you behave yourself, I don't mind doing something for you.

> (COOMBE *digs* CORKETT *in ribs.* CORKETT *digs him back.*
> COOMBE *then sits.*)

CORKETT: All right, I'm fly! Let's have some dinner to start with. I've got rats inside of me. What time do you dine, Spider?

SKINNER: Seven. (*Rises.*) But pray don't wait for me. (*Rings.*)

CORKETT: I won't; I'll have some lunch now, and then I'll dine with you by and by.

SKINNER: We always dress for dinner. Mrs Skinner makes a point of it.

CORKETT: Very sorry, Spider, I've left my dress togs with my uncle. You'll have to excuse morning dress this time.

> (*Enter* SERVANT.)

SKINNER: Some lunch for this gentleman.

CORKETT: And some wine, Spider.

SKINNER: Some claret for the gentleman.

CORKETT: Claret be blowed. Let's have some champagne.

SKINNER: Some champagne for the gentleman.

CRIPPS: (*rising*) I think I'll join the gentleman. I've had one dinner, but mine's a wonderful accommodating sort of stomach.

> (*Exeunt* SERVANT *and* CRIPPS.)

CORKETT: *Au revoir* — (*going*) — Spider — meet you at dinner. Seven, I think you said. (*aside*) If I can't take it out of Spider, I'll take it out of his champagne. (*Exit.*)

SKINNER: (*by fire, looking after him*) The brute! If he gets a spoonful of wine into him, it'll fly into the place where his brains ought to be, and he may open his mouth too wide. Coombe, you'd better go and look after him. (*Gets to centre.*)

---

bang-up: first-rate.
seven: the fashionable hour for the evening meal.
my uncle: the pawnbroker.

COOMBE: All right, my dear boy. Anything for an honest living. (*Exit.*)

SKINNER: (*alone, centre*) That cursed Corkett turned up again! Am I always to be reminded of that? I wish they'd all die. I'll cut the whole gang after my next 'coup', disappear, retire to some quiet country place, go to church regularly, turn churchwarden and set an example to all the parish. (*Goes to fire and sits in armchair.*)

> (*Enter* OLIVE, *showing in* NELLY. *She is haggard, pale, and very poorly dressed.*)

OLIVE: (*to* NELLY) Come in. Here is my husband — you shall speak to him yourself.

SKINNER: What is it now? Do shut that door. (NELLY *shuts door.*) What is it?

OLIVE: (*at back of his chair*) This is the poor woman who lives in the gardener's old cottage.

NELLY: Mercy, sir, mercy on a starving woman and a dying child.

SKINNER: My good woman, you'll be much better off in the workhouse. You will be provided with food and your child will be attended by a doctor.

NELLY: But he will die — it will kill him to move him this bitter weather. Have mercy, sir, have mercy!

SKINNER: Now please don't make a scene. I've made up my mind to pull down that cottage. It isn't fit for a dog to live in.

NELLY: Then let me live in it, and my children, only for a few days — only till my child is better — or dead.

SKINNER: Yes, that's just it! Your child may die — and I don't wish him to die on my property, a hundred yards from my door. I dislike death, it's a nuisance, and I don't wish to be reminded of it.

NELLY: Ah, but think of it, it's the last chance for my child. If you turn us out tonight, my boy will die.

OLIVE: Oh, Herbert, think what you are doing!

NELLY: (*turning to her*) Oh, thank you for that. Beg him to let me stay.

OLIVE: I have no influence over my husband.

SKINNER: (*to* NELLY) Have the goodness to believe I mean what I say. (*Rises and stands with back to fire.* NELLY *kneels to him.*) Now get up, there's no need to kneel to me.

NELLY: Yes! yes! there is much need. You shall not say me 'no'. Oh, I'm sure you are good and kind at heart — you do not wish my boy, my brave, beautiful boy to die. Ah, you are listening — you will have mercy — yes, yes, yes!

SKINNER: (*after a pause*) Very well. If you don't bother me any more you can stay till your child gets better.

NELLY: (*Rises.*) God bless you! God bless you!

SKINNER: Yes, we know all about that. Now go away and don't make any more fuss.

NELLY: Oh, but I can't help thanking you and — (*turning to* OLIVE) you too with my whole heart.

SKINNER: There, that'll do. Olive, show the woman out.

OLIVE: Will you come this way, Mrs — I don't know your name.

NELLY: My name is — Nelly. (*to* SKINNER) Thank you again and again. you have saved my child's life. (*Exit, with* OLIVE. COOMBE *enters, almost instantaneously, looking scared.*)

SKINNER: What's the matter now?

COOMBE: (*pointing after* NELLY) That woman! That woman!

SKINNER: Well, what of her? What's the matter, man? Have you seen a ghost?

COOMBE: I knew her again in a moment.

SKINNER: Who is she?

COOMBE: Denver's widow.

SKINNER: You must be mistaken. How do you know her?

COOMBE: They pointed her out to me at the inquest on Ware's body. I'm not
likely to forget her.

SKINNER: (*aside*) That man's widow here at my door. (*Stands pale and speechless
for a few moments, then, in a low, hoarse voice speaks to* COOMBE.)
Coombe, you can do this job for me.

COOMBE: What? What?

SKINNER: My wife has got a maggot in her brain about that Hatton Garden — accident. If she finds out that this woman is Denver's widow, she'll make my life
a purgatory and the whole business'll leak out.

COOMBE: What's to be done?

SKINNER: She's living in that old tumble-down cottage of mine — you know. She
can't pay her rent — she's had notice to quit for the last fortnight — go and
get some men and turn her and her belongings out of my place.

COOMBE: All right, leave it to me.

SKINNER: Do it at once.

COOMBE: It's done. (*Exit.*)

SKINNER: Denver's widow! Lucky I found it out and can bundle them out. They
can do their starving somewhere else — they shan't do it on my property.
(*Music. Exit.*)

        Scene changes.

    SCENE 2.   NELLY DENVER*'s home. Winter. Cottage interior and
exterior of schoolhouse, with lane between them and stile at back of stage. Lights
three-quarters up. Enter* NELLY *from inner room of cottage. She pauses at the
door and looks in again, speaking as she looks.*)

NELLY: Sleep on, my darling boy! You are happier so. You do not feel you are
hungry, and you do not tear your poor mother's heart by begging for the
food she has not got to give.

        (*Enter* JAIKES *through stile with bundle of sticks and some coal in
an old sack. He is beating himself to keep warm.*)

JAIKES: This is a freezer and no mistake. (*Enters cottage.*)

NELLY: (*eagerly*) Well, Jaikes, any success?

JAIKES: (*hanging his hat on a peg*) Success, missus, rather! Things is looking up.
What do you think? I've been and earned a shilling this afternoon.

NELLY: (*joyfully*) A shilling, Jaikes?

JAIKES: Yes, a whole shilling, straight off! Earned it all in a couple of hours. There
it is! (*Puts shilling on table.*)

NELLY: Oh, Jaikes, isn't that lucky! I was just wondering whether we should have
anything to eat tonight.

JAIKES: Eat! Lor' bless you, we'll have a reg'lar Lord Mayor's Banquet. What did the gentleman say about letting us stay on?

NELLY: At first he was very hard and cruel and said we must go, but I went down on my knees to him and begged so hard and wouldn't take 'no', till he was obliged to say we might stay till Ned was better.

JAIKES: Bless your sweet, pale face, missus, he must have had a heart made of brickbats if he could have said 'no' to you. (*Crosses to fireplace.*)

NELLY: And so you see we haven't got to turn out after all, Jaikes. (*He begins to put sticks and lay fire.*) You have brought some wood and some coals?

JAIKES: Yes; you see it gets a bit chilly towards the evening, and I thought a fire 'ud look cheerful.

NELLY: Where did you get the firing from, Jaikes? (*Gets matches from the mantelpiece.*)

JAIKES: I begged it off Bodgers the baker.

NELLY: Bodgers the baker — that dreadful, hard-hearted man?

JAIKES: Oh, Bodgers is all right once you get the right side of him, though judging from Bodgers's squint you'd think he was capable of anything.

NELLY: And how did you manage to get the soft side of him? (*Lights match and gives it to* JAIKES.)

JAIKES: Well, I went to work artful; you see, Bodgers's missus is a regular downright tartar.

NELLY: Is she?

JAIKES: Oh, yes, she leads Bodgers a dreadful life. It's no wonder he squints (*Lights fire.*) with such a wife as he's got. Well I hangs about the bakehouse and sympathises with Bodgers, and says all the hard things as I could invent about womenkind. Oh, I laid it on thick! (*Rises and puts sack up stage.*)

NELLY: (*Kneels by fire.*) But you didn't mean it, Jaikes?

JAIKES: (*coming down*) Not I, missus. My private opinion of women is as they're angels, you in particular, missus. Well, I kept on helping Bodgers and a-sympathising with him, and Bodgers, he says, 'I know what you're after, you old vagabond', says he.

NELLY: He called you an old vagabond?

JAIKES: Yes, but I didn't take no notice of that.

NELLY: No, put it down to his ignorance.

JAIKES: Yes, that's what I did. 'You're after a job, you old scarecrow', says he. 'Now be off! Get out, 'cos I shan't employ you', and he takes a shilling out of the till and chucks it down at me, and I picks it up and I says, 'I takes it, Mr Bodgers, just to show the respect I've got for you and 'cos I know you'd be offended if I didn't.'

NELLY: That was clever of you, Jaikes, to earn a shilling in that way. (*Rises.*)

JAIKES: It was artful, wasn't it? And now, missus, what shall we do with it?

NELLY: (*Sits.*) Well, Jaikes, it's your money.

Lord Mayor's Banquet: held annually in Guildhall to celebrate the installation of the new Lord Mayor of the City of London.

JAIKES: No, missus, I only earned it for you and the dear little master and missy.

NELLY: Well, what do you think, Jaikes?

JAIKES: Faggots is cheap and relishing.

NELLY: I don't think they like faggots.

JAIKES: No? What do you say to some nice red herrings — soft-roed 'uns?

NELLY: Yes, red herrings are nice, but do you think, Jaikes, there is enough support in them for growing children?

JAIKES: Well, perhaps there ain't, but there's plenty of flavour. (*suddenly*) I've got it, missus!

NELLY: Well, what, Jaikes?

JAIKES: Saveloys! After all, there's nothing like saveloys, is there? Talk about your partridge, your venison, and your 'are, why, I've tasted saveloys as 'ud give 'em all a start if it came to a question of game. But there, missus, you take the shilling and spend it how you think proper.

NELLY: (*Rises and puts back chair.*) You may be sure I shan't forget half an ounce of tobacco. (*Puts on her bonnet and shawl.*)

JAIKES: Tobacco — now don't you, missus, I've given up smoking.

NELLY: Given up smoking, Jaikes?

JAIKES: Yes; you see, missus, there's so many boys have took to it lately — I thought it was about time for men to leave off. (*Gets to fire.*)

NELLY: Well, I shall insist on your having a good hearty meal with us.

JAIKES: Now don't you, missus. I ain't hungry. I've been smelling the dinners at Bodgers' all day, and what with his roast beef and Yorkshire pudding, his beefsteak and kidney pie, roast duck and stuffing, I sniffed and sniffed at them till I got a reg'lar attack of indigestion.

NELLY: Well, if you don't manage to find a great big appetite before I come back, there'll be such a to-do in this house as never was.

JAIKES: Don't I tell you, missus, I ain't hungry? Now you make haste and get something for Master Ned — by when he wakes.

NELLY: (*going to inner door and looking off*) Look, Jaikes, how pretty he looks in his sleep.

JAIKES: (*going to inner door*) Yes, bless his heart. How much he do remind me of — but I mustn't say that, must I?

NELLY: Yes, say it, Jaikes — I like to think of him — my dear, dead Will! Whatever his faults, he was always the best of husbands to me. (*crying a little, then wiping away her tears*) But there, I mustn't cry today now we've been so fortunate. Oh, Jaikes, I feel so much happier. I think we shall weather the storm after all.

JAIKES: Why, of course we shall, now I can go and earn shillings off-hand like that.

NELLY: (*taking his hands and swinging them backwards and forwards in her own*) And the cruel winter will soon be over.

JAIKES: And the nice warm spring days will come.

---

faggots: liver, etc., chopped, seasoned, rolled into a ball and baked.

saveloys: highly-seasoned, dried sausages.

the dinners at Bodgers': refers to the practice of preparing the ingredients of a meal and paying for it to be cooked in the oven of the local baker.

NELLY: And darling Ned will get well and strong again.

JAIKES: And I shall get lots of work and earn heaps of money.

NELLY: How happy we shall be!

JAIKES: Lor' bless you, missus, we shall get on like a house afire now.

NELLY: Dear old Jaikes! Wait here, Jaikes, I'll be back soon, and then we'll have our Lord Mayor's Banquet all together. (*Opens door, crosses, and exit.*)

JAIKES: (*crossing to fire*) Blow up, Bodgers! (*Pokes fire.*) There! That's a-blazing up beautiful. We shall soon have quite a Fifth of November. Master Ned's a-sleeping as sound as a top — Miss Cissy will be out of school soon and she'll take care of him. I wish I could earn another sixpence. We can't have much of a Lord Mayor's Banquet with a shilling, but with eighteen pence, what a treat we could have. (*Leaves cottage, crossing the stage as he speaks.*) I'll try! I'll try! There's life in the old dog yet. (*Exit, running feebly and beating his arms.*)

> (CHILDREN *in school sing the following hymn. After first verse enter* DENVER. *He has changed very much, his hair is almost white and his face worn, his manner grave and subdued. He enters listening to the children's voices. The hymn is sung to the accompaniment of an harmonium.*)
> > *1st verse*

What though my sins as mountains rise
  And reach and swell to Heaven,
Yet Mercy is above the skies,
  I may be still forgiven.
> > *2nd verse*

Then let me stay in doubt no more
  Since there is sure release,
For ever open stands the door,
  Repentance, Pardon, Peace.

DENVER: (*sinking on bench*) Repentance, Pardon, Peace! The old, old message! The sweet old message! That must be for me — yes — even for me. (*Noise of children in school.*) They are coming out. Perhaps I shall be able to get some news of my dear ones. I have tracked them so far, from one wretched home to another — Shall I ever find them, or find them only in the grave? (*Retires up stage.*)

> (CHILDREN *come out of school, skipping, shouting, laughing etc.*
> CISSY DENVER *comes out among the others; they are laughing, romping and playing. She stands apart for a moment and then goes timidly up to them.*)

CISSY: Let me play with you!

BIG GIRL: No, come away from her, girls! Nobody is to speak to her. (*to* CISSY) Our fathers and mothers are respectable. Come on girls! (*Exeunt all schoolgirls but one.*)

> (CISSY *is left sobbing when the little schoolgirl who has stayed behind goes up to her and offers her a piece of cake.*)

What though my sins . . . : the hymn appears to be of Jones's own devising.

LITTLE GIRL: There, Cissy, don't you cry. I've got a piece of cake. There —
(*giving cake*) don't you tell anybody — I love you if the others don't. (*Kisses*
CISSY *and runs off.* CISSY *is crying.*)

DENVER: (*Comes down to* CISSY.) Why are you crying, my dear?

CISSY: The girls won't play with me. They won't speak to me.

DENVER: Why, how's that? What makes them so cruel? (CISSY *is silent.*) Come,
tell me all about it. You're not afraid of me, are you?

CISSY: (*looking up into his face*) No, I like you.

DENVER: That's right. I thought we should get on together. Now tell me all your
troubles — why won't they play with you?

CISSY: (*looking cautiously round*) You won't tell anybody, will you?

DENVER: No, I promise you — it shall be a secret.

CISSY: (*in a whisper*) They say my father killed a man. (DENVER *starts up stung*
with pain and turns away his face.) Ah! that makes you turn away from me.

DENVER: No! No, my dear, don't think that. Tell me quick — what is your name?

CISSY: Cissy Denver.

DENVER: (*aside*) My own child! The sins of the father are visited upon the children. Oh, heaven, is it just? What has this innocent lamb done that she should
be hounded for my crime?

CISSY: Why are you crying?

DENVER: Never mind me! Never mind me! Where do you live?

CISSY: (*Points.*) In here.

DENVER: In there?

CISSY: Yes, will you come in? (*Goes inside the cottage, leaves the door open. As*
soon as she sees the fire, she runs to it.)

DENVER: My own little Cissy that I left a toddling baby. (*Enters cottage.*)

CISSY: (*kneeling by fire and clapping hands*) Oh, look! A fire! A fire! We haven't
had a fire for I don't know how long. (*Warms her hands.*)

DENVER: (*at back of table, aside*) In this wretched hole, and without a fire!
(*Comes to* CISSY — *aloud*) Who else lives with you, Cissy?

CISSY: Mother and Ned, and our old Jaikes. You don't know our old Jaikes. I do
love him!

DENVER: God bless him! Where are the others, Cissy?

CISSY: I daresay Jaikes has gone to get some work, and mother is in the next room
nursing Ned, I'll tell her you're here. (*Rises and goes to door at back.*)

DENVER: (*Goes towards door.*) No, no, I must go — I have no business here (*at the*
door, preparing to go).

CISSY: (*who has been to inner door, opened it and looked in*) No — mother isn't
at home. Oh, I know, we can't pay our rent, and she's gone to ask the gentleman to let us stop on for a few days.

DENVER: (*aside*) To stay on here!

CISSY: (*Runs to door.*) Ned's in there, he's asleep. (DENVER *is going to door to*

The sins of the fathers . . . : cf. Exodus, XXXIV, 7: ' . . . visiting the iniquity of the fathers
upon the children, and upon the children's children, unto the third and the fourth generation'.

look. CISSY *closes door and comes away.*) Hush! you mustn't wake him. He's been very ill.

DENVER: Ill! Not very ill? Not dangerously ill?

CISSY: (*Goes to him.*) Yes, but he's getting better. Won't you sit down and warm yourself? There's only one chair, but you may have that. (*Gets chair, places it by fire, dusting it with pinafore.*)

DENVER: (*Sits.*) May I? And will you come and sit on my knee? (*Holds out his arms.*) Don't be afraid — come!

CISSY: (*going to him*) Oh, I'm not a bit afraid of you.

DENVER: What has been the matter with your little brother?

CISSY: (*sitting on* DENVER's *knee*) The doctor says he has not had enough to eat. We have been so poor; sometimes we have scarcely had anything for days. Mother tried to get a living by teaching, but when people found out who my father was, they wouldn't let her teach any more.

DENVER: (*aside*) The fiends! (*aloud*) But your mother has had some money — some friends have sent her some, eh?

CISSY: No, she has no friends.

DENVER: Yes, Cissy, yes — think again. She has had some money sent her?

CISSY: No; who would send her money?

DENVER: (*aside*) It has never reached her. (*aloud*) And does the doctor think your little brother will get better?

CISSY: (*Gets off his knee.*) Yes; if he could have nice things to eat.

DENVER: So he shall! Everything that money can buy. (*Takes out purse.*) Here, take this, you'll find plenty of money in that.

CISSY: Is that for mother? Oh, that is kind.

DENVER: No, my dear, don't say that. Wait a minute. I've got some more money loose in my pocket. (*Taking it out and putting it in purse.*) There, now you've got all my money.

CISSY: And what will you do without it?

DENVER: Oh, I've got plenty more at home; and now — (*looking hungrily at her and longing to embrace her*) I wonder if you'll give me a kiss?

CISSY: Yes, that I will.

DENVER: (*Takes her in his arms and kisses her hungrily.*) Don't take any notice of me, dear — don't mind my kissing you. I had a little girl of my own once, and when I kiss you it seems as if she came back to me again.

CISSY: Is she dead then?

DENVER: Yes, dead — (*aside*) — to me. Suppose, Cissy, that you — I mean that I — (*aside*) — I can't say it!

CISSY: I know I should have been very fond of you if you had been my father.

DENVER: (*Clasps her in his arms eagerly and kisses her again and again.*) God bless you, my darling; you mustn't mind when your schoolfellows speak unkindly of your dead father.

CISSY: I won't — I don't believe it's true. I don't believe he was a bad man, because if he had been, Jaikes and mother wouldn't have been so fond of him.

DENVER: Always think that, my dear, always think that. How thin your clothes are, dear. (*He takes his muffler off and puts it round* CISSY.) There, dear, that will keep a little of the cold out.

CISSY: Oh, isn't it pretty?

DENVER: There, now run and find your mother and give her that purse.

CISSY: And who shall I tell her gave it to me?

DENVER: Say somebody gave it to you who happened to see you and thought you were like a little girl he had lost, and say, too, that — (*breaking down, aside*) Oh, my wife, if I could but send you one word from my living grave!

CISSY: Yes, what else shall I say?

DENVER: (*rising*) I dare not! No, dear, there is no other message. Your mother does not know me. (*Kisses her.*) Run along, dear, make haste and tell her of your good fortune.

CISSY: Yes, that I will! (*coming out of cottage*) She's gone to Mr Skinner's — that nice big house across the field. (*Exit.*)

DENVER: (*following her to door*) Run on then, my brave little queen. (*He watches her off and then looks carefully and cautiously around.*) My boy, I must see my boy! (*Re-enters cottage cautiously.*) Just one look, one kiss. Nobody is about.

> (DENVER *goes into inner room, is absent a few moments then returns in tears.* JAIKES *enters, rubbing his hands to warm them.*)

JAIKES: (*crossing stage*) Artfulness ain't done it this time. Not a blessed ha'penny! Whew! it gets colder and colder. (*Goes up to stile.*) I wonder where the missy is?

DENVER: (*coming out*) My little baby boy that I left, grown so thin, so pale, so wasted — is there no end to my sin, no end to its bitter fruit? (*Sees* JAIKES — *aside*) Jaikes!

JAIKES: Hillo! What are you doing in there?

DENVER: (*Turns away his face from* JAIKES *and muffles it partly with his cape so that he does not see his features.*) Excuse my intrusion, I was passing your cottage and happened to come in. I take a great interest in the sick poor. There's a little boy in that room — he's dangerously ill — send for the doctor to see him at once. Have the best advice you can get and give him some nourishing food, the best of everything (*still keeping his face averted from* JAIKES *and speaking in slightly disguised tones*).

JAIKES: Oh, yes, that's all very well, but where's the money to come from?

DENVER: (*aside*) Cissy has my purse. (*aloud*) I will pay for whatever is required. I have just given away all the money I have about me, but you can have the bills sent in to me. John Franklin, Kensington Gardens, London.

JAIKES: Oh, yes, it's likely I can get tick on the strength o' that, ain't it? 'A pound of tea and a quartern loaf and put it down to Mr John Franklin, Kensington Gardens, London.'

DENVER: Do as I tell you — you will find it all right.

JAIKES: Who is Mr John Franklin? If you want to help us, why don't you give us some money and let's have a look at your face? (*Peers round* DENVER's

---

I take a great interest in the sick poor: this claim to be an amateur social worker would not have seemed implausible in the 1880s.

tick: credit

quartern loaf: large loaf, made from a quarter of a peck of flour and weighing about 4 lb.

muffler and recognises him.) Master Will! (*Drops on his knees.*) Master Will! God forgive me! It's Master Will come back from the dead. Say it's really you, Master Will!

DENVER: Yes, it is I, come back, as you say from the dead. My wife! Is she well? How is she? Has she suffered much? Does she ever speak of me?

JAIKES: Oh, Master Will, I can't tell you what she's had to go through. It's been a terrible hard fight for her, but she's borne up like an angel. Oh, sir, you've come back at the right time. We're nearly starving.

DENVER: (*Helps* JAIKES *to seat on bench.*) Starving? That's all over now. I'm rich, Jaikes, I'm rich! When I left England I went to the Silver Mines of Nevada — I had to struggle hard at first and could only send you a few dollars — I was almost starving myself, but one morning I struck a rich vein of silver; today I'm richer than I can count; and then I sent you a thousand dollars, and so — none of it reached you?

JAIKES: No, sir, you see we've changed our home so often and she always took care not to leave our address for fear —

DENVER: For fear my wretched story should follow you, I see.

JAIKES: Ah, sir, don't say any more about that — that's all past now. Oh, don't you mind my crying, sir; to see you come back like this is too much for me — I can't believe it, sir. (*Rises.*) And Miss Nelly — she'll go mad with joy.

DENVER: She must not know, Jaikes.

JAIKES: Not know? Not tell her, Master Will?

DENVER: Not yet! Not yet. Listen, Jaikes, I have come back to England with one thought, with one resolve — to make her happy. Whatever happens to me, that I will do. Shall I ask her to share my nightmare of a life, put her on a ceaseless rack of anxiety and suspense, torture her as I am tortured? Heaven forbid!

JAIKES: But surely, Master Will, you are safe after all these years?

DENVER: I shall never be safe till I stand in the dock to answer for my crime — I shall be safe then. I've started a hundred times to give myself up, but I have always been held back by the thought that I was not myself that night; but it will come, Jaikes.

JAIKES: What will come, sir?

DENVER: Detection. It may be tomorrow, or it may not be for years, but it will come, and if I were to join her, suspicion would be aroused at once. I might be discovered, dragged from her side, tried, condemned and hanged.

JAIKES: Master Will! But if missus could but know. If she could but know.

DENVER: Not yet, Jaikes. Listen, you shall take her from this poverty and put her in her old home with everything that money can buy, and then, when I have made her rich, cheerful, contented, I will ask myself whether I may dare to throw the shadow of my life across her happiness. In the meantime, promise me, swear to me that she shall not know.

JAIKES: Why, of course, Master Will, if you wishes it.

DENVER: Jaikes, I must see her — I am dying to look on her dear face, to hear one word from her lips — to see her without being seen.

JAIKES: That's easily managed. Stand here (*indicating exterior of cottage window*), you'll be able to see her and hear her and she'll never be none the wiser.

DENVER: God bless you, my dear old Jaikes, for all your kindness. God bless you, I shall never be able to repay you.

JAIKES: There now, don't you talk nothing about that, Master Will. Why, to see you come back like this pays me fifty times over. I allus said you would. (*crying with joy*) I allus said – (*Music. Looks off.*) Here comes Miss Nelly.

> (DENVER *and* JAIKES *go up and get behind cottage. Enter* NELLY, *crosses stage and goes into cottage.*)

DENVER: (*coming from behind*) My wife! My poor wife!

> (NELLY *in cottage puts her purchases on table.*)

NELLY: There, my precious ones, you shall have a meal tonight at any rate. (*Goes up to door of inner room, looks inside, shows content and shuts door.*) I wonder where Jaikes and Cissy are? (*Takes off bonnet and shawl and hangs them up.*)

DENVER: My own Nell, the girl who left her own bright home to follow my cursed fortunes. Oh, if I look another moment I must rush to her and hold her in my arms!

> (*Enter* OLIVE, *quickly crosses stage and enters cottage.* DENVER *retires behind cottage and comes out again after she has entered.*)

OLIVE: I am the bearer of bad news. My husband has repented of his kindness. He will not let you stay here.

NELLY: Not let me stay here?

OLIVE: No – since you left he has learned who you are. He has found out that you are the wife of a –

> (DENVER *turns aside as if stabbed with pain.*)

NELLY: (*Checks* OLIVE.) Ah no, no, for pity's sake don't say it. I have heard the word so often. Yes, it is true – I am the widow of such a man, and for that I am to be punished, it seems (*sobbing*).

OLIVE: Who knows it is true? Who knows that your husband did really kill that man?

DENVER: (*eagerly*) What's that?

NELLY: Why, what doubt can there be?

OLIVE: It was never proved. He was never tried. Who knows but that there might have been some terrible mistake?

DENVER: (*outside*) Some terrible mistake?

NELLY: What do you mean? What do you know?

OLIVE: (*recovering herself quickly*) Nothing – I thought it might comfort you to think your husband was innocent. It could do no harm now that he is dead; but I am forgetting my errand. I came here to help you and I dare not stay. (*Takes out purse.*)

> (COOMBE'*s voice is heard off.*)

COOMBE: (*outside*) You can wait here. Be ready if I want you. (COOMBE *enters. As* DENVER *hears and sees* COOMBE *he retires.*) But we'll try persuasion first. (*Enters cottage.*)

DENVER: (*coming away from cottage*) The man who showed me into Geoffrey Ware's room that dreadful night. What does it mean?

OLIVE: There are three pounds five shillings. It is all I have. (*Takes money out of purse and shows it empty.* COOMBE, *who has entered unseen by* NELLY *or* OLIVE, *gets to back of table and picks up money.*)

COOMBE: It won't be necessary, ma'am. I'll take it to your husband. Your husband wants you — you'd better go. (*Holds door of cottage open for* OLIVE.)

OLIVE: Oh, if he were not my husband! (*Exit quickly from cottage and crosses stage, going off.*)

COOMBE: (*calling after her*) Ah! you shouldn't have took your place for life. (*Shuts door and turns to* NELLY.)

DENVER: What now? If I stop this ruffian he'll call his men and there may be a disturbance, and I may be involved. What can I do?

COOMBE: Now, my dear good lady, there's a pleasant way of doing things and a unpleasant, and I always try the pleasant way first.

NELLY: Oh, don't make any words about it. You have come to turn me out, is it not so?

COOMBE: Oh, dear no. I've only come to ask you in the kindest manner possible to pay your rent. Three pounds five shillings.

NELLY: How can I pay it? I haven't a shilling in the world, and you know I haven't.

DENVER: (*outside*) Where is Cissy? Where is the money?

COOMBE: Ah, that's a pity! Because as you can't pay you must go.

NELLY: No, no! Let me stay tonight — only tonight. I will go tomorrow morning. My child is in that room very ill, and if he is moved in this bitter weather, it will kill him. Let me stay tonight, I will do no harm.

COOMBE: Now look here, my dear good lady — it's no good your begging and praying to me, 'cos go you must.

NELLY: Oh, is there no tenderness, no pity on the earth? (*going up stage*)

COOMBE: (*Gets round front of table to fire.*) Now, look sharp! Are you going to pack up?

NELLY: Yes, yes, give me a little time, I will go. (*Goes into inner room, re-entering almost immediately very determinedly.*) No, I will not go. My child is sleeping. He is getting better. I will not wake him and take him into the bitter cold to kill him. (*She bolts the door and stands with her back to it.*)

COOMBE: (*Stands with his back to the fire.*) Will you go quietly, or shall I have to send for my men to turn you out?

NELLY: I tell you I will not go. Go back and tell your master that here I stay — I and my children — till he drags our bodies out and flings them into the streets.

COOMBE: Oh very well, we must try the unpleasant way then. (*Goes towards door.*)

NELLY: Merciful Father, help me now!

DENVER: (*outside*) I can bear it no longer. (*Comes to door, is about to open it when* CISSY *enters and runs to him.*) Quick, my child, give your mother the money! (*Pushes her through door, which he has opened.*)

CISSY: (*running round to* NELLY) Mother, look what the kind gentleman gave me!

NELLY: (*Seizes money eagerly.*) An angel from heaven has sent it. (*Music. To* COOMBE, *as she throws money on the table*) Here. Take your money! Now you go! (*Points to the door.* COOMBE, *baffled, picks up money.*)
       End of act III.

ACT IV

SCENE 1.   *Room in* DENVER*'s house, Kensington Gardens. Doors right and left. Window to left. Music to open. Lights full up. Enter* FRANK SELWYN, *showing in* BAXTER.

BAXTER: Mr John Franklin not in, eh?

SELWYN: No. I am his private secretary.

BAXTER: (*looking at him keenly*) Oh! you are his private secretary? (*aside*) This is the young sprig I'm after.

SELWYN: Perhaps I might do.

BAXTER: No. I think not. When can I see Mr Franklin?

SELWYN: It's uncertain. What's your business?

BAXTER: That's my business! I'll wait. (*Turns back to audience and stands looking at picture on wall, whistling.*)

SELWYN: (*aside, looking at* BAXTER) Can he have come about that cursed cheque? It must come sooner or later. Mr Franklin must find me out, find out that I have repaid his goodness by robbing him, returned his trust by forging his name!

BAXTER: (*turning round*) I suppose you've got a nice comfortable berth as Mr Franklin's private secretary?

SELWYN: Yes.

BAXTER: Very rich man, isn't he?

SELWYN: Very.

BAXTER: Made his money in silver mining, didn't he?

SELWYN: Yes.

BAXTER: Ah! so I've heard. Went to bed one night a common miner, and the next a millionaire.

SELWYN: I've heard so. They call him the Silver King.

BAXTER: Gives a lot of money away, doesn't he?

SELWYN: His whole life is spent in doing good. He's as noble and generous as he is rich.

BAXTER: Ah! employs you to look after the deserving cases — trusts you with his purse, and his chequebook occasionally, eh?

SELWYN: (*wildly*) What do you mean?

BAXTER: Nothing, only you must take care he doesn't get imposed on. (*aside*) It's all right — the young idiot!

SELWYN: (*aside*) It must come!

(*Enter* DENVER.)

DENVER: Somebody wishes to see me, Frank?

BAXTER: Mr John Franklin? (*looking at* DENVER)

DENVER: Yes, I am John Franklin. What do you want?

BAXTER: I beg pardon. That is my card. (*Gives card.*) Sam Baxter, Scotland Yard. (*Aside, as* DENVER *takes card.*) I've seen you before somewhere, my gentleman.

DENVER: (*wincing under* BAXTER*'s steady gaze*) Well, what is your business? I must beg you to make haste as I have to catch a train into the country.

BAXTER: Then I'll come to the point at once. (*Opens his pocketbook, takes out papers.* SELWYN *is going,* BAXTER *stops him.*) Mr Private Secretary, you needn't go. We may want you. (*aside, looking at papers*) Now where have I seen you before, Mr Franklin? (*aloud, taking a cheque from pocketbook*) Oh, here it is!

SELWYN: The cheque I forged!

BAXTER: You bank at the County and Metropolitan?

DENVER: Yes.

BAXTER: This cheque was presented yesterday for payment in the ordinary way. The clerk refused to cash it, detained the presenter and sent for you immediately. You were not at home, and so the affair was placed in my hands.

> (DENVER *comprehends the situation, and as* SELWYN *makes a movement as if to speak, stops him with a look of caution and silences him.*)

DENVER: (*to* BAXTER) Give me the cheque. (BAXTER *gives the cheque.* DENVER *looks at it.*) Well?

BAXTER: That signature, sir?

DENVER: Well?

BAXTER: Is it in your handwriting, sir?

> (SELWYN *makes a movement, as if to speak, but* DENVER *stops him with a glance.*)

DENVER: Yes, it's quite right. (SELWYN *gives a sigh and shows immense relief, and is about to blab out his gratitude.* DENVER *stops him with a look.*) Yes, the signature is a little awkward. I must have been in a hurry. (BAXTER *still looks incredulous.*) Do you doubt me?

BAXTER: Oh, no, sir, if you say so, sir, of course it's all right – if you wrote the cheque – why, there's an end of the matter, isn't there, sir?

DENVER: I think so. You may take the cheque back to the bank, tell the cashier it is all right. If necessary I'll call at the bank tomorrow and make the matter right. Will you accept a five-pound note for your trouble? (*Gives* BAXTER *note.*)

BAXTER: Thank you, sir, and if ever you should want my assistance in any little matter of business, sir, I shall be happy to oblige you, sir, and to keep my mouth shut. (*In putting the note in his pocket he intentionally drops a piece of paper.*)

DENVER: Thank you, I have your card.

BAXTER: (*aside to* DENVER) Keep your eye on that youngster – he's got mixed up with a bad lot. (*aloud*) Good day, Mr Franklin (*going*).

DENVER: Good day, Mr Baxter. (*Turns to* SELWYN.)

BAXTER: (*glancing back at* DENVER, *aside*) I've had you through my hands somewhere. (*Exit.*)

DENVER: (*Crosses to* SELWYN *and puts his hand on his shoulder.*) Don't do it again, my boy, don't do it again!

SELWYN: I never will, sir! Oh, sir, your kindness breaks my heart! I've been such a bad fellow, sir! I don't deserve that you should forgive me. I shall be ashamed to meet you in the future, sir.

DENVER: I hope not. This was your first step downwards – Pray that it may be your last.

SELWYN: It shall! It shall!

DENVER: Remember, I still trust you! (*Exit.*)

SELWYN: I'll make a fresh start today. God bless him! (*Exit.*)

    (*Re-enter* BAXTER, *from opposite door.*)

BAXTER: I beg pardon, I must have dropped a paper here! Nobody here! (*Picks up the paper he had previously dropped, creeps to the window and looks out.*) There goes Mr Franklin in a cab. Drives off! Now when and where have I had that man through my hands? Deuce take my memory! (*Comes slowly away from window.*) Dear! Dear! (*Snaps his fingers and taps his forehead to aid his memory as he crosses the stage, then stops suddenly.*) Good heavens! Yes! That's the man! Derby night four years ago! The skittle alley at the Wheatsheaf — the revolver, whew! Here's a find! John Franklin, millionaire, philanthropist and Silver King, an unhung murderer. The hair grown grey but the same face. By Jove! What a catch for me! (*Music. Exit very swiftly and with great animation.*)

    Scene changes.

SCENE 2.   *Exterior of the Grange. Lights full up. Discover* OLD VILLAGE PEOPLE. JAIKES *enters, very respectably dressed.*

JAIKES: Well, Gaffer Pottle! Mrs Gammage! Hillo, Tabby!

GAFFER: (*an ancient, decrepit villager*) My humble respects, Muster Jaikes. (*turning to* TABBY) Curtsy, Tabitha! Curtsy! Curtsy, you old fool! Don't you know Muster Jaikes is Master of the Grange and Lord of the Manor?

TABBY: Ah, Daniel Jaikes and me was brought up together. I ain't going to curtsy to Dan'l Jaikes. I'm going to shake hands with him. (*Crosses to* JAIKES.) Don't you remember how fond we was of one another when we was boy and girl together, eh, Dan'l dear?

JAIKES: No, I don't. It's too many years ago — and don't call me Dan'l. (TABBY *goes up stage.*) Tabby's a-setting her cap at me again, I must put a stop to that.

GAFFER: I hopes Miss Nelly is pretty tolerable?

JAIKES: Oh, she's all right! Your dinner ain't ready yet. You can wait here a few minutes, and mind you all behaves yourselves! (*very severely to* TABBY) Tabby, let those flowers alone. I'll tell Mrs Denver you have arrove. (*Exit.*)

GAFFER: Dan'l Jaikes seems to be rather 'igh and mighty now he's come into his fortin'!

MRS GAMMAGE: Ah! Fancy Dan'l Jaikes coming and buying the Grange and being Lord of the Manor, and bringing Miss Nelly back to live in it.

GAFFER: I can't make out who this here Uncle Samiwell was as has died and left Dan'l all this money.

MRS GAMMAGE: Aye, Dan'l never had no Uncle Samiwell as ever I heered on.

TABBY: (*coming down stage*) Ah, you folks don't know nothin' about it. Dan'l's master of the Grange, ain't he? And I wouldn't say as I mightn't be missus afore long.

GAFFER: I wouldn't say as you mightn't, Tabby. Pigs might fly, but I've kept pigs for up'ards of fifty years, and I never see 'm make a start.

MRS GAMMAGE: No, Tabby, Muster Jaikes don't seem to be noways particler smit with you just now.

GAFFER: Aye, aye, Tabby, you've had three husbands and buried 'em all. You let well alone. (*Music.*)

> (*Enter from house* NELLY, *well dressed, with* CISSY *and* NED *clinging to her, one on each side,* JAIKES *following them.* OLD PEOPLE *bow and curtsy.*)

NELLY: Well, you have come, all of you? That's right! How do you do, all of you? (*shaking hands with some of them*) How do you do, Tabby?

TABBY: We're all well and hearty, thank you kindly, and we be mortal glad to see you back at the Grange, bain't we, Gaffer?

GAFFER: Aye, we didn't like they folks as come here when you and Muster Denver left.

MRS GAMMAGE: They was mean, they was.

TABBY: Aye, no beef and coals at Christmas, no pea soup, no blankets, no flannel petticoats, no nothing!

> (CISSY *runs off with* NED *into shrubbery.*)

GAFFER: Aye, we knowed when you come back, Miss Nelly, there'd be plenty for everybody.

NELLY: I hope so. You see, my friends, I have known what it is to be poor myself. Since I left you I have heard my children cry for bread; indeed, if it were not for the kindness of my old friend here — (*indicating* JAIKES, *who shuffles about and looks very uncomfortable*)

JAIKES: Yes, yes, missus! We'll drop the subject.

NELLY: No, we will not. You know I owe everything to you. (*to the* OLD PEOPLE) Go and have your dinner, all of you. You'll find it ready in the hall. It is Jaikes that provides it for you, not I. First thank the Giver of all good, and then thank our dear old Jaikes. (*Crosses to seat and sits.*)

JAIKES: No, no, I won't be thanked! (*Hurries them into house.*) Be off, you old vermints, be off! (TABBY *stops behind.*) Now, Tabby!

NELLY: What do you want?

TABBY: (*curtsying to* NELLY) Oh! if you please, Miss Nelly, we liked that bit of beef you sent us so much. The next time we hopes it'll be a little larger and not quite so fat. And I'm getting short o'tea and candles, and a little drop of gin is comforting after washing all day. And my best gown's wore out.

JAIKES: Good job, too! I wish it was your tongue instead.

NELLY: Very well, Tabby, I won't forget you.

JAIKES: Now will you be off and get your dinner, or else you shan't have none! Be off! (*Hurries her off. Exit* TABBY.) The old hussy! You mustn't let her impose on you, missus.

NELLY: Ah, Jaikes, it is for you to say — you are master here.

JAIKES: Yes, yes — of course, so I am — I forgot that! Still, you know, missus, all this money is, as you may say, yours.

NELLY: Mine, Jaikes?

JAIKES: Yes, you see, my Uncle Samuel left particular instructions in his will —

---

beef and coals . . . pea soup . . . blankets . . . flannel petticoats: customary items in the charity traditionally dispensed by the gentry to their poorer tenants.

well, never mind my Uncle Samuel, we'll drop the subject. Ain't you 'appy
now you're back in your old home, missus?

NELLY: Yes, Jaikes, I am happy! (*Sighs.*)

JAIKES: Quite happy, missus?

NELLY: (*Sighs.*) Yes, Jaikes, happier than I ever hoped to be.

JAIKES: There's some'ut, missus! I can see — something you miss now, ain't there?
Tell the truth.

NELLY: Yes, Jaikes, there is.

JAIKES: What is it, missus? I've ordered 'em to lay out the garden just as it used to
be and to plant a new chestnut tree where the old 'un was blown down —

NELLY: It isn't that, Jaikes.

JAIKES: The old fish-pond as they folks filled up — I'll have it dug out again?

NELLY: Ah, no, don't trouble about that.

JAIKES: Then what is it, missus? You shall have it if it costs a mint of money.
(*Music.*)

NELLY: Oh, Jaikes, can't you see what it is? I'm back in my old home without the
man who made it all dear to me — without my Will! Oh, I love him still — yes,
I love him as much today as the day I married him in the church yonder. It
was under this tree I promised to be his wife. Oh, Jaikes, I remember it as if it
were yesterday. Everything here, every tree, every brick in the old house,
every little nook and corner brings back to me his dear handsome face until I
can sometimes hardly stop myself from running all through the grounds and
fields and calling out, 'Will! Will! come back to me, come back to me, if it
were but for a moment!' Now you know what it is I miss in my old home,
my husband's love — and you can't give that back to me, Jaikes, no, no, not
that, not that! (*Exit.*)

JAIKES: (*looking after her*) Can't I? Oh, yes, I can, and I will, too, this very day!
I've wrote and told him I can't keep his secret no longer — he's on his way to
you now as fast as the train can bring him! You wait a bit, missus, and I'll dry
up them tears for you! You shall be the happiest woman in England afore this
day's over, that you shall! Make haste, Master Will, make haste and come!
(*Re-enter* TABBY. JAIKES *has his back to her: she taps him on the back.*)
Hillo! what now, Tabby?

TABBY: (*very affectionately*) Oh, Dan'l dear! I'm so glad you've come back again.
Ain't you glad to be back among your old friends, Dan'l dear?

JAIKES: (*cautiously edging from her*) Yes — yes — middling!

TABBY: Don't you remember when we used to go cowslipping, eh, Dan'l?

JAIKES: (*resolutely*) No, I never went cowslippin' along of you, Tabby.

TABBY: Oh, yes, you did, Dan'l. And our games at hide and seek?

JAIKES: No!

TABBY: Oh, yes, Dan'l, I used to hide and you used to try and find me.

JAIKES: Oh, no, Tabby! I used to hide and you used to try and find me!

TABBY: Oh, Dan'l, you don't know how fond I've allays been of you, and now
you're gettin' old and I'm gettin' old —

JAIKES: Yes, you are, Tabby, and precious ugly into the bargain!

TABBY: And I've been thinking how nice it 'ud be if we could end our days
together.

JAIKES: I'm much obliged, Tabby, but I don't want to end my days just at present.

TABBY: Ah, but Dan'l dear — me to take care of you and nurse you up, and you to take care of me and nurse me up — wouldn't that be nice?

JAIKES: (*resolutely*) No, no, you might like it; but I ain't ambitious, Tabby, I'm very content as I am.

TABBY: Ah, Dan'l — you've never been married.

JAIKES: And you have — three times.

TABBY: And the best of wives I've made, I'm sure. Ask my three good men else.

JAIKES: It 'ud be a sin to disturb 'em now they've got a bit of peace.

TABBY: And I should make a better wife now than ever.

JAIKES: You ought, Tabby, you've had plenty of experience.

TABBY: (*taking his arm affectionately*) Well, then, what do you say, lovey — when shall we be married?

JAIKES: (*aghast*) Married! Me marry you! Why, you old Mormon, (TABBY *starts back horrified.*) you old female Henry the Eighth! You old wolf in sheep's clothing! You — you, you old Bluebeard in petticoats! Me marry you! Never! Never! Be off with you! Be off! (*Frightens her off. Exit* TABBY.) I've had a narrow squeak that time!

    (*Enter* CISSY *with flowers.*)

CISSY: Look, Jaikes, for mamma! Aren't they pretty? Oh, Jaikes, it was kind of you to bring us to this beautiful home!

JAIKES: Ah! It ain't me, little missy, it isn't me as is doing it all!

    (*Exit* CISSY. DENVER *appears at gate.*)

DENVER: Jaikes!

JAIKES: Master Will!

DENVER: Is anybody about? Can I come in?

JAIKES: Yes, come in, Master Will! Miss Nelly's gone to give her poor people their dinner and I'm all alone.

DENVER: You're sure I shan't be seen?

JAIKES: No fear, sir, I'll keep a good look out.

DENVER: How is she? Is she quite well and happy — and the children?

JAIKES: Yes, they're all quite well. Oh, Master Will, I'm so glad you've come. I can't hold out much longer! Uncle Samuel has got me into a dreadful mess! I wish we hadn't invented him. And then there's all that money as you sent her anenonymously from America.

DENVER: Yes?

JAIKES: Well, it didn't turn up while we was starving, but now we're rolling in money and it's a nuisance, it all turns up as bold as brass. Oh, Master Will, don't hide it from her no longer — tell her as you're alive — you wait here — I'll go and fetch her to you.

DENVER: Stop, Jaikes, you mustn't go!

JAIKES: Master Will, when you brought her back here and spent all that money to make the old place just like it used to be when she was a girl you thought you was going to make her happy, didn't you?

Mormon: i.e. polygamist.

DENVER: (*Crosses slowly to seat near* JAIKES.) And have I not made her happy? What more can I do?

JAIKES: Why, sir, don't you see. — Home ain't four walls and the ceiling and the furniture — home's the place where them as loves us is — and it was you what made this place home for her, and she's breaking her heart 'cause it's her home no longer.

DENVER: Jaikes, I will tell you why my wife must not know that I am alive, and when I have told you never speak of it again. Last night I went down to the river to a place owned by that man Coombe.

JAIKES: What, the man as was going to turn the missus out?

DENVER: Yes, I've been following him up for the last six months, ever since I recognised him as the man that showed me into Geoffrey Ware's room that night. Just as drowning men catch at straws, I have caught at the straw of a hope that I might find out something. I don't know what — something that might give me a right to believe that I did not shed that man's blood —

JAIKES: Ah, how happy it would make her!

DENVER: And so night after night I go to that place and watch, and watch, and watch. I've tried to get in, all in vain, it's a hopeless task. Well, when I got back last night, I found your letter waiting for me — begging me to make myself known to my wife. I read the letter again and again, and the more I tried to persuade myself that for her dear sake I must keep silence, the more my heart cried out, 'I must have her! I will have her! If I die for it, she shall be my own again!' And then I thought I would take her out to Nevada, to the city that I have built, where every man would shed his blood for me, and every child is taught to reverence the name of John Franklin. 'There', I thought, 'I shall be free from the past, safe from the law — there', I said, 'we will live the rest of our days honoured, happy, beloved, in peace with ourselves and all the world.' And so I spent half the night planning out a happy future with her and my children. Oh, Jaikes, I was so happy — I couldn't sleep for joy of it, and when at last I put my head on my pillow, my one thought was, 'Tomorrow I will tell her I am alive! Tomorrow I will take her in my arms and call her my wife again!'

JAIKES: And so you shall, Master Will! Let me fetch her to you! Let me fetch her to you!

DENVER: Stay! I fell asleep, Jaikes — do you know what a murderer's sleep is? It's the waking time of conscience! It's the whipping-post she ties him to while she lashes and stings his poor helpless guilty soul! Sleep! It's a bed of spikes and harrows! It's a precipice over which he falls sheer upon the jags and forks of memory! It's a torchlight procession of devils, raking out every infernal sewer and cranny of his brain! It's ten thousand mirrors dangling round him to picture and re-picture to him nothing but himself. Sleep — oh! God, there is no hell like a murderer's sleep! (*holding* JAIKES'*s hand*) That's what my sleep has been these four years past. I fell asleep last night and I dreamed that we were in Nevada and we were seated on a throne, she and I; (*Releases* JAIKES'*s hand and rises.*) and it was in a great hall of justice, and a man was brought before me charged with a crime; and just as I opened my mouth to pronounce sentence upon him, Geoffrey Ware came up out of his grave, with his eyes staring, staring, staring, as they stared at me on that night, and as they will stare at me till I die, and he said, 'Come down! Come down! you whited sepulchre! How dare you sit in that place to judge men?' And he leapt up in his grave — close to the throne where I was — and seized me by the throat and dragged me down, and we struggled and fought like wild beasts — we seemed to be fighting for years — and at last I mastered him, and held him down and wouldn't let him stir. (*Sits again.*) And then I saw a hand coming out of the sky, a long, bony hand with no flesh on it, and nails like eagle's claws, and it came slowly (*raising his hand*) — out of the sky, reaching for miles it seemed, slowly, slowly it reached down to the very place where I was, and it fastened on my heart, and it took me and set me in the justice hall in the prisoner's dock, and when I looked at my judge, it was Geoffrey Ware! And I cried out for mercy, but there was none! And the hand gripped me again as a hawk grips a wren, and set me on the gallows, and I felt the plank fall from my feet, and I dropped, dropped, dropped — and I awoke! (*Puts his hand across his eyes.*)

JAIKES: For mercy's sake, Master Will —

DENVER: Then I knew that the dream was sent for a message to tell me that though I should fly to the uttermost ends of the earth — (*holding* JAIKES*'s arm*) as high as the stars are above, or as deep as the deepest seabed is below, there is no hiding-place for me, no rest, no hope, no shelter, no escape! (*Drops into garden seat and sobs.*)

        (*A pause.* CISSY *runs on.*)

CISSY: Jaikes, who's that? (DENVER *looks up and strives to hide his tears.*) Oh! it's you! (*She runs to him and sits on his knee.*) You've come to see us in our new home! But you are crying — what's the matter? Are you unhappy?

DENVER: (*putting his arms round her*) Not now, Cissy — not now! Not now!

CISSY: Jaikes, do you know the kind gentleman?

JAIKES: (*who has gone up stage and is keeping watch, looking off*) No, missy, no!

CISSY: I'm so glad you've come! You shall come and live with us, will you?

DENVER: What would you do with me?

CISSY: You shall play with Ned and me. We've got a rocking horse and soldiers, and lots of things.

DENVER: What games we could have, couldn't we?

CISSY: (*clapping her hands*) Yes! Oh, do stay, will you! Do! Do!

DENVER: And your mother?

CISSY: Oh, I know she'd be glad to have you. She's always talking about you and wondering who you are. Who are you?

DENVER: Who am I?

CISSY: Yes, tell me — tell me true!

DENVER: Well, I'm a king.

CISSY: But what king are you?

DENVER: I'm the Silver King! At least that's what men call me.

JAIKES: (*looking off*) The other way, Gaffer Pottle — this (*Calls out severely.*) is private! (*looking at* DENVER *warningly*)

DENVER: (*starting up*) I must go — goodbye, Cissy! (*Kisses her.*)

CISSY: (*holding* DENVER*'s hand*) No, no, you mustn't go! Mamma does want to see you so badly! Wait here! I'll go and fetch her. (*Runs off to house calling.*) Mamma!

JAIKES: Master Will, won't you stay?

DENVER: No, Jaikes — let me go! Not a word, for her sake! Let me go! (*Exit quickly.*)

          (*Enter* CISSY *from house.*)

CISSY: Come on, mamma! (*Looks round.*) Where is he, Jaikes?

          (*Enter* NELLY *from house.*)

NELLY: Where is he?

JAIKES: Where's who, missus?

NELLY: The gentleman who was here who gave the purse to Cissy.

JAIKES: Oh, yes, missus, there was a gentleman here, but as — as he was rather pressed for time he had to go — to — to — catch his train.

NELLY: (*going up towards gate*) Why did you let him go, Jaikes, when you knew how much I wanted to thank him? He can't have gone far — I'll go after him. (*Is preparing to go after* DENVER. JAIKES *goes before her.*)

JAIKES: No, don't you go, missus! I'll run after him and bring him back. I shall catch him before he gets to the station. (*Exit* JAIKES *after* DENVER.)

NELLY: (*At gate, slowly comes down to seat.* CISSY *is at gate, looking after* JAIKES.) Who can it be, this unknown friend, this silent, unseen protector, this guardian who is ever watching over my path? Cissy, (CISSY *comes down to her mother.*) what was the gentleman like?

CISSY: Oh, he was a very nice old gentleman!

NELLY: Old?

CISSY: Oh, yes, his hair was nearly white, and he was crying so much.

NELLY: Crying? Why should he cry? (*With sudden joy, aside*) Can it be? Oh, if it were he, if it could be, if it might be, if it were possible! (*Eagerly snatches locket from her neck, opens it, shows it to* CISSY *very eagerly.*) Cissy, was he like this?

CISSY: Why, that's my father's likeness, mamma!

NELLY: Yes, was he like that?

CISSY: (*after looking at it for a moment or two*) Oh, no, mamma! The Silver King's hair is nearly white.

NELLY: But the face, Cissy, the face?

CISSY: (*looking again*) No, my father's face is quite young and happy, and the Silver King's face is so sad and old. No, the Silver King isn't a bit like that. (*Kneels by* NELLY.)

NELLY: (*shutting up the locket*) Of course not, I knew it was impossible! I was mad to dream of such a thing.

CISSY: Mamma, it wasn't true, was it, what the schoolgirls used to say?

NELLY: What, dear?

CISSY: That my father had killed a man.

NELLY: (*aside*) I can't tell her the truth, I will not tell her a lie!

          (*Enter* JAIKES *at gate.*)

JAIKES: (*panting, breathless*) I couldn't catch him, missus. (CISSY *goes up to gate and looks off.*) I followed him right up to the station and the train had just started!

(*Whistle heard.*)

CISSY: (*at gate, looking off*) Oh, Jaikes, that is a story! The train's only just started, for I heard the whistle and I can see the smoke. (*Points off. She runs off and returns immediately with* NED. *They sit in arbour.* NELLY *goes up to gate, looks at* JAIKES, *who shuffles about and looks guilty and miserable.*)

NELLY: (*at gate*) Why are you playing me false? Why don't you tell me the truth?

JAIKES: (*aside, very uncomfortable*) It'll come out — it'll come out!

NELLY: (*coming down to* JAIKES) Who is this man? Your uncle who died? This gentleman who gave the purse to Cissy, this unknown friend who sent me all that money from America — who is he?

JAIKES: How should I know? I hates folks as sends anenomymous letters — I'd string 'em all to the nearest lamp-post without judge or jury!

NELLY: Jaikes, I will take no more money from you, no more food, no more shelter till I know where it comes from. As bare and helpless as we came into this Grange, I and my children will leave it this very day and go out again to starve unless I know who it is that is loading me with all this wealth and kindness. Who is he, Jaikes? Who is he? Who is he, I say?

JAIKES: Oh, missus, can't you guess?

NELLY: (*frantically*) Ah, I know it! I knew it! He is alive! Take me to him! Make haste! I cannot wait a moment! (*catching* CISSY *and* NED *in her arms*) Ned! Cissy! My darlings, kiss me, kiss me — your father is alive! (*Music. She kisses them eagerly, crying with joy. Picture.*)

   Scene changes.

  SCENE 3. *Front scene. The exterior of* COOMBE's *wharf, with gate leading into the wharf yard. Lights half up. Enter* CRIPPS *from yard, looking round.*

CRIPPS: Now I wonder whether Father Christmas intends to turn up or whether I'm to be kept here all the night? (*Enter* COOMBE.) Oh, here you are!

COOMBE: My dear boy, I hope I ain't kept you waiting very long, my dear boy.

CRIPPS: Yes, you 'ave, and the next time just you give me the straight tip and I'll go and get drunk instead of wasting my time.

COOMBE: Where's the Spider?

CRIPPS: He's just gone, and he wanted to know why the blazes you don't get somebody to look after this crib and let us in instead of keeping us hangin' about the place as if we was suspicious characters.

COOMBE: I wish I could get hold of a likely party.

CRIPPS: I thought you had got your heye upon a man —

COOMBE: So I had, little Johnny Piper, the very man for the job.

CRIPPS: Well, why didn't you have him?

COOMBE: He got the clinch only last week — eighteen months. You see it's no good having anybody here as ain't got a unblemished character. We don't want to have the bluebottles come sniffing round here, do we?

CRIPPS: Not likely!

He got the clinch: 'He was sent to prison.'
bluebottles: police.

COOMBE: I suppose the Spider's comin' back?

CRIPPS: Yes, he didn't seem much to relish the prospect of spending his time with me in your back-yard here, so he's gone off to his club — he said he'd be back here at ten.

COOMBE: Ah! the Spider always keeps Greenwich time.

CRIPPS: Yes, other folks' Greenwich time, when he can nobble 'em. Ah! the Spider's a deep 'un! He was never bred up on pidgin's milk, Spider wasn't.

COOMBE: Spider's too grasping. We shall have to take him down a peg or two.

CRIPPS: It's that viller residence of his what swallows up all our hard-won earnings. Why, you and me might take viller residences if we liked, couldn't we?

COOMBE: Yes, of course.

CRIPPS: And we could keep our cooks and buttons, and 'arf a dozen 'osses, and mix with the gentry if we felt so disposed, couldn't we?

COOMBE: Yes, to be sure we could — but we don't.

CRIPPS: No — 'cos why? 'Cos the less we mix with the gentry the better — except in the way of business.

COOMBE: Yes, Master Spider's a-flying too high for us. You back me up tonight and we'll clip his wings a bit.

CRIPPS: All right. I'll back you up. Come on inside. (*Crosses and is going in.*)
(DENVER *enters, dressed as a ragged, shabby, old porter.*)

DENVER: (*Crosses to* COOMBE.) Here's poor deaf Dicky (*grinning to* COOMBE).

COOMBE: No! nothing for you tonight, Dicky!

DENVER: Yes, guv'nor, find a job for Dicky. Poor deaf Dicky! Find a job for poor deaf Dicky, guv'nor!

CRIPPS: Who the blazes is this cove?

COOMBE: Oh, he's been knocking about here on and off for the last six months. (*Crosses to* CRIPPS.) He's handy to run errands and take letters to the sea captains that want to buy my old iron, d'ye see? (*winking and nudging* CRIPPS) He's as deaf as a post, and he ain't quite right in his upper storey.

DENVER: Don't be hard on poor deaf Dicky, guv'nor — give Dicky a job! Dicky run very fast and get back in no time. Find a job for poor deaf Dicky.

COOMBE: (*shaking his head vigorously*) No! no! no!

DENVER: Mr Coombe shakes his head and says 'No! no! no!' But Dicky says 'Yes! yes! yes!' Poor Dicky, so hungry! Dicky hasn't had a job all day.

COOMBE: (*entering wharf*) No, no, I've got no jobs tonight.

DENVER: (*imploringly, stopping him*) Dicky only wants a master to treat him kind and dry bread to eat and rags to wear — Dicky's so cold.

CRIPPS: Well, be off and get what you want at the workhouse, you forty horse-power idiot!

COOMBE: Oh, he's useful to me sometimes. (*Takes out money.*) There's a sixpence. Go and get some supper; and don't make a beast of yourself.

DENVER: Thank you, guv'nor, thank you! Dicky do anything for you, guv'nor! Dicky very fond of you! Dicky likes —

---

bred up on pidgin's milk: from the expression 'to milk a pigeon' (to attempt an impossible task).
buttons: page-boy.

COOMBE: (*pointing him off*) Be off with you!

DENVER: (*running off*) Dicky's got a sixpence! Dicky's got a sixpence!

CRIPPS: (*looking after him*) He's as daft as forty blessed hatters. Come in, Father Christmas! (*Music.* COOMBE *and* CRIPPS *go into gate, which closes with a clang.* DENVER, *who has returned, endeavours to follow them, but the door is slammed in his face.*)

DENVER: Shut out! Shut out! Shall I never worm myself in? I must be mad to dream that ever I shall wring this man's secret from him; and yet he was in Geoffrey Ware's room that night! Let me think of that! Let me beat it into my brain. This man led me up those stairs — why? why? Oh, if only I could but remember after that! (*passing his hand over his forehead*) No! no! All's dark! All's uncertain. To think that within a dozen yards of me there is a man whose word might give me wife, children, home, all! All! And I stand here and can do nothing!

(*Enter* CORKETT *loudly dressed.*)

CORKETT: (*aside*) Now I wonder which is old Coombe's shanty? I know it's somewhere about here!

DENVER: (*sauntering by him in apparent carelessness and recognising him*) Geoffrey Ware's old clerk! What has he to do with this man? Can this be another link in the chain?

CORKETT: (*aside*) I can see their little dodge. They mean to cut 'Enery Corkett. Spider's never at home when I call, and when I met him in Regent's Street the other day, he wouldn't so much as give me a friendly nod; stared at me as if I was so much dirt. I ain't going to be treated like so much dirt, and I ain't going to be cut, or else I shall cut up rough. I'll just let Master Spider see as 'Enery Corkett's as good as he is. Now I wonder where Father Christmas hangs out? (*Sees* DENVER.) Hillo! I say, my good fellow!

DENVER: (*Comes to him, holding his hand to his ear.*) Eh?

CORKETT: (*aside*) He's deaf! (*Shouts.*) Can you tell me where I can find a party by the name of Coombe — a marine store dealer? Coombe!

DENVER: Deaf Dicky got no home — no friends.

CORKETT: (*aside*) He's a blooming idiot! (*Shouts.*) Well, find me a party by the name of Coombe. He lives in the Gray's Inn Road, and he's got a wharf somewhere down here — Coombe!

DENVER: (*nodding*) Coombe! Dicky knows Mr Coombe! White hair, red nose, spectacles, nice kind gentleman, good old gentleman!

CORKETT: That's him! A perfect beauty, old Coombe is. Where is he?

DENVER: Dicky mustn't tell. Dicky take message — give Dicky letter and sixpence and Dicky take it to Mr Coombe — let Dicky take letter to Mr Coombe.

CORKETT: Oh, I see — caution's the word! Father Christmas don't want to be smelt out. I'll go into a pub and write a letter to Coombe and give it to this

---

(*s.d.*) *loudly dressed*: this finery is described on p. 92 below: in this scene it may be concealed under a greatcoat.

I ain't going to be cut: ignoring ('cutting') a person in public was a ruthless but socially acceptable way of showing unwillingness to continue their acquaintance.

daffy to take, and then I'll follow him up and see where he goes. (*Shouts.*)
Well, come on, old dunderhead, I'll give you a letter to take to him.

DENVER: Thank you, thank you! Dicky take it to Mr Coombe! (*Exit* CORKETT.)
At last! At last! At last! (*Music. Exit after* CORKETT.)
    Scene changes.

SCENE 4.   *Interior and exterior of* COOMBE*'s wharf. Lights half up.*
Discover COOMBE *and* CRIPPS *inside hut.* COOMBE *standing by table,* CRIPPS
seated behind it.

CRIPPS: I say, let's have some wet. (*Lights pipe.*)

COOMBE: Put a name on it.

CRIPPS: Oh, beer, gin, rum, whisky, brandy, anything as has got some taste in it.

COOMBE: I'll give you a wee drop of prime Highland whisky, my dear boy. (*Exit
at inner door.*)

CRIPPS: (*shouting after him*) Bring the jar while you are about it. (SKINNER
enters in yard outside and whistles.) The Spider! (CRIPPS *rises and goes to
door, unlocks it, admits* SKINNER, *then closes door and relocks it.*)

SKINNER: (*crossing to front of table*) Well! (*taking off gloves*) Where is the venerable Coombe?

CRIPPS: (*Seats himself at back of table.*) The venerable Coombe is getting this
child some whisky.

SKINNER: (*dropping his voice*) Between ourselves, I half suspect Mr Coombe
means to execute a double shuffle on his own account with those diamonds
of Lady Blanche.

CRIPPS: He'd better not try it on.

SKINNER: Just so! You back me up and we'll get at the truth tonight.

CRIPPS: All right! I'll back you up.
    (COOMBE *re-enters with whisky jar and water jug and glass, which
he sets down in front of* CRIPPS, *who helps himself largely.*)

COOMBE: (*cordially holding out his hand to* SKINNER) My dear boy, I'm
delighted to see you.

SKINNER: Reciprocated, Mr Coombe — there's something magical in the grasp of
your hand. It's horny and damned dirty — what of that? It's honest! The
shake of an honest hand does me good. (*Takes out his handkerchief and
wipes his hand behind his back.*)
    (*Enter* DENVER *outside with letter. Knocks at door.* SKINNER
puts out light.)

CRIPPS: Who the blazes is that?

COOMBE: (*Goes behind table to door communicating with wharf, calls out.*)
Who's there? Who's there?

DENVER: (*Knocks.*) Poor deaf Dicky got letter for Mr Coombe. Let Dicky in
please.

COOMBE: All right, Spider, it's only a deaf idiot that brings messages for me!
(*Opens door.* SKINNER *lights candle and sits at table.*)

---

daffy: fool, madman.

DENVER: (*at door*) Letter, guv'nor. Gentleman wanted to know where Mr
    Coombe lived. Dicky wouldn't tell him. Dicky wanted to bring letter and earn
    sixpence — gentleman give Dicky twopence, gentleman hadn't got any more.
    (*Has been trying to enter, but* COOMBE *stops at the door.*)
COOMBE: All right! Give me the letter! Wait! (DENVER *is coming inside.*
    COOMBE *shoves him out.*) No, outside! (*Shuts door in* DENVER'*s face.*)
DENVER: (*outside*) How long! How long!
COOMBE: (*Sits, opens letter.*) It's from the Duke of New York.
SKINNER: Curse the fellow! To think how many good people die off every day,
    and yet that young blackguard persists in living on.
        (DENVER, *outside, is listening at door until* COOMBE *opens it.*)
COOMBE: (*Reads.*) 'Dear Father Christmas: — I'm cleaned out and I want a little
    of the rhino. You ain't treating me fair. I must see you tonight, so send me
    back a message by the idiot who brings this.'
SKINNER: (*snatching the letter*) Tell him to go to the devil! Now, Coombe, sharp's
    the word! Let's get to business.
COOMBE: I'll send off deaf Dicky first.
CRIPPS: (*suddenly struck with an idea*) Boil me down into mock turtle soup!
    (*Strikes table with his fist.*)
SKINNER: What's the matter, Cripps?
CRIPPS: Why, the deaf chap would be just the man to keep this here crib.
SKINNER: We ought to have somebody here. What's the fellow like?
COOMBE: He's deaf and an idiot. The police'd never be able to get anything out of
    him, and he could never tell any lies against us.
SKINNER: That's the sort of man we want. Bring him in! Let's have a look at him.
    (COOMBE *opens the door and beckons* DENVER *in. He comes in grinning
    and touching his cap to* SKINNER *and* CRIPPS.) What's your name?
    (DENVER *touches his cap and grins.*) What's your name?
DENVER: (*nodding and grinning*) Yes, guv'nor!
CRIPPS: What's your confounded name, you thick-headed hoddy-dod? (*shouting*)
DENVER: He's round at the public house. Dicky go and fetch him, guv'nor?
SKINNER: This man would be a perfect treasure in the witness box.
DENVER: Dicky go there if you like, guv'nor.
SKINNER: I should like to see him under cross-examination.
DENVER: Dicky take him an answer?
SKINNER: (*shaking his head*) No answer. Listen! You want work — don't you —
    WORK! (*shouting*)
DENVER: Work? Oh, yes, guv'nor! Dicky work very hard — scrub the floor, run
    messages. Dicky do what you tell him.
SKINNER: Coombe, this man is like you. He'll do anything for an honest living.
COOMBE: Shall we have him?
DENVER: Dicky be as faithful as a dog. Dicky follow you about everywhere and
    never leave you — never leave you.

---

rhino: ready money.
hoddy-dod: fool.

SKINNER: The devil you won't! That would be rather awkward!

DENVER: Give poor Dicky a chance, guv'nor.

SKINNER: He's as safe as anybody we can get. All right, Coombe, give him a trial!

DENVER: What did you say, guv'nor?

SKINNER: (*indicating* COOMBE) No, he'll tell you. I can't shout any more.

COOMBE: (*Crosses towards* DENVER, *shouting.*) You can come here as porter and sleep on the premises. (*Takes a shilling and counts on his fingers.*) Look! Fifteen shillings a week — fifteen shillings!

DENVER: Oh, thank you! thank you! Dicky so glad! so glad! so glad!

COOMBE: (*beckoning* DENVER) Come this way, I'll show you where you've got to sleep. Sleep! (COOMBE *goes up stage and off.* DENVER *follows him.*)

DENVER: Dicky stay here always — Dicky very fond of Mr Coombe — Dicky stay here always! Thank you, Mr Coombe — thank you, too, sir! Thank you, too! (*Exit at inner door, after* COOMBE.)

SKINNER: (*Sits at table. To* CRIPPS, *taking out moulds*) Cripps, I want you to make me some keys to fit these moulds. (*Explains to* CRIPPS *in dumb-show.*) (*Enter* CORKETT *outside.*)

CORKETT: That idiot's a long time gone. This was the place he went in at. (*Looks through the keyhole.*) There's a light inside. (*Knocks.*)

SKINNER: (*Puts out light.*) Who the plague is that? (CORKETT *knocks again, and whistles in peculiar manner.*)

CRIPPS: It's that blessed Duke of New York.

SKINNER: (*relighting*) You'd better let him in or else he'll kick up a row. (CRIPPS *goes to door, unlocks it, admits* CORKETT, *who is very loudly dressed, with outrageous tweed suit, eyeglass, crutch-stick, white hat, light kid gloves.* CRIPPS *locks door, leaving key, and returns to his seat at head of table.*)

CORKETT: How do, dear boys! Ah, Spider, old chummy! (*waving his hand to* SKINNER) Bless you, bless you!

SKINNER: Bless yourself! Pray for some brains. What do you want here?

CORKETT: L.s.d., especially the L.

SKINNER: What have you done with that last twenty pounds?

CORKETT: Blued it!

SKINNER: (*looking at* CORKETT's *clothes*) You've been to my tailor's again, I see.

CORKETT: Yes. Neat, ain't they? Told him to put 'em down to your account. Hope you don't mind it, dear boy!

SKINNER: (*venomously*) Take care, you brute! You're nearly at the end of your tether! (*Enter* COOMBE.)

COOMBE: (*Seeing* CORKETT, *shakes hands with him.*) Why, it's our young friend, 'Enery Corkett.

---

fifteen shillings a week: a decent wage for the job, by the standards of the time.

(s.d.) crutch-stick: short cane with a handle shaped like the arm-rest of a crutch: like the *eyeglass* (monocle), a favourite accoutrement of the 'swell'.

L.s.d.: pounds, shillings and pence: these abbreviations were derived from the Latin names of the denominations used before decimalisation.

CORKETT: (*Goes up and sits on table.*) Dear old Father Christmas!

SKINNER: Now, Coombe, have you stowed away your March hare?

COOMBE: Yes, I've took him up to the cock-loft and give him some bread and cheese and left him. He seems happy enough.

SKINNER: Then business, sharp. Where's the money-box?

(COOMBE *takes cash-box out of chimney, opens it and takes out money.*)

CRIPPS: How much?

COOMBE: A hundred and eighty.

SKINNER: Only a hundred and eighty for all that plate? I'd better have left it on Sir George's sideboard − I shall miss it the next time I dine with him.

COOMBE: (*giving money to* CRIPPS *and* SKINNER) That clears Sir George's plate.

SKINNER: (*pocketing money*) Right! (*to* COOMBE) Now, my venerable chum, just one word with you about Lady Blanche's jewels − where are they?

(COOMBE *shuts cash-box with a bang.*)

COOMBE: (*uneasily*) Well, you see, my dear boy, I didn't like to leave them here and − and so I took 'em to my own place − my shop in the Gray's Inn Road. I thought they'd be safe there. (COOMBE *returns cash-box to chimney.*)

SKINNER: Now, Coombe, you're telling lies, you know. Lies! And setting a bad example to Cripps here!

CRIPPS: Yes. Father Christmas, don't you try any hanky-panky tricks with this child. You know me. Handle me gentle, use me well, fair and square, I've got the temper of a sucking lamb, haven't I, Spider?

SKINNER: You have, Mr Cripps, and also its playfulness and innocence.

CRIPPS: But rub me the wrong way − come any dodge, try to do me out of my fair share of the swag, and then − ! (*Brings fist down on table with tremendous force.*)

SKINNER: Then you have the ferocity of the British lion in mortal combat with the apocryphal unicorn. Now, Coombe, once more, where are Lady Blanche's diamonds?

COOMBE: My dear boy, I've got a gentleman coming to see 'em next week − a gentleman from Amsterdam.

CRIPPS: Damn Amsterdam!

SKINNER: Never mind that, I want my property!

CORKETT: (*up stage, aside*) There's a reward of a thousand pounds offered for them jewels, I'll have a cut in here! (*Comes down. Music.*)

(DENVER *creeps on and hides behind bales and listens with great interest.*)

SKINNER: Those jewels are worth six thousand pounds, and once more for the last time, where are they?

COOMBE: Don't get into a temper, Spider! I tell you I may have a customer for 'em next week − we'll settle for 'em then (*banging fist on table*).

SKINNER: No, we won't settle for them then, we'll settle for them now! (*banging fist on table*)

---

hanky-panky: legerdemain, trickery.

CRIPPS: Yes, we'll settle for 'em now! (*banging fist on table*)

CORKETT: (*joining in*) Yes, we'll settle for 'em now! (*banging fist on table*)

SKINNER: (*turning sharply on* CORKETT) You infernal jackanapes, what business is it of yours?

CORKETT: Every business of mine, Mr Spider, look there! (*Turns out pockets, shows they are empty.*) That's what business it is of mine! I mean to have fifty quid out of this!

SKINNER: Oh, you do, do you?

CORKETT: (*promptly*) If you don't give it me I'll let on about Hatton Garden four year ago.

(DENVER *starts violently and shows great interest.*)

SKINNER: (*with deadly rage.*) If you say half a word more —

CORKETT: (*promptly*) Half a word more!

(SKINNER *seizes* CORKETT *by the throat and swings him round into* CRIPPS's *arms.* COOMBE *seizes* SKINNER *from behind and restrains him.*)

COOMBE: (*alarmed*) Come, come, my dear boys, this won't do!

CRIPPS: (*holding* CORKETT) Stow it, Spider, stow it!

SKINNER: I've given you rope enough, Mr Corkett!

CORKETT: (*still held by* CRIPPS) Don't you talk about rope, Spider! If it comes to hanging, it won't be me, it'll be you!

(DENVER *shows great interest.* SKINNER *tries to get at* CORKETT. COOMBE *interposes.*)

SKINNER: Curse you, will you never give me peace till I kill you?

CORKETT: Yes, as you killed Geoffrey Ware!

(DENVER, *no longer able to restrain himself, leaps up with a terrific scream of joy.*)

DENVER: Ah! innocent! Innocent! Thank God!

SKINNER: (*Turns round and sees* DENVER.) Who is it? Who is it?

DENVER: Wilfred Denver! (*To* CRIPPS *and* CORKETT, *who are in front of door to wharf.*) Stand from that door! (*They do not move.* DENVER *flourishes crowbar — they retreat down stage.*)

ALL: (*overcome, helpless*) Stop him! Stop him!

DENVER: Stop me! The whole world shall not stop me now! (*Gets through door and bangs it to. Picture.*)

End of act IV.

ACT V

SCENE 1.   SKINNER's *villa, as in the first scene of act III. Moonlight. Music to open. Enter* SKINNER *with a lighted candle and bag by door. He crosses stage to opposite door and calls off.*

SKINNER: Olive! (*pause*) Olive! Olive!

OLIVE: (*outside*) Yes!

SKINNER: Come down at once, I want you. (*Comes to chair, centre, and sits. Takes jewel-case and cash-box out of bag.*) Now, have I got everything? Yes, I think so, everything worth taking. Coombe's private cash-box. (*Takes a jemmy from his pocket and prises cash-box open. Takes out jewels.*) As I thought — Lady Blanche's jewels! The old fox! The old sweep! I knew he meant to rob me. (*Takes out a bag of money from cash-box.*) Hillo, Mr Coombe's private savings! That's lucky. They'll come in handy at a pinch. (*Puts bag in his pocket.*)

> (*Enter* OLIVE. *She is in a dressing-gown and with her hair down, as if newly aroused from sleep.*)

OLIVE: What do you want?

SKINNER: Shut the door.

OLIVE: Herbert! Something has happened. What is it?

SKINNER: The worst. That man Denver is alive.

OLIVE: Alive! No — impossible!

SKINNER: Yes, and has got on our scent. Knows everything.

OLIVE: Have I not always said a day of retribution would come?

SKINNER: For heaven's sake don't preach now. Listen to me, and if you make one mistake in carrying out my instructions, it's death and ruin to me. Now will you obey?

OLIVE: Oh, Herbert!

SKINNER: No sermons. Will you do as I tell you?

OLIVE: You know I will — if it's to save you.

SKINNER: You see all this? (*Opens cabinet — puts all the jewels, etc., into it.*)

OLIVE: Yes.

SKINNER: While this is safe, I'm safe. If it's found, I'm ruined — you understand?

OLIVE: Yes.

SKINNER: (*locking cabinet and giving the key to* OLIVE) There's the key. The moment I leave this house, take all that, sew it securely in your dress, walk to Lewisham, take the first train to Charing Cross and the morning express to Paris — go to the old address, I'll join you as soon as I can. Remember what's at stake. If you find yourself watched or followed, get rid of it — burn it, plant it on somebody else, for heaven's sake, don't be found with it on you. Don't write to me. Now, is that all? Yes, that's all.

OLIVE: I shall not see you again?

SKINNER: Not for a week or two. Goodbye! (*Kisses her.*)

OLIVE: Goodbye, Herbert. Take care!

SKINNER: It's you who must take care. I can trust you, Olive?

OLIVE: Yes, I will make no mistake. It shall not be found.

SKINNER: Good girl! I shall make something of you yet. (*Whistle heard off.*) Coombe! (*to* OLIVE) Now be off. The moment the house is clear set to work. (*Exit* SKINNER.)

OLIVE: Oh, Herbert, what am I doing for your sake? (*Exit.*)

> (*Enter* SKINNER *at the other door, followed by* COOMBE, CRIPPS *and* CORKETT.)

COOMBE: My dear boy! What luck! Did you follow him up?

Lewisham: suburb to the south-east of London, approximately 6 miles from Bromley.

SKINNER: Yes, to a big place in Kensington Gardens; he's John Franklin, the millionaire. The Silver King!

COOMBE: Well, what did you do, my dear boy?

SKINNER: Checked it out, went into the place and asked for him — gave my name and was shown up.

CORKETT: And what did he say, Spider?

SKINNER: He's just driven off into the country — heaven knows why; but I got his address and I can put my hand on him when I choose.

CRIPPS: Yes, but can you stop his jaw?

SKINNER: Yes, I can stop his, if I can stop yours! Now look here, you three — we are perfectly safe while we hold our tongues. There's not a fraction of evidence against us, and there never will be if we keep quiet. But the moment one of us opens his mouth, it's transportation for us all. Now, do we stick together?

CRIPPS: Yes, of course we will, Spider.

SKINNER: Right! Now there's not a moment to waste. Coombe, you go to your place in the Gray's Inn Road. You may get a visit from the police tomorrow — be ready for them; destroy every scrap that could tell a tale. Sharp's the word — off you go!

COOMBE: But the swag at the wharf?

SKINNER: The swag is not at the wharf. It's safe. Now will you go? (*Hustles* COOMBE *off.*) Now you, Cripps, you go to the Lawn, Kensington, and watch the house.

CRIPPS: Whose house?

SKINNER: Denver's — Franklin's, or whatever he calls himself — take the Moucher with you and send him to the Carr Lane crib to report every three hours.

CRIPPS: But the blessed swag — what about that?

SKINNER: Don't I tell you the swag is safe?

CRIPPS: Yes, but where is it? What do you call safe?

SKINNER: I call a thing safe, Cripps, when that thing is in my possession and its whereabouts is known only to myself. Now the swag is safe in that sense.

CRIPPS: That's all my eye!

SKINNER: You shall have your share when the time comes.

CORKETT: (*aside*) Yes, and I'll have mine.

SKINNER: (*to* CRIPPS) No words — Bundle off! (*Shoves* CRIPPS *off.*)

CORKETT: And what am I to do, Spider?

SKINNER: You! It was your cursed blabbing that brought us into this infernal mess. Now I'll give you just one word of caution. If you ever open your mouth one single half inch, it's all up with you. If that Hatton Garden business ever comes to light — if it's ever known that Denver didn't do it,

---

transportation: the wholesale transportation of convicts to Australia had ceased in the 1850s, but it is possible that the old threat still has power for such long-established malefactors as Coombe and Cripps.

the Moucher: a 'moucher' is a beggar: in one of the drafts of the play Skinner lures Denver to a house owned by a character of this name, intending to have him killed when he arrives.

it will be known that Corkett did. We've made up our minds that if one of us has to swing for it, it'll be you. Now you're warned.

CORKETT: Oh, yes, Spider, I'll take my davy I'll never mention it again.

SKINNER: (*taking money bag from pocket*) Now, if I let you have a sufficient sum, do you think you can manage to make yourself scarce for three months?

CORKETT: I'll try, Spider, I should like to go on the Continent if I'd got coin enough. I've got a pal in Amsterdam.

SKINNER: Very well, I'll let you have fifty pounds.

CORKETT: Fifty pounds! Oh, come, Spider, don't be stingy! Three months! — And they're sure to cheat me. I can't speak a word of Dutch. Make it a hundred and I'll be off slick tomorrow morning.

SKINNER: I shall give you sixty and not a penny more. (*Begins to count money. Aside*) Coombe's money comes in handy.

CORKETT: (*watching him, aside*) That's one of old Coombe's bags. How did Spider get that? He must have brought the swag here.

SKINNER: (*giving him money*) There you are, and don't reckon on getting any more from me. I've had just as much of you as I can swallow. There's a train from Liverpool Street to Harwich at eight o'clock. You'd better go by it.

CORKETT: All right, Spider, I'm off. Ta, ta. (*Exit.*)

SKINNER: I think I've shut his mouth for the time; but the moment he's spent the money he'll come back. Curse them, I won't trust any of them. Now let me see! Olive is safe! The swag is safe! Nothing can touch me. The Grange, Gardenhurst, Bucks. Now then, for Mr John Franklin. (*Puts out light and exit.*)

(*A pause. Enter* BAXTER *cautiously by window.*)

BAXTER: The light out. Which way did they go? He brought that stuff here. It must be in the house somewhere. Oh, if I could only nab you, Spider. To think that I know that that rascal has had his finger in every jewel robbery for the last ten years, and I've never been able to lay my hands on him. But I think I shall be one too many for you this time. There's some big swag about here tonight, and I don't leave this house till I've smelt it out. (*Hears footsteps and retreats to window. Enter* OLIVE. BAXTER *speaks aside.*) The Spider's wife!

OLIVE: They have left the house — now is the time. (*Goes to cabinet and unlocks it.*) Oh, how my heart beats. Courage — for Herbert's sake. Hark, who's that? Somebody at that window. Who can it be? (*Leaves cabinet open, stands back, touches* BAXTER — *screams.*) Who's there?

BAXTER: Silence for your life. (*Struggles with* OLIVE, *who would scream out, but that he puts his hand over her mouth and hustles her off.*) Who's this coming? Is it Spider? Steady, Sam, steady! (*Hides behind curtain.*)

(*Enter* CORKETT.)

CORKETT: Spider's safe off. He's all right — the swag must be here — he couldn't have carted it nowhere else. Now where's he put it? All's quiet — if I can only collar it I will make myself scarce. I'll go to the Continent and enjoy myself.

I'll take my davy: 'I'll be sworn' ('davy' = affadavit).

(*Knocks against cabinet.*) What's that? Why, it's the blessed cabinet. Crimes! It's open! (*Feels inside.*) These are the cases! Here's a lucky squeeze. (*Takes jewel-cases, etc., out.*) Golly, here's all the blessed lot of it. Why, it'll be a perfect little goldmine to me. (*Kneels down to look at jewels and stuffs them into his pockets quickly.*) I can be honest now for the rest of my life. After all, honesty is the best policy. (*Stuffs one case under his waistcoat.*) Won't old Spider be jolly mad when he finds it out. I'm off — my name's Walker!

> (*During the latter part of* CORKETT's *speech,* LARKIN, *a detective, has sneaked round from the window. As* CORKETT *rises and is going off he confronts him. Tableau.* CORKETT *then turns to escape right and is met by* BAXTER, *who pounces on him.*)

BAXTER: No, it isn't! It's Corkett! I know you, you young blackguard. (*to* LARKIN) Turn on the light.

CORKETT: Nobbled — Baxter — fourteen years!

BAXTER: Now, my young friend, turn out. Let's see what's in your pockets.

CORKETT: I've only got my handkerchief.

BAXTER: Let's have a look at it.

CORKETT: And a bunch of keys!

BAXTER: Turn out — produce! (CORKETT *begins to gingerly fumble about and produces nothing.*) Now, will you hand over?

CORKETT: Yes, sir. (*Produces a jewel-case from coat pocket.*)

BAXTER: (*Opens it.*) The Honourable Mrs Farebrother's rings. Stolen from her maid while travelling.

CORKETT: I don't know neither her nor her maid.

BAXTER: Fire away! The next! (CORKETT *produces another from coat pocket.* BAXTER *looks at it.*) Hunt and Gask. Bracelets! Bond Street robbery last autumn.

CORKETT: I can prove an alibi. I was in quod at the time.

BAXTER: The next? Look alive! Here, I've got no time to waste. (*Taps* CORKETT's *waistcoat where case is.*) What's this? (*Takes out case and looks at it.*) By Jove, Lady Blanche Wynter's jewels!

CORKETT: Yes, I was just a-going to take 'em to her.

BAXTER: I'll save you the trouble.

CORKETT: There's a reward of a thousand pounds offered for them jewels.

BAXTER: I'll save you the trouble of taking that too.

CORKETT: I say, you know, I'll just tell you how this happened — now it ain't my fault, it's my misfortune —

BAXTER: Oh, yes, you're a very much injured young man. Now, my sweet innocent, you just come along nicely with me.

CORKETT: Yes, so I will, I'll come like a lamb. But I say, you know, this ain't my swag — not a blessed bit of it. It's all Spider's.

My name's Walker: 'I'm going!'
Hunt and Gask: there was in fact a firm of jewellers in Bond Street called Hunt and Roskell: cf. *The Case of Rebellious Susan*, p. 116 below.

BAXTER: (*Takes hold of* CORKETT *by the collar and hustles him off.*) We'll talk
about Spider by and by. Trot! (*Exeunt all through window. Music.*)
Scene changes.

SCENE 2.   *The Grange, Gardenhurst, as in the second scene of act IV.*
Early morning. Lights full up. Music. NELLY *discovered at gate, looking anxiously*
off.
NELLY: Make haste, Jaikes, make haste and bring him to me. (*Comes and sits on*
seat.) What if Jaikes could not find him — or if Will would not come? Oh, yes,
he will — the train is whirling him to me. He is coming — he is coming!
(*Enter* DENVER *and* JAIKES.)
DENVER: (*to* JAIKES, *as they enter*) Go round to the front and bring her to me.
(*Exit* JAIKES. DENVER, *at gate, sees* NELLY. *Aloud*) Ah, there she is.
(NELLY, *turning, sees him, does not recognise him for a minute —*
he holds out his arms and she drops gradually into them.)
NELLY: Is it — my Will? My Will — this face — this white hair — my Will alive?
DENVER: (*clasping her*) Nell! (*Kisses her hungrily — a long embrace.*)
NELLY: (*hysterically*) Oh, Will — don't speak. Don't say a word. Only let me look
at you. Oh, let me cry or else my heart will break. Don't stop me, Will. Ha, ha,
ha! (*sobbing and laughing in his arms*)   *214860*
(*Enter* JAIKES)
JAIKES: (*aside*) I can't find her nowhere — she ain't at home. (*Sees* NELLY *in*
DENVER'*s arms.*) Ah, yes, she's home at last (*creeping quietly off on tip-toe*).
DENVER: (*to* JAIKES) Where are you going?
JAIKES: I'm going to have a look at the weather, Master Will! (*Exit.*)
DENVER: (*sitting on seat,* NELLY *at his feet, soothing her*) That's right, have a
good cry and ease your heart. Oh, Nell! Nell! I've such news for you — the
best news ever spoken. There is no other news — think of it — I never killed
that man, I am innocent!
NELLY: Oh, Will, can it be so? Oh, Will, it seems to me as if I were dreaming. I can
only look in this dear changed face and ask — 'Is it true?'
DENVER: Yes, my own. Do you think I am changed?
NELLY: Yes, and no — changed and not changed — you are always the same to me
— you are always my Will! You are not changed a bit.
DENVER: Nell, our children — our little Ned and Cissy — where are they?
NELLY: I was waiting for you to ask that, I've been watching them all night. Come,
we'll go and wake them.
(*Enter* JAIKES, *with* CISSY *and* NED, *one on each side, dragging*
him by each hand.)
JAIKES: Gently — gently, missy — gently, Master Ned! That's my old rheumaticky
arm. Don't you pull it out of joint, you young Turk.
DENVER: (*Meeting* CHILDREN *and taking them to seat, puts them on his knees.*)
Ned, Cissy, do you know me? I'm your father that was dead — I am alive
again and I have come home to you, my brave boy, my dear little girl; put
your arms round my neck, both of you. Quite, quite close — that's it, my
darlings!
CISSY: I know who that little girl was that you lost!

DENVER: Well, tell me — who was she?

CISSY: Why, me — wasn't she?

DENVER: Yes, I've found her now — I shall never lose her again.

CISSY: No, we shall never let you go away again, shall we, mamma?

NED: But you are crying?

CISSY: And Jaikes, you too? What is there to cry for?

JAIKES: Don't you take no notice of me, missy. (*blubbering*) I'm not crying — I'm only laughing the wrong way.

NELLY: Cissy, when you were a little baby and could just run about, you used to call somebody upstairs and down — all over the house — don't you remember? Who was it?

CISSY: (*hugging* DENVER) Daddy!

JAIKES: Yes, missy, and I can remember when your daddy used to go toddling a-calling 'Jaikes' all over the house. Ah, Master Will, I can just remember your great-great-grandfather. I've seen five generations of you and I've never had a happier moment than this in all my life.

> (*Enter* SKINNER *by path. He stands at gate, looking anxiously round. His face is livid and his whole appearance betokens his intense anxiety.*)

NELLY: (*At back of seat, sees* SKINNER.) Look, Will, that man!

DENVER: (*Starts up, sees* SKINNER. *To* JAIKES) Jaikes, take my children away! (*Exit* JAIKES, *with* CHILDREN. *To* NELLY) Go into the house, Nell. I will come to you when I have sent this man away.

NELLY: No, let me stay — I would rather stay!

SKINNER: (*advancing*) Mr John Franklin!

DENVER: Denver, sir. (*to* NELLY) Come, Nell, I have no business with this man!

SKINNER: Mrs Franklin, I hold your husband's life in my hands. If you value it, beg him to hear what I have to say.

NELLY: Oh, Will, is it true? Are you in danger? Yes, let us hear what he has to say.

SKINNER: What I have to say must be said to him alone.

NELLY: Oh, Will, listen to him — for my sake!

DENVER: Remain within sight, within call. (*Exit* NELLY. *To* SKINNER) Now, sir!

SKINNER: Look here, Mr Franklin!

DENVER: Denver, sir!

SKINNER: I thought I had better not mention that name — I do not want to get you into trouble.

DENVER: I'll take care you don't do that!

SKINNER: (*aside*) He seems calm — he means mischief. (*aloud*) You appear to misunderstand me.

DENVER: Not at all! I understand you perfectly. I've watched you day and night for the last five months.

SKINNER: (*whose self-confidence is shaken by* DENVER's *coolness*) What do you know? What have you seen?

DENVER: Enough for my purpose.

SKINNER: And you mean to use it?

DENVER: I do.

SKINNER: Take care! I warn you, don't quarrel with me. I'll give you a chance —
   if you're wise, you'll take it before it's too late.
DENVER: Go on.
SKINNER: We are both in a devil of a mess. Why not make a mutual concession,
   silence for silence — you keep quiet on my affairs, I will keep quiet on yours
   — you allow me to pursue my business, I allow you to pursue yours.
DENVER: And the alternative?
SKINNER: You fight me — I fight you. You proclaim me a thief and get me a
   possible five or seven years — I proclaim you a murderer and get you hanged.
   Take care, it's an edged tool we are playing with. It cuts both ways, but the
   handle is in my hands, and the blade towards you. You had better remain
   John Franklin — Wilfred Denver is dead — let him remain so.
DENVER: You lie! Down to your very soul, you lie! Wilfred Denver is alive, and
   today all the world shall know it. (*Calls.*) Nell! (NELLY *comes to him.*)
   There stands the murderer of Geoffrey Ware! He wants to bargain with me —
   Shall I hide myself or shall I tell the truth to the world? Shall I make peace
   with him or shall I fight him? Give him his answer, Nell!
NELLY: You shall fight him!
DENVER: You have your answer — go!
SKINNER: I shall go straight from here and give information to the police that
   Wilfred Denver is alive.
DENVER: Nell, send Jaikes to me. (*Exit* NELLY. DENVER *takes pocketbook and
   writes hurriedly, speaking as he writes.*) 'From Wilfred Denver, The Grange,
   Gardenhurst, Bucks. To Superintendent, Criminal Investigation Department,
   Scotland Yard. I surrender myself to take my trial on the charge of the
   murder of Geoffrey Ware, of which I am innocent, and I know the where-
   abouts of the real murderer.' (*Enter* JAIKES *and* NELLY *from house.*)
   Jaikes, take this telegram at once.
           (BAXTER *appears at gate.*)
BAXTER: (*entering garden*) I'll take that. (*Holds out his hand, takes the telegram
   from* JAIKES, *who is going towards gate.*)
DENVER: Baxter!
SKINNER: (*aside*) Baxter! Now for my chance! (*aloud*) Mr Baxter, do your duty
   and arrest the murderer of Geoffrey Ware! (*pointing to* DENVER)
BAXTER: (*Moves towards* DENVER, *taking out handcuffs.*) Very well, I will do
   my duty and arrest the murderer of Geoffrey Ware! (*Turns sharply on
   SKINNER, who is advancing up stage, and handcuffs him. SKINNER is much
   surprised and drops his stick. Two detectives walk on at gate.*)
SKINNER: (*struggling*) What do you mean?
BAXTER: I mean that your dear friend Mr Henry Corkett has turned Queen's
   evidence.
SKINNER: And you believe him?
BAXTER: Oh, yes, I always believe what's told me — especially when it's proved.
SKINNER: And what proof have you of this tale?
BAXTER: The evidence of your other friends, Mr Coombe and Mr Cripps. Thanks
   to Mr Corkett, I've bagged the lot of 'em and they all tell the same tale. Is
   that enough, Spider?

SKINNER: The blackguards, hang the lot.

BAXTER: Well, no. 1 think that may happen to you, but I fancy they'll get off.

JAIKES: Oh, don't let 'em off, Master. Hang the lot of 'em.

> (BAXTER *advances slightly towards* DENVER, *who has dropped down stage with* NELLY. BAXTER *raises his hat.*)

BAXTER: Mr Wilfred Denver, I believe?

DENVER: That is my name.

BAXTER: I shall want you as a witness against this man.

DENVER: I shall be ready to come when called upon; but I've no desire for revenge — my only wish is to clear my name.

BAXTER: That is already done. (*Picks up* SKINNER'*s stick.*) Come, Spider, I want to catch the up train — I've got a call to make on Lady Blanche Wynter in town this morning.

SKINNER: (*glancing at handcuffs*) Is this necessary?

BAXTER: (*giving him his walking-stick*) Well, yes, I think so, if you don't mind. (*to* DETECTIVE) Take good care of him, Bob. (*Turns to* DENVER.) You've had a very narrow escape, sir. Good morning, sir. (*Exit* SKINNER *and* TWO DETECTIVES, *followed by* BAXTER. *They go off by the gate.*)

DENVER: (*as they go*) Good morning, Mr Baxter! (JAIKES *goes off during the above and returns with* CISSY *and* NED.) Come, let us kneel and give thanks on our own hearth in the dear old home where I wooed you, and won you in the happy, happy days of long ago. Come, Jaikes — Cissy, Ned, Nell — come in — Home at last!

> *Curtain.*

Come, let us kneel: see appendix (pp. 222–3 below) for earlier versions of this speech.

IV *The Case of Rebellious Susan*, Lyceum Theatre, New York, 1894. Fritz Williams (Pybus), Herbert Kelcey (Kato) and Bessie Tyree (Elaine) in act III

THE CASE OF REBELLIOUS SUSAN

A comedy in three acts

by HENRY ARTHUR JONES

TO MRS GRUNDY

Dear and honoured madam,

In dedicating this little comedy to you I have no other object in view than that of bribing and blinding your well-known susceptibilities, and of endeavouring to win over and conciliate that large body of English playgoers who take their opinions and morals ready-made from you, the august and austere effigy of our national taste and respectability.

The truth is, my dear lady, I am a little fearful that without some such shelter as your powerful protection, many excellent persons may be in doubt as to the exact moral which this comedy sets forth, or indeed may go further and doubt whether there is a moral in it at all, or, dreadest and cruellest alternative, may actually proclaim that it is *im*-moral. The mere possibility of this latter alternative is so painful to me, that I am obliged to recall a conversation which I recently overheard in a railway carriage.

'Ah, who wrote that play?' I heard one passenger inquire of another.

'That man Henry Arthur Jones', replied his neighbour.

'I hate that fellow', said the other. 'He's always educating the people.'

Now though I cannot honestly credit myself with any such unselfish motive in writing plays as my fellow-passenger ascribed to me, I could not help feeling a glow of virtuous pride when I found that my natural ingrained tendencies were so salutary and so patriotic. And if I have in any way contributed to the State Education grant, or even abated the School Board rate in any parish, I hope I shall not be deprived of the glory that attaches to such public benefactions merely because they have been quite involuntary and unsuspected on my part.

Now, my dear Mrs Grundy, I will not go so far as to say that I know with any degree of certainty what the moral of this comedy is. I prefer to leave that for you and the public to discover. And I am very hopeful in this respect when I remember that one of our keenest and most analytical critics, in interpreting for us a recent masterpiece of the lobworm-symbolic school, declared that though he could not be

---

TO MRS GRUNDY: the dedicatory letter reflects Jones's annoyance at Wyndham's insistence on changes in the text (see note to p. 129 below) as well as his habitual frustration at the limitations imposed by public prudery. *Mrs Grundy* is a personage often referred to in Morton's comedy *Speed the Plough* (1800). She never appears, but her supposed and reported opinions set the standard by which behaviour is measured.

the lobworm-symbolic school: i.e. Ibsen, and other 'advanced' dramatists. In the preface to *The Tempter* (1898) Jones used the phrase to describe the theatrical tastes and enthusiasms of William Archer.

quite sure what the play did mean, yet he was quite sure that it meant a devil of a lot. And so, my dear ma'am, I will not pin myself down to any one, definite, precise, hard-and-fast, cut-and-dried moral in this comedy. Why should I? Why should I needlessly limit the possible scope of its beneficent operation, or curb my boundless desire that all sorts of unexpected collateral good may haphazardly visit those who witness its representation?

I know of no task wherein the generosity and the ingenuity of the critical play-goer may be more profitably employed than in finding a profound significance in passages where the author himself would never have detected it, and in dragging to light profound moral truths from hiding-places where the author himself would never have imagined them to be lurking. Therefore, my dear Mrs Grundy, if you will be pleased to wink at any little outside indiscretion, and if the public will set its wits to work, I have no doubt a very serviceable moral is to be extracted from this comedy.

Look at life itself, my dear lady. The moral of it is not very obvious at first sight, but there must be a tremendous moral hidden somewhere in it. Nay, there must be hundreds of morals in it, and I am not without a suspicion that in claiming only one moral for this comedy I have done myself a very grave injustice. For all I know it may be teeming with morals.

But perhaps you will say that my comedy is quite unlike life. I am aware that I have no warrant in the actual facts of the world around me for placing on the English stage an instance of English conjugal infidelity. There is, I believe, madam, a great deal of this kind of immorality in France, but I am quite sure you will rejoice to hear that a very careful and searching inquiry has not resulted in establishing any well-authenticated case in English life. And even had the inquiry revealed a quite opposite state of things, I am sure you will agree with me that it would be much better to make up our minds once for all that the facts are wrong and stick to that, rather than allow the possibility of anything hurtful to our continued self-esteem and self-righteousness. I am too sensible, madam, of the honour of belonging to the same nation as your own revered self to do anything to impair its holy self-respect and worship of its own conviction that it is the most moral, most religious, most heaven-favoured nation under the sun.

Happily, as I say, there is not the slightest necessity for disturbing our cherished national belief that immorality is confined to the Continent, and especially to France. Let us, therefore, again thank heaven that we are not as other nations are, and let us avoid seeing or hearing anything that might disturb our belief in our own moral superiority.

So, my dear madam, I have to frankly own that I have not the slightest justification in fact for laying the scene of my comedy in England, and I am again justly open to the charge, so often made against me, of being quite false to life as my countrymen see it.

And now, my dear lady, having endeavoured to win your approbation by every means in my power, let me again say that all I am anxious is that you should not too hastily condemn the piece because its morality is intrinsic and not extrinsic. For I do stoutly affirm, adorable arbitress of British morals, that there is a profound moral somewhere in this piece. Only, if I dare hint so much to you, dear lady, it is well at times not to be too ferociously moral. There is a time to be ferociously moral, and a time to refrain. The present, my dear Mrs Grundy, is an eminently suitable time to refrain. Let us not be always worrying books and plays for their morals. Let us not worry even life itself for too plain, or too severe a moral. Let us look with a wise, sane, wide-open eye upon all these things, and if a moral rises naturally from them let us cheerfully accept it, however shocking it may be; if not, let us not distress ourselves.

If, my dear ma'am, you cannot see any moral in this little comedy, take it for granted there is one, and — go and see the play again. Go and see it, my dear Mrs Grundy, until you do find a moral in it. And remember that it is not only careless trifles like this that are naturally repugnant to you. Remember how hateful to you are all the great eternal things in literature and art. So much so, that if our grand English Bible itself were to be now first presented to the British public you would certainly start a prosecution against it for its indecency and its terrible polygamistic tendencies.

Refrain, my dear lady! Refrain! Refrain! And if you must have a moral in my comedy, suppose it to be this — that as women cannot retaliate openly, they may retaliate secretly — and *lie*!

And a thoroughly shocking moral it is, now we have got it. But oh, my dear Mrs Grundy, Nature's morality is not your morality, nor mine. Nature has ten thousand various morals, all of them as shocking as truth itself. The very least of them would fright our isle from its propriety if it were once guessed at.

Refrain, my dear madam! Refrain! And — excuse me — isn't that foot of yours rather too near that tender growing flower — I mean the English drama? And your foot is so heavy! Don't stamp out the little growing burst of life. Refrain, my dear lady! Refrain! Adieu!

Yours, with the deepest reverence for all things worthy of
reverence,
Henry Arthur Jones

Dieppe,
28.8.1894
P.S. My comedy isn't a comedy at all. It's a tragedy dressed up as a comedy.

THE CASE OF REBELLIOUS SUSAN

A comedy in three acts

by HENRY ARTHUR JONES

First produced at the Criterion Theatre, London, on 3 October 1894, with the following cast:

SIR RICHARD KATO, Q.C.	*Uncles to*	Charles Wyndham
ADMIRAL SIR JOSEPH DARBY	*Lady Susan*	Henry Kemble
JAMES HARABIN		C.P. Little
FERGUSSON PYBUS		Fred Kerr
LUCIEN EDENSOR		Ben Webster
MR JACOMB		E. Dagnall
KIRBY		Markham
FOOTMEN		
HOTEL WAITER		
LADY SUSAN HARABIN		Miss Mary Moore
LADY DARBY		Miss Fanny Coleman
MRS QUESNEL (INEZ)		Miss Gertrude Kingston
ELAINE SHRIMPTON		Miss Nina Boucicault

ACT I – Drawing-room at Mr Harabin's in Mayfair.

(*Ten months pass.*)

ACT II – Sir Richard Kato's sitting-room at the St Mildred's Hotel, Westbay.

(*Fifteen months pass.*)

ACT III – At Sir Richard Kato's house in Harley Street.

ACT I

SCENE.   *Drawing-room at Mr* HARABIN's; *an elegantly furnished room in Mayfair. At back, in centre, fireplace, with fire burning. To right of fireplace a door leading to* LADY SUSAN's *sitting-room. A door down stage left. Enter* FOOTMAN, *left, showing in* LADY DARBY, *a lady of about fifty.*

LADY DARBY: Where is Lady Susan now?

FOOTMAN: Upstairs in her sitting-room, my lady (*indicating door, right*).

LADY DARBY: Where is Mr Harabin?

FOOTMAN: Downstairs in the library, my lady.

(*Enter* SECOND FOOTMAN *showing in* INEZ, *a widow of about thirty, fascinating, inscrutable.*)

LADY DARBY: (*to* FIRST FOOTMAN) Tell Lady Susan I wish to see her at once.

INEZ: And will you say that I am here too?

(*Exit* FIRST FOOTMAN *at door, right. Exit* SECOND FOOTMAN *at door, left.*)

LADY DARBY: (*going affectionately to* INEZ, *shaking hands very sympathetically*) My dear Mrs Quesnel, you know?

INEZ: Sue wrote me a short note saying that she had discovered that Mr Harabin had — and that she had made up her mind to leave him.

LADY DARBY: Yes, that's what she wrote me. Now, my dear, you're her oldest friend. You'll help me to persuade her to — to — look over it and hush it up.

INEZ: Oh, certainly. It's the advice everybody always gives in such cases, so I suppose it must be right. What are the particulars?

LADY DARBY: I don't know. But with a man like Harabin — a gentleman in every sense of the word — it can't be a very bad case.

(*Enter* LADY SUSAN, *about twenty-seven, door, right, followed by* FIRST FOOTMAN, *who crosses and goes off at door, left.* LADY DARBY *goes to* LADY SUSAN *very affectionately and sympathetically, kisses her in silence.* LADY SUSAN, *having kissed* LADY DARBY, *goes to* INEZ, *kisses her.*)

LADY SUSAN: Inez! I'm so glad you've come! I knew I could rely upon you.

INEZ: Yes, dearest — naturally! What can I do?

LADY SUSAN: (*taking a bundle of letters from her pocket*) Read those letters. I found them in his *secretaire*. They explain it all. And then tell me if you wouldn't do as I am going to do.

LADY DARBY: (*very sympathetically*) My poor girl! My poor girl!

LADY SUSAN: Oh! please don't. I'm not an object of pity. At least, if I am now, I won't be one very long.

LADY DARBY: What do you mean?

LADY SUSAN: I'm going to follow Jim's example. I'm going to pay him back in his own coin.

(s.d.) drawing-room: principal reception room, usually on the first upstairs floor.
(s.d.) shaking hands: the usual greeting between close friends.

LADY DARBY: (*soothingly*) Yes, dear, yes! That's what we all say at first, but we don't mean it. And it can't be as bad as that.

LADY SUSAN: As bad as what?

LADY DARBY: Mr Harabin may have been indiscreet —

LADY SUSAN: Indiscreet! (*ironic laugh*)

LADY DARBY: And infatuated —

LADY SUSAN: Infatuated! (*ironic laugh*)

LADY DARBY: And led away —

LADY SUSAN: Indiscreet! Infatuated! Led away!

LADY DARBY: My dear, we may call it what we like, but men are men, and they are led away, and the rest of it.

LADY SUSAN: Very well, I'm going to be indiscreet, and infatuated, and the rest of it.

LADY DARBY: My dear child, that's impossible.

LADY SUSAN: Not at all, my dear aunt.

> (INEZ *gives back the letters to* LADY SUSAN *with a little sigh and a sympathetic look, and a little shake of the head.* LADY SUSAN *takes them.*)

LADY DARBY: My dear Sue, of course you're angry and upset for the moment — and quite right — quite right! I don't blame you — but after all it can't be such a very bad case.

LADY SUSAN: Every case is a bad case.

LADY DARBY: Oh, no, my dear! Some cases are much worse than others; and when you come to my age you'll be thankful that yours is no worse than a respectable average case.

LADY SUSAN: Respectable average case! No! that's just what my case shall not be. It shan't be average, and perhaps it won't be respectable. Read those letters. (*Giving letters to* LADY DARBY, *who takes them and reads them apart. To* INEZ) Well?

INEZ: Well, dearest, it is rather dreadful —

LADY SUSAN: Rather?

INEZ: But look at poor dear Mrs Barringer!

LADY SUSAN: (*enraged*) Ah! that's it! And in a few days all my friends will be saying, 'Look at poor dear Lady Sue!' They shan't say that. They shall say, 'Look at poor dear Jim Harabin!' If somebody is to be pitied, it shall be Jim.

INEZ: But, dear, you won't do anything in a hurry!

LADY SUSAN: If I don't, I can't do anything at all. I can't rake it up in a year's time.

INEZ: No, but I should wait till —

LADY SUSAN: Till the next time. No! I've made up my mind. I'm going back home with you now — that is, if you'll have me for a day or two till I can make my plans.

INEZ: Certainly, dearest; you know you're welcome.

LADY SUSAN: There's a dear! Phillips is packing my things. I shall be ready in an hour.

INEZ: Of course, dear, I'm delighted. But I'm going to Egypt in a few days.

LADY SUSAN: Oh, that's splendid! We can go together, and have a good time. Ah,

Inez, how lucky you've been! (INEZ *looks surprised.*) No, I don't mean that, dear, but still a widow's position has some advantages, hasn't it?

LADY DARBY: (*Having read the letters, sighs very deeply, and shakes her head.*) The old story!The old story! (*Gives them back to* LADY SUSAN.)

LADY SUSAN: (*taking letters, putting them in her pocket*) And what would you advise me to do?

LADY DARBY: I should give him a good sound talking to. I should make his life a misery to him for a fortnight; then — I should never mention the matter again.

LADY SUSAN: (*enraged laugh*) Ha, ha! Ha, ha! (*to* INEZ) And what would you advise me to do?

INEZ: Well — I shouldn't nag him. I should be utterly broken-hearted and mutely reproachful. I should look more intensely interesting, and a little paler, and wear prettier frocks, and give him a better dinner each evening, and when he had begged forgiveness for a long while, I should find it in my heart to — to forgive him.

LADY SUSAN: (*outburst of ironic laughter*) Ah! that's it! We are such traitors to ourselves. If we could only bind ourselves together —

LADY DARBY: A trades union of our sex? My dear, seven-eighths of us are natural blacklegs to start with.

LADY SUSAN: Yes, and that's why men are spoilt. It's our cowardice and weakness and falsehood that make them such brutes.

LADY DARBY: They are brutes!

INEZ: Yes, but that's God's fault more than woman's.

LADY DARBY: I don't know whose the fault is, but there's no denying they are brutes.

INEZ: (*Sighs.*) I'm afraid they are; but I don't see what we are to do except take them as we find them and make the best of them.

    (*Enter* FOOTMAN *announcing 'Sir Richard Kato'.* SIR RICHARD KATO, *a bright, shrewd man of the world, about fifty-five, enters. Exit* FOOTMAN.)

SIR RICHARD: (*very sympathetically*) My dear Sue! (*Goes to her, kisses her very tenderly.*) How d'ye do, Lady Darby? How d'ye do, Mrs Quesnel? (*Shakes hands — a pause —* SIR RICHARD *looks keenly from one to the other.*) Anything important under discussion?

LADY SUSAN: You may speak out, Uncle Dick; they know all about it.

SIR RICHARD: Then I'm sure they are of the same opinion that I am.

LADY DARBY: I've strongly advised Sue to — to make the best of it.

INEZ: And so have I.

LADY SUSAN: Oh, yes! 'Patch it up!' 'Don't make a fuss about it!' That's what outsiders always say to a woman.

SIR RICHARD: And, my dear Sue, as outsiders see most of the game, you may depend, in ninety-nine cases out of a hundred, outsiders are right.

    (LADY DARBY *and* INEZ *talk together a little apart.*)

---

give him a better dinner: i.e. arrange for him to be given a better dinner: a woman of Lady Susan's rank would issue directives to cook and housekeeper but would not herself participate in the cooking of meals.

LADY SUSAN: Ah, you've never been deceived.

SIR RICHARD: Well, I've never been *married*. But I've had twenty-five years' practice in the Divorce Court, and if I'm not qualified to give advice in a matter of
this kind, I don't know any man in England who is.

LADY SUSAN: (*impetuously*) I don't want advice. I want sympathy.

SIR RICHARD: Well, I am sure you will have the deepest sympathy from all —

LADY SUSAN: (*enraged*) I don't want sympathy. I won't have it.

SIR RICHARD: My dear Sue, what do you want?

LADY SUSAN: I want somebody to show me some way of paying him back without — without —

SIR RICHARD: Without losing your place in society and your self-respect. Ah!
that's the difficulty. There's an immense reputation to be made as a moralist
by any man who will show you ladies the way to break the seventh commandment without leaving any ill effects upon society.

LADY SUSAN: Well, he'd better make haste, or we shall find out the way ourselves.

SIR RICHARD: (*Shakes his head.*) My dear Sue, believe me, what is sauce for the
goose will never be sauce for the gander. In fact, there is no gander sauce, eh,
Lady Darby?

LADY DARBY: No. If there had been, our grandmothers would have found it out
and left us the receipt for it.

SIR RICHARD: (*very affectionately*) Come, come, Sue! (*putting his arm very
tenderly on hers*) Come, now! Let us talk this over quite calmly and sensibly
(*with great tenderness*).

LADY SUSAN: Oh, yes! I know what you mean. But I won't listen to another
word unless you promise you won't advise me to patch it up.

SIR RICHARD: I promise. Now, what is the exact point at which we have arrived?
Where are we? What were you saying when I came in? (*looking from one to
the other*)

LADY SUSAN: I'd just said that men are brutes.

LADY DARBY: And I had agreed.

INEZ: And I too — with some qualifications.

SIR RICHARD: And I agree with you — without any qualifications. Men are brutes.
Once recognise that simple fact in all its bearings, and we start on a basis of
sound philosophy.

LADY SUSAN: I don't want any basis, or any sound philosophy. I want my
revenge. (*Throws herself desperately on the sofa.*)

SIR RICHARD: (*to* LADY DARBY) Leave her to me for a little while, and come
back again.

LADY DARBY: And what's to be done with Mr Harabin?

SIR RICHARD: What can be done with him?

LADY DARBY: Somebody ought to give him a good sound talking to.

SIR RICHARD: Leave him to me, too.

LADY DARBY: (*suddenly bethinking herself*) Good gracious!

---

the seventh commandment: i.e. the prohibition of adultery.
receipt: recipe.

INEZ: What's the matter?

LADY DARBY: I was going to Waterloo to meet Sir Joseph when Sue's letter came, and I forgot all about him. His ship's just come into Portsmouth. I shall miss him now (*taking out watch*). And I haven't seen the dear man for six months. (*Exit very hurriedly.* INEZ *is following.*)

LADY SUSAN: Inez.

INEZ: Yes, dearest.

LADY SUSAN: I'm coming with you.

INEZ: No, dearest — I'll go and get your room ready, and come back in half-an-hour, and if you are still in the same mind —

LADY SUSAN: You'll take me with you?

INEZ: We'll see about it. (*Exit.*)

SIR RICHARD: (*very tenderly*) Come, Sue, I've only your welfare at heart. I've no personal interest to serve.

LADY SUSAN: Why did you let me get married?

SIR RICHARD: My dear, if you remember, you were so anxious and so sure of happiness —

LADY SUSAN: But why didn't you tell me what marriage was?

SIR RICHARD: My dear, in the first place you wouldn't have listened —

LADY SUSAN: (*confidently*) Oh, yes, I should.

SIR RICHARD: In the second place you wouldn't have heeded —

LADY SUSAN: Oh, yes, I should — if you had painted marriage in its true colours.

SIR RICHARD: It has so many true colours.

LADY SUSAN: No, it hasn't. It's a hateful, wretched institution.

SIR RICHARD: Marriage is not a hateful, wretched institution. On the contrary, after twenty-five years' constant practice in the Divorce Court, I am prepared to affirm that marriage is a perfect institution —

LADY SUSAN: (*aghast*) What?

SIR RICHARD: — worked by imperfect creatures. So it's like a good ship manned by a mutinous crew.

LADY SUSAN: It's men that make it what it is.

SIR RICHARD: Yes — and women. And the result is a condition that varies in each case with all the varying tastes, tempers, dispositions, infirmities, prejudices, habits, etc., etc., etc., of the contracting parties. Now you yourself are a perfect woman. —

LADY SUSAN: I? perfect? I've never pretended to that.

SIR RICHARD: Well, you see, dear, that introduces one little kink into the working of the institution in your case. Still, however, as Jim Harabin is perfect —

LADY SUSAN: Jim perfect?

SIR RICHARD: You thought him perfect at the time of your engagement, if you remember.

LADY SUSAN: Never!

SIR RICHARD: Well, you see, that introduces another little kink into the working of the institution in your case. So you saw his faults?

LADY SUSAN: Always — heaps of faults.

SIR RICHARD: Then, my dear, if that didn't stop you from marrying him, do you think it would have stopped you if I had hinted at, or even described, certain other faults? No; you would have been shocked and grieved. He would have promised amendment. And in the end you would have forgiven him. And at this very precise moment we should be at the very precise point at which we have now arrived.

LADY SUSAN: Oh, no! I shouldn't have forgiven him.

SIR RICHARD: Then, my dear, you'd have been on the high way to be an old maid, and at this precise moment you would have been railing at me for having spoilt your chances. And that reminds me, while you're blaming me for letting you marry, Elaine is blaming me for trying to stop her from throwing herself away on this — what's the fool's name? — Fergusson Pybus.

LADY SUSAN: She's written to him to come to see you at once.

SIR RICHARD: What for?

LADY SUSAN: She knows there has been a misunderstanding between Jim and me, and she knows that I am leaving the house. When I've gone. of course I can't chaperon her any longer.

SIR RICHARD: And so you intend to throw her back on my hands. (*perplexed*) Now, my dear Sue, do be a sensible girl, and — and —

LADY SUSAN: No. You promised me you wouldn't advise me to patch it up.

SIR RICHARD: Well, will you listen to what Jim has to say?

LADY SUSAN: I have. It's no use.

SIR RICHARD: Have you thoroughly rowed him?

LADY SUSAN: Not so much as he deserves.

SIR RICHARD: No — no — but still considerably, eh? And he's thoroughly ashamed of himself?

LADY SUSAN: Not so much as he ought to be.

SIR RICHARD: No — no — but still considerably, eh? Well now (*making a dart at the bell-handle and pulling it*) — we'll have him up.

LADY SUSAN: (*very decidedly*) No. I won't meet him.

SIR RICHARD: My dear Sue, if you're going to leave him, don't give him a chance to say that you didn't thoroughly explain your reasons for taking the step. (FOOTMAN *appears at door, left.*) Will you tell Mr Harabin I should like to see him for a minute? (*Exit* FOOTMAN.)

LADY SUSAN: It's no use — (*going off*)

SIR RICHARD: (*going to door, left, stopping her*) My dear Sue, let's hear what the accused has to say.

LADY SUSAN: I have heard.

SIR RICHARD: Well, perhaps there is something else.

LADY SUSAN: Yes; he has thought of some fresh excuses.

SIR RICHARD: Perhaps he's more sorry and ashamed.

LADY SUSAN: Well, what then?

SIR RICHARD: Then you'll forgive him. (LADY SUSAN *shakes her head.*) It will come to that at the last, my dear Sue. Why not spare yourself and all of us no end of trouble and anxiety, and forgive him at first?

I can't chaperon her any longer: an engaged couple would not normally appear together in public without a chaperon.

LADY SUSAN: (*decidedly*) No! Not till I have something to be forgiven on my side.
(SIR RICHARD *shrugs his shoulders.*)
> (*Enter* JAMES HARABIN, *an average English gentleman about forty,*
> *a little inclined to stoutness. He comes in hesitatingly, evidently very*
> *uncomfortable and ashamed, his eyes averted.*)

SIR RICHARD: (*The moment he has entered begins very sternly.*) Now, Harabin,
this is really disgraceful. I haven't words to characterise your conduct. Sue has
my countenance in all she is saying and doing. Frankly, I don't counsel her to
forgive you, and you'll be very lucky indeed if you can persuade her. Now
what have you got to say for yourself? At least, don't try to excuse yourself.
The only thing to do is to throw yourself on her mercy, and if she does forgive you, it's a thousand times more than you deserve. And let me tell you
it's only one woman in a thousand who would be magnanimous enough to do
it. Now!

HARABIN: (*very tamely and hesitatingly*) I know I've behaved in a very foolish
and blackguardly way —

SIR RICHARD: You have. Go on.

HARABIN: (*same distressed, uncomfortable manner*) And I'm very sorry now —
that —

LADY SUSAN: Now that you're found out. Yes, that is a pity.

SIR RICHARD: (*same stern, sharp tone*) But are you genuinely sorry — deeply,
sincerely, truly, lastingly penitent?

HARABIN: I am indeed.

LADY SUSAN: Of course. But can he give me any reason for his conduct — one
single little reason?

SIR RICHARD: No, he can't. I'm sure he can't.

LADY SUSAN: Then I don't see any reason that I should look over it. (*She is going
off left.* SIR RICHARD *gets towards the door and stops her.*)

SIR RICHARD: (*to* HARABIN, *very sternly*) Can you give one single little reason
for your conduct?

LADY SUSAN: Is my company unpleasant? Is my temper bad? Has he found me
flirting with anybody? Have I given him his dinners badly cooked? He must
surely be able to give some shadow of a reason.

SIR RICHARD: Come, sir, you must surely be able to give some shadow of a
reason.

HARABIN: (*fumbling, uncomfortable*) I must own, Sir Richard, that I can't.

SIR RICHARD: I thought not. I'm glad you have the grace to own that.

LADY SUSAN: What, no reason?

HARABIN: Except (*Turns to* SIR RICHARD.) — Well, Kato, you'd find it out if
you were married yourself —

SIR RICHARD: Stick to the point. I'm not married. Find out what?

HARABIN: Well — married life, even with the best and sweetest of wives, does
grow confoundedly unromantic at times.

LADY SUSAN: (*with a peal of ironic laughter*) Unromantic! Ha! ha! ha! If it comes
to romance, I think I'm a more romantic person to live with than you.
Unromantic! Married life isn't very romantic with you, Jim.

SIR RICHARD: Married life isn't very romantic anywhere, with anybody, and it ought not to be. When it is, it gets into the Divorce Court. You ought to have finished with romance long ago, both of you.

LADY SUSAN: Jim is twelve years older than I am, so if he hasn't finished with it, I'm twelve years to the good yet. Unromantic! Don't you think that married life grows unromantic for women? Don't you think we want our little romance as well as you? Unromantic! Ha! ha! (*She is going off again,* SIR RICHARD *again stops her.*)

SIR RICHARD: (*stopping her and turning sternly to* HARABIN) There, Harabin, you see what your conduct has done! See the extremities to which you are driving the best of wives. The unwomanly, unfeminine attitude you have forced her to take up —

LADY SUSAN: Unwomanly! Unfeminine!

SIR RICHARD: (*soothingly*) Yes, my dear, but it isn't your fault. Your language and behaviour are quite natural under the circumstances. (*very sternly turning to* HARABIN) Harabin! why don't you do something to repair your fault?

HARABIN: (*same lame uncomfortable manner*) I've offered to take the villa at Cannes she liked last year.

LADY SUSAN: Ha! (*contemptuously*)

HARABIN: And I have asked her to go to Hunt and Roskell's and choose something. I don't mind what I do to show my regret.

SIR RICHARD: Well, that's something. If I were Sue, I should accept the villa at Cannes and a diamond ring and bracelet from Hunt and Roskell's; not in the least as any reparation of your fault — nothing can repair that — but as a sign of belief in the genuineness of your — your remorse. What else can you do?

HARABIN: Anything that you can suggest.

SIR RICHARD: You have of course absolutely broken off —

HARABIN: Absolutely. I have given Sue assurances and proofs of that.

SIR RICHARD: And you promise that nothing shall ever induce you to renew the acquaintance?

HARABIN: I promise.

SIR RICHARD: You hear, Sue?

LADY SUSAN: Oh, yes. Of course. But will he promise that nothing of this kind shall ever happen again? (*looking at* HARABIN)

HARABIN: Yes, certainly.

LADY SUSAN: Will you give me your word of honour as a gentleman that it shall never happen again? Your sacred word — Uncle Dick, listen to this! — now, sir, your sacred word of honour as a soldier, your parole. (HARABIN *is about to promise, then checks himself. Fiercely*) Ha! (*to* SIR RICHARD) There! You see! I knew! He promises it shall never happen again — until the next time. (*to* HARABIN) You needn't give your promise — I'll save you the trouble of breaking it. (*Exit fiercely, left.*)

(HARABIN *and* SIR RICHARD *stand and look at each other non-plussed for some moments without speaking.*)

SIR RICHARD: I gave it to you hot, Jim, but, upon my word, you deserve it.

Hunt and Roskell's: Bond Street jewellers.

HARABIN: I know I do.

SIR RICHARD: Why didn't you make haste and give your word of honour it should not happen again?

HARABIN: So I should in another moment. But hang it all, Kato, I didn't like to pledge myself irrevocably – in case, you know –

SIR RICHARD: But don't you mean it never to happen again?

HARABIN: Yes, of course. But, after giving my word of honour as a gentleman, I should have felt so jolly uncomfortable if it had. I say, Kato, what can I do?

SIR RICHARD: I don't know. I've done all I can to bring her round.

> (*Enter* FOOTMAN, *announcing 'Sir Joseph Darby'. Enter* ADMIRAL SIR JOSEPH DARBY, *a jovial English gentleman of about sixty. Exit* FOOTMAN.)

ADMIRAL: (*very cordially*) My dear Jim – (*Shakes hands.*) Sir Richard. Is Lady Darby here?

SIR RICHARD: She left a little while ago to meet you at Waterloo.

ADMIRAL: I've been home, and they told me she'd come here. I haven't seen her for six months, bless her heart! Well, I'll be off back (*going*).

SIR RICHARD: You'd better wait. She's coming back here.

ADMIRAL: Coming back here?

SIR RICHARD: Yes. The fact is, we've had a little – matrimonial upset.

ADMIRAL: What's the matter, eh, Jim?

HARABIN: Lady Susan and I –

ADMIRAL: That's bad! That's very bad! You've been married six years. There never ought to be any quarrels after the first year.

SIR RICHARD: Or even then.

ADMIRAL: Oh, yes. I allow every married couple twelve months for what I call the shaking-down process, that is, to learn each other's tempers, to learn the give and take of married life. In all well-regulated households, for the woman to learn that she has got a master. In all ill-regulated households, for the man to learn that he has got a master. The first year of our married life Lady Darby and I lived a thorough cat and dog life. (*a roar of reminiscent laughter*) We had a battle-royal, I assure you, every day of our life. Ho! Ho! Ho! But we shook down comfortably after that – God bless her! God bless her! You're sure she's coming back here?

SIR RICHARD: Oh, yes.

ADMIRAL: (*turning to* HARABIN) Now, Jim, how is it the shaking-down process isn't complete in your case? What is it? Extravagance? debts? incompatibility of temper? jealousy? She's jealous, eh?

HARABIN: Worse, I'm afraid, Sir Joseph, and – I regret to say I've given her only too much cause.

ADMIRAL: That's awkward, that's very awkward. So she's found you out. Well, then, you must own up like a man. And, above all, mind your p's and q's till things have shaken down again.

HARABIN: But she won't let things shake down.

ADMIRAL: Oh, yes, she will. That's what it always comes to. Women are noble creatures – bless 'em! bless 'em! My wife, now – I've been a sad rascal, Jim – I won't mince matters – I've been a thorough out and out rascal. (*much affected*) I can't forgive myself. But she's forgiven me. Ah! what angels women are! Yes, she's forgiven me freely! (*slight pause*) I haven't told her all. But she's forgiven me freely what I have told her. So I thought I wouldn't grieve her by telling her any more. (*Sits in his chair and ponders his past transgressions, much affected.*)

(*Enter* FOOTMAN.)

FOOTMAN: (*to* SIR RICHARD) I beg pardon, Sir Richard, Mr Fergusson Pybus is below and would like to speak to you.

SIR RICHARD: Jim, here is this creature that is running after Elaine. Can I see him here for a few moments?

HARABIN: Certainly. (*to* FOOTMAN) Show Mr Pybus up. (*Exit* FOOTMAN.)

SIR RICHARD: I've done my best to break off the match, but Elaine seems determined to have him. Why I should saddle myself with another ward when I'd already got Sue to look after, is a mystery to me.

(*Enter* FOOTMAN, *announcing 'Mr Fergusson Pybus'. Enter* FERGUSSON PYBUS, *a lank, dreamy young man of twenty-five, with longish light hair, with precise, nervous, and rather affected manner. He wears a black velvet coat and a bright yellow tie. Exit* FOOTMAN.)

PYBUS: How d'ye do, Sir Richard! (SIR RICHARD *gives a curt nod in return.* PYBUS *bows to* ADMIRAL, *who is seated in gloomy reflection on his past transgressions, and takes no notice. Goes very sympathetically with timid, ingratiating manner to* HARABIN.) My dear Harabin, (*Takes* HARABIN's *hand, holds it between both of his for a moment with an expression of the deepest sympathy.*) you have my deepest, most heartfelt sympathy.

HARABIN: (*gruffly*) What for?

PYBUS: Miss Shrimpton has acquainted me with the regrettable fact that there is a serious misunderstanding between you and Lady Susan. (HARABIN *roughly withdraws his hand.*) I trust I am not indiscreet. (*to* ADMIRAL) Sir Joseph Darby, I believe. (ADMIRAL *bows.*) Then I'm speaking *en famille.* My dear Harabin, I can't say how much I regret this. I do not seek to know the nature of this misunderstanding − I do not ask who is to blame. There is to me in all matrimonial disagreements such a want of − of symmetry, a want of − a − proportion − of harmony − a want of beauty, so to speak. It affects me like a wrong note in music, like a − (*descriptive gesture*) like a faulty dash of colour in a picture − it distresses me.

SIR RICHARD: Does it?

PYBUS: Woman is to me (ADMIRAL *begins to listen.*) something so priceless, so perfect, so rare, so intolerably superior in every way to man, that I instinctively fall upon my knees before her.

ADMIRAL: (*in a tone of contemptuous irony*) Are you married, sir?

PYBUS: (*undecidedly*) No − no − not at present. Now my dear Harabin, may I

(s.d.) FERGUSSON PYBUS: Pybus's costume shows his disregard for the conventions of 'society' (especially considering that he is calling on Elaine's guardian) and his manner suggests the much-parodied 'intensity' of the Aesthetes.

offer my services as a — what shall I say — ambassador between you and Lady Susan?

HARABIN: Thank you, that's not necessary.

PYBUS: I'm delighted to hear it. But I do implore you to lose no time in placing yourself in the most abject position before your offended deity. (HARABIN *looks at* PYBUS *with rather angry impatience, turns his back on him and goes up stage.* PYBUS *follows him up.*) Pardon me, I have never disguised from you or Sir Richard (*turning to* SIR RICHARD) that it is only by the constant companionship and influence of Miss Shrimpton in the tenderest union that I can hope to gain that power over myself, that ascendancy over my fellows, that — that divine afflatus which — which will, I trust, enable me to — a — to stamp myself upon the age.

HARABIN: Sir Richard is Miss Shrimpton's guardian. I'll leave you to speak to him. (*Goes over to* SIR RICHARD. *In a low tone*) What can I do about Sue?

SIR RICHARD: Try another coax.

ADMIRAL: (*pulling out his watch*) Are you sure, Sir Richard, that Lady Darby is coming back here?

SIR RICHARD: Oh, yes. Go up with Jim and see Sue, and get her to listen to reason.

HARABIN: Yes, Sir Joseph, perhaps she'll listen to you.

ADMIRAL: I can't think what's coming over women. They never used to make this fuss. I never had any nonsense of this sort with Lady Darby. She used to make things very uncomfortable for about a fortnight, and then she dropped it. Ah! what an angel my wife is! (*Exeunt* HARABIN *and* ADMIRAL.)

PYBUS: (*to* SIR RICHARD) I cannot tell you how an affair of this kind distresses me. It seems to me so strange, so extraordinary, so impossible, that a man and a lady, united in the tenderest bonds, with every inducement to make each other supremely happy, with nothing to offer but worship and reverence on the man's side, nothing but courtesy and divine condescension on the lady's side, it seems so strange that two such beings should bicker and wrangle and bring discord into the harmony of life. Why should they do it? Why should they do it?

SIR RICHARD: Ah! why should they?

PYBUS: Sir Richard, I have already approached you with regard to — to — her —

SIR RICHARD: (*Rings bell.*) Let me see, what is your exact position?

PYBUS: I have now been her humble suitor for more than six months.

SIR RICHARD: Yes, I know. But your pecuniary position?

PYBUS: My father left me a modest annual income in consols.

(FOOTMAN *appears at door, left.*)

SIR RICHARD: Will you ask Miss Shrimpton to come here for a few moments? (*Exit* FOOTMAN.) What is the amount of this modest annual income?

PYBUS: It is not so much the exact amount of my income as the fact that with —

---

a modest annual income in consols: his capital is invested in safe government stocks, yielding a reliable but modest return. £275 was an adequate but by no means substantial income for the circles in which the characters move.

with her to inspire me, I feel I shall be able to – a – in some way – stamp
myself upon the age.

SIR RICHARD: And is that likely to be very lucrative?

PYBUS: What?

SIR RICHARD: Stamping yourself upon the age. What's it likely to bring in?

PYBUS: (*undecidedly*) Well – of course – that would depend upon the way I – a
– stamp myself upon the age.

SIR RICHARD: Just so. It seems a trifle problematic. So I'm afraid we must come
back to the precise amount of this modest annual income. How much?

PYBUS: Well – a – it is a capitalised sum of – a – ten thousand pounds.

SIR RICHARD: Bringing in an annual income of two hundred and seventy-five
pounds. Miss Shrimpton's fortune is – perhaps you know the amount?

PYBUS: I do not seek to know. There is something inexpressibly repulsive to me in
the bare idea of receiving money with Elaine. It seems like a crime. I want
my wife to be a fairy creature, incessantly, perpetually, a fairy creature.

SIR RICHARD: (*drily*) Ah!

PYBUS: I should wish her to come to me penniless, shoeless, without even rags –
> (*Enter* ELAINE SHRIMPTON, *a raw, self-assertive modern young
> lady, with brusque and decided manner.* PYBUS *assumes an attitude
> of devotion, props his head upon his hand, and worships her from
> afar.*)

ELAINE: How d'ye do, Sir Richard? Fergusson has told you of our decision?
(*looking enquiringly at* PYBUS)

PYBUS: (*nervously*) I have hinted to Sir Richard that – (*Leaves off nervously.*)

ELAINE: In a few months I shall be twenty-one. I find I cannot stay any longer
with Lady Susan, so I wish to know definitely if you will give your consent to
our immediate marriage.

PYBUS: (*same nervous, timid, deprecating manner*) Of course – we should wish to
be guided by your advice, Sir Richard – that is – if –

SIR RICHARD: That is, if my advice coincides with your own wishes.

PYBUS: Yes; and even if it did not, we would at least – a – a –

SIR RICHARD: You would at least listen to it. Thank you.

ELAINE: (*very decidedly*) At the same time we feel that we have duties and
responsibilities that we shall allow no worm-eaten conventionalities of society
to interfere with.

PYBUS: I feel that it is only by the – a – the – a – constant stimulus and charm
of her presence that I can – a – (*musingly, looking at her devotedly*) Ye – es
– Ye – es –

ELAINE: Fergusson has a career before him; I, too, have a career before me. Why
should we blind our eyes to the plainest and most sacred duties that lie before
us – duties to ourselves?

SIR RICHARD: (*trying to get a word in*) Well – I –

ELAINE: (*stopping him*) Why should we check the natural, self-ordained, self-
consecrated development of our characters?

(s.d.) ELAINE SHRIMPTON: see introduction, p. 17 above.

SIR RICHARD: Well —

ELAINE: Why should we dwarf and stunt ourselves physically, morally, intellectually, for the sake of propping up a society that is decrepit and moribund to its core? Why should we?

SIR RICHARD: I wouldn't if I were you.

PYBUS: I trust you don't think, Sir Richard, that we are taking up this attitude in any disrespect to you as Elaine's guardian.

SIR RICHARD: No, but —

ELAINE: (*stopping him*) We have thoroughly sifted the matter, and we are prepared to argue it out point by point, and step by step, from beginning to end, if you wish to discuss it.

SIR RICHARD: Not at all, thank you.

ELAINE: Then, as you have nothing to say —

SIR RICHARD: Excuse me, as I'm your guardian, and as I have command of your fortune until you're twenty-five, I have just a word or two to say.

ELAINE: (*Resigns herself in a bored attitude.*) Well?

SIR RICHARD: In the first place I should advise you not to marry. (ELAINE *suddenly turns round on him.*) At least, not at present.

ELAINE: I thought we had already dismissed that point as settled, eh, Fergusson?

PYBUS: Ye — es — I really thought — I assure you, Sir Richard, we value your advice immensely — but —

SIR RICHARD: But you won't take it. Very well, we'll consider that point settled. You marry as soon as Elaine's twenty-one.

PYBUS: And I assure you when we find ourselves in any difficulty we shall always come to you, shan't we, Elaine?

ELAINE: We are scarcely likely to find ourselves in any difficulty where our own good sense will not be an ample guide.

PYBUS: No, no! but if we do we'll come to you, Sir Richard.

SIR RICHARD: Thank you. Well, we'll consider you married. Mr Pybus, you have an annual income of two hundred and seventy-five pounds. I shall allow Elaine precisely the same sum annually until she is twenty-five.

ELAINE: What? You will hold back my money! It's cowardly! But so like a man! Brute force! — brute force! — never anything but brute force! Never any other argument!

SIR RICHARD: My dear Elaine, an allowance of two hundred and seventy-five pounds a year —

ELAINE: (*taking him up quickly*) Is at bottom, when you analyse it, nothing more or less than an exhibition of brute force. What else is it? — Analyse it.

SIR RICHARD: (*very calm*) Thank you, no! We'll adopt the synthetic method, and call it brute force. Well, that point's settled. I think that's all. I had a little advice to bestow.

ELAINE: Advice? Well, go on.

SIR RICHARD: On second thoughts I really feel I'm taking a mean advantage of my age and experience.

ELAINE: No — no. We'll hear what you have to say.

PYBUS: I assure you, Sir Richard, that although we haven't adopted your advice we have the highest opinion of it.

SIR RICHARD: Thank you. (*They both assume a bored expression, half super-cilious, half benevolent.*) I hope you won't mind my telling you, Mr Pybus, that Elaine is a rather ignorant, impulsive girl, with a smattering of pseudo-scientific knowledge, chiefly picked up from unwholesome feminine novels (ELAINE *looks defiant.* PYBUS *coughs, a bored, distressed, supercilious, remonstrative cough.* SIR RICHARD, *taking no notice, continues.*) If you want to be happy with her, you'll put her with some good housewife for a few months, where she will gain some rudimentary knowledge of house-keeping, and learn those little arts which are necessary to make a home com-fortable on an income of five hundred and fifty pounds a year. A few cook-ing lessons might not be out of place. (ELAINE *throws up her arms with a gesture of contemptuous despair at* SIR RICHARD's *stupidity.* PYBUS *exchanges glances with her, and coughs the same cough, fidgets.* SIR RICHARD, *taking no notice, continues.*) And I hope you won't mind my telling you, Elaine, that Mr Pybus, although doubtless a very clever and talented man — (PYBUS *coughs his cough.*)

ELAINE: Fergusson is a genius, if ever there was a genius on this earth!

SIR RICHARD: (*same calm tone*) I've no doubt! I've no doubt! And I'm sure he will stamp himself upon the age in some highly interesting and original way. (PYBUS *coughs again.*) I should advise him to choose the most lucrative, and stick to that. (PYBUS *again coughs, with more pity and contempt.*)

ELAINE: Have you anything more to say?

SIR RICHARD: So much for you individually. For the pair of you, as a mere matter of duty, and quite in a perfunctory way, without expecting you to pay the least attention to what I am saying, let me assure you that you'll find marriage a very trying and difficult position, full of cares and anxieties, that this romantic attachment of yours will probably wear away before long — (*incredulous and benevolent pity and protestation on the part of both*) And then you will have to face the coarse and brutal bread-and-cheese realities of life. You'll find that you have tempers to train and subdue, whims and obstinacies of your own to check, whims and obstinacies of your partner to indulge. There will be the need of daily, hourly, forbearance and kindliness, a constant overlooking of each other's faults and imperfections. And if towards the close of your married life you can look back upon it, not indeed without regrets, but without remorse, and on the whole with pleasure and thankfulness, it will only be because you have shut your eyes to much, for-given much, and utterly forgotten a good deal more.

ELAINE: Sir Richard, you're talking about what you have absolutely no experience of.

SIR RICHARD: (*rather angrily*) No experience?

ELAINE: You have never been married. (SIR RICHARD *makes an impatient gesture.*) And why do you advise us?

SIR RICHARD: (*hurriedly*) I don't! I don't! Kindly let me know when you have

---

and utterly forgotten a good deal more: an s.d. in French's seems designed to allow for a round of applause after this: '*Picks up hat and gloves from table, R.* PYBUS *looks at his watch,* ELAINE *rises, crosses to C.*'

fixed the date of your marriage, and if I can be of the least use in any possible way, pray command me. (*Exit very hurriedly.*)

ELAINE: (*looking after him*) Sir Richard grows more brutally cynical every day. And to refuse me my money!

PYBUS: My dear Elaine, let us at the very outset of our married life make it a rule to avoid all that is mean and petty and commonplace in life. What I want you to do, my dearest, is to surround me with — (*descriptive gesture*) — with all that is sweet and dainty and graceful and beautiful. Do you understand, my darling?

ELAINE: (*dubiously*) Ye — es.

PYBUS: To create a lovely lonely world for me to dwell in, so that I may be able to bring all my powers to their full fruition. Do you see, my dearest?

ELAINE: Yes, dearest, we will help each other. I feel, too, that I have a message for this age.

PYBUS: Ye — es. Ye — es. Still, I think, darling, it would be more profitable — I don't use the word in a pecuniary sense — if you were chiefly to devote yourself to — as I say — (*descriptive gesture*) — as it were — do you see, dear?

ELAINE: Oh, yes. But still, of course, I shall be free to develop my own character.

PYBUS: Of course, dearest, of course. Still, I think —
    (ADMIRAL *enters right, very excited, and hurriedly.*)

ADMIRAL: Excuse me, I've just seen Lady Darby drive up in a cab.
    (*Enter* FOOTMAN *showing in* LADY DARBY, *left. Exit* FOOTMAN.)

ADMIRAL: My dear girl — (*embracing her very effusively*)

LADY DARBY: My dear Jo —
    (PYBUS *coughs and seems uncomfortable.*)

ADMIRAL: (*Glances at him and speaks very sternly.*) I have not seen Lady Darby for some months, sir. (*Takes* LADY DARBY *up stage.*)

PYBUS: (*to* ELAINE) Come, dearest, we will go into the morning room. I do not like these coarse manifestations of affection. (*Exeunt* PYBUS *and* ELAINE.)

ADMIRAL: My darling girl, (*Looks at her with great admiration.*) how well you're looking! Upon my word, Victoria, you're worth forty bread-and-butter misses! You are! Now, come, sit down, my dear; tell me all the news.
    (*Enter* FOOTMAN *showing in* INEZ. ADMIRAL *shows great impatience.*)

INEZ: How d'ye do, Sir Joseph?

ADMIRAL: How d'ye do? (*Beckons* LADY DARBY *to get her away. Shows signs of impatience all through the scene.*)
    (*Re-enter* SIR RICHARD *right, very downcast.*)

INEZ: Well, Sir Richard?

SIR RICHARD: (*Shakes his head.*) Sue is determined to leave him.

INEZ: What's to be done?

SIR RICHARD: Nothing, except give her her head till she comes round.

LADY DARBY: We must keep people from knowing it; and, above all, we must keep it out of the papers. What can we do? (*Sits down and begins to write hurriedly.*)

SIR RICHARD: Mrs Quesnel, since there's no help for it, will you take care of her for a few weeks, and bring her round to a sensible frame of mind?

INEZ: Of course, anything that I can do —
    (*Re-enter* LADY SUSAN, *apparently in very bright spirits, dressed as for a journey, followed by* MAID *with parcels and bandboxes.*)
LADY SUSAN: Now, Inez, I'm ready. Is your carriage outside?
INEZ: (*doubtfully*) Ye — es, but —
LADY SUSAN: (*to* MAID) Phillips, put them in Mrs Quesnel's carriage, and come back and bring the rest of my luggage. (*Exit* MAID, *left, with bandboxes and parcels.*) Goodbye, Uncle Jo! (*kissing* ADMIRAL) Goodbye, Uncle Dick! (*kissing him*) Goodbye, auntie!
LADY DARBY: You foolish woman!
LADY SUSAN: What are you writing?
LADY DARBY: (*Reads.*) 'Lady Susan Harabin, whose health has been in a very delicate state for some time past, has left for Egypt with Mrs Quesnel.' (HARABIN *enters, looking half wretched and half defiant.* LADY DARBY *continues to read.*) 'Mr James Harabin has gone to Yorkshire for a few weeks' shooting before rejoining Lady Susan.'
LADY SUSAN: (*Shrugs her shoulders.*) I've said goodbye to everybody, haven't I?
HARABIN: (*sternly*) You have not said goodbye to me, madam.
LADY SUSAN: (*with great politeness*) Goodbye, my dear sir. Come, Inez. (INEZ *protests a little.* LADY SUSAN *gently pushes her off, left, and is going after her.*)
HARABIN: (*trying to assume a tone of stern authority*) Where are you going, madam?
LADY SUSAN: (*same tone of extremely calm politeness*) I am going to find a little romance, and introduce it into our married life (*going off*).
HARABIN: (*loud, angry*) I forbid you, madam! I forbid you!
    (LADY SUSAN, *in the most graceful, calm, and polite way, snaps her fingers three times at him, each time with a larger action, then backs out door left, bowing profoundly and politely to him.* HARABIN *makes an angry dash after her, realises he is powerless, stops, stands in a state of helpless, pathetic bewilderment for a few moments, then turns and appeals in turn for sympathy to* LADY DARBY, *who slowly and sympathetically shakes her head and sighs deeply; to the* ADMIRAL, *who purses his lips and pulls a long face; to* SIR RICHARD, *who shrugs his shoulders.* HARABIN *stands helpless.*)
    A very slow curtain
(*Ten months pass between acts I and II.*)

ACT II

SCENE.   SIR RICHARD KATO'*s sitting-room at the St Mildred's Hotel, Westbay, a comfortable room in a good-class seaside hotel. A door, right. A*

---

bandboxes: hatboxes.

large window, left, opening upon balcony and giving exit to gardens. Discover SIR
RICHARD *writing at table. Enter* WAITER, *showing in* INEZ. *Exit* WAITER.

SIR RICHARD: (*rising, shaking hands very cordially*) My dear Mrs Quesnel!

INEZ: What has brought you to Westbay, Sir Richard?

SIR RICHARD: An appeal from Elaine, who seems to have made a bad start in
    matrimony —

INEZ: Oh yes, she and Mr Pybus are down here in separate apartments —

SIR RICHARD: My wish to see my young friend Lucien, my wish to see Sue, my
    wish to see you — first of all, how is Sue?

INEZ: In the rudest health. We've had a glorious time.

SIR RICHARD: You've been away from England ten months. Weren't you and Sue
    getting a little homesick, eh?

INEZ: (*meditating*) N—o, n—o. I don't think so.

SIR RICHARD: I'm sorry. Tell me everything about Sue.

INEZ: I've told you everything in my letters.

SIR RICHARD: Yes, but what are her feelings towards her husband?

INEZ: I haven't the key of her heart.

SIR RICHARD: But so far as you can judge?

INEZ: So far as I can judge, Sue is in a state of the most perfect indifference
    towards every man alive. But that is the attitude which you men force us to
    assume to you, to ourselves, to everybody except the one man alive.

SIR RICHARD: But there is no *one-man-alive* in Sue's case?

INEZ: Not that I know of. But don't trust either my eyesight or my penetration,
    because —

SIR RICHARD: Because?

INEZ: Because if I were in Sue's place I should take good care that nobody knew.
    And I credit Sue with the common or garden powers of deception. (SIR
    RICHARD *walks about, a little perplexed and uncomfortable.*) It's charming
    of me to give away my sex to you like this, isn't it?

SIR RICHARD: It is. I assure you I appreciate it. After a lifetime's practice in the
    Divorce Court I still feel myself like Newton, a mere child on the seashore,
    with all the boundless ocean of woman's mysterious nature stretching silent,
    and innavigable, and inexplorable before me.

INEZ: Perhaps the Divorce Court isn't the best place to learn what unsuspected
    depths and treasures there are in woman's nature.

SIR RICHARD: (*very winning and confidential*) Well, now tell me — I'm only
    asking in the purest spirit of scientific inquiry — are there any depths and
    treasures which we mere outsiders, men, never suspect?

INEZ: Shall I tell you? Yes, treasures of faithfulness, treasures of devotion, of self-
    sacrifice, of courage, of comradeship, of loyalty. And above all, treasures of
    deceit — loving, honourable deceit, and secrecy and treachery.

Newton: 'I do not know what I may appear to the world, but to myself I seem to have been
only a boy playing on the sea-shore, and diverting myself in now and then finding a smoother
pebble or a prettier shell than ordinary, whilst the great ocean of truth lay all undiscovered
before me.' (Sir David Brewster, *Memoirs of . . . Sir Isaac Newton* (revised edn, 1875) II, 407).

SIR RICHARD: I had already suspected there might be an occasional jewel of that sort in the dark, unfathomed caves.

INEZ: You're laughing at me. You men never will see anything but a comedy in it. So we have to dress up our tragedy as a comedy just to save ourselves from being ridiculous and boring you. But we women feel it is a tragedy all the same.

SIR RICHARD: (*with real feeling*) Surely you have no tragedy in your life?

INEZ: (*Laughs.*) Oh! dear no. And you? (*very searchingly*)

SIR RICHARD: I? Oh! dear no. (*Pause – a shadow of recollection crosses his face.*) None that I cannot hide, or better still, laugh at.

INEZ: Ah, that's it! Our own hearts aren't sacred to us. That's our real modern tragedy – we laugh at the tragedy of our own lives!

SIR RICHARD: No, no, that's our real modern comedy and our truest wisdom. (INEZ *shakes her head.*) Yes, yes, believe me, it is so. We'll keep on dressing it up as a comedy for fear of boring people and making ourselves ridiculous. To come back to Sue –

INEZ: Where is Mr Harabin?

SIR RICHARD: You'll keep my secret?

INEZ: (*giving hand*) Honour!

SIR RICHARD: On his way here.

INEZ: On his way here?

SIR RICHARD: (*Nods.*) Sir Joseph and Lady Darby are bringing him. I came last evening to reconnoitre, but I didn't get in till midnight. Now, can't you and I, like good Samaritans, pour in wine and oil upon the wound?

INEZ: I'm always pouring in oil, but Sue doesn't seem to trouble very much about the wound.

SIR RICHARD: You don't rub it in. Not enough elbow-grease, eh?

INEZ: Perhaps. It's very absurd to make a fuss about other people's love-affairs.

SIR RICHARD: But when a husband and wife have quarrelled – ?

INEZ: Then it's clearly one's duty to advise them to make it up. And one does it, the same as one goes to church, because it is one's duty, not because there is any result from it.

SIR RICHARD: (*Takes out watch*) You'd better send Sue to me, but don't tell her that Harabin is coming. (*Enter* WAITER. *He brings card to* SIR RICHARD.) Where are you staying?

INEZ: 7, Marine Gardens – it's just opposite (*going towards window*).

SIR RICHARD: (*to* WAITER) Show Mr Edensor in.

        (*Exit* WAITER.)

INEZ: Edensor? There was a Mr Edensor staying at the hotel at Cairo last year.

SIR RICHARD: This is Lucien Edensor.

INEZ: It must be the same.

SIR RICHARD: He's the son of my old friend Danby Edensor. His father died in India last year, and I've got him a government appointment in New Zealand. He wrote to me from Eastgate, so I asked him to come over and see me. Do you know him?

INEZ: Very slightly, only a *table d'hôte* acquaintance. This is my nearest way. I'll send Sue to you. (*Exit at balcony.*)

> (*Enter* WAITER, *announcing 'Mr Lucien Edensor'. Enter* LUCIEN EDENSOR, *a handsome young man about twenty-five. Exit* WAITER.)

SIR RICHARD: (*coming down from balcony*) Ah! my dear boy (*shaking hands very warmly*).

LUCIEN: Sir Richard, how can I thank you?

SIR RICHARD: By saying nothing at all about it, and proving that you are the right man for the post.

LUCIEN: I shall do all I can to justify your recommendation.

SIR RICHARD: I'm sure you will. When do you start?

LUCIEN: Next Thursday.

SIR RICHARD: It will be a wrench to leave England for so many years.

LUCIEN: I'm rather glad of it. The truth is, Sir Richard, I'm awfully down in the mouth.

SIR RICHARD: What's the matter? A woman? (LUCIEN *nods.*) Poor boy! Ah well, at your age you'll get over that.

LUCIEN: I shall never get over it.

SIR RICHARD: That's what we all say at twenty-five, and it does credit to our youthful innocence.

LUCIEN: I shall never forget her.

SIR RICHARD: No; but you'll wonder what the devil you could have seen in her to rave about.

LUCIEN: You don't know how I love her.

SIR RICHARD: Yes I do, my boy. I've been twenty-five. I've had my illusions. At twenty-five you have the delight of your illusions, and you laugh at the fogies. But at fifty you'll have the far greater delight of seeing through your illusions and laughing at the youngsters. Take my word for it, fifty is the age when a healthy man begins to enjoy life.

LUCIEN: (*bitterly*) And when instead of loving a woman with all his heart he can laugh at her!

SIR RICHARD: No, no! when he can love her and laugh at her too. When he can love 'em all very much more, and when, damn 'em, they can plague him very much less.

LUCIEN: I shall never love but this one woman as long as I live.

SIR RICHARD: So you say! So you say!

LUCIEN: (*rather angrily*) You don't believe me!

SIR RICHARD: My dear young friend, I bought all there was of your father's very excellent Madeira. Today is the fifth of September. Write to me every fifth of September and say, 'On my honour, I love her still', and on *my* honour I'll

---

table d'hôte: meal provided for hotel guests at a fixed time and price: it was common in European hotels for the guests making use of this tariff to share a large table.

send you half-a-dozen bottles of that excellent Madeira every year. Is it a
bargain?

LUCIEN: Yes. (*Shakes hands, suddenly remembers.*) There was only two dozen of
that Madeira left! It won't last out!

SIR RICHARD: My boy, it will last out your love.

LUCIEN: Sir Richard, when you talk like that, I feel, in spite of all you have done
for me, I feel I — I hate you. I love her, and if my love is an illusion I hope I
shall die in it!

SIR RICHARD: (*with a change in manner, very softly and tenderly*) You're right.
(*long sigh*) Love her, my dear boy, love her as long as you can!

LUCIEN: Do you say that, Sir Richard? even if —

SIR RICHARD: If what?

LUCIEN: If she's the wife of another man.

SIR RICHARD: The devil! No!

LUCIEN: I can't help it. I must keep on loving her.

SIR RICHARD: Very well then, keep on loving her. But pack off to New Zealand
next Thursday. Now let's drop her. You'll want the agreement and the letter
of instructions. They're upstairs. (*He is going to the door when the* WAITER
enters, showing in LADY SUSAN. LUCIEN *starts a little, unnoticed by* SIR
RICHARD. *Exit* WAITER.)

LADY SUSAN: (*Begins very affectionately.*) My dear Uncle Dick! (*Sees* LUCIEN,
starts rather violently. SIR RICHARD *sees her confusion.* LUCIEN, *behind*
SIR RICHARD'*s back, makes her a sign of warning.*) You have a visitor.

SIR RICHARD: You know Mr Edensor?

LADY SUSAN: (*who has a little recovered*) No.

SIR RICHARD: Then let me introduce you. Mr Lucien Edensor, Lady Susan
Harabin.

LADY SUSAN: I thought at first that I had met you, but —

LUCIEN: I don't think I've had the pleasure.

              (*an awkward little pause*)

SIR RICHARD: I'll fetch those instructions, Lucien. (*He turns suddenly at door,
sees they are both watching him furtively. Exit* SIR RICHARD. *They watch
him off. The moment he has left the room they turn to each other.*)

LADY SUSAN: (*pleased, excited, very frightened*) Lucien!

LUCIEN: Lady Sue!

LADY SUSAN: (*alarmed*) We haven't — betrayed ourselves?

LUCIEN: No — I don't think so.

LADY SUSAN: What brings you here? Why didn't you let me know you were
coming? Why haven't you sent me a message all these months?

LUCIEN: You said I was not to write.

LADY SUSAN: (*reproachfully*) And you obeyed me!

LUCIEN: When my father died Sir Richard was such a brick to me I felt I couldn't
behave like a blackguard and bring disgrace to his family. But now I've seen
you again — (*trying to clasp her*)

LADY SUSAN: (*repulsing him*) Hush! We shall be heard! What can we do?

LUCIEN: Go back to the old sweet days of last year, let it all be as it was then.
That last Sunday at Cairo —

LADY SUSAN: (*frightened, looking round*) Hush! You're sure nobody suspected?

LUCIEN: How could they? We were always so careful.

LADY SUSAN: Oh, I should kill myself if anyone knew! You have never spoken of me — boasted to any of your men friends — ?

LUCIEN: Lady Susan, I'm not a cad.

LADY SUSAN: Forgive me, I know you wouldn't — and you never will?

LUCIEN: Be sure you will never be (*looking at her with great intentness*) misjudged through me.

LADY SUSAN: Thank you. No one will ever guess —

LUCIEN: No one shall ever guess *what — never — happened.*

> (*She looks at him very gratefully and affectionately, presses his hand with great gratitude.*)

LADY SUSAN: Thank you! Thank you! Shush!

> (*Enter* SIR RICHARD *with papers in his hands. Throughout the act his outward demeanour to the persons on the stage is that of great frankness and entire absence of suspicion, but whenever the business of the stage allows it, he shows the audience that he is most keenly watching every word, movement, and glance of* LADY SUSAN, INEZ *and* LUCIEN.)

SIR RICHARD: Lucien, my boy, you'll stay to lunch with us?

LUCIEN: Yes. No, I don't think — at least — (*Glances at* LADY SUSAN.)

SIR RICHARD: Oh, I insist. I've brought the agreement and instructions. You'll have time to study them carefully on your way out to New Zealand.

LADY SUSAN: New Zealand?

LUCIEN: I am leaving for New Zealand next Thursday.

LADY SUSAN: For long?

LUCIEN: For some years, perhaps for life.

LADY SUSAN: Indeed!

SIR RICHARD: You had better take these — (*Is about to cross and give papers to* LUCIEN, *when* WAITER *enters, showing in* INEZ. *Exit* WAITER. SIR RICHARD *watches very closely to see if* INEZ *and* LUCIEN *recognise each other.* INEZ *slightly bows to* LUCIEN. LUCIEN *returns bow in same unembarrassed manner.* SIR RICHARD, *papers still in hand, speaks to* INEZ.) Didn't you say that Mr Edensor was staying at your hotel at Cairo last year?

INEZ: (*quite frankly*) Yes. (*to* LUCIEN) If you remember, we used to sit opposite you at *table d'hôte.*

LADY SUSAN: (*suddenly, a little overdoing it*) Of course! I could not imagine where I had met Mr Edensor. Now I remember quite well!

> (SIR RICHARD *turns and looks at her.*)

LUCIEN: (*a little lamely*) Yes, but really it had escaped me.

> (SIR RICHARD *turns and looks at him.*)

SIR RICHARD: Very natural. Well, you'll sit opposite each other again at lunch

---

I should kill myself if anyone knew: Wyndham asked Jones to omit this line, and to rewrite the second sentence of Lady Susan's speech to read: 'You have never spoken of me to any of your men friends?' (*Life and Letters*, pp. 162–3).

with me today. (*giving papers*) Take these into the smoking-room and look
through them. Wait for me there.

LUCIEN: (*Has taken papers. To* INEZ) Then I shall meet you again at lunch.

SIR RICHARD: Yes, you'll meet her again at lunch. (*Exit* LUCIEN.) My dear Sue,
welcome to England! I'm delighted to see you. Quite well and happy, eh?
(*Looks at her.*)

LADY SUSAN: Quite well and *perfectly* happy.

SIR RICHARD: (*between her and* INEZ) That's right. So you didn't remember
Lucien? (*In a tone of affected carelessness, the tone of a skilful cross-
examiner who is leading his witness unsuspectingly on.*)

LADY SUSAN: Yes, I did, but I could *not* recall where it was I had met him.

SIR RICHARD: (*turning to* INEZ) *You* remembered him at once?

INEZ: (*very frankly*) Oh, yes. He sat almost opposite to us at *table d'hôte* for a
month. Then he was called away suddenly to India to his father, who was
dying.

LADY SUSAN: Was he? I'd forgotten.

> (SIR RICHARD *watches the following scene unobtrusively, but
> most intently.*)

INEZ: My dear Sue, where is your memory? Nearly everyone in the hotel went to
see him off at the —

LADY SUSAN: I'm sure I didn't.

INEZ: Everybody except you. That was the Monday night, if you recollect —

LADY SUSAN: (*very quickly and pettishly*) My dear Inez, you seem strangely
interested in this young fellow.

INEZ: I seem interested! I scarcely spoke to him.

LADY SUSAN: Neither did I.

INEZ: At any rate, you were at church with him on the Sunday night.

LADY SUSAN: (*confused*) I'm sure I — who told you that?

INEZ: You told me you were going to church on the Sunday evening. I stayed at
home. Did you go?

LADY SUSAN: (*confused*) Did I? Let me think — Yes, yes, I did.

INEZ: After dinner Mr Edensor came into the drawing-room. Mrs Grantham asked
him where he had been. He said, 'To church.' She said, 'Isn't it very late?'
He said, 'The sermon was a very long one.' You hadn't come in. I asked him
if he had seen you at church, and he said, 'Yes,' you sat in the next pew to
him. When I got upstairs you had just come in. I said, 'You're late.' You said,
'The sermon was a very long one', and —

LADY SUSAN: Oh, my dear Inez, it was an awful, awful, awful sermon. It was just
as boring as this rigmarole of yours. Now do, please, stop, and let us finish
with this terrible young fellow.

INEZ: (*a little angry*) My dear Sue, the young fellow is no concern of mine.

LADY SUSAN: And I'm sure he's none of mine.

INEZ: (*a little nettled*) I didn't say he was.

(s.d.) SIR RICHARD watches . . . intently: in French's edition he is consulting Bradshaw's
railway guide.

LADY SUSAN: Then why do you wish to make out that we went to church together?

INEZ: My dear Sue, why do you make such a fuss about it?

SIR RICHARD: (*interposing, soothing them down*) Tsch! Tsch! Tsch! Tsch! Tsch! My dear Mrs Quesnel, you are making a mountain out of a molehill. Sue went to church, as I understand, this particular Sunday night. Eh, Sue?

    (INEZ *begins to watch very intently.*)

LADY SUSAN: Yes.

SIR RICHARD: And by the merest chance Mr Edensor went to the same church?

LADY SUSAN: Yes.

SIR RICHARD: You neither went with him nor came back with him?

LADY SUSAN: (*Hesitates a little.*) N—o.

SIR RICHARD: But by the merest chance he happened to sit in the same pew with you?

LADY SUSAN: Yes. No. I'm not sure. I can't remember.

INEZ: It was the next pew, at least so Mr Edensor said.

LADY SUSAN: Yes, the next pew. I remember now. It was the next pew. (*getting more and more confused*) He sat on this side — no, on this — no — I — (*Meets* SIR RICHARD'*s look.*) I forget, and there's an end of it. (*Goes up to balcony in a temper, stands there with her back to* SIR RICHARD *and* INEZ.)

    (*Enter* WAITER *with cards on tray, hands them to* SIR RICHARD. *He takes cards, looks at* LADY SUSAN, *whose back is to him, shows them to* INEZ.)

INEZ: (*in a low voice*) Mr Harabin!

SIR RICHARD: (*cautiously*) Shush! don't tell her. (*to* WAITER) I'll come and speak to them. (*Exit* WAITER. *Exit* SIR RICHARD.)

LADY SUSAN: (*to* INEZ) Inez, it's mean of you to spread such stories about me. I thought you were my friend.

INEZ: So, I am, dearest. Sue, if you have been — foolish —

LADY SUSAN: Foolish?

INEZ: With this Mr Edensor —

LADY SUSAN: (*very indignant*) Inez!

INEZ: Dearest, I said, 'if'. You know, dear, you may rely upon me. We women must stick by each other. I'll say anything to help you —

LADY SUSAN: (*dignified innocent tone*) Thank you. If you will only say the simple truth, that will be quite sufficient to clear my conduct of all suspicion. (*suddenly, eagerly*) You never saw anything to lead you to suppose —

INEZ: No, not at the time. The idea never came to me till this moment. There was nothing between you, dearest? (*very searchingly*)

LADY SUSAN: (*emphatically*) No, not even so much as an innocent flirtation. You know, Inez, if there were I should tell you. I tell you everything.

INEZ: Do you?

LADY SUSAN: Yes. And you tell me everything, don't you, dearest?

The idea . . . this moment: French's s.d. suggests the degree of intimacy between Inez and Lady Susan: '*going to* SUSAN, *taking her hands and looking into her eyes*'.

INEZ: Yes, dearest, everything. (*Kisses her.*)

    (*Re-enter* SIR RICHARD.)

SIR RICHARD: You'll stay to lunch, Sue? I'm going to have quite a pleasant little party.

LADY SUSAN: Who's coming?

SIR RICHARD: Isn't there one very old friend, and a dear good fellow whom you would be pleased to meet again?

LADY SUSAN: My husband! Uncle Dick, how can you insult me by asking me to meet my husband?

SIR RICHARD: My dear Sue, why shouldn't you meet your husband?

LADY SUSAN: Because — because it's impossible.

SIR RICHARD: Why? You haven't carried out your threat?

LADY SUSAN: What threat?

SIR RICHARD: To introduce a little romance into your married life.

LADY SUSAN: (*with the greatest indignation*) Uncle Dick!

SIR RICHARD: But you threatened —

LADY SUSAN: Threatened! What else can we poor women do? Oh! and you could believe that I could be guilty of — (*horror-stricken*) Oh! oh! Will men never understand a woman?

    (*Exit very indignantly at balcony.* SIR RICHARD *and* INEZ *look at each other nonplussed.*)

INEZ: Our oil doesn't seem to be lubricating.

SIR RICHARD: Mrs Quesnel, honour — (INEZ *gives him her hand.*) Was there anything between Sue and young Edensor at Cairo?

INEZ: On my honour, I believe no.

    (*Enter* WAITER *at door.*)

WAITER: Mr and Mrs Fergusson Pybus are here and would like to see you, Sir Richard.

SIR RICHARD: Show them in. And let me know when Sir Joseph and Lady Darby and Mr Harabin return.

    (*Exit* WAITER.)

INEZ: What's to be done about Sue?

SIR RICHARD: More oil. A constant gentle application. (*Strokes the back of her hand.*) Go and soothe her down and bring her over to lunch if you can.

INEZ: If we don't succeed what a lot of oil we shall have wasted! (*Exit at balcony.*)

    (SIR RICHARD, *left alone for some moments, walks up and down room very perplexed, indicating that he is putting together the links of a chain of evidence, and puzzling them out in his own mind, walks, stops suddenly, slightly scratches his forehead, puts one forefinger on the other, puts head on one side, walks again, puzzles. Enter* WAITER, *announces 'Mr and Mrs Pybus'. Enter* ELAINE *and* PYBUS *slowly and a little sulkily, as if on bad terms with each other. Exit* WAITER.)

SIR RICHARD: (*cordially*) Well? (*shaking hands with both of them*) Well? (*looking from one to the other*) What's the matter? Nothing serious, I hope?

PYBUS: We told you, Sir Richard, that we should come to you if any difficulty arose.

SIR RICHARD: Thank you. (*to him*) Sit down. (*to her*) Sit down. (*They sit down one on each side of him. Genially*) Now tell me all about it.

> (*During the following scene* SIR RICHARD *is quietly seated between the two. He does not interfere in the least, but merely turns his head from one to the other as each begins to speak.*)

ELAINE: The whole thing is in a nutshell. Is the mistress of the house to be consulted on a purely domestic arrangement, or is she not? Is she to be treated as a rational creature, or is she not?

PYBUS: My darling, I have always wished to treat you as something entirely sweet and perfect and gracious, something sainted and apart, but when you insist on getting on a chair and breaking the looking-glass — you do make it a little difficult, my darling, for me to — to — (*descriptive gesture*) to cherish my ideal of you.

ELAINE: It was your pushing that broke the looking-glass.

PYBUS: My darling, I was quite gentle. I merely held the corner of the dressing-table in a firm position while you struggled.

ELAINE: Just so. You merely asserted your superior brute force. Brute force! Brute force! When will Woman hear any other argument from Man?

PYBUS: My dear Elaine, I did argue with you for nearly three-quarters of an hour. I explained how impossible it is for me to — to concentrate myself, to bring all my manifold powers to bear upon the problems of this age while you are shaking the washing-stand, and letting the breakfast get quite cold merely for the sake of indulging your own whims.

ELAINE: Whims? I have no whims. I have only convictions.

PYBUS: My dear Elaine, what is it but a whim when you —

ELAINE: Really, Fergusson, it is impossible — (*rising angrily*)

PYBUS: (*also rising angrily*) Really, my darling, I cannot —

SIR RICHARD: (*Interposing, soothes them down.*) Tsch! Tsch! Tsch! Tsch! Sit down. Sit down, both of you. (*motioning them into their chairs again*) Sit down. There is to me in all matrimonial disagreements a want of harmony, a want of beauty, so to speak, which I am quite sure, Mr Pybus, must be as distressing to you as it is to me.

PYBUS: That is what I am always explaining to Elaine. We made it a rule when we were married to avoid all that is petty and mean and commonplace in life.

SIR RICHARD: (*soothingly*) An excellent rule. It ought to be incorporated in the marriage service. (*Throughout the scene he assumes a perfectly calm and judicial bearing.*) Well now. You were married on the second of February. After your honeymoon, you took up residence at —

PYBUS: At Clapham.

SIR RICHARD: At Clapham. You made it a rule to avoid all that is mean and petty and commonplace in life, and you took up your residence at Clapham. I forget the exact address?

Clapham: by the 1890s speculative building had turned Clapham into a by-word for drab, lower-middle class suburbia. In *The Dancing Girl* Goldspink owns houses in 'Gladstone Terrace, Freetrade Road, Peckham', and the financier Greenslade in *The Crusaders* has had 'large building speculation' in Clapham, Wimbledon, Peckham and Camberwell.

PYBUS: The Nest, Gladstone Road, Clapham.

SIR RICHARD: The Nest, Gladstone Road, Clapham.

PYBUS: (*plaintively*) I cannot say that Clapham appeals to me.

ELAINE: Clapham is intolerably suburban. The inhabitants of Clapham are entirely conventional persons. They do not live in the realm of ideas at all. And Fergusson will not join me in rousing —

PYBUS: (*interrupting*) My angel, I do think it is of more importance that you should — (*Ends with a feeble descriptive gesture.*)

ELAINE: And I think that it is of more importance that you should assist me in organising my society.

PYBUS: I cannot see, my dear —

ELAINE: (*stopping him*) No, Fergusson, you cannot see. That is the difficulty with men. They cannot see.

PYBUS: Really, my darling — (*rising again angrily*)

ELAINE: Really —

SIR RICHARD: (*soothing them down*) Tsch! Tsch! Tsch! Tsch! (*Gets them seated again. To* ELAINE) What is this society you are organising?

ELAINE: The Clapham Boadicean Society for the Inculcation of the New Morality among the Women of Clapham.

SIR RICHARD: What is the New Morality? Has it anything to do with the Ten Commandments?

ELAINE: It is not based precisely upon those lines. (*beginning oratorically*) There is an immense future for Woman —

SIR RICHARD: (*hurriedly stopping her*) I'm sure there is! I'm sure there is! But we must not discuss the future of Woman just now. Well now, you agree upon one thing. You both dislike Clapham.

ELAINE: It is your unwarranted retention of my fortune, Sir Richard, that —

SIR RICHARD: (*Interrupts, stopping her.*) Yes, yes, — we must not discuss my conduct just now.

ELAINE: But it is your conduct that compels us to exist in a jerry-built villa, in a wretched suburb surrounded by suburban persons with entirely suburban ideas —

SIR RICHARD: My dear Elaine, we must not discuss Clapham just now. (*taking out watch*) I want to hear the history of this unfortunate disagreement between you and Mr Pybus.

ELAINE: But it all arises from living in Clapham.

SIR RICHARD: Oh! I thought you said it was a purely domestic affair.

ELAINE: So it is. We live in Gladstone Road, Clapham.

SIR RICHARD: But how does that produce disagreements between you and Mr Pybus?

PYBUS: I am of an intensely nervous and artistic temperament, and I cannot shave in the morning unless the blind is fully drawn up so that I can perceive, with the utmost nicety, the exact position of any pimple — otherwise I cut myself.

ELAINE: But it is very inconvenient that the blind should be drawn up, because of the neighbours in the rooms of the opposite house.

PYBUS: I am sure Sir Richard will agree that it is highly desirable that the blind should be drawn up.

SIR RICHARD: (*judicially*) It is highly desirable, Mr Pybus, that you should not cut yourself while shaving.

PYBUS: (*to* ELAINE, *triumphantly*) There!

ELAINE: But if the blind is drawn up, the people in the opposite house –

SIR RICHARD: It is highly desirable that the good folks who live in Clapham should not be shocked.

ELAINE: (*triumphantly, to* PYBUS) There! And every morning Fergusson will insist –

PYBUS: My dear, it is you who will insist. And really –

SIR RICHARD: Tsch! Tsch! Tsch! Tsch!

PYBUS: (*plaintively*) It affected my health so much I was obliged to leave Clapham. And I cannot consent to return to the Nest unless Elaine – (*descriptive gesture*)

ELAINE: Nor can I – unless –

SIR RICHARD: Tsch! Tsch! Tsch! Tsch! (*in a very calm and judicial tone*) Is there only one blind to this window, or is there also a small muslin blind?

ELAINE: There is a small muslin blind.

(PYBUS *nods acquiescence.*)

SIR RICHARD: What is the distance from the top of the muslin blind to the top of the window?

ELAINE: Four feet.

PYBUS: Three, my dear.

ELAINE: Four.

PYBUS: I'm sure, my darling –

ELAINE: I measured.

PYBUS: I'm sure – my dear, if you will contradict – (*piteously*)

SIR RICHARD: Tsch! Tsch! Tsch! Tsch! We'll have it measured. (*to* PYBUS) The looking-glass is immediately under the window?

PYBUS: (*pathetically*) The looking-glass is unfortunately broken.

SIR RICHARD: Kindly replace it at my expense. (*Proceeds judicially.*) If the roller blind were drawn down each morning to exactly half the distance between the top of the window and the top of the muslin blind, it would allow plenty of light for you to shave by, Mr Pybus.

PYBUS: Yes – yes, I think so, but really I cannot –

SIR RICHARD: Tsch! Tsch! Tsch! Tsch! (*turning to* ELAINE) And it would also protect anyone inside the room from the observation of the neighbours opposite.

ELAINE: Yes. Unless anyone went near the window.

SIR RICHARD: Well, now, it seems to me it would be convenient if during the time Mr Pybus is shaving in the morning the roller blind is drawn down exactly half the distance. And during that time it would be convenient if you, Elaine, did not go within two yards of the window.

(*Enter* WAITER.)

WAITER: Sir Joseph Darby and Mr Harabin are outside, Sir Richard.

SIR RICHARD: Show them in. (*Exit* WAITER.) Now, won't that arrangement enable you to return in perfect agreement like doves to the nest?

PYBUS: (*doubtful*) Yes, perhaps, but –

ELAINE: Well, that depends —

SIR RICHARD: Go and take a pleasant little stroll in the gardens, (*getting them off at window*) and arrange in future for the blind to be just half-way up — that is to say, neither up nor down! (*Gets them off at window.*)

>   (*Enter* WAITER, *showing in* ADMIRAL *and* LADY DARBY. *Exit* WAITER.)

SIR RICHARD: (*to* ADMIRAL) Well, how does he seem now?

>   (ADMIRAL *shakes his head very sympathetically, and points to* JAMES HARABIN, *who enters very slowly, hands in pockets, very downcast and miserable. He walks despondently to armchair, drops into it listlessly, and stares in front of him with the pathetic expression of a man very much ill-used by the world.*)

ADMIRAL: (*pointing to* HARABIN *as to a martyr*) There! There you see the result of all this tomfoolery of woman's higher education! There you see what happens when a woman takes the bit into her mouth. A man's peace and happiness utterly ruined!

>   (HARABIN *sits in plaintive silence, taking no notice.*)

LADY DARBY: Quite true, Jo, but (*with a severe look at* HARABIN) that does not excuse a man for forgetting that he has got a good wife, and —

ADMIRAL: (*quickly*) No, my darling; when a man has a good wife it's a rascally shame to forget her. And to think that next Saturday I shall be compelled to leave you for — (*He is much affected.*) Ah, Victoria, if you had only been a good sailor!

LADY DARBY: I'm not so sure that we should have been any happier, Jo. You never seem to appreciate me so much as you do the week before you leave me, and the week after you return.

ADMIRAL: Well, perhaps it's best as it is, my love, perhaps it's best as it is!

HARABIN: (*feebly, pathetically*) Kato, I'm all to pieces. I couldn't eat any breakfast.

SIR RICHARD: (*ringing bell*) My dear Jim! What shall it be? A chop, steak, bacon and eggs —

HARABIN: (*shuddering, shakes his head piteously*) Could they manage an anchovy sandwich, and a glass of dry champagne?

>   (*Enter* WAITER.)

SIR RICHARD: Anchovy sandwich, and a small bottle of the best dry champagne.

ADMIRAL: Do you know, Kato, I feel that an anchovy sandwich and a glass of champagne would just keep me going till lunch.

SIR RICHARD: Anchovy sandwiches for two, and a large bottle of the best dry champagne.

>   (*Exit* WAITER.)

ADMIRAL: My appetite is something remarkable.

HARABIN: I haven't made a decent meal for months.

ADMIRAL: (*Very sympathetically, again points to* HARABIN *as to a martyr.*) Ah! there it is, you see. A woman runs away from her duties. What happens? Everything goes to rack and ruin! A man's meals, a man's health, all his little home comforts and luxuries completely sacrificed!

HARABIN: What did Sue say about meeting me, Kato?

SIR RICHARD: Well, the fact is, Jim, I – I believe Mrs Quesnel is talking very kindly about you. And perhaps, if Lady Darby were to go over to Sue and help the negotiations, we might induce Sue to come over to lunch and make it up.

LADY DARBY: I'll go and see what I can do. But really, there is no excuse for a man –

ADKIRAL: No, my love, none whatever! And when I think – (*Much affected, breaks off.*) Go and put it very nicely to her, dear. I'll come over as soon as I have had my anchovy sandwich, and we'll go for a nice little stroll together, shall we? Ah! how this place reminds me of old days! (*much affected again*)

LADY DARBY: Don't be foolish, Jo. (*Exit at door.*)

ADMIRAL: (*as he closes the door after her*) There goes the best woman in England! Ah, Jim, it's a great pity for you young men that the good old stamp of English girl and wife is getting extinct!

(*Enter* WAITER, *with a tray of anchovy sandwiches, and a bottle of champagne; pours out three glasses.*)

ADMIRAL: What do you think of English women today, Kato?

SIR RICHARD: I have met with some of all sorts.

(ADMIRAL *comes up to table, takes up a glass of champagne.* HARABIN *sits and looks gloomily in front of him.*)

ADMIRAL: (*glass in hand*) You've had a great deal of experience in the marriage question.

SIR RICHARD: (*taking glass*) Outsiders' experience – yes.

(*Exit* WAITER.)

ADMIRAL: What is to become of society – (*Drinks.*) A very good glass of champagne, Kato! What is to become of society if women insist on turning everything topsy-turvy, eh? (*Takes an anchovy sandwich.*)

SIR RICHARD: (*Drinks.*) I don't know. Have a glass of champagne, Jim. (*Giving champagne to* HARABIN, *who takes it moodily and gloomily, sits holding it in his hand without drinking.*)

(*During the following scene the* ADMIRAL *helps himself very freely to champagne, and eats nearly all the plate of sandwiches.* HARABIN *sits very moody and gloomy, scarcely touches one or the other.*)

ADMIRAL: Where are we going, eh? (*Eats a large mouthful of anchovy sandwich.*)

SIR RICHARD: Ah, just so. Take a sandwich, Jim. (*Gives a sandwich to* HARABIN, *who takes it, makes a face at it, and sips a little wine, gloomily.*)

ADMIRAL: That's what I ask myself. (*another mouthful*) Where are we going?

SIR RICHARD: Ah! Where are we? Well, I can afford to look on with the complacent curiosity of an intelligent rustic who sees the coach rattling down hill at the devil of a rate with runaway leaders and no brake. I can only mildly speculate whether there will be a smash-up.

ADMIRAL: (*very solemnly*) Kato, take my word for it, there will be a smash-up.

SIR RICHARD: I shouldn't wonder. Of what?

ADMIRAL: Of the marriage coach – if we men don't keep a tight hold of the reins. And a devil of a smash-up it will be!

SIR RICHARD: Ah! Thank God I'm not a passenger.

ADMIRAL: (*taking another sandwich*) Here's an instance of it. (*Points to*
HARABIN, *who is toying with a sandwich, and vainly trying to get a mouth-*
ful of it down.) Jim has his little failings. But because a man has his little
failings, is that any reason for his wife running amuck among all the conventions and proprieties of social life, eh? What's your opinion?

SIR RICHARD: I have no opinion. I take no side. I merely watch the game.

ADMIRAL: And looking round I ask myself where are we going, eh, Jim? (*Takes*
another sandwich.)

HARABIN: (*moodily*) I know where I'm going. I'm going to the dogs. Has Kato
told you how they've cheated and swindled me?

ADMIRAL: Who?

HARABIN: Everybody. My servants, my tradesmen, and confounded womenkind.

ADMIRAL: (*sympathisingly, sandwich in hand*) Ah! (*Points him out again as a*
martyr to SIR RICHARD.)

HARABIN: Why the deuce a man who has a perfect wife like I had, for Sue was as
near perfection as possible, wasn't she, Kato? —

SIR RICHARD: You're her husband. You ought to know.

HARABIN: She was. Perfect manners! Perfect taste! And the best of tempers! What
on earth could induce me — ?

SIR RICHARD: The advantages and delights of a steady and unflinching course of
strictly respectable monogamy are so many and so obvious, that I have never
been able to understand in the least how any man or woman alive could
possibly deviate from it for one moment.

ADMIRAL: (*more sandwich*) If ever there was a jewel of a wife it's Lady Darby.
God bless her! Here's her health. (*Drinks.*) I don't deserve her. She's too good
for me. When I remember what an unfaithful rascal I've been, and the lies I've
had to tell — the awful lies — (*Is overcome with painful reminiscences and*
weeps.)

HARABIN: I never knew what a good wife was till Sue left me.

ADMIRAL: (*getting very confidential, and a little maudlin*) You wouldn't believe
me, Jim, (*pawing* HARABIN *affectionately*) if I were to tell you half of the
particulars of my — my unfortunate history. (*crying a little*) Of course, in
these matters (*turning to* SIR RICHARD, *and taking him in*) we must all
make great allowances for men (SIR RICHARD *acquiesces.*), especially for
sailors. How do you account for it, Jim, (*suddenly brightening into great*
joviality and pride) that the best Englishmen have always been such devils
amongst the women? Always! I wouldn't give a damn for a soldier or a sailor
that wasn't, eh? How is it, Jim?

HARABIN: (*still absorbed in his own woes*) I don't know, and I jolly well don't
care.

ADMIRAL: Yes. Taking all things into consideration I can forgive myself a good
deal. But when all's said and done, nothing can disguise from me awfu' fac',
Kato, that I have behaved like a disgraceful scoundrel, best of wives. (*Is again*
overcome, and weeps.) And if I knew any possible way in which I could blot
out the past, I'd do it freely and willingly. What would you advise me to do,
Kato?

SIR RICHARD: In the absence of any possible amendment of conduct in the past, or any probable amendment of conduct in the future, I think a good display of hearty repentance in the present is all that can be reasonably demanded from any man.

ADMIRAL: If I were to go down on my knees to her I couldn't express a thousandth part of the sorrow I'm feeling at this moment.

HARABIN: If I can only get Sue to settle down comfortably again with me, I'll reform and make a model husband for the rest of my life.

ADMIRAL: Ah, that's just what I've said to myself scores of times. And once or twice I've kept my word — for a considerable period, I may say a very considerable period.

HARABIN: But I mean it. Never again! These last ten months since Sue left me, I've had such a lesson of the treachery, the extravagance, and the heartlessness of womankind, that from this time forward I am fully determined I will never again — (*Enter* LADY DARBY.) What does Sue say?

LADY DARBY: She says she'll have nothing to say to you.

HARABIN: Very well. (*Rises resolutely, takes hat, goes to door, suddenly stops.*) Lady Darby, do you suppose that — she refuses to return to me because — she has — introduced —

LADY DARBY: Oh, no, you may make yourself quite easy on that point.

HARABIN: You're quite sure?

LADY DARBY: Quite sure.

HARABIN: Very well. (*Goes to door.*)

SIR RICHARD: Where are you going, Jim?

HARABIN: To the telegraph office. You'll bear me witness, Kato, how awfully cut up I was, and how thoroughly I had determined to turn over a new leaf. But now I feel justified in taking advantage of any course of conduct that may present itself. (*Exit.*)

ADMIRAL: (*Points to* HARABIN*'s exit as to that of a martyr, then turns to* LADY DARBY *with resolute voice and manner.*) Where is Sue staying?

LADY DARBY: At number 7, Marine Gardens, just opposite.

ADMIRAL: (*with great resolution*) Take me to her.

SIR RICHARD: What are you going to do?

ADMIRAL: I'm going to bring her back to her senses. A woman has no right to shake the foundations of society in this way. I shall tell her very plainly that this kind of behaviour must be put a stop to!

SIR RICHARD: That tune won't do with Sue. Send her over to me.

ADMIRAL: But, my dear Kato —

SIR RICHARD: Send her to me. I shall handle her better than you will.

ADMIRAL: Very well. (*Turns to* LADY DARBY.) Ah! What a comfort it is to have a wife of the good old-fashioned sort like you, Victoria. (*Exeunt* ADMIRAL *and* LADY DARBY *at balcony.* SIR RICHARD *is left alone, walks up and down, puzzled. A knock at door.*)
(LUCIEN *enters.*)

LUCIEN: (*letters in hand*) I've looked through the letters, Sir Richard, and —

SIR RICHARD: Lucien, I've got a case that is puzzling me a great deal.

LUCIEN: Indeed!

SIR RICHARD: It may never come into court, but — it's puzzling me. It has just occurred to me that you might help me.

LUCIEN: Anything that I can do.

SIR RICHARD: It is concerned with the extraordinary practices of an English clergyman at Cairo. This English clergyman, the Reverend Samuel it seems — I forget his church — Saint — Saint — Saint Something. What are the English churches at Cairo?

LUCIEN: I don't remember.

SIR RICHARD: (*still pretending to be puzzled*) Saint — ha, — you can't remember the English churches?

LUCIEN: No. I never went into one all the while I was there.

SIR RICHARD: Then I'm afraid you can't help me. So you never went to church at Cairo? Bad boy! Bad boy! You never went to church!

LUCIEN: (*innocently*) No, not once. (*Suddenly remembers, shows a little alarm.*) Yes, I went the last Sunday night I was there. I remember now.

SIR RICHARD: (*carelessly*) What was the name of the church?

LUCIEN: Saint — Saint — Something.

SIR RICHARD: What was the church like?

LUCIEN: The inside?

SIR RICHARD: Yes.

LUCIEN: The inside? (*beginning to flounder*) There was nothing remarkable about the inside.

SIR RICHARD: Was it a large church?

LUCIEN: Yes — rather — rather a large church — a medium-sized church — (*Catches* SIR RICHARD's *eye.*) You're pumping me!

SIR RICHARD: Pumping you, my dear boy? I only wanted to get a few particulars. If you don't care to tell me, it's of no consequence.

LUCIEN: (*getting a little angry*) I'll tell you all I remember. There was an aisle, and — I've an impression, but I can't be quite sure, that there were large pillars — and — and — (*Gets a little more confused under* SIR RICHARD's *glance.*) the sermon was a very long one.

SIR RICHARD: (*looking at him*) Ah!

           (*Enter* PYBUS *at balcony.*)

PYBUS: I beg pardon, Sir Richard, but if you will kindly help us a little, I think we might arrange some basis for our returning together to the Nest.

SIR RICHARD: Very well, Mr Pybus.

LUCIEN: Goodbye, Sir Richard (*offering hand*).

SIR RICHARD: (*offering him 'The Times'*) No, sit down. I want to have a little more talk about this long sermon. (*Pushes 'The Times' into his hands and gently pushes him into the armchair.*) Now, Mr Pybus.

PYBUS: (*confidentially to* SIR RICHARD *as they go off at balcony*) If you wouldn't mind hinting to Elaine that if she could surround me with that necessary atmosphere —

SIR RICHARD: Ah!

PYBUS: Really, she does not give me any impetus, any afflatus.

SIR RICHARD: (*sympathisingly*) Ah! Ah! Come along, we'll see about it. (*Exeunt*

SIR RICHARD *and* PYBUS *by balcony.* LUCIEN *is seated behind the paper. Short pause.*)

       (*Enter* WAITER, *showing in* LADY SUSAN. *Exit* WAITER. LUCIEN *rises, puts down paper, comes to her.*)

LADY SUSAN: (*embarrassed*) My uncle sent for me —

LUCIEN: He's outside in the garden. We've only a few moments. (*coming to her*)

LADY SUSAN: No, no. (*Breaks away from him.*) Oh, you'll go! You'll be kind to me and go!

LUCIEN: I shall do what you tell me, if it is to kill myself.

LADY SUSAN: How can you talk so rashly?

LUCIEN: Because I mean it. I'll go if you tell me. It will be a harder parting than the last, but I'll do it. It will break my heart, but I'd rather break my heart with longing for you than win all the other women in the world. (*Her face shows great pleasure.*) You needn't think you'll have any trouble in getting rid of me (*going from her*).

LADY SUSAN: You'll break *my* heart if you talk like this.

LUCIEN: You love me still?

LADY SUSAN: Is there any need to ask that? And you — you love me still?

LUCIEN: I've never loved any woman but you, I never shall if I live a thousand years. You don't know how you have sweetened all my life. Those weeks at Cairo! They're like a splendid dream. All's dull grey with me now for the rest of my life.

LADY SUSAN: All's dull grey with me for the rest of my life. What am I saying?

LUCIEN: (*Clasps her, takes her hand, sees ring on it.*) The ring I gave you. (*Kisses her finger.*) Give me something in return.

LADY SUSAN: Will you leave me then? Oh, this is madness. You'll go? You'll go? Oh, promise me!

LUCIEN: If you bid me.

LADY SUSAN: (*taking off a ring*) Here's a ring Uncle Dick gave me ten years ago. I've worn it ever since. You'll never part from it? (*taking ring off finger and giving it him*)

LUCIEN: Never. (*Takes it, is about to put it on his finger.*)

LADY SUSAN: No, don't put it on now. Uncle Dick would recognise it. Put it on the moment you have left me, and wear it always.

LUCIEN: Always. To my last breath.

LADY SUSAN: You'll never speak of me?

LUCIEN: I have never breathed your name to a living soul from the moment I left you. I never will. Don't you see, I cannot speak of you? I must hide you. I shall hide you in my heart till I die.

LADY SUSAN: And I shall hide you in my heart till I die. (*looking off at balcony*) We've only a moment.

LUCIEN: One moment in all our lives.

LADY SUSAN: Goodbye.

LUCIEN: Goodbye. (*clasping her*) No! by God, I can't give you up! Sue, we belong to each other. I'll give my whole life to make you happy.

LADY SUSAN: (*struggling in his arms*) No, no! I daren't! I daren't! What will become of me?

LUCIEN: Trust me. You're mine already. You can't trust me more than you have trusted me. You shan't deny me! You shan't cheat yourself and me of all that makes life worth living. I cannot leave you! I will not!

LADY SUSAN: (*desperately*) What can I do? What can I do?

LUCIEN: Meet me tomorrow night at eight — the Continental mail, Cannon Street Station. We'll go over to the Continent. You'll come? You must! You shall!

LADY SUSAN: (*desperately*) Yes. (*He takes her hand, kisses it.*) Hush!

LUCIEN: Tomorrow night — Cannon Street Station. (*She nods.*)

>   (*Enter* SIR RICHARD *at window.* LADY SUSAN *and* LUCIEN
>   *show a little confusion.* SIR RICHARD *looks keenly from one to
>   the other and back again.*)

SIR RICHARD: (*in a very calm, matter-of-fact tone*) Lucien, I've been consulting the time-tables, and I find if you leave tomorrow by the eleven o'clock train, you'll have time to make those inquiries for me about the clergyman in Cairo, and still catch next Thursday's boat to New Zealand.

LUCIEN: I'm very sorry, Sir Richard; it's impossible.

SIR RICHARD: Not a bit, my dear boy. Now go back to Eastgate at once, up to town by the two-fifteen, dine with me at Brooks's tonight at eight, and off you go tomorrow at eleven.

LUCIEN: I'm very sorry — I can't.

SIR RICHARD: I'm very sorry, but you can, and you will.

LUCIEN: I've certain things to do.

SIR RICHARD: And certain things to leave undone (*very sternly*). Come, sir, you leave at eleven tomorrow (*very firmly*).

LUCIEN: (*more firmly*) No.

SIR RICHARD: (*still more firmly*) Yes. I say, yes.

LUCIEN: But I —

SIR RICHARD: But I say 'Yes'. (*in a very kind but firm tone*). Come, my lad, understand me, I mean it. Off you go. (*Opens the door, stands with it open.*) Pack! Pack! Pack! (LUCIEN *has a moment or two's indecision, exchanges one last agonised look with* LADY SUSAN, *and then is about to rush off.* SIR RICHARD *at door intercepts him, offers his hand.* LUCIEN, *after another moment's indecision, takes it, wrings* SIR RICHARD's *hand. Cordially shaking hands*) There's a good lad! (LUCIEN *rushes off.* SIR RICHARD *closes door after him, comes to* LADY SUSAN, *with great decision. Very resolutely*) Now, my very dear Sue, I'm going to have a little talk with *you*.

LADY SUSAN: (*a little alarmed, a little cowed, a little defiant*) What about?

SIR RICHARD: It's time this pretty little escapade of yours was ended. People are beginning to talk about you, and you've gone just as far as is possible to go without running the risk of becoming déclassé.

LADY SUSAN: Déclassé?! There are plenty of women who are not good, and who are not déclassé.

SIR RICHARD: Very likely. Women are divided into two classes.

Brooks's: i.e. at Sir Richard's club.

déclassé: cf. Sir Christopher Deering's description of the consequences of loss of caste in *The Liars*, pp. 215–16, below.

LADY SUSAN: Good and bad!

SIR RICHARD: Not at all. Those who have lost their reputation, and those who have kept it. I'm determined you shall keep yours.

LADY SUSAN: Thank you, dear Uncle Dick. I've kept my reputation, such as it is, up to now, and I assure you, it's quite safe in my keeping for the future.

SIR RICHARD: Very likely. But I'm going to make sure of it.

LADY SUSAN: (*provokingly*) Oh, indeed! And how will you do that?

SIR RICHARD: Your husband is here. He's anxious for you to return to him and your home.

LADY SUSAN: (*defiantly*) I've told you, no, no, no.

SIR RICHARD: Very well. Then, my dear Sue, as I've seen nothing of you for the last ten months, supposing you come on a little visit to me.

LADY SUSAN: When?

SIR RICHARD: At once. This afternoon by the four-thirty.

LADY SUSAN: No. I'll come in two or three weeks.

SIR RICHARD: What are you going to do in the meantime?

LADY SUSAN: Do? Nothing.

SIR RICHARD: Where are you going?

LADY SUSAN: Going? Nowhere.

SIR RICHARD: You're going to stay here?

LADY SUSAN: Yes — of course.

SIR RICHARD: How long?

LADY SUSAN: Just as long as I feel inclined.

SIR RICHARD: Very well. I'll come and stay with you.

LADY SUSAN: You can't. There's no room in the house.

SIR RICHARD: I'll get rooms next door.

LADY SUSAN: What for?

SIR RICHARD: Just to be near you.

LADY SUSAN: It's ridiculous! Impossible!

SIR RICHARD: Not a bit. My dear girl, make up your mind that, at all costs, you're going to have my company for the next few weeks.

LADY SUSAN: Indeed I won't. I won't have you in my house. I'll turn you out.

SIR RICHARD: I'll stay on the doorstep. Understand me, my dear Sue. I shall haunt you like your shadow, and there will be no escaping from me. Now you know what is in store for you, so behave like a good girl and give me a hearty welcome.

LADY SUSAN: Indeed I won't! I'll run away from you. (*getting into a temper, walking up and down with great indignation, uttering little cries*) Really! Of all the absurd. — Well! — What next! I never — Oh! (*Turns round and faces him, very resolutely.*) Now, Uncle Dick, I love you very much, but don't drive me to kick over the traces.

SIR RICHARD: My dear Sue, I'm going to take very good care that you don't.

LADY SUSAN: Really, of all the unwarrantable — (*Bursts into a fit of angry laughter.*) Once for all understand me, Uncle Dick, I'm my own mistress, and I'm going to do just as I please.

SIR RICHARD: No, my dear Sue, you are going to do just what is suitable for my niece, and for an English lady with her own reputation and the reputation of her family to consider.

LADY SUSAN: No, I'm not. I'll — I'll — (*Bursts into a fit of angry tears.*) I'll do something that will make you horribly ashamed of me. I will, Uncle Dick. I'll — (*Steps up to him, is about to snap her fingers at him.*)

SIR RICHARD: Ah! (*Catches her hand and puts it down.*) My dear Sue, you may snap your fingers at your husband, but you must not snap your fingers at me!

LADY SUSAN: (*struggling to get her hand*) I hate you, Uncle Dick! I hate you! (*stamping her foot at him*)

SIR RICHARD: (*complacently*) Very well, my dear Sue, hate me as much as you please, but understand, there are three proverbial courses open to you, and one of those three courses you'll take, and no other. Firstly, you can return to your home with your husband —

LADY SUSAN: (*defiantly*) No.

SIR RICHARD: Or, secondly, you can stay here in my very delightful and constant company.

LADY SUSAN: No.

SIR RICHARD: Or, thirdly, you can return to Harley Street with me, and I'll give you a comfortable home as long as you please. Which of these three courses will you take?

LADY SUSAN: Neither! Neither! Neither!
    (*Enter HARABIN at door.*)

HARABIN: (*coming in*) I say, Kato — (*Sees LADY SUSAN.*) I beg your pardon. (*Beats a hasty retreat, shuts the door after him.*)

SIR RICHARD: (*in an alarmed tone, to LADY SUSAN*) For heaven's sake. Sue, don't be a fool!

LADY SUSAN: (*frightened*) What do you mean?

SIR RICHARD: I'm trying to save you. Take care that Jim — (*Stops.*)

LADY SUSAN: (*still more frightened*) Jim doesn't know?

SIR RICHARD: Not at present. But take care. One false step and you're lost.

LADY SUSAN: Lost? What do you mean? What do you know?

SIR RICHARD: (*very solemnly*) That last Sunday evening at Cairo!

LADY SUSAN: (*in an agony of fright*) Uncle Dick, I've done nothing wrong. You believe me, don't you? There wasn't even so much as an innocent flirtation. There wasn't, indeed. You believe me, don't you? (*very much agitated*)

SIR RICHARD: Yes, I believe you, but — (*very mysteriously*) appearances!

LADY SUSAN: (*in an agony of fright*) Appearances? Appearances? What appearances?

SIR RICHARD: (*very solemnly, very mysteriously*) The sermon was a very long one!

LADY SUSAN: (*frightened*) E—h?

SIR RICHARD: (*very decidedly*) Which of the three courses will you take?

LADY SUSAN: (*in a quiet, humble voice*) I'll go back to Harley Street with you.
    Curtain
(*Fifteen months pass between acts II and III.*)

I'll go back to Harley Street with you: in French's edition she 'sinks slowly into chair'.

ACT III

SCENE.   *At* SIR RICHARD KATO's *at Harley Street. Very snug bachelor's apartment, handsomely furnished. Door right. Door left. Fireplace at back. Window in corner up left. A winter evening. Lamps lighted. Large fire burning. Discover* KIRBY *showing in* INEZ *left in handsome winter dress and fur cloak.*

KIRBY: I'll tell Sir Richard you are here, ma'am. (*Exit left.*)
                    (*As* KIRBY *is going out,* LADY SUSAN *enters right.*)
LADY SUSAN: Dearest, I heard your voice. (*Kisses her.*)
INEZ: I've been out all day. When I got home I found a note from Sir Richard asking me to come round.
LADY SUSAN: You're to take me out to dinner this evening.
INEZ: Oh! Then Sir Richard has a family party?
LADY SUSAN: Yes, my husband is coming. So of course I must go.
INEZ: Why must you go?
LADY SUSAN: Why should I stay?
INEZ: Why shouldn't you? Is there any particular reason that you shouldn't meet your husband?
LADY SUSAN: (*considering the matter in an indifferent tone*) N—o. But, on the other hand, is there any particular reason that I should?
INEZ: You don't hate him?
LADY SUSAN: (*indifferently*) N—o.
INEZ: You love him? (LADY SUSAN *shakes her head.*) Just a little bit?
LADY SUSAN: Not a *tiny little* bit.
INEZ: You don't dislike him?
LADY SUSAN: (*same careless, indifferent tone*) No. Rather the reverse. The longer Jim and I are parted the more I find a mild sort of liking for him stealing over me.
INEZ: Why won't you meet him and talk things over? He would give guarantees for the future.
LADY SUSAN: Really I don't wish to demand anything so unreasonable.
INEZ: Unreasonable?
LADY SUSAN: Considering what the creatures are, isn't it rather unreasonable of us to demand faithfulness from men?
INEZ: (*after a little pause, with considerable feeling*) I know one man who was faithful.
LADY SUSAN: (*Sighs.*) Well, perhaps there is one in a million. Yes, Inez, I do believe there is one in a million. But no woman has ever married him!
                    (*Enter* SIR RICHARD.)
SIR RICHARD: How d'ye do? (*to* INEZ, *shaking hands cordially*)
LADY SUSAN: She has done her duty, Uncle Dick.
SIR RICHARD: What duty?
LADY SUSAN: Begged me to stay and dine with my husband.
SIR RICHARD: Oh!
LADY SUSAN: And as that is impossible, she will now do the further duty of

taking me to dine at the Bristol, and to the Lyceum afterwards. (*Enter KIRBY, left, with card, which he brings to* SIR RICHARD.) Come, Inez, I'll dress and come back with you (*taking* INEZ *off, right*).

SIR RICHARD: (*to* KIRBY) Show Mr Jacomb up.
> (*Exit* KIRBY, *left.*)

LADY SUSAN: (*Shows interest, stops at door, comes back.*) Jacomb? Isn't that the man − who −

SIR RICHARD: Yes, that's the man who − You'd better stay.

LADY SUSAN: It's no business of mine. Inez, this is some man who has met that Mr Edensor in New Zealand, and − (*Enter* KIRBY, *left, announcing 'Mr Jacomb'. Enter* MR JACOMB, *left. Exit* KIRBY.) Very well, Uncle Dick. As you seem to wish it, I will stay.

JACOMB: (*a genial, rosy old fellow, about sixty.*) Sir Richard Kato? (SIR RICHARD *bows.*) I'm glad to meet you (*shaking hands*). As I wrote I have a message for you from Mr Lucien Edensor, and also one for Lady Susan Harabin.

LADY SUSAN: (*startled, a little agitated*) For me? impossible!

JACOMB: And one for Mrs Quesnel.

INEZ: For me?

SIR RICHARD: (*introducing*) Mr Jacomb. Mrs Quesnel. Lady Susan.
> (*They bow.*)

LADY SUSAN: (*agitated*) I'm quite sure you can have no message for me. (*Seeing that* SIR RICHARD *is watching her, she turns to him.*) What message can he have for me?

SIR RICHARD: Let's hear. (*Motions her to a seat. She sits down so that her face is hidden from* SIR RICHARD, INEZ *and* JACOMB, *but quite in full view of audience.* SIR RICHARD *motions* INEZ *to a chair, taking chair himself and placing it so that he can see* LADY SUSAN's *face. She turns away from him.*) Now we are all attention. (*Moves his chair a little forward so that he can again see* LADY SUSAN's *face. She again turns a little further away from him. During the following scene he watches her very closely, constantly edging his chair to get her face in view.*)

JACOMB: A year ago last September I sailed for New Zealand with my brother Frank and his wife and daughter, his only daughter. Frank I must tell you is the head of Jacomb, Perrin and Co. You may know the firm.

SIR RICHARD: New Zealand shippers, a very first-rate firm.

LADY SUSAN: But what has all this to do with me?

SIR RICHARD: Let's hear.

JACOMB: Well, on board there was a young fellow, Mr Lucien Edensor. I noticed that he seemed very homesick, poor fellow.
> (*Seeing that* SIR RICHARD *is watching her,* LADY SUSAN
> *pretends to be bored, gazes at ceiling, yawns, etc.*)

LADY SUSAN: (*assumed indifference*) Did he?

---

the Bristol: restaurant in Cork Street, off Bond Street.
the Lyceum: Irving's theatre, in Wellington Street at the east end of the Strand.

JACOMB: Yes, wouldn't eat, wouldn't talk, wouldn't play poker, wouldn't make chums, wouldn't do anything. Well, one night, over a cigar and a glass of whisky, I drew him out, and of course it was all about a woman, poor fellow.

SIR RICHARD: All about a woman! Poor fellow!

LADY SUSAN: All about a woman! Poor fellow! (*Yawns, looks at ceiling.*)

JACOMB: His heart was broken, life was a hopeless blank, and he'd a great mind to end it there and then —

LADY SUSAN: Indeed!

JACOMB: Well, I took him into Frank's private cabin, and Mrs Jacomb and Annie seemed to take a great fancy to him.

LADY SUSAN: Did they?

JACOMB: And to make a long story short, the next day, just for the sake of whiling away the time on board ship, I made a sporting bet of fifty pounds with my brother Frank that there would be a match between his daughter Annie and young Edensor.

LADY SUSAN: Indeed! (*same tone*) Did you win?

JACOMB: You shall hear. My wife and I set to work, and from morning till night we did nothing but lay our heads together to bring it off. You wouldn't believe how interesting it was to watch them.

LADY SUSAN: It must have been. What was the result?

JACOMB: He held out. He couldn't forget this other woman. (LADY SUSAN *hides her face from those on stage, shows great delight.*) Yes, he held out, for over three weeks. (LADY SUSAN*'s face changes.*) I thought I should lose my fifty pounds.

> (SIR RICHARD *is most keenly watching* LADY SUSAN *all the time.*)

INEZ: And at the end of the three weeks — ?

JACOMB: He began to thaw. My fifty pounds was safe.

LADY SUSAN: You seem to have been alarmed for your fifty pounds (*rather pettishly*).

JACOMB: It wasn't the money. I couldn't bear to be beaten. I wouldn't have lost that bet for a thousand pounds. I was determined he should marry her.

LADY SUSAN: And — did he?

JACOMB: (*Fumbles in his overcoat pocket, brings out three little parcels tied round with white satin ribbon, looks at the addresses.*) I promised him I'd deliver these in person (*offering one to* LADY SUSAN).

LADY SUSAN: For me? What is it?

JACOMB: Open it.

> (LADY SUSAN *takes parcel, comes down stage out of view of others, opens it, pulls out a piece of wedding-cake, she looks for a letter, cannot find one, shows disappointment, crumbles the wedding-cake between her fingers in her anger, finds in it the ring she had given* LUCIEN *in act II, shows great pain. Meantime* JACOMB *has given the other two parcels to* INEZ *and* SIR RICHARD *respectively; they have taken them and opened them, finding in them also tiny pieces of wedding-cake.*)

INEZ: Wedding-cake? Why should Mr Edensor send wedding-cake to me?

LADY SUSAN: Or to me? (*Takes* LUCIEN's *ring off her finger, puts it in the box with the cake, wraps paper round it, goes up to fireplace.*)

SIR RICHARD: Very good wedding-cake it is, too. Won't you try it, Sue?

LADY SUSAN: You know I never eat sweets. (*Throws box and all into fire.*)

INEZ: (*putting hers in her pocket*) I'll sleep with mine under my pillow.

SIR RICHARD: And so they married and lived happy ever afterwards (*putting his parcel on table at back*). Why didn't Lucien write and tell me?

JACOMB: He said you had chaffed him so much about the other one, and he didn't like you to know that he'd changed his mind so soon.

LADY SUSAN: So soon! But he was three weeks. He must have been genuinely attached to the other woman to have held out for so long as three weeks. What is your niece like?

JACOMB: I'd forgotten. I've a photograph of them taken together. (*pulling photograph out of his breast pocket*) There they are — (*showing* SIR RICHARD *the photograph*)

SIR RICHARD: He looks confoundedly happy, the rascal!

JACOMB: Never was a happier couple in this world!

LADY SUSAN: (*looking at photograph over their shoulders*) Will you allow me? (JACOMB *gives her the photograph. She takes it.*) Is your niece fair or dark?

JACOMB: Rather fair, Lady Susan, and she's a sweet-tempered little body.

LADY SUSAN: (*looking at photograph*) Hm, so she seems. Such women make the best wives. And Mr Edensor held out for three weeks against those attractions. How could he? (*giving back the photograph*) Thank you. Very interesting.

JACOMB: Well, I've delivered my message, Sir Richard.

SIR RICHARD: (*Rings bell.*) Thank you, Mr Jacomb. I'll write Lucien and tell him I've received it safely.

JACOMB: (*shaking hands*) Delighted to have made your acquaintance. Good day, Mrs Quesnel. Good day, Lady Susan.

        (LADY SUSAN *and* INEZ *bow.* KIRBY *appears at door.*)

SIR RICHARD: Kirby, remind me to send half-a-dozen of that old Madeira to Mr Edensor in New Zealand. The door.

JACOMB: (*going off*) You can't believe what trouble I had to make him understand he was in love with her. But I landed him! I landed him! And I won my fifty pounds! (*Exit left, followed by* KIRBY.)

LADY SUSAN: I must go and dress, Inez.

INEZ: I'll come with you, dearest.

LADY SUSAN: (*pettishly*) No, go and dress at home and come back for me, and we'll dine at the Café Royal, shall we?

INEZ: I don't mind.

LADY SUSAN: Yes, and we'll go to something merry and rakish, not to a tragedy. I hate tragedies. (*Exit right.* SIR RICHARD *opens the door for her. He closes the door after her, stands perplexed.*)

INEZ: What's puzzling you?

Café Royal: in Regent Street. Opened in 1865, one of the earliest of the grill-rooms and restaurants that proliferated in the West End in the later decades of the century.

SIR RICHARD: Mrs Quesnel, what was the exact nature of Sue's acquaintance with Lucien?

INEZ: What does it matter? You needn't trouble about Sue. We women know the value of appearances. We are awful cowards, and have terrible leanings towards respectability. Sue won't shatter Mr Harabin's family gods on his family hearth, or burst up Mr Harabin's family boiler with any new-fangled explosive. And so long as Mr Harabin's family boiler remains intact, why should you meddle with Sue? I must go and dress. My cloak, please.

SIR RICHARD: (*helping her on with cloak*) It's a brutal night. I wish you were going to stay and dine with us. How well you look in furs! (SIR RICHARD *sighs.*)

INEZ: Why do you sigh?

SIR RICHARD: Alas! My family gods! My family hearth! My family boiler!

INEZ: What of it?

SIR RICHARD: There is no one to tend it! (*pointing to his fireside*)

INEZ: And nobody to burst it up.

SIR RICHARD: It would not burst up if it were in the right person's care.

INEZ: (*mischievously*) Ah, but who would be the right person?

SIR RICHARD: Yourself, for instance?

INEZ: I wouldn't lark with the safety-valve (*going*).

SIR RICHARD: (*taking her hand*) Stay. Would you really undertake the charge — of — (*pointing to hearth*) — my family gods and family boiler?

INEZ: That depends. First of all I should like to know a little about the previous engineers. You are terribly concerned about Sue. How about yourself?

SIR RICHARD: Won't you trust me?

INEZ: No, I won't. You're a sensible man. I'm a sensible woman. I don't expect you have lived till — how old are you?

SIR RICHARD: Say forty-five — it's a few years more, but say forty-five.

INEZ: Till forty-five without having loved any woman. But I should like to know —

SIR RICHARD: What?

INEZ: Well, some particulars.

SIR RICHARD: (*Walks about a little perplexed.*) You don't want to know everything?

INEZ: No, not everything. But a good deal.

SIR RICHARD: If I tell you the leading outlines quite truthfully, will you tell me the leading outlines quite truthfully?

INEZ: Yes. How many times have you really loved?

SIR RICHARD: Only once, and that is at the present moment (*looking at her*).

INEZ: Goodbye. I wanted to know the truth.

SIR RICHARD: Don't go. I'll tell you — the truth.

INEZ: Honour? I really mean to be quite truthful with you.

SIR RICHARD: Yes, but I hope your case won't — won't —

INEZ: Won't be as bad as yours? Oh, no, it won't. Rest assured of that. No woman's case ever is as bad as a man's. Now go on.

SIR RICHARD: I've thought myself in love scores of times, but I've only really loved once, and that was — (*longish pause with great feeling*) — I won't tell you. It's too sacred. I did love that woman with all my heart and soul. And she loved me.

(*pause*)

INEZ: And those scores of cases when you *thought* you were in love?

SIR RICHARD: Oh, they don't count.

INEZ: But I should like to get some — some general impression.

SIR RICHARD: What does it matter? There was a light girl —

INEZ: And a dark girl? Come, the whole catalogue.

SIR RICHARD: (*Rattles away, half seriously, half jestingly.*) A light girl, a dark girl, a red-haired girl; a tall girl, a short girl; a merry girl, a sad girl; a lean girl, a fat girl; a girl in mauve, a girl in white, a girl in green; a blonde, a brunette; a girl with eyes as blue as heaven, and a girl with eyes as black as jet; a quaker girl, a *danseuse*; a pale girl, a sallow girl, a rosy-cheeked girl; a peer's daughter, a milliner; a Scotch girl, an Irish girl, an Italian girl; and — some others. You can't say I haven't made a clean breast of it.

INEZ: And you have thought yourself in love with all these? What does remain of your heart?

SIR RICHARD: All that doesn't belong to that one woman whom I did really love.

INEZ: Ah!

SIR RICHARD: Now it's your turn.

INEZ: Suppose I follow your example and lump them as you've done, and say that in vagrant hours I've had vagrant fancies for — (*Rattles them off very glibly as he has done.*) — a light man, a dark man, a red-haired man; a tall man, a short man; a merry man, a sad man; a man in a blouse, a man in knickerbockers, a man in a kilt; a hunter in pink, and a bicyclist; a Scotchman, an Irishman, and — I won't say an Italian, but just to fill out the list I'll throw you in a couple of Spaniards, a Hindoo prince, and a young Japanese. Suppose I were to own up to all these?

SIR RICHARD: But, good heaven, you don't?

INEZ: No. But if I did?

SIR RICHARD: I should ask for further details.

INEZ: If I asked you for further details?

SIR RICHARD: I should decline to give them.

INEZ: And let me fill them in according to my wildest imaginations — let me guess how much of this spacious heart of yours was given to this stray companion, and how much to that stray companion. Ah, no, no, no, no! Let's draw a veil.

SIR RICHARD: But you haven't told me anything.

INEZ: I will. Sincerely I have loved once. And I should like to remain constant, if constancy were not such a dream.

SIR RICHARD: Is constancy a dream?

INEZ: What else is it? You have loved once, and yet with her consecrated image in your heart's holy of holies, you have opened its outer courts to a rabble of petticoats, drunk the wine and broken the bread with sluts, tossed off life's sacrament with any strange priestess that offered it — look at the remains of the feast! Oh, no, no, no, my dear friend! if constancy is not a dream, if faithfulness is not a shadow, where are they to be found?

SIR RICHARD: Not in my heart. Yet I have loved once. Thank God for it!

INEZ: And I have loved once. Thank God for it! (*A long pause. They look at each other seriously, then smile, and then gradually laugh in each other's face.*)

SIR RICHARD: To come back to —

INEZ: To Harley Street?

SIR RICHARD: And the previous question. What do you say?

INEZ: I'll think it over. (*suddenly*) Dear me! I've stayed here gossiping with you, and now if I don't make haste I shall be too late to get Sue away before her husband comes. My cloak! Quick!

SIR RICHARD: (*helping her on with it*) You do look well in furs.

INEZ: (*fastening her cloak*) Shall I tell you a secret? All women do. (*She blows him a kiss and runs off.* SIR RICHARD *stands looking after her, blows a kiss after her, sighs, closes door, goes to window, looks outside, draws curtain, takes out his watch, changes coat for smoking-jacket, lights pipe, sits down at fire, sighs, looks at the fire, looks at the door where* INEZ *has gone off, blows another kiss after her, pokes the fire.*)

> (*Enter* FERGUSSON PYBUS, *shown in by* KIRBY. PYBUS *is very pale and bilious, with a look of settled gloom on his face, a large black patch over one eye, carelessly and seedily dressed. Exit* KIRBY.)

SIR RICHARD: Good heaven, Mr Pybus! What's the matter?

PYBUS: Haven't you heard? The Boadicean Society — my wife has got all the telegraph girls and shop girls in Clapham out on strike.

SIR RICHARD: Yes, so I see in the paper. Well?

PYBUS: I thought perhaps you might sympathise with me.

SIR RICHARD: (*cordially*) I do. (*Shakes his hand.*) What's the matter with your eye? Not — not *domestic*, I trust?

PYBUS: No. Mr Cupples our butcher (*piteously*) — I'm in a state of extreme nervous prostration. Cupples —

SIR RICHARD: Yes.

PYBUS: Elaine persuaded Mrs Cupples to join her Boadicean Society. Cupples had been in the habit of spending his evenings at the King's Head. Last week the Boadicean Society went round to the King's Head, and sung temperance songs at Cupples, and then escorted him home. The next morning Cupples came round to the Nest and demanded an interview with me. I declined to see him, but he stayed outside, and as soon as I appeared, without waiting for me to disclaim all responsibility for my wife's actions, he took advantage of my state of nervous prostration, and —

SIR RICHARD: Poor fellow! Poor fellow! (*Pats* PYBUS'*s shoulder sympathisingly.*)

PYBUS: What would you advise me to do?

SIR RICHARD: With regard to Cupples? Do you owe him anything?

PYBUS: There is a little bill.

SIR RICHARD: What sort of a man is he?

PYBUS: He is a coarse, powerful man with a copious supply of very abusive epithets.

SIR RICHARD: I should pay him his little bill. Then I should utterly refuse to have anything more to do with him. I should cut him dead.

I should cut him dead: cf. note to *The Silver King*, p. 89 above.

PYBUS: Ye – es. Perhaps that would be best. And Elaine?

SIR RICHARD: Where is she?

PYBUS: I left her at the Nest this morning, addressing the post office girls from my bedroom window, and urging them to make an example of the Clapham postmaster. Sir Richard, you might have warned me of the nature of Elaine's temper.

SIR RICHARD: Ah! Didn't I mention something about tempers?

PYBUS: At the time I became engaged to her my prospects were most brilliant. If she had given me the least afflatus I feel sure I should have stamped myself on the age in some way.

SIR RICHARD: I'm sure you would!

PYBUS: But so far from giving me any afflatus, she will not even give me a light and easily assimilated course of diet. I cannot nourish my peculiar gifts on tinned mutton of the cheapest brands, and the more stringy portions of an underdone ham.

SIR RICHARD: Ah! Didn't I mention something about cooking lessons?

> (*Enter* KIRBY, *left, with evening paper.*)

KIRBY: I beg pardon, Sir Richard, I thought you might like to see – (*giving paper*)

SIR RICHARD: What?

KIRBY: (*pointing to article in paper*) The Clapham post office has been completely wrecked by the telegraph girls on strike.

> (*Exit* KIRBY. PYBUS *groans and rolls round in his chair.*)

SIR RICHARD: (*reading*) 'Progress of the strike. The Clapham postmaster put to flight, takes refuge in a coal cellar. Destruction of telegraphic communication with Clapham.'

PYBUS: (*Looks up piteously.*) Am I liable?

SIR RICHARD: Somebody will have to pay the piper. And as your wife called the tune – (PYBUS *groans.*)

> (*Re-enter* KIRBY, *left.*)

KIRBY: Sir Richard, Mrs Pybus has come in (PYBUS *jumps up.*) and says she must see you at once.

PYBUS: Go and remonstrate with her, Sir Richard, and ask her – (ELAINE *enters,* PYBUS *sees her, has a furious outburst.*) – ask her what the Devil will be the end of all this damned silly behaviour! (*Exit* KIRBY.)

ELAINE: (*Looks* PYBUS *up and down with the utmost contempt.*) The old weapons! Abuse and brute force! No other argument!

PYBUS: (*rather more mildly*) So it is – a damned silly – (*Growls the end of the sentence under his breath to himself.* ELAINE, *merciless, contemptuous, looks at him. He meekly subsides into his chair.*)

ELAINE: (*Turns to* SIR RICHARD.) When today's revolution is complete it will no longer be *safe* for men to swear at their wives.

SIR RICHARD: I shall be sorry to note the disappearance of another picturesque old custom.

---

tinned mutton . . . underdone ham: indicative of Elaine's poor housekeeping rather than the couple's poverty: fresh mutton, at about ninepence a pound, should have been well within their means.

ELAINE: (*severely*) Please do not trifle. You have doubtless followed the recent
course of events in Clapham —

SIR RICHARD: Yes. You seem to have been using a great deal of brute force with
that poor devil of a postmaster.

ELAINE: It was the only argument he could understand. I have called to make a
formal demand for the remainder of my fortune. (PYBUS *jumps up.*) I have
immediate use for it.

SIR RICHARD: What use, may I ask?

ELAINE: To accelerate the progress of the new epoch.

PYBUS: (*protesting*) Sir Richard —

ELAINE: (*Just glances at* PYBUS, *then turns her back contemptuously on him.*)
We had perhaps better discuss this matter apart from Mr Pybus, as it is no
concern of his.

PYBUS: (*Appeals.*) Sir Richard —

SIR RICHARD: Tsch! tsch! tsch! We won't discuss it at all. Rest assured I shall not
hand over your fortune for any such nonsense.

ELAINE: Nonsense! He calls our new epoch nonsense!

PYBUS: (*venturing*) So it is! (ELAINE *looks fiercely at him. He mutters and subsides.*)

ELAINE: (*to* SIR RICHARD) You will find that we are in earnest.

SIR RICHARD: About what?

ELAINE: About re-organising society.

SIR RICHARD: I don't quite follow — how will wrecking Clapham post office re-
organise society?

ELAINE: We must make a start somewhere.

SIR RICHARD: Begin at home, in your own lives. There's no other way of re-
organising society. Go back to the Nest, and give Mr Pybus a nice comfortable
dinner.

ELAINE: No man shall receive dinner from me while the present inequalities
between the sexes remain unredressed.

SIR RICHARD: (*to* PYBUS) We shall all starve.

ELAINE: Please be serious. Do you deny that Woman has been most shamefully
treated by Man?

SIR RICHARD: It isn't Man that's ungallant to Woman. It's Nature that is so
ungallant and unkind to your sex.

ELAINE: We will correct Nature.

SIR RICHARD: By changing your sex? What is it that you ladies want? You are
evidently dissatisfied with being women. You cannot wish to be anything so
brutal and disgusting as a man. And unfortunately there is no neuter sex in
the human species. *What do you want?*

ELAINE: We want freedom to develop our real selves.

SIR RICHARD: Hum — sounds like a deadly dull, unwholesome process. Still, for
my part, you are quite welcome. But if that is your ideal, why did you marry
Mr Pybus? I don't see that he is necessary.

ELAINE: Mr Pybus is not necessary. (PYBUS *jumps up protestingly.*) There is an
immense future for Woman —

SIR RICHARD: (*interrupting*) At her own fireside. There is an immense future for women as wives and mothers, and a very limited future for them in any other capacity. While you ladies without passions — or with distorted and defeated passions — are raving and trumpeting all over the country, that wise, grim, old grandmother of us all, Dame Nature, is simply laughing up her sleeve and snapping her fingers at you and your new epochs and new movements. Go home! Be sure that old Dame Nature will choose her own darlings to carry on her schemes. Go home! Go home! Nature's darling woman is a stay-at-home woman, a woman who wants to be a good wife and a good mother, and cares very little for anything else. (ELAINE *is about to speak,* SIR RICHARD *silences her with a gesture.*) Go home! Go home, and don't worry the world any longer about this tiresome sexual business, for, take my word, it was settled once for all in the Garden of Eden, and there's no more to be said about it. Go home! Go home! Go home!

ELAINE: (*furious*) Sir Richard, you are grossly indelicate!

SIR RICHARD: (*blandly*) I am. So's Nature. (*cheerfully*) Now I must go and dress for dinner.

　　　　(*Re-enter* KIRBY *with another paper in his hand.*)

KIRBY: Beg pardon, Sir Richard. Latest edition. I see there's a warrant issued for the apprehension — (*Indicating* ELAINE. ELAINE *shows great consternation.*

ELAINE: Not for me?

KIRBY: Yes, ma'am. (*Exit.*)

PYBUS: There, you see. I thought your Boadicean Society —

ELAINE: Silence. This is my affair. (*to* SIR RICHARD) Do you think they will send me — away?

SIR RICHARD: (*paper in hand*) It looks uncommonly like it.

　　　　(PYBUS *begins to look pleased.*)

ELAINE: How long — do you suppose?

SIR RICHARD: The ringleaders at Birmingham got eighteen months.

ELAINE: (*in a fright*) Eighteen months!

SIR RICHARD: Of course, I shall defend you, and I shall do my best to get you off lightly. But you must take great care in the meantime, and, above all, no public speaking.

PYBUS: And she's such a good public speaker.

ELAINE: I cannot sacrifice my principles, nor will I be muzzled.

SIR RICHARD: (*angry*) Then, frankly, I won't defend you.

ELAINE: (*After a pause, has a great inspiration.*) I will defend myself!

SIR RICHARD: (*horrified*) Defend yourself! Don't talk such nonsense. You'll get five years.

ELAINE: The longer the better. Our cause demands a martyr. I will surrender tonight. Please ring the bell.

　　　　(PYBUS *rings the bell with great alacrity.*)

SIR RICHARD: You silly woman! Do you know what you are doing?

PYBUS: (*remonstrating*) Sir Richard, do please let her know what is the best for herself.

The ringleaders at Birmingham: this does not appear to refer to any actual incident.

ELAINE: If I defend myself I shall be allowed to speak.

SIR RICHARD: (*satirically*) Oh, yes!

    (KIRBY *appears, door left.*)

ELAINE: (*to* KIRBY) A hansom at once, please. I have a message for this age!

    (*Exit proudly, in a glow of martyrdom, followed by* KIRBY.)

SIR RICHARD: (*having watched her off*) Good heaven! How is it that women never will understand the Woman question? (*Turns to* PYBUS.) What do *you* intend to do?

PYBUS: I shall now return to the Nest. It is not naturally a noisy spot, nor are the inhabitants of Clapham an unruly class, except when they are incited by seditious persons. I may now perhaps be able to stamp myself upon the age.

SIR RICHARD: I dare say.

PYBUS: (*Going off at door, turns.*) — Sir Richard — (*very nervously*) In view of a period of quietude at the Nest, I really think it advisable for my wife to conduct her defence in person — (*looking very imploringly at* SIR RICHARD) I do, indeed. (*Continues to look very imploringly at* SIR RICHARD. SIR RICHARD *at length cordially grasps his hand.*) Thank you. Thank you. (*Exit delighted, left, as* LADY SUSAN *in handsome evening dress and cloak re-enters by the other door.*)

SIR RICHARD: (*Looking at her, takes her hands.*) You look very handsome, Sue. Hillo! Then you've found my ring!

LADY SUSAN: Yes, it turned up the other day.

SIR RICHARD: Where?

LADY SUSAN: (*a little confused*) Oh, I was turning over some old rubbish and there it was.

SIR RICHARD: (*Looks at her keenly, her eyes drop, and she goes to the window, draws aside the curtains, discovers a thick fall of snow outside.*) What a night! Why do you insist on going out to dine?

LADY SUSAN: Why do you insist on asking people to dinner whom I cannot possibly meet?

    (*Enter* KIRBY, *showing in* HARABIN. KIRBY *announces 'Mr Harabin'. Exit* KIRBY. *The three stand looking at each other rather embarrassed.*)

LADY SUSAN: (*very indignantly*) Uncle Dick!

HARABIN: I beg pardon. I see there's a mistake (*going back to door, left*).

SIR RICHARD: (*Stopping* LADY SUSAN *at door, right, calls across to* HARABIN.) Harabin, one moment. It's my fault. Let me frankly apologise to both of you. (*getting* LADY SUSAN *down stage, driving them nearer to each other*) First of all let us own there has been a mistake. And now the mistake is made let us make the best of it. (*to* HARABIN) Lady Susan is dining out with Mrs Quesnel, but as Mrs Quesnel has not arrived, naturally Lady Susan is obliged to wait. (*getting them nearer to each other all the time — to* LADY SUSAN) Mr Harabin is dining with me. He has come a little too early, but I am sure you would not wish me to send him out on such a night as this. (*drawing her closer to* HARABIN) Therefore he is obliged to wait. And so as you are both here don't you think you could manage — I won't say to entertain each other — but to endure each other's company for a few minutes? And if there is any

little natural disinclination to make each other's acquaintance, let me give
you a formal introduction. (*to* LADY SUSAN) Mr Harabin, a gentleman
whose profound attachment and admiration for you has been steadily growing for the last two years. (*to* HARABIN) Lady Susan Harabin, who I am sure
in her heart has no violent dislike for you. (*suddenly*) I must go and dress for
dinner. (*Bolts off very hurriedly, right, leaving them together. The two stand
looking at each other in an embarrassed way for some moments. Then* LADY
SUSAN *sits down, takes up an illustrated paper. Pause.* HARABIN *sits down.
She looks at him over the paper.*)

HARABIN: It is extremely cold.

LADY SUSAN: Extremely.

HARABIN: There is every indication of a very heavy snowfall.

LADY SUSAN: Indeed.

> (*longish pause*)

HARABIN: I have never seen you looking so remarkably well.

LADY SUSAN: Indeed.

HARABIN: Really beautiful. I hope you don't think me rude in making remarks on
your personal appearance.

LADY SUSAN: (*in an indifferent tone*) No.

HARABIN: (*with great politeness*) Wouldn't it be advisable to take off that heavy
cloak while you remain in this hot room? (LADY SUSAN *rises and slips it
off.*)

HARABIN: (*rushing towards her*) Allow me. (*By the time he gets to her the cloak
is off. Reproachfully*) You might have permitted me the honour – (LADY
SUSAN *reseats herself with great composure, and turns over the newspaper,
looking at him from the corners of her eyes. He remains standing over her
rather embarrassed. At length he bursts out.*) Confound it, Sue, you might
have a little pity on a poor devil!

LADY SUSAN: I cannot allow you to call me by my Christian name. If you do, I
shall be compelled to wait in another room.

> (*pause*)

HARABIN: But do talk to me.

LADY SUSAN: What is there to discuss?

HARABIN: Ourselves – at least, yourself. Sue, do put down that paper.

LADY SUSAN: (*rising, going towards door*) I told you I should go if you called me
by my Christian name. (*Is going off, right.*)

HARABIN: Let me open the door for you. (*He goes hastily after her, she rushes to
the door, tries to open it.*)

LADY SUSAN: Uncle Dick has locked the door!

> (*He again comes towards her, she rushes away towards the door, left.*)

HARABIN: No, don't go. (*Places her a chair with great politeness.*) Do sit down
again. (*She sits.*) I cannot tell you how much I have suffered during your
absence.

LADY SUSAN: Indeed.

HARABIN: And I have thoroughly determined to be the best of men in the future.

LADY SUSAN: I am sincerely glad to hear it.

HARABIN: You might give a fellow a little encouragement.

LADY SUSAN: Encouragement?

HARABIN: To be good. No man can be good unless a woman encourages him.

LADY SUSAN: And not many men even then, it seems.

HARABIN: I could be very good if you were to encourage me a little. Sue —
(LADY SUSAN *rises.*) Lady Sue — Lady Susan — (*He offers her the chair, she sits down again.*) You have never really understood me.

LADY SUSAN: No? (*Looks at him attentively.*)

HARABIN: I'm not at all a bad sort of fellow. You don't know how awfully sorry I am for the past. And I'm really devoted to you.

LADY SUSAN: Indeed.

HARABIN: It's a beastly night outside. You'll only catch a bad cold if you go out. I say, Sue; let's all have a jolly comfortable dinner together, and let bygones be bygones.
(*Pause.* LADY SUSAN *considers.*)

LADY SUSAN: On both sides?

HARABIN: Yes, on both sides. Of course there are no — no bygones on your side?

LADY SUSAN: Of course not. I suppose there are a good many on your side?

HARABIN: Eh? Eh? Well —

LADY SUSAN: You seem unwilling for me to touch upon your bygones.

HARABIN: (*embarrassed pause*) I assure you, I'm not a bad sort of fellow. And I've cherished your image throughout.

LADY SUSAN: Throughout a course of flirtations with all sorts of women?

HARABIN: Oh, not a course — and not all sorts. I assure you — there's nothing for you to trouble about.

LADY SUSAN: What do you mean by 'nothing'?

HARABIN: Well, well — oh, very well, let bygones be bygones.

LADY SUSAN: (*placidly*) Very well.

HARABIN: You will? I cannot tell you how delighted I am that you've forgiven me.
(*Is about to embrace her.*)

LADY SUSAN: Stay. We are to take each other for better or worse, as we did when we were married, and the past is never to be once mentioned between us?

HARABIN: Never. You've forgiven me, haven't you?

LADY SUSAN: Yes.

HARABIN: Very well, what more is there to be said? (*with sudden alarm*) Sue —

LADY SUSAN: What?

HARABIN: You — you haven't been — flirting with anyone in the meantime?

LADY SUSAN: I thought the past was not to be mentioned —

HARABIN: No. But — (*Shows great uneasiness.*)

LADY SUSAN: I see, we had better remain strangers. I'll wait in the next room (*going*).

HARABIN: No, no. Sue, of course I trust you. But perhaps it would be best to — to have a thorough understanding once for all. Then we shall never have occasion to return to the subject again. Now! Have you anything to tell me?

LADY SUSAN: Have *you* anything to tell *me*?

HARABIN: Well — of course — (*Stops, then suddenly*) Perhaps you'd better begin, as yours will be so much simpler. The whole truth, mind. (*Listens in deadly earnest, impatiently.*)

LADY SUSAN: One evening at Cairo —

HARABIN: (*eagerly*) Yes —

LADY SUSAN: I'd been playing a nocturne of Chopin's in the dusk —

HARABIN: In the dusk? Where?

LADY SUSAN: In the drawing-room.

HARABIN: The public drawing-room?

LADY SUSAN: Yes. And as I finished —

HARABIN: Yes —

LADY SUSAN: Signor Massetti, the musician, who was staying in the hotel, started up from a chair at the back — I didn't know he was in the room —

HARABIN: (*fiercely*) Well —

LADY SUSAN: And — don't look so ferocious —

HARABIN: (*maddened*) Go on! Go on!

LADY SUSAN: He kissed —

HARABIN: Kissed you?

LADY SUSAN: My hand.

HARABIN: Your hand?

LADY SUSAN: Yes — several times.

HARABIN: Did he? Did he? (*pacing up and down the room*)

LADY SUSAN: Yes, don't be in such a temper. He's quite an elderly man.

HARABIN: So much the worse.

LADY SUSAN: And devoted to music.

HARABIN: I dare say, the old blackguard! How many times did he kiss your hand?

LADY SUSAN: Five or six.

HARABIN: (*tortured*) Five or six!

LADY SUSAN: Yes, but I had really played very well.

HARABIN: The old scoundrel! And — what did he say?

LADY SUSAN: I forget exactly.

HARABIN: (*fiercely*) You forget?

LADY SUSAN: He complimented me upon my playing.

HARABIN: Yes, but — what else?

LADY SUSAN: Nothing. That's all.

HARABIN: All? Really? Really, really all?

LADY SUSAN: All, until I've heard all you have to tell me. (*Long pause. He paces up and down rather agitated.*) Come. Aren't you going to begin?

HARABIN: I'm so much upset about your flirtation.

LADY SUSAN: You're not upset about your own — flirtations?

HARABIN: Yes, I am. I feel quite a touch of remorse when I remember them.

LADY SUSAN: My dear Jim, you don't feel anything like so much remorse for your own transgressions as you do for mine.

HARABIN: Naturally not. (*Goes to her very solemnly.*) Will you give me your word, your sacred word of honour, that it went no further than a kiss on the hand with this confounded old Signor What's-his-name?

LADY SUSAN: My sacred word of honour, it went no further than a kiss on the hand with Signor Massetti.

HARABIN: (*Looks at her, much relieved.*) I'm glad to hear it. And there is nothing else?

LADY SUSAN: Yes, a good deal.

HARABIN: (*bristling up furiously*) A good deal! (*fiercely*) Go on! Go on! What else is there?

LADY SUSAN: There's all your side.

HARABIN: We'll finish with your side first. I must insist upon knowing —

LADY SUSAN: You must insist! (*Laughs at him.*) My dear Jim, don't be absurd. If it comes to that, I must insist upon knowing — First of all this: when I was a good, faithful wife to you, why did you run after other women? Secondly, how have you employed yourself in the last two years? And thirdly, how are you going to make me confess what I will have my tongue cut out rather than I will confess — that is, if there were anything to confess?

HARABIN: (*tortured*) If there were anything to confess! — then there is nothing to confess?

LADY SUSAN: I don't say that.

(HARABIN *takes two or three desperate turns about the room in agony.*)

HARABIN: Very well. I had thoroughly determined to be the best husband in England for the future. (KIRBY *shows in* ADMIRAL *and* LADY DARBY *at door, left. Exit* KIRBY.) Yes, madam. You have lost the greatest chance of happiness that was ever offered to a woman on this earth, and you have wrecked my whole future. (*Is going off.*)

ADMIRAL: (*Seizes him gently.*) Shake down! Shake down! Shake down!

HARABIN: Let me go, Sir Joseph — (*trying to get off*)

ADMIRAL: (*Turns him round.*) Shake down! Shake down! Shake down!

HARABIN: I wanted to let things shake down. I've wanted to let them shake down for the last two years. But she won't let them.

ADMIRAL: Now, Sue, how is it that you won't let things shake down?

LADY SUSAN: I am quite willing to let things shake down, but he won't let them.

ADMIRAL: Now, Jim, how is it that you won't let things shake down?

HARABIN: You can't expect me while —

ADMIRAL: While what?

HARABIN: While she won't tell me —

ADMIRAL: What?

HARABIN: (*fiercely at* LADY SUSAN) How many elderly musicians kissed her hand in Cairo!

ADMIRAL: Sue, how many elderly musicians kissed your hand in Cairo?

LADY SUSAN: Only one, and Mr Harabin knows all about him.

ADMIRAL: There you are, Jim. Only one, and you know all about him. Now shake down.

HARABIN: Very well — only — (*very uneasy*) — then — there was — only one?

LADY SUSAN: (*very coldly*) Will you give me my cloak, Uncle Jo? Aunt Vic, we'll wait in the drawing-room.

HARABIN: No — no!

LADY DARBY: (*stopping her*) Mr Harabin, you don't suppose that Lady Susan during her absence from you has done anything that needs to be concealed.

HARABIN: Certainly not. Certainly not. But still — (*Looks very uneasy. The lock of the door, right, is heard to turn. Enter* SIR RICHARD *in evening dress.*)

SIR RICHARD: Sir Joseph, Lady Darby (*shaking hands with them: to* LADY SUSAN). Well, how do we stand now?

LADY SUSAN: As we were.

HARABIN: Sir Richard, I wish to ask Lady Susan one solemn question in the presence of you all.

LADY SUSAN: My dear Jim, I shall never answer it.

HARABIN: Then am I to think — ?

LADY SUSAN: Just whatever you please to think.

    (HARABIN *goes in great distress to* SIR RICHARD.)

HARABIN: Kato, one moment. (*Draws* SIR RICHARD *down stage.* ADMIRAL *and* LADY DARBY *expostulate with* LADY SUSAN.) Sue won't say whether she has anything to confess, unless I confess everything to her.

SIR RICHARD: Very well. Confess everything to her.

HARABIN: Oh! That's impossible, you know.

SIR RICHARD: You don't suppose there is anything to confess on Sue's side?

HARABIN: No, I feel sure there isn't. But I should like to know. What shall I do?

SIR RICHARD: Sue looks very handsome.

HARABIN: Exquisite! Exquisite!

SIR RICHARD: I should stretch a point or two rather than send her out in the snow when you can have a cosy dinner with her here and — make it up.

    (*Enter* KIRBY, *showing in* INEZ *in evening dress.*)

KIRBY: (*announcing*) Mrs Quesnel.

INEZ: My dear Sue, ten thousand apologies. It's an awful night, and I couldn't get a cab for love or money. But — (*Looks at* HARABIN, *then looks inquiringly at* LADY SUSAN.)

KIRBY: Shall I serve dinner, Sir Richard?

SIR RICHARD: Lay covers for six instead of four, and then serve.

    (*Exit* KIRBY.)

LADY SUSAN: Come, Inez. I'm quite ready.

HARABIN: No, don't go, Sue. Sir Richard — (*appealing to* SIR RICHARD)

SIR RICHARD: (*Goes to* LADY SUSAN.) Sue, can't you give Mr Harabin some assurance —

LADY SUSAN: I have told him that bygones shall be bygones, and that I will be a good faithful wife to him, if he will be a good faithful husband to me. He can take me or leave me on those terms.

SIR RICHARD: (*Looks very earnestly at* LADY SUSAN *for some moments.*) I think, Jim, your happiness will be quite safe in her hands (*passing her over to* HARABIN).

HARABIN: I intend to be the best of husbands in the future. I'll give you my word —

LADY SUSAN: Your word of honour, as a gentleman?

HARABIN: (*very quickly*) Yes! yes! — my word of honour as a gentleman.

LADY DARBY: Why didn't you forgive him at first, Sue, and save us all this trouble?

LADY SUSAN: (*Sighs.*) I wonder why I didn't.

LADY DARBY: You see, dear, we poor women cannot retaliate.

LADY SUSAN: I see.

LADY DARBY: We must be patient.

INEZ: And forgive the wretches till they learn constancy.

LADY SUSAN: I see.

LADY DARBY: And, dear, yours is a respectable average case after all.

LADY SUSAN: Yes, a respectable average case after all.

>   (*Enter* KIRBY.)

KIRBY: Dinner is served, Sir Richard. (*Exit* KIRBY.)

SIR RICHARD: Take your wife in to dinner, Jim.

>   (HARABIN *gives his arm to* LADY SUSAN.)

ADMIRAL: Victoria, I have only another fortnight on shore. Give me the pleasure and the honour of taking in to dinner the best woman and the best wife in England! (LADY DARBY *gives her arm to* ADMIRAL.) Ah, Victoria! When I remember —

LADY DARBY: That's enough, Jo. Don't be foolish.

ADMIRAL: I can't help it. My conscience troubles me. Some day, when I can summon courage, I will endeavour to tell you — (*Takes her off very affectionately.*)

LADY SUSAN: Uncle Dick, have you ever had a love affair of your own?

SIR RICHARD: Just one.

LADY SUSAN: You never speak about it.

SIR RICHARD: It's too sacred.

LADY SUSAN: (*Sighs.*) Ah! One does not speak of the most sacred things! (*to* HARABIN) Now, sir, your arm, and don't forget I'm going to be a good wife to you.

HARABIN: I won't. How well you look, Sue! I'll take you down Bond Street tomorrow morning and buy you — the whole street! I have never loved you so much as I do at this moment.

LADY SUSAN: How long will your love last? For three weeks?

HARABIN: For three weeks? For life!

LADY SUSAN: Are you sure? Love me, Jim! I want to be loved! (*Exeunt* LADY SUSAN *and* HARABIN.)

SIR RICHARD: (*to* INEZ) Then I must take you?

INEZ: I don't see any alternative.

SIR RICHARD: (*more puzzled than ever*) What *was* there between Lucien and Sue at Cairo?

INEZ: *Honi soit qui mal y pense.*

SIR RICHARD: Yes, but that sermon was a very long one! Do women ever tell the truth about their little love affairs?

INEZ: Do men?

SIR RICHARD: No wise man ever tells.

INEZ: No wise woman ever tells.

SIR RICHARD: I wonder —

INEZ: Wonder at nothing that you find in the heart of a woman, or the heart of a man. God has put everything there.

SIR RICHARD: Let us leave these problems (*Kisses her hand very tenderly.*) and go in to dinner. (*Giving his arm to her. Curtain falls as they go off.*)

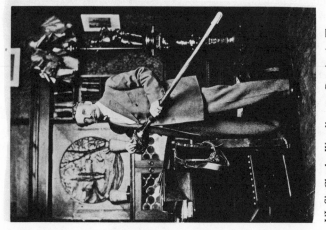

VI Sir Charles Wyndham as Deering in *The Liars*, Criterion Theatre, London, 1897: act IV

V *The Liars*, Empire Theatre, New York, 1898. Falkner (Arthur Byron, far right) has received the message from the Colonial Office. This appears to be the moment before his exit at the end of act I; John Drew (Deering) stands in the centre, Isabel Irving (Lady Jessica) and Blanche Burton (Beatrice) are left and right, respectively

THE LIARS

An original comedy in four acts

by HENRY ARTHUR JONES

'Above all things, tell no untruth; no, not in trifles; the custom of it is naughty.'

Sir Henry Sidney's letter to his son, Philip Sidney

First produced at the Criterion Theatre, London, on 6 October 1897, with the following cast:

COLONEL SIR CHRISTOPHER DEERING	Charles Wyndham
EDWARD FALKNER	T.B. Thalberg
GILBERT NEPEAN, *Lady Jessica's husband*	Herbert Standing
GEORGE NEPEAN, *Gilbert's brother*	Leslie Kenyon
FREDDIE TATTON, *Lady Rosamund's husband*	A. Vane Tempest
ARCHIBALD COKE, *Dolly's husband*	Alfred Bishop
WAITER, *at the Star and Garter*	Paul Berton
GADSBY, *footman at Freddie Tatton's*	C. Terric
TAPLIN, *Sir Christopher's servant*	R. Lambert
FOOTMAN, *at Cadogan Gardens*	A. Eliot
LADY JESSICA NEPEAN	Miss Mary Moore
LADY ROSAMUND TATTON, *her sister*	Miss Irene Vanbrugh
DOLLY COKE, *their cousin*	Miss Sarah Brooke
BEATRICE EBERNOE	Miss Cynthia Brook
MRS CRESPIN	Miss Janette Steer
FERRIS, *Lady Jessica's maid*	Miss M. Barton

ACT I – Tent on the lawn of Freddie Tatton's house in the Thames Valley, after dinner, on a summer evening.

ACT II – Private sitting-room number 10 at the Star and Garter at Shepperford on the following Monday evening.

ACT III – Lady Rosamund's drawing-room, Cadogan Gardens, Chelsea, on the Tuesday morning.

ACT IV – Sir Christopher Deering's rooms in Victoria Street on the Tuesday evening.

Time – the present.

ACT I

SCENE.   *Interior of a large tent on the lawn of* FREDDIE TATTON'*s house in the Thames Valley. The roof of the tent slopes up from the back of the stage. An opening at back discovers the lawn, a night scene of a secluded part of the Thames, and the opposite bank beyond. Small opening left. The tent is of eastern material, splendidly embroidered in rich eastern colours. The floor is planked and some rugs are laid down. The place is comfortably furnished for summer tea and smoking-room. Several little tables, chairs and lounges, most of them of basket-work. On the table spirit-decanters, soda-water bottles, cigars, cigarettes, empty coffee cups, match-box, etc. Some plants in the corners. Lamps and candles lighted. Time: after dinner on a summer evening. Discover* ARCHIBALD COKE *and* 'FREDDIE' TATTON. COKE, *a tall, pompous, precise man, about fifty, is seated at side table smoking.* FREDDIE, *a nervous, weedy little creature about thirty, with no whiskers, and nearly bald, with a squeaky voice, is walking about.*

FREDDIE: (*very excited, very voluble, very squeaky*) It's all very well for folks to say, 'Give a woman her head; don't ride her on the curb.' But I tell you this, Coke, when a fellow has got a wife like mine, or Jess, it's confoundedly difficult to get her to go at all, without a spill, eh?

COKE: It is perplexing to know precisely how to handle a wife (*Drinks, sighs.*) — very perplexing!

FREDDIE: Perplexing? It's a d—ee—d silly riddle without any answer! You know I didn't want to have this house-party for the Regatta — (COKE *looks at him.*) — I beg your pardon. Of course I wanted to have you and Dolly, and I didn't mind Gilbert and Jess. But I didn't want to have Falkner here. He's paying a great deal too much attention to Jess, and Jess doesn't choke him off as she should. Well, I thoroughly made up my mind if Jess came, Falkner shouldn't.

COKE: Yes?

FREDDIE: Well, Rosamund said he should. So I stuck out, and she stuck out, in fact we both stuck out for a week. I was determined he shouldn't come.

COKE: Then why did you give in?

FREDDIE: I didn't.

COKE: But he's here!

FREDDIE: Yes; but only for a few days. Rosamund invited him, unknown to me, and then — well — you see, I was obliged to be civil to the fellow. (*very confidential*) I say, Coke — we're tiled in, aren't we? Candidly, what would you do if you had a wife like Rosamund?

COKE: (*sententiously*) Ah! Just so! (*Drinks.*)

FREDDIE: You're the lucky man of us three, Coke.

COKE: I must own my wife has some good points —

FREDDIE: Dolly got good points! I should think she has!

COKE: But she's terribly thoughtless and frivolous.

FREDDIE: So much the better. Give me a woman that lets a man call his soul his

---

the Regatta: Henley Regatta, held annually at Henley-on-Thames in the first week of July: a major event in the social season.
tiled in: safe from interruption or overhearing (the phrase is derived from Masonic ritual).

own. That's all I want, Coke, to call my soul my own. And — (*resolutely*) some of these days — (*very resolutely*) I will, that's all!

> (*Enter* MRS CRESPIN, *a sharp, good-looking woman between thirty and thirty-five.*)

MRS CRESPIN: Is Mr Gilbert Nepean leaving for Devonshire tonight?

FREDDIE: Yes. He takes the eleven thirty-four slow and waits for the down fast at Reading.

MRS CRESPIN: Tonight?

FREDDIE: Yes. His steward, Crampton, has been robbing him for years, and now the fellow has bolted with a heap of money and a farmer's wife.

MRS CRESPIN: Mr Nepean must go tonight?

FREDDIE: Yes. Why?

MRS CRESPIN: Lady Jessica and Mr Falkner have gone for a little moonlight row. I thought Mr Nepean might like to stay and steer.

FREDDIE: Oh, Lady Jessica knows the river well.

MRS CRESPIN: Ah, then Mr Nepean can look after the steward. After all, no husband need emphasise the natural absurdity of his position by playing cox to another man's stroke, need he?

> (*Enter* COLONEL SIR CHRISTOPHER DEERING, *a genial, handsome Englishman, about thirty-eight, and* GEORGE NEPEAN, *a dark, rather heavy-looking man about the same age.*)

SIR CHRISTOPHER: Oh, nonsense, Nepean; you're mistaken!

GEORGE: You'd better say a word to Falkner —

SIR CHRISTOPHER: (*with a warning look*) Shush!

GEORGE: If you don't, I shall drop a very strong hint to my brother.

SIR CHRISTOPHER: (*more peremptorily*) Shush, shush!

FREDDIE: What's the matter?

SIR CHRISTOPHER: Nothing, Freddie, nothing! Our friend here (*Trying to link his arm in* GEORGE's — GEORGE *stands off.*) is a little old-fashioned. He doesn't understand that in all really innocent flirtations ladies allow themselves a very large latitude indeed. In fact, from my very modest experience with the sex — take it for what it's worth — I should say the more innocent the flirtation, the larger the latitude the lady allows herself, eh, Mrs Crespin?

MRS CRESPIN: Oh, we are all latitudinarians at heart.

SIR CHRISTOPHER: Yes; but a lady who practises extensively as a latitudinarian rarely becomes a — a — a longitudinarian, eh?

MRS CRESPIN: Oh, I wouldn't answer for her! It's a horrid, wicked world; and if once a woman allows one of you wretches to teach her the moral geography of it, it's ten to one she gets her latitude and longitude mixed before she has time to look at the map. (*Goes up to opening, and looks off.*)

FREDDIE: (*to* SIR CHRISTOPHER) I say, I'm awfully sorry about this. You know I told Rosamund how it would be if we had Falkner here —

---

the down fast: an express train from London.
latitudinarians: Church of England clergy who were indifferent to nice distinctions of creed or form.

SIR CHRISTOPHER: (*Draws* FREDDIE *aside.*) Shush! Tell Lady Rosamund to caution Lady Jessica —

FREDDIE: I will. But Rosamund generally does just the opposite of what I tell her. Don't be surprised, old fellow, if you hear some of these days that I've — well, don't be surprised.

SIR CHRISTOPHER: At what?

FREDDIE: Well, I shall — now, candidly, old fellow — we're tiled in, quite between ourselves — if you found yourself landed as I am, what would you do?

SIR CHRISTOPHER: You mean if I found myself married?

FREDDIE: Yes.

SIR CHRISTOPHER: I should make the best of it.

> (GEORGE *comes up to them.* MRS CRESPIN *comes from back of tent.*)

GEORGE: (*to* SIR CHRISTOPHER) Then it's understood that you'll give Falkner a hint?

SIR CHRISTOPHER: My dear fellow, surely your brother is the best judge —

GEORGE: Of what he doesn't see?

SIR CHRISTOPHER: He's here.

GEORGE: He's leaving for Devonshire tonight — unless I stop him. Will that be necessary?

SIR CHRISTOPHER: No. Falkner is my friend. I introduced him to Lady Jessica. If you insist, I'll speak to him. But I'm sure you're wrong. He's the very soul of honour. I didn't live with him out there those three awful years without knowing him.

GEORGE: I don't see what your living three years in Africa with him has got to do with it, eh, Mrs Crespin?

MRS CRESPIN: Let's see how it works out. Falkner behaves most gallantly in Africa. Falkner rescues Mrs Ebernoe. Falkner splendidly avenges Colonel Ebernoe's death, and strikes terror into every slave-dealer's heart. Falkner returns to England covered with glory. A grateful nation goes into a panic of admiration, and makes itself slightly ridiculous over Falkner. Falkner is the lion of the season. Therefore we may be quite sure that Falkner won't make love to any pretty woman who comes in his way. It doesn't seem to work out right.

SIR CHRISTOPHER: But Falkner is not an ordinary man, not even an ordinary hero.

MRS CRESPIN: My dear Sir Christopher, the one cruel fact about heroes is that they are made of flesh and blood! Oh, if only they were made of waxwork, or Crown Derby ware, or Britannia metal; but, alas and alas! they're always made of flesh and blood.

COKE: Where did Falkner come from? What were his people?

SIR CHRISTOPHER: His grandfather was what nonconformists call an eminent divine, his father was a rich city merchant; his mother was a farmer's daughter. Falkner himself is a — well, he's a puritan Don Quixote, mounted on Pegasus.

Britannia metal: alloy resembling silver in appearance.

MRS CRESPIN: Put a puritan Don Quixote on horseback, and he'll ride to the — Lady Jessica, eh?

SIR CHRISTOPHER: Hush! He'll love and he'll ride away.

MRS CRESPIN: (*significantly*) I sincerely hope so.

COKE: I must say that Falkner is less objectionable than dissenters generally are. I have an unconquerable aversion to dissenters.

SIR CHRISTOPHER: Oh, I hate 'em! But they saved England, hang 'em! And I'm not sure whether they're not the soundest part of the nation today.

MRS CRESPIN: Oh, pray don't tell them so, just as they're getting harmless and sensible — and a little artistic.

> (*A piano is played very softly and beautifully at a distance of some twenty yards. They all listen.*)

MRS CRESPIN: Is that Mrs Ebernoe?

SIR CHRISTOPHER: Yes.

MRS CRESPIN: What a beautiful touch she has!

SIR CHRISTOPHER: She has a beautiful nature.

MRS CRESPIN: Indeed! I thought she was a little stiff and unsociable. But perhaps we are too frivolous.

SIR CHRISTOPHER: Perhaps. And she hasn't quite recovered from poor Ebernoe's death.

> (*Enter* LADY ROSAMUND *and* DOLLY COKE *in evening dress.*
> DOLLY *is without any wrap on her shoulders.*)

MRS CRESPIN: But that's nearly two years ago. Is it possible we still have women amongst us who can mourn two years for a man? It gives me hopes again for my sex.

FREDDIE: (*his back to* LADY ROSAMUND) I know jolly well Rosamund won't mourn two years for me.

LADY ROSAMUND: (*a clear-cut, bright, pretty woman*) You're quite right, Freddie, I shan't. But if you behave very prettily meantime, I promise you a decent six weeks. So be satisfied, and don't make a disturbance down there (*with a little gesture pointing down*) and create the impression that I wasn't a model wife.

> (FREDDIE *makes an appealing gesture for sympathy to* SIR CHRISTOPHER.)

COKE: (*in a very querulous, pedantic tone to* DOLLY) No wrap again! Really, my dear, I do wish you would take more precautions against the night air. If you should take influenza again —

DOLLY: (*a pretty, empty-headed little woman*) Oh, my dear Archie, if I do, it is I who will have to cough and sneeze!

COKE: Yes; but it is I who will be compelled to listen to you. I do wish you would remember how very inconvenient it is for me when you have influenza.

DOLLY: My dear, you can't expect me to remember *all* the things that are inconvenient to you. Besides, other people don't wrap up. Jessica is out on the river with absolutely nothing on her shoulders.

MRS CRESPIN: Is it not a physiological fact that when our hearts reach a certain temperature our shoulders may be, and often are, safely left bare?

> (GEORGE NEPEAN *has been listening. He suddenly rises, comes*

some steps towards them as if about to speak, stops, then turns and
exit with great determination.)

SIR CHRISTOPHER: Mrs Crespin, you saw that?

MRS CRESPIN: Yes. Where has he gone?

SIR CHRISTOPHER: I suppose to tell his brother his suspicions. I'm sure you
meant nothing just now, but — (*glancing round*) — we are all friends of Lady
Jessica's, aren't we?

MRS CRESPIN: Oh, certainly. But don't you think you ought to get Mr Falkner
away?

SIR CHRISTOPHER: He'll be leaving England soon. These fresh outbreaks amongst
the slave-traders will give us no end of trouble, and the Government will have
to send Falkner out. Meantime —

MRS CRESPIN: Meantime, doesn't Mrs Ebernoe play divinely? (*going off*)

SIR CHRISTOPHER: (*politely intercepting her*) Meantime it's understood that
nothing more is to be said of this?

MRS CRESPIN: Oh, my dear Sir Christopher, what more can be said? (*Exit.*)

SIR CHRISTOPHER: (*Holds the tent curtains aside for her to pass out; looks after
her, shakes his head, perplexed, then turns to* COKE.) Coke, what do you say,
a hundred up?

COKE: (*rising*) I'm agreeable! Dolly! Dolly!

(LADY ROSAMUND, DOLLY *and* FREDDIE *are chattering very
vigorously together.*)

DOLLY: (*Doesn't turn round to him.*) Well? (*Goes on chattering to* LADY ROSA-
MUND *and* FREDDIE.)

COKE: You had a tiresome hacking cough, dear, during the greater portion of last
night.

DOLLY: Did I? (*same business*)

COKE: It would be wise to keep away from the river.

DOLLY: Oh, very well, dear. I'll try and remember. (*same business*)

COKE: (*Turns, annoyed, to* SIR CHRISTOPHER) I'm a painfully light sleeper. The
least thing disturbs me, and — (*Looks anxiously at* DOLLY, *who is still
chattering, and then turns to* SIR CHRISTOPHER.) Do you sleep well?

SIR CHRISTOPHER: (*Links his arm in* COKE's.) Like a top. Never missed a night's
rest in my life. (*Takes* COKE *off at opening.*)

FREDDIE: (*Has been talking angrily to* LADY ROSAMUND.) Very well then,
what am I to do?

DOLLY: Oh, do go and get a whisky and soda, there's a dear Freddie!

FREDDIE: That's all very well, but if Jessica goes and makes a fool of herself in my
house, people will say it was my fault.

LADY ROSAMUND: What — example or influence, or sheer desperate imitation?

FREDDIE: (*Pulls himself up, looks very satirical, evidently tries to think of some
crushing reply without success.*) I must say, Rosamund, that your continued
chaff of me and everything that I do is in execrable taste. For a woman to

a hundred up: i.e. at billiards.

chaff her husband on all occasions is — well, it's very bad taste, that's all I can say about it! (*Exit at back.*)

DOLLY: Freddie's getting a dreadful fidget. He's nearly as bad as Archie.

LADY ROSAMUND: Oh, my dear, he's ten times worse. One can't help feeling some small respect for Archie.

DOLLY: Oh, do you think so? Well, yes, I suppose Archie is honourable and all that.

LADY ROSAMUND: Oh, all men are honourable. They get kicked out if they aren't. My Freddie's honourable in his poor little way.

DOLLY: Oh, don't run Freddie down. I rather like Freddie.

LADY ROSAMUND: Oh, if you had to live with him —

DOLLY: Well, he always lets you have your own way.

LADY ROSAMUND: I wish he wouldn't. I really believe I should love and respect him a little if he were to take me and give me a good shaking, or do something to make me feel that he's my master. But (*Sighs.*) he never will! He'll only go on asking everybody's advice how to manage me — and never find out. As if it weren't the easiest thing in the world to manage a woman — if men only knew.

DOLLY: Oh, do you think so? I wonder if poor old Archie knows how to manage me!

LADY ROSAMUND: Archie's rather trying at times.

DOLLY: Oh, he is! He's so frumpish and particular, and he's getting worse.

LADY ROSAMUND: Oh, my dear, they do as they grow older.

DOLLY: Still, after all, Freddie and Archie aren't quite so awful as Gilbert.

LADY ROSAMUND: Oh, Gilbert's a terror. I hope Jessica won't do anything foolish —

> (*A very merry peal of laughter heard off, followed by* LADY JESSICA'*s voice.*)

LADY JESSICA: (*heard off*) Oh, no, no, no, no, no! Please keep away from my dress! Oh, I'm so sorry! (*laughing a little*) But you are — so — so — (*another peal of laughter*)

FALKNER: (*heard off, a deep, rich, sincere, manly tone*) So ridiculous? I don't mind that!

LADY JESSICA: (*heard off*) But you'll take cold. Do go and change!

FALKNER: (*heard off*) Change? That's not possible!

> (LADY JESSICA *appears at opening at back, looking off, smothering her laughter. She is a very bright, pretty women about twenty-seven, very dainty and charming. Piano ceases.*)

LADY JESSICA: Oh, the poor dear, foolish fellow! Look!

LADY ROSAMUND: What is it?

LADY JESSICA: My ten-and-sixpenny brooch! He kept on begging for some little souvenir, so I took this off. That quite unhinged him. I saw he was going to be demonstrative, so I dropped the brooch in the river and made a terrible fuss. He jumped in, poor dear, and fished it up. It was so muddy at the bottom! He came up looking like a *fin-de-siècle* Neptune

---

fin-de-siècle: in this context, late eighteenth century.

— or a forsaken merman — or the draggled figurehead of a penny Thames
steamship.

LADY ROSAMUND: (*very seriously*) Jess, the men are talking about you.

LADY JESSICA: (*very carelessly*) Ah, are they? Who is?

LADY ROSAMUND: My Freddie says that you —

LADY JESSICA: (*interrupting on 'says'*) My dear Rosy, I don't mind what your
Freddie says any more than you do.

LADY ROSAMUND: But George has been fizzing up all the evening.

LADY JESSICA: Oh, let him fizz down again.

LADY ROSAMUND: But I believe he has gone to give Gilbert a hint —

LADY JESSICA: (*showing annoyance*) Ah, that's mean of George! How vexing!
Perhaps Gilbert will stay now.

LADY ROSAMUND: Perhaps it's as well that Gilbert should stay.

LADY JESSICA: What? My dear Rosy, you know I'm the very best of wives, but
it does get a little monotonous to spend all one's time in the company of a
man who doesn't understand a joke — not even when it's explained to him!

LADY ROSAMUND: Jess, you really must pull up.

DOLLY: Yes, Jess, Mrs Crespin was making some very cattish remarks about you
and Mr Falkner.

LADY JESSICA: Was she? Rosy, why do you have that woman here?

LADY ROSAMUND: I don't know. One must have somebody. I thought you and
she were very good friends.

LADY JESSICA: Oh, we're the best of friends, only we hate each other like poison.

LADY ROSAMUND: I don't like her. But she says such stinging things about my
Freddie, and makes him so wild.

LADY JESSICA: Does she? I'll ask her down for the shooting. Oh! I've got a
splendid idea!

LADY ROSAMUND: What is it?

LADY JESSICA: A new career for poor gentlewomen. You found a school and
carefully train them in all the best traditions of the gentle art of husband-
baiting. Then you invite one of them to your house, pay her, of course, a
handsome salary, and she assists you in 'the daily round, the common task' of
making your husband's life a perfect misery to him. After a month or so she
is played out and retires to another sphere, and you call in a new — lady-help!

LADY ROSAMUND: Oh, I don't think I should care to have my Freddie system-
atically henpecked by another woman.

LADY JESSICA: No; especially as you do it so well yourself. Besides, your Freddie
is such a poor little pocket-edition of a man — I hope you don't mind my saying so —

LADY ROSAMUND: Oh, not at all. He's your own brother-in-law.

LADY JESSICA: Yes; and you may say what you like about Gilbert.

---

forsaken merman: in Arnold's poem of that title, a merman whose mortal lover has returned to
the land.

for the shooting: i.e. in September, at the end of the London season.

'the daily round, the common task': a common misquotation from Keble's hymn 'New Every
Morning' ('the trivial round, the common task').

DOLLY: Oh, we do, don't we, Rosy?

LADY JESSICA: Do you? Well, what do you say?

DOLLY: Oh, it wouldn't be fair to tell, would it, Rosy? But Mrs Crespin said yesterday —

> (LADY ROSAMUND *glances at* DOLLY *and stops her.*)

LADY JESSICA: About Gilbert?

DOLLY: Yes.

LADY JESSICA: Well, what did she say?

> (DOLLY *glances at* LADY ROSAMUND *inquiringly.*)

LADY ROSAMUND: No, Dolly, no!

LADY JESSICA: Yes, Dolly! Do tell me.

LADY ROSAMUND: No, no!

LADY JESSICA: I don't care what she said, so long as she didn't say that he could understand a joke. That would be shamefully untrue. I've lived with him for five years, and I'm sure he can't. But what did Mrs Crespin say, Rosy?

LADY ROSAMUND: No, it really was a little too bad.

DOLLY: Yes. I don't much mind what anybody says about Archie, but if Mrs Crespin had said about him what she said about Gilbert —

LADY JESSICA: But what did she say? Rosy, if you don't tell me, I won't tell you all the dreadful things I hear about your Freddie. Oh, do tell me! There's a dear!

LADY ROSAMUND: Well, she said — (*Begins laughing.*)

> (DOLLY *begins laughing.*)

LADY JESSICA: Oh, go on! go on! go on!

LADY ROSAMUND: She said — no, I'll whisper!

> (LADY JESSICA *inclines her ear,* LADY ROSAMUND *whispers;*
> DOLLY *laughs.*)

LADY JESSICA: About Gilbert? (*beginning to laugh*)

LADY ROSAMUND: Yes (*laughing*).

> (*They all join in a peal of laughter which grows louder and louder.
> At its height enter* GILBERT NEPEAN. *He is a man rather over
> forty, much the same build as his brother* GEORGE; *rather stout,
> heavy figure, dark complexion; strong, immobile, uninteresting
> features; large, coarse hands; a habit of biting his nails. He is dressed
> in tweeds, long light ulster and travelling cap, which he does not
> remove. As he enters, the laughter, which has been very boisterous,
> suddenly ceases. He goes up to table without taking any notice of
> the ladies; very deliberately takes out cigar from case, strikes a
> match which does not ignite, throws it down with an angry gesture
> and exclamation; strikes another which also does not ignite; throws
> it down with a still angrier gesture and exclamation. The third match
> ignites, and he deliberately lights his cigar. Meantime, as soon as he
> has reached table,* LADY JESSICA, *who stands behind him,*

(s.d.) *takes out cigar from case*: it is impolite of Nepean to smoke in the presence of a lady without first asking her permission.

exchanges glances with DOLLY *and* LADY ROSAMUND, *and makes a little face behind his back.* DOLLY *winks at* LADY JESSICA, *who responds by pulling a mock long face.* DOLLY *steals off.* LADY ROSAMUND *shrugs her shoulders at* LADY JESSICA, *who pulls her face still longer.* LADY ROSAMUND *steals quietly off after* DOLLY. GILBERT *is still busy with his cigar.* LADY JESSICA *does a little expressive pantomime behind his back.*)

GILBERT: What's all this tomfoolery with Falkner?

LADY JESSICA: Tomfoolery?

GILBERT: George says you are carrying on some tomfoolery with Falkner.

LADY JESSICA: Ah! That's very sweet and elegant of George. But I never carry on any tomfoolery with any one — because I'm not a tomfool, therefore I can't.

GILBERT: I wish for once in your life you'd give me a plain answer to a plain question.

LADY JESSICA: Oh, I did once. You shouldn't remind me of that. But I never bear malice. Ask me another, such as — if a herring and a half cost three ha'pence, how long will it take one's husband to learn politeness enough to remove his cap in his wife's presence?

GILBERT: (*Instinctively takes off his cap, then glancing at her attitude, which is one of amused defiance, he puts the cap on again.*) There's a draught in here.

LADY JESSICA: The lamp doesn't show it. But perhaps you are right to guard a sensitive spot.

GILBERT: I say there's a confounded draught.

LADY JESSICA: Oh, don't tell fibs, dear. Because if you do, you'll go — where you *may* meet me; and then we should have to spend such a very long time together.

GILBERT: (*Nonplussed, bites his nails a moment or two; takes out his watch.*) I've no time to waste. I must be down in Devonshire tomorrow to go into this business of Crampton's. But before I go, I mean to know the truth of this nonsense between you and Falkner.

LADY JESSICA: Ah!

GILBERT: Shall I get it from you — or from him?

LADY JESSICA: Wouldn't it be better to get it from me? Because he mightn't tell you *all*?

GILBERT: *All*? Then there is something to know?

LADY JESSICA: Heaps. And if you'll have the ordinary politeness to take off that very ugly cap I'll be very sweet and obedient and tell you *all*.

GILBERT: Go on!

LADY JESSICA: Not while the cap sits there! (*pointing to his head*)

GILBERT: I tell you I feel the draught.

(LADY JESSICA *rises, goes to the tent opening, carefully draws the curtains. He watches her, sulkily biting his nails.*)

LADY JESSICA: There! Now you may safely venture to uncover the sensitive spot.

GILBERT: (*firmly*) No.

LADY JESSICA: (*serenely seated*) Very well, my dear. Then I shan't open my lips.

GILBERT: You won't?

LADY JESSICA: No; and I'm sure it's far more important for you to know what is going on between Mr Falkner and me than to have that horrid thing sticking on your head.

GILBERT: (*Takes a turn or two, bites his nails, at length sulkily flings the cap on the chair.*) Now!

LADY JESSICA: Mr Falkner is very deeply attached to me, I believe.

GILBERT: He has told you so?

LADY JESSICA: No.

GILBERT: No?

LADY JESSICA: No; but that's only because I keep on stopping him.

GILBERT: You keep on stopping him?

LADY JESSICA: Yes; it's so much pleasanter to have him dangling for a little while, and *then* —

GILBERT: Then what?

LADY JESSICA: Well, it is pleasant to be admired.

GILBERT: And you accept his admiration?

LADY JESSICA: Of course I do. Why shouldn't I? If Mr Falkner admires me, isn't that the greatest compliment he can pay to your taste? And if he spares you the drudgery of being polite to me, flattering me, complimenting me, and paying me the hundred delicate little attentions that win a woman's heart, I'm sure you ought to be very much obliged to him for taking all that trouble off your hands.

GILBERT: (*Looks furious.*) Now understand me. This nonsense has gone far enough. I forbid you to have anything further to say to the man.

LADY JESSICA: Ah, you forbid me!

GILBERT: I forbid you. And, understand, if you do —

LADY JESSICA: Ah, take care! Don't threaten me!

GILBERT: Do you mean to respect my wishes?

LADY JESSICA: Of course I shall respect your wishes. I may not obey them, but I will respect them.

GILBERT: (*Enraged, comes up to her very angrily.*) Now, Jessica, once for all —
　　　　　(*Enter* GEORGE. GILBERT *stops suddenly.*)

GEORGE: The dog-cart's ready, Gilbert. What's the matter?

GILBERT: Nothing. (*to* LADY JESSICA) You'll please to come on to me at Teignwick tomorrow.

LADY JESSICA: Can't. I've promised to go to Barbara, and I must keep my promise, even though it parts me from you.
　　　　　(*Enter* SERVANT *at back.*)

SERVANT: You've only just time to catch the train, sir.

GILBERT: I'm not going.

SERVANT: Not going, sir?

GILBERT: No.
　　　　　(*Exit* SERVANT.)

LADY JESSICA: (*Appeals to* GEORGE.) Isn't it dear of him to stay here on my

---

dog-cart: light carriage, so named on account of its provision for the conveyance of hunting dogs.

account when he knows he ought to be in Devon? Isn't it sweet to think that after five long years one has still that magnetic attraction for one's husband?

GILBERT: No. I'm hanged if I stay on your account. (*Goes up to opening, calls out.*) Hi! Gadsby! I'm coming! (*Comes back to* LADY JESSICA.) Understand, I expect you at Teignwick tomorrow.

LADY JESSICA: Dearest, I shan't come.

GILBERT: I say you shall!

LADY JESSICA: 'Shall' is not a pretty word for a husband to use. (*Takes up the cap he has thrown down and stands twiddling the tassel.*)

GILBERT: George, I expect this business of Crampton's will keep me for a week, but I can't tell. Look after everything while I'm away. (*glancing at* LADY JESSICA — *to her*) You won't come to Teignwick?

LADY JESSICA: I've promised Barbara. Here's your cap.

GILBERT: Goodbye, George! (*Shakes hands with* GEORGE, *looks at* LADY JESSICA, *and is then going off at back.*)

LADY JESSICA: Ta ta, dearest (*going up to him*).

GILBERT: (*Turns, comes a step or two to* LADY JESSICA, *livid with anger; speaks in her ear.*) You'll go just one step too far some day, madam, and if you do, look out for yourself, for, by Jove! I won't spare you! (*Exit.* LADY JESSICA *stands a little frightened, goes up to opening at back, as if to call him back, comes down, takes up an illustrated paper.* GEORGE *stands watching her, smoking.*)

LADY JESSICA: (*after a little pause*) George, that was very silly of you to tell Gilbert about Mr Falkner and me.

GEORGE: I thought you had gone far enough.

LADY JESSICA: Oh, no, my dear friend. You must allow me to be the best judge of how far —

GEORGE: How far you can skate over thin ice?

LADY JESSICA: The thinner the ice the more delicious the fun, don't you think? Ah, you're like Gilbert. You don't skate — or joke.

GEORGE: You heard what Gilbert said?

LADY JESSICA: Yes; that was a hint to you. Won't it be rather a tiresome task for you?

GEORGE: What?

LADY JESSICA: To keep an eye on me, watch that I don't go that one step too far. And not quite a nice thing to do, eh?

GEORGE: Oh, I've no intention of watching you — (*Enter* FALKNER *at back.* GEORGE *looks at the two.*) Not the least intention, I assure you. (*Exit.*)

LADY JESSICA: So tomorrow will break up our pleasant party.

FALKNER: (*About forty, strong, fine, clearly-cut features, earnest expression, hair turning gray, complexion pale, and almost grey with continued work, anxiety and abstinence.*) And after tomorrow?

LADY JESSICA: Ah, after tomorrow!

FALKNER: When shall we meet again?

LADY JESSICA: Shall we meet again? Yes, I suppose. Extremes do meet, don't they?

FALKNER: Are we extremes?

LADY JESSICA: Aren't we? I suppose I'm the vainest, emptiest, most irresponsible creature in the world —

FALKNER: You're not! You're not! You slander yourself! You can be sincere, you can be earnest, you can be serious —

LADY JESSICA: Can I? Oh, do tell me what fun there is in being serious! I can't see the use of it. There you are, for instance, mounted on that high horse of seriousness, spending the best years of your life in fighting African slave-traders and other windmills of that sort. Oh do leave the windmills alone! They'll all tumble by themselves by and by.

FALKNER: I'm not going to spend the best years of my life in fighting slave-traders. I'm going to spend them — in loving you (*approaching her very closely*).

LADY JESSICA: Oh, that will be worse than the windmills — and quite as useless. (*He is very near to her.*) If you please — you remember we promised to discuss all love matters at a distance of three feet, so as to allow for the personal equation. Your three feet, please.

FALKNER: When shall we meet again?

LADY JESSICA: Ah, when? Where do you go tomorrow night, when you leave here?

FALKNER: I don't know. Where do you?

LADY JESSICA: To my cousin Barbara's.

FALKNER: Where is that?

LADY JESSICA: Oh, a little way along the river, towards town; not far from Staines.

FALKNER: In what direction?

LADY JESSICA: About two miles to the nor'-nor'-sou' west. I never was good at geography.

FALKNER: Is there a good inn near?

LADY JESSICA: There's a delightful little riverside hotel, the Star and Garter, at Shepperford. They make a speciality of French cooking.

FALKNER: I shall go there when I leave here tomorrow. May I call at your cousin's?

LADY JESSICA: It wouldn't be wise. And I'm only staying till Monday.

FALKNER: And then?

LADY JESSICA: On Monday evening I go back to town.

FALKNER: Alone?

LADY JESSICA: No; with Ferris, my maid. Unless I send her on first.

FALKNER: And you will?

LADY JESSICA: No; I don't think so. But a curious thing happened to me the last time I stayed at Barbara's. I sent Ferris on with the luggage in the early after-noon, and I walked to the station for the sake of the walk. Well, there are two turnings, and I must have taken the wrong one.

FALKNER: What happened?

Staines: in Surrey, 6 miles from Slough and situated on the Thames.
Shepperford: a fictitious place-name, reminiscent of Shepperton.

LADY JESSICA: I wandered about for miles, and at half-past seven I found myself, very hot, very tired, very hungry, and in a very bad temper, at the Star and Garter at Shepperford. That was on a Monday, too.

FALKNER: That was on a Monday?

LADY JESSICA: Yes — hark! (*Goes suddenly to back, looks off.*) Oh, it's you, Ferris! What are you doing there?

> (FERRIS, *a perfectly-trained lady's maid, about thirty, dark, quiet, reserved, a little sinister-looking, appears at opening at back with wrap in hand.*)

FERRIS: I beg pardon, my lady. But I thought you might be getting chilly, so I've brought you this.

LADY JESSICA: Put it on the chair.

FERRIS: Yes, my lady. (*Puts wrap on chair and exit.*)

LADY JESSICA: (*Yawns.*) Heigho! Shall we go into the billiard room? (*going*)

FALKNER: No. (*stopping her*) How long do you mean to play with me?

LADY JESSICA: Am I playing with you?

FALKNER: What else have you done in the last three months? My heart is yours to its last beat. My life is yours to its last moment. What are you going to do with me?

LADY JESSICA: Ah, that's it! I'm sure I don't know. (*smiling at him*) What shall I do with you?

FALKNER: Love me! love me! love me!

LADY JESSICA: You are very foolish!

FALKNER: Foolish to love you?

LADY JESSICA: No; not foolish to love me. I like you for that. But foolish to love me so foolishly. Foolish to be always wanting to play Romeo, when I only want to play Juliet sometimes.

FALKNER: Sometimes? When?

LADY JESSICA: When I am foolish too — on a Monday evening.

> (*She is going off; he intercepts her, clasps her.*)

FALKNER: Ah! Will you drive me mad? Shall I tear you to pieces to find out if there is a heart somewhere within you?

LADY JESSICA: (*struggling*) Hush! Someone coming.

> (FALKNER *releases her.* SIR CHRISTOPHER *saunters in at back, smoking. Exit* LADY JESSICA.)

SIR CHRISTOPHER: Drop it, Ned! Drop it, my dear old boy! You're going too far.

FALKNER: (*going off after* LADY JESSICA) We won't discuss the matter, Kit.

SIR CHRISTOPHER: (*putting his arm in* FALKNER'*s, and holding him back*) Yes we will, Ned. George Nepean has been making a row, and I — well, I stroked him down. I said you were the soul of honour —

FALKNER: (*disengaging himself*) You were right. I am the soul of honour.

SIR CHRISTOPHER: And that you didn't mean anything by your attentions to Lady Jessica.

FALKNER: You were wrong. I do mean something.

SIR CHRISTOPHER: Well, what?

FALKNER: (*going*) That's my business — and Lady Jessica's.

SIR CHRISTOPHER: You forget — I introduced you here.

FALKNER: Thank you. You were very kind (*going off*).

SIR CHRISTOPHER: (*stopping him*) No, Ned; we'll have this out, here and now, please.

FALKNER: (*angrily*) Very well, let's have it out, here and now.

SIR CHRISTOPHER: (*with great friendship*) Come, old boy, there's no need for us to take this tone. Let's talk it over calmly, as old friends and men of the world.

FALKNER: Men of the world! If there is one beast in all the loathsome fauna of civilisation that I hate and despise, it is a man of the world! Good heaven, what men! what a world!

SIR CHRISTOPHER: Quite so, old fellow. It is a beastly bad world, — a lying, selfish, treacherous world! A rascally bad world every way. But bad as it is, this old world hasn't lived all these thousands of years without getting a little common sense into its wicked old noddle — especially with regard to its love affairs. And, speaking as an average bad citizen of this blackguardly old world, I want to ask you, Ned Falkner, what the devil you mean by making love to a married woman, and what good or happiness you expect to get for yourself or her? Where does it lead? What's to be the end of it?

FALKNER: I don't know — I don't care! I love her!

SIR CHRISTOPHER: But, my good Ned, she's another man's wife.

FALKNER: She's married to a man who doesn't value her, doesn't understand her, is utterly unworthy of her.

SIR CHRISTOPHER: All women are married to men who are utterly unworthy of them — bless 'em! All women are undervalued by their husbands — bless 'em! All women are misunderstood — bless 'em again!

FALKNER: Oh, don't laugh it off like that. Look at that thick clown of a husband. They haven't a single idea, or thought, or taste in common.

SIR CHRISTOPHER: That's her lookout before she married him.

FALKNER: But suppose she didn't know, didn't understand? Suppose experience comes too late?

SIR CHRISTOPHER: It generally does — in other things besides marriage!

FALKNER: But doesn't it make your blood boil to see a woman sacrificed for life?

SIR CHRISTOPHER: It does — my blood boils a hundred times a day. But marriages are made in heaven, and if once we set to work to repair celestial mistakes and indiscretions, we shall have our hands full. Come down to brass tacks. What's going to be the end of this?

FALKNER: I don't know — I don't care! I love her!

SIR CHRISTOPHER: You don't know? I'll tell you. Let's go over all the possibilities of the case. (*ticking them off on his fingers*) Possibility number one — you leave off loving her —

FALKNER: That's impossible.

SIR CHRISTOPHER: Possibility number two — you can, one or the other, or both of you, die by natural means; but you're both confoundedly healthy, so I'm afraid there's no chance of that. Possibility number three — you can die together by poison, or steel, or cold Thames water. I wouldn't trust *you* not to do a fool's trick of that sort; but, thank God, she's got too much sense. By the way, Ned, I don't think she cares very much for you —

FALKNER: She will.

SIR CHRISTOPHER: Well, well, we shall see. Possibility number four — you can keep on dangling at her heels, and being made a fool of, without getting any — 'forrarder'.

FALKNER: Mine is not a physical passion.

SIR CHRISTOPHER: (*Looks at him for two moments.*) Oh, that be hanged!

FALKNER: I tell you it is not.

SIR CHRISTOPHER: Well then, it ought to be.

FALKNER: (*very angrily*) Well then, it is! And say no more about it. What business is it of yours?

SIR CHRISTOPHER: Possibility number five — a liaison with her husband's connivance. Gilbert Nepean won't make a *mari complaisant*. Dismiss that possibility.

FALKNER: Dismiss them all.

SIR CHRISTOPHER: Don't you wish you could? But you'll have to face one of them, Ned. Possibility number six — a secret liaison. That's nearly impossible in society. And do you know what it means? It means in the end every inconvenience and disadvantage of marriage without any of its conveniences and advantages. It means endless discomfort, worry, and alarm. It means constant sneaking and subterfuges of the paltriest, pettiest kind. What do you say to that, my soul of honour?

FALKNER: I love her. I shall not try to hide my love.

SIR CHRISTOPHER: Oh, then you want a scandal? You'll get it! Have you thought what sort of a scandal it will be? Remember you've stuck yourself on a pedestal, and put a moral toga on. That's awkward. It wants such a lot of living up to. Gilbert Nepean is a nasty cuss and he'll make a nasty fuss. Possibility number seven, tableau one — Edward Falkner on his moral pedestal in a toga-esque attitude, honoured and idolised by the British public. Tableau two — a horrible scandal, a field day for Mrs Grundy; Edward Falkner is dragged from his pedestal, his toga is torn to pieces, his splendid reputation is blown to the winds, and he is rolled in the mud under the feet of the British public, who, six months ago, crowned him with garlands and shouted themselves hoarse in his praise. Are you prepared for that, my soul of honour?

FALKNER: If it comes.

SIR CHRISTOPHER: (*Shakes his head, makes a wry face, then proceeds.*) Possibility number eight. Last remaining possibility, only possible possibility — pull yourself together, pack up your traps, start tomorrow morning for Africa or Kamtschatka, Jericho or Hong-Kong. I'll go with you. What do you say?

FALKNER: No.

SIR CHRISTOPHER: No?

FALKNER: I wonder at you, Deering — I wonder at you coming to lecture me on love and morality.

SIR CHRISTOPHER: Ah, why?

Mrs Grundy: cf. note to p. 105 above.
Kamtschatka: peninsula in eastern Siberia.

FALKNER: (*with growing indignation*) I love a woman with the deepest love of my heart, with the purest worship of my soul. If that isn't moral, if that isn't sacred, if that isn't righteous, tell me, in heaven's name, what is? And you come to lecture me with your cut-and-dried worldly-wise philosophy, your mean little maxims, you come to lecture me on love and morality — you!

SIR CHRISTOPHER: Yes, I do! I may have had my attachments, I may have done this, that and the other. I'm not a hero, I'm not on a pedestal, I never put on a moral toga. But I owe no woman a sigh or a sixpence. I've never wronged any friend's sister, or daughter, or wife. And I tell you this, Ned Falkner, you're a fool if you think that anything can come of this passion of yours for Lady Jessica, except misery and ruin for her, embarrassment and disgrace for you, and kicking out of decent society for you both.

FALKNER: (*very firmly*) Very well. And will you please be the first to cut me? Or shall I cut you?

SIR CHRISTOPHER: You mean that, Ned?

FALKNER: Yes; if I'm a fool, leave me to my folly. (*very strongly*) Don't meddle with me.

SIR CHRISTOPHER: You do mean that, Ned? Our friendship is to end?

FALKNER: Yes. (*Sits, takes up paper.*)

SIR CHRISTOPHER: Very well. You'll understand some day, Ned, that I couldn't see an old comrade, a man who stood shoulder to shoulder with me all these years — you'll understand I couldn't see him fling away honour, happiness, reputation, future, everything, without saying one word and trying to pull him up. Goodbye, old chap (*going off*).

> (FALKNER *springs up generously, goes to him warmly, holding out both hands.*)

FALKNER: (*Cries out.*) Kit!

SIR CHRISTOPHER: Ned!

> (*The two men stand with hands clasped for some time, then* FALKNER *speaks in a soft, low, broken voice.*)

FALKNER: I love her, Kit — you don't know how much. When I see her, that turn of her head, that little toss of her curls, the little roguish face she makes — God couldn't make her like that and then blame a man for loving her! If He did — well, I'd rather miss heaven than one smile, one nod, one touch of her finger-tips!

SIR CHRISTOPHER: Oh, my poor dear old fellow, if you're as far gone as that, what the deuce am I to do with you?

> (*Enter at back* BEATRICE EBERNOE, *a tall, dark woman, about thirty, very beautiful and spiritual.*)

BEATRICE: Ned, here's a messenger from the Colonial Office with a very urgent letter for you.

FALKNER: For me?

> (*Enter* SERVANT *at back, bringing letter to* FALKNER.)

---

spiritual: the private edition, the licensing copy and French's read 'spirituelle'.

SERVANT: Important, sir. The messenger is waiting in the hall for your answer.

FALKNER: (*taking letter*) Very well, I'll come to him.

      (*Exit* SERVANT.)

FALKNER: (*reading letter*) More trouble out there. They want me to go out at once and negotiate. They think I could win over the chiefs and save a lot of bloodshed.

SIR CHRISTOPHER: You'll go, Ned?

FALKNER: I don't know.

SIR CHRISTOPHER: (*to* BEATRICE) Help me to persuade him.

BEATRICE: Can I? Have I any influence? Ned, for the sake of old days —

FALKNER: Ah no — let me be — I must think this over. (*Exit with distracted manner.*)

BEATRICE: Have you spoken to him?

SIR CHRISTOPHER: Yes; I gave him a thorough good slanging. Not a bit of use. When one of you holds us by a single hair, not all the king's horses and all the king's men can drag us back to that beggarly dusty old tow-path of duty.

BEATRICE: I won't believe men are so weak.

SIR CHRISTOPHER: Aren't we? There never was so sensible a man as I am in the management of other men's love affairs. You should have heard me lecture Ned. But once put me near you and I'm every bit as bad as that poor fool I've been basting! (*indicating* FALKNER *by inclination of the head towards the direction he has gone*)

BEATRICE: Oh no, Kit, I won't have you say that.

SIR CHRISTOPHER: But I am. How beautifully you played just now!

BEATRICE: Did I?

SIR CHRISTOPHER: Don't do it again.

BEATRICE: Why not?

SIR CHRISTOPHER: It's taking an unfair advantage of me. You oughtn't to arouse those divine feelings in a man's heart. You oughtn't to make me feel like a martyr, or a king, or a saint in a cathedral window, with all heaven's sunlight streaming through me! You oughtn't to do it! Because devil a ha'porth of a king, or a martyr, or a saint is there in me — and after you've been playing to me and lifted me into that seventh heaven of yours, I feel so mean and shabby when I drop down to earth again, and find myself a hard, selfish man of the world.

BEATRICE: Oh, I think there's a great deal of the martyr and saint and king in you.

SIR CHRISTOPHER: Do you? I believe there is! I know there would be if you'd only screw me up to it — and keep me screwed up. Beatrice there's nothing I couldn't do if you would only —

BEATRICE: (*going away from him*) Kit, you mustn't speak of this again. I can't quite forget.

SIR CHRISTOPHER: There's no need. While he was alive I never had one disloyal thought towards him. Now he's dead who could be so fitted to take care of his dearest treasure as his oldest friend?

BEATRICE: (*going away*) I can't quite forget.

SIR CHRISTOPHER: But you're young. What do you mean to do with your life?

BEATRICE: I'd some thoughts of entering a sisterhood.

SIR CHRISTOPHER: Ah no! Surely there are plenty of dear good ugly women in the world who can do that.

BEATRICE: But I must enjoy the luxury of self-sacrifice. Tell me how I can drink the deepest of that cup.

SIR CHRISTOPHER: Marry me. I'll give you the most splendid opportunities. Now if you and I were to join our forces, and take our poor Ned in hand, and —

BEATRICE: Hush!

(FALKNER *re-enters, evidently very much distracted.*)

SIR CHRISTOPHER: (*After a little pause, goes up to him.*) Well, Ned, what are you going to do?

FALKNER: (*in an agony of indecision*) I don't know! I don't know!

SIR CHRISTOPHER: You'll go, Ned? I'll go with you!

(*Enter* LADY JESSICA *at back.*)

BEATRICE: You'll go, Ned?

LADY JESSICA: Go? Where?

FALKNER: Nowhere. I shan't go, Kit. The man's waiting. I must give him my answer. (*Exit.* LADY JESSICA *looks after him.* SIR CHRISTOPHER *shrugs his shoulders at* BEATRICE.)

   Curtain

(*Five days pass between acts I and II.*)

  ACT II

  SCENE. *Private sitting-room in the Star and Garter, Shepperford-on-Thames, a room in a small high-class riverside hotel, furnished in the usual incongruous hotel fashion. Large French windows both right and left take up a good part of the back of the stage, and open upon a veranda which runs along outside. The pillars and roof of the veranda are smothered with trails of flowers and creeping plants. Beyond the veranda and very near to it is the Thames with opposite bank. Door down stage right. A sofa down stage right. A sideboard left. On the sideboard, plates, knives, forks, etc., dishes of fine peaches, grapes and strawberries, and a bottle each of hock, claret and champagne, as described in the text. A small table with writing materials at back between windows. A small table with white cloth laid, down stage, a little to the left of centre. A fireplace down stage left. Enter* FALKNER *in evening dress and French* WAITER.

FALKNER: (*menu in hand*) Crème à la Reine. We might have some trifle before the soup.

WAITER: Anchovy salad? Caviare?

FALKNER: Caviare.

WAITER: *Bien, m'sieu.* At what hour will *m'sieu* dine?

FALKNER: I don't know; I'm not sure that my friend will come at all. But tell the

---

(s.d.) SIR CHRISTOPHER shrugs . . . : French's and the promptbooks add a line for him: 'Not all the king's horses, nor all the king's men.' This may well have been used by Wyndham in performance to give himself the curtain-line.

Crème à la Reine: chicken soup made with cream.

cook to have everything prepared, so that we can have dinner very soon after my friend arrives.

WAITER: *Bien, m'sieu.*

FALKNER: (*reading menu*) Caviare. *Crème à la Reine. Rouget à l'Italienne.* Whitebait. *Petites Timbales à la Lucullus. Mousse de Foies Gras en Belle Vue.* Is your cook equal to those *entrées*?

WAITER: Oh, sir, he is equal to anything. Trust to me, sir. The cook shall be *magnifique.* The dinner shall be *magnifique.*

FALKNER: (*continuing*) *Poulardes poêlées, sauce Arcadienne. Selle de Mouton. Ortolans. Salade. Asperges en Branches. Pouding Mousseline, sauce Eglantine. Soufflé Glacé à l'Ananas.* Dessert. (WAITER *points to the dessert on the sideboard.*) And the wines?

WAITER: (*pointing to the wines on the sideboard*) Ayala, seventy-five, Johannisburg, sixty-eight. Château Haut-Brion, seventy-five. I have brought them from London myself. We have not these vintages here.

FALKNER: Good.

WAITER: It is but one friend that *m'sieu* expect?

FALKNER: Only one friend.

WAITER: *Bien, m'sieu.* (*Exit.*)

> (FALKNER *alone walks restlessly about the room for a few seconds, comes down; is arrested by something he hears outside the door, shows great delight. Re-enter* WAITER.)

WAITER: A lady; she say will Mr Falkner please to see her? She have lost her way.

FALKNER: Show her in.

> (*Exit* WAITER. FALKNER *alone walks eagerly about the room for a few seconds; his manner very eager and impatient, and quite different from what it had been before. Re-enter* WAITER, *showing in* LADY JESSICA, *most charmingly and coquettishly dressed in summer outdoor clothes. She comes in rather tempestuously, speaking as she enters, and going up to* FALKNER.)

LADY JESSICA: (*all in a breath*) Oh, my dear Mr Falkner, I've been staying with my cousin, and I was walking to the station, and by some unlucky chance I must have taken the wrong turning, for instead of finding myself at the station

---

Rouget à l'Italienne: red mullet in an Italian sauce.
Petites Timbales à la Lucullus: small pastry moulds filled with minced chicken or meat and served in a rich sauce.
Mousse de Foies Gras en Belle Vue: goose-liver pâté.
Poulardes poêlées: chicken cooked on top of the stove in a rich stock. The *sauce Arcadienne* appears to be Jones's invention.
Selle de Mouton: saddle of mutton.
Asperges en Branches: boiled asparagus.
Pouding Mousseline: steamed pudding of lemon, sugar, butter, eggs, etc., served with a sweet or whip sauce. In this case the name of the sauce (which means 'wild rose') appears to be Jones's invention.
Soufflé glacé à l'Ananas: iced pineapple soufflé.
Ayala . . . Johannisburg . . . Château Haut-Brion: the champagne, hock and claret referred to in the first s.d. of the act.

I found myself here; and as I'm very hungry, would you think it very dreadful if I asked you to give me just a mere mouthful of dinner?

FALKNER: (*intensely in calm low voice*) I'm delighted. (*to* WAITER) Will you let us have dinner as soon as it is ready?

WAITER: In half an hour, sir. And the friend, sir?

FALKNER: The friend?

WAITER: The friend that *m'sieu* expect — the friend of the dinner?

FALKNER: Oh, yes — if he comes, show him in.

LADY JESSICA: (*alarmed*) You don't expect —

FALKNER: (*glancing at* WAITER) Hush!

WAITER: (*absolutely impassive face*) *Bien, m'sieu!* (*Exit.*)

FALKNER: I'm so glad you've come. Look. (*holding out his hand*) I'm trembling with delight. I knew you would be here.

LADY JESSICA: I'm sure you didn't, for I didn't know myself two hours ago. It was only by chance that I happened to take the wrong turning.

FALKNER: No; the right turning. And not by chance. It was not chance that brought you to me.

LADY JESSICA: Oh, please, not that strain. I can't play up to it. Sit down and let us discuss something mundane — say dinner.

FALKNER: (*giving her the menu*) I hope you'll like what I've ordered. I sent the waiter up to London for some of the dishes and the wines.

LADY JESSICA: (*Takes menu, looks at it, shows much terror.*) What? You surely don't expect my poor little appetite to stand up to this dinner. Oh, let me be a warning to all, never to take the wrong turning when it may lead to a menu like this.

FALKNER: That's for your choice. You don't suppose I'd offer you anything but the very best.

LADY JESSICA: Yes, but a little of the very best is all I want; not all of it.

FALKNER: Take all of it that I can set before you.

LADY JESSICA: Oh, but think — there may be other deserving ladies in the world.

FALKNER: There is but you.

LADY JESSICA: (*Looks at him very much amused.*) And I came here to cure you of this folly. Ah, me! (*reading the menu*) *Mousse de Foies Gras. Poulardes poêlées, sauce Arcadienne* — what is *sauce Arcadienne*?

FALKNER: I don't know. Love is the sauce of life. Perhaps it's that.

LADY JESSICA: Yes, but don't dish it up too often or too strong. It's sure to be wasted.

FALKNER: My love for you is not wasted.

LADY JESSICA: No?

FALKNER: You'll return it. You'll love me at last.

LADY JESSICA: Shall I? *Crème à la Reine. Rouget à l'Italienne.* And if I did, what then?

FALKNER: Join your life to mine. Come to Africa with me.

LADY JESSICA: (*Shakes her head.*) Impossible! We should only shock the British public. They wouldn't understand us. *Ortolans. Salade. Asperges en Branches.* Besides, what would everybody say?

FALKNER: We shouldn't hear them.

LADY JESSICA: No; but they'd be talking all the same. Ha, ha! They'd call us the eloping philanthropists.

FALKNER: Would that matter?

LADY JESSICA: Oh, yes. A philanthropist may not elope. A tenor may. Doesn't it show the terrible irony there is in the heart of things, that the best meaning philanthropist in the world may not elope with his neighbour's wife? *Pouding Mousseline, sauce Eglantine.* What makes you so eager to go hunting slave-traders in Africa?

FALKNER: My father spent half his fortune putting slavery down. My grandfather spent half his life and died a pauper for the same cause.

LADY JESSICA: Well then, you should send a subscription to the Aborigines' Protection Society. That is how I keep up our family traditions.

FALKNER: How?

LADY JESSICA: My father had a shocking reputation, and my grandfather, Beau Lillywhite — Oh! (*shrug*) So I follow in their footsteps — at a respectful distance. I flirt with you. *Soufflé Glacé à l'Ananas.* There's no flirting in Central Africa, I suppose?

FALKNER: No flirting. Only heat and hunger and thirst, and helpless misery prolonged to a horrible death.

LADY JESSICA: (*genuinely moved*) Oh, I'm so sorry! Don't think me heartless about *that*. Perhaps if I had lived amongst it as you have —

FALKNER: Ah, if you had! you'd do as I ask you. You'd give all your heart to me, you'd give all your woman's care and tenderness to them, and you'd never hear one whisper of what people said of you.

LADY JESSICA: (*looking at him with real admiration*) How earnest you are! How devoted!

> (*Enter* WAITER *with knives and forks; he goes to table and begins laying it. They move away from each other.*)

LADY JESSICA: (*to* WAITER) What is *sauce Arcadienne*?

WAITER: *Pardon*! The cook is splendid. He is *magnifique* — but he has (*gesture*) *renversé* the *sauce Arcadienne* all over the shop.

FALKNER: It doesn't matter.

LADY JESSICA: Oh, I had set my heart on *sauce Arcadienne*.

FALKNER: The cook must make some more *sauce Arcadienne*.

WAITER: Ah, that is impossible till the middle of the night.

LADY JESSICA: Ah, what a pity! It is the one thing I long for, *sauce Arcadienne*.

FALKNER: Why?

LADY JESSICA: Because I don't know what it is.

WAITER: He will give you some *sauce Marguerite*.

LADY JESSICA: What is *sauce Marguerite*?

WAITER: (*all the while laying table*) Ah, it is *délicieuse*. It is the very best sauce that is in all the world.

LADY JESSICA: *Va pour la sauce Marguerite!* Oh, this dinner!

Aborigines' Protection Society: an influential organisation dedicated to the abolition of slavery and the well-being of colonised peoples.

(*A barrel organ strikes up outside.*)

WAITER: Ah, there is the beast of the organ man.

LADY JESSICA: No, let him be. I like music — and monkeys. (*to* FALKNER) Tell them to make haste.

FALKNER: Hurry the dinner.

WAITER: *Bien, m'sieu!* (*Exit.*)

LADY JESSICA: (*taking out watch*) Half-past seven, I've not an hour to stay.

FALKNER: Yes, your life if you will.

LADY JESSICA: Ah, no! You must be sensible. Think! What could come of it if I did love you? I should only break your heart or — what would be far worse — break my own.

FALKNER: Break it then — or let me break it. It's better to feel, it's better to suffer, than to be meanly happy. I love you, but I'd rather smother you in tears and blood than you should go on living this poor little heartless, withered life, choked up with all this dry society dust. Oh, can't I make you feel? Can't I make you live? Can't I make you love me?

LADY JESSICA: (*after a moment's pause, looking at him with great admiration*) Perhaps I do in my heart of hearts!

FALKNER: Ah! (*Springs to seize her; she struggles with him.*)

LADY JESSICA: Mr Falkner! Mr Falkner! If you please. Do you hear? Mr Falkner! (*Tears herself free.*) Will you please go and stop that horrid organ? Will you please?

> (FALKNER *bows, exit at door.* LADY JESSICA *panting, flurried, out of breath, goes up to the window fanning herself with handkerchief, passes on to veranda, stays there for a few moments fanning herself, suddenly starts back alarmed, comes into room, stands frightened, listening.* GEORGE NEPEAN *appears on veranda, comes up to window, looks in.*)

LADY JESSICA: (*trying to appear indifferent*) Ah, George!

GEORGE: I thought I caught sight of you. May I come in?

LADY JESSICA: Certainly.

GEORGE: (*entering*) I'm not intruding?

LADY JESSICA: Intruding? Oh, no. Have you heard from Gilbert?

GEORGE: Yes, I had a letter this morning. He may be back in two or three days.

LADY JESSICA: (*embarrassed*) Yes?

> (*A pause. The organ outside stops in the middle of a bar.*)

GEORGE: (*glancing at table*) You're dining here?

LADY JESSICA: Yes; just a small party. What brings you here?

GEORGE: I was going on to some friends at Horsham. I was waiting for the ferry when I caught sight of you. (*glancing at table and sideboard*) You're giving your friends rather a good dinner.

LADY JESSICA: H'm, rather. I've heard the cooking's very good here. (*a little pause*) There's a nest of cygnets outside. Have you seen them?

GEORGE: No.

Horsham: market-town in Surrey, about 17 miles from Guildford.

LADY JESSICA: Do come and have a look at them; they are so pretty. (*Going off at window followed by* GEORGE *when* FALKNER *enters at door. The two men look at each other.* LADY JESSICA *shows very great confusion and embarrassment. A long awkward pause.* GEORGE *looks very significantly at the sideboard and table.*)

GEORGE: (*to* LADY JESSICA) Gilbert must know of this. You understand? (*Bows. Exit by window and veranda.*)

LADY JESSICA: (*who has stood frightened and confused*) Did you hear? What can I do? What can I do?

FALKNER: (*calm, triumphant*) You must join your life to mine now.

LADY JESSICA: No, no! If you wish me ever to have one kind thought of you, get me out of this! Do something, find somebody to dine with us. Understand me, I know myself, if this leads to a scandal, I shall hate you in a week. Oh, do something! Do something!

FALKNER: Be calm. Be sure I'll do all I can to save you from a scandal. If that is impossible, be sure I'll do all I can to protect you from it.

LADY JESSICA: Ah, no! Save me from it. I can't face it. I can't give up my world, my friends. Oh, what can I do? I'll go back to town —

FALKNER: What good will that do? You had far better stay now. Sit down, be calm. Trust to me.

LADY JESSICA: Oh, you are good, and I'm such a coward.

FALKNER: Let us think what is the best thing to do.

LADY JESSICA: Can't we get somebody to dine with us?

LADY ROSAMUND: (*heard outside*) Oh, can't you wait, Freddie?

LADY JESSICA: (*looking off*) Hark! Rosy! (*Goes up to window.*)

FREDDIE: (*heard off*) What! Row two more miles without a drink?

LADY JESSICA: She's there in a boat with Freddie and another man. The men are landing. If we could only get them to stay and dine with us! We must! Go and find George Nepean and bring him back here. Make haste. When you come back, I'll have Rosy here.

FALKNER: In any case rely on me. I'm as firm as the earth beneath you. (*Exit at door.*)

LADY JESSICA: (*Goes up to window. Calls off.*) Rosy! Rosy! Come here! Yes, through there. Shush!

(LADY ROSAMUND *appears in the veranda.*)

LADY ROSAMUND: Jess! What's the matter? (*entering room*)

LADY JESSICA: Everything. You and Freddie must stay and dine here.

LADY ROSAMUND: We can't, we're going on to dine with Mrs Crespin at her new place, and we've got Jack Symons with us.

LADY JESSICA: *Va pour* Jack Symons, whoever he may be! He must stay and dine too!

LADY ROSAMUND: Impossible. Mrs Crespin has asked some people to meet us. As her place is on the river Jack proposed we should row down and dress there. What are you doing here? I thought you were at Barbara's.

LADY JESSICA: I was going back to town tonight. I thought I'd walk to the station — it's so delightful across the fields. Well, you know the path, I went on all right till I came to those two turnings, and then — I must have taken the wrong one, for, instead of finding myself at the station, I found myself here.

LADY ROSAMUND: Well?

LADY JESSICA: I'd been wandering about for over an hour, I was very hungry; I remembered Mr Falkner was staying here; so I came in and asked him to give me some dinner.

LADY ROSAMUND: It was very foolish of you!

LADY JESSICA: Yes, especially as George Nepean was waiting for the ferry and caught sight of me on the veranda.

LADY ROSAMUND: George Nepean!

LADY JESSICA: He came in, saw Mr Falkner, put a totally wrong construction on it all, and threatened to let Gilbert know.

LADY ROSAMUND: How could you be so imprudent, Jess? You must have known that —

LADY JESSICA: Oh, don't stand there rowing me. Help me out of this and I promise you I won't get into another.

LADY ROSAMUND: Why didn't you explain to George how it happened?

LADY JESSICA: So I would. Only when he came in I was alone. I felt sure he would put a wrong construction on it, so I told him I was dining here with a little party — then Mr Falkner came in, and I was too confused to say anything. Besides, I couldn't very well tell him the truth, because —

LADY ROSAMUND: Because what?

LADY JESSICA: Well, it's very curious, but the last time I was staying with Barbara the very same thing happened.

LADY ROSAMUND: What?

LADY JESSICA: I was walking to the station, and I must have taken the wrong turning, for, instead of finding myself at the station, I found myself here.

LADY ROSAMUND: What, twice?

LADY JESSICA: Yes.

LADY ROSAMUND: Oh, impossible!

LADY JESSICA: No, it isn't; for it actually happened.

LADY ROSAMUND: Do you mean to tell me that you —

LADY JESSICA: (*taking her up on the 'tell'*) Yes, I do. The sign-post is most deceptive.

LADY ROSAMUND: It must be.

LADY JESSICA: But the other time it was really a mistake, and I dined here all alone.

LADY ROSAMUND: Honour?

LADY JESSICA: Really, really honour!

LADY ROSAMUND: I cannot imagine how you, a woman of the world —

LADY JESSICA: Oh, do not nag me. Mr Falkner has gone for George. You must stay here and tell George you are dining with me.

LADY ROSAMUND: What about Freddie and Jack? See if they've come back to the boat.

LADY JESSICA: (*looking off at window*) Not yet. Here's Mr Falkner — alone. (*Re-enter* FALKNER *at window.*) — Well, where is he?

FALKNER: (*to* LADY ROSAMUND) How d'ye do? (*to* LADY JESSICA) He took

a fly that was waiting outside and drove to the post office. I went there and
made inquiries. He stopped, sent off a telegram –

LADY JESSICA: That must have been to Gilbert.

FALKNER: Then he drove off towards Staines. Shall I follow him?

LADY JESSICA: Yes. No. What's the use? He may be anywhere by now.

LADY ROSAMUND: Besides we can't stay to dinner.

LADY JESSICA: You must – you must! I must be able to tell Gilbert that somebody dined with me.

LADY ROSAMUND: Jess, I'll write to George when I get back tonight, and tell
him that I dined with you here.

LADY JESSICA: Oh, you good creature! No! Write now, on the hotel paper. Then
he'll see you were actually here.

LADY ROSAMUND: Pen, ink, and paper.

FALKNER: (*at table up stage*) Here!

                (LADY ROSAMUND *seats herself at table.*)

LADY JESSICA: Rosy, I've got a better plan than that.

LADY ROSAMUND: What?

LADY JESSICA: Could you be in town tomorrow morning?

LADY ROSAMUND: Yes – why?

LADY JESSICA: Write to George to call on you there. I'll drop in a little before he
comes. Then we can see what frame of mind he is in, and explain things
accordingly. We can manage him so much better between us.

LADY ROSAMUND: Very well, make haste. (*Looks off at window.*) Mr Falkner,
will you go into the bar, run up against my husband and his friend, and keep
them busy there till I get back into the boat.

FALKNER: Very well. (*Exit at door.*)

LADY ROSAMUND: Now, what shall I say?

LADY JESSICA: (*dictating*) 'My dear George – '

LADY ROSAMUND: (*writing*) 'My dear George' – Oh, this pen! (*Throws away the
pen, takes up another, tries it.*)

LADY JESSICA: We must make it very short and casual, as if you didn't attach
much importance to it.

LADY ROSAMUND: (*Throws away second pen.*) That's as bad!

LADY JESSICA: (*taking out a gold stylograph, giving it to* LADY ROSAMUND.)
Here's my stylograph. Take care of it, it was a birthday present.

LADY ROSAMUND: 'Monday evening. My dear George – '

LADY JESSICA: (*dictating*) 'Jess has told me that you have just been here and that
you were surprised at her presence. She fears you may have put a wrong construction on what you saw. She was too flurried at the moment to explain.
But if you will kindly call on me tomorrow, Tuesday morning, at Cadogan
Gardens at' – what time will suit you?

LADY ROSAMUND: Twelve?

LADY JESSICA: Yes, and I'll be there a few minutes before.

---

stylograph: a form of fountain-pen.
Cadogan Gardens: the Cadogan estate, extending west of *Sloane Street* in Chelsea was devel-
oped from the mid-1870s as a wealthy and fashionable residential district.

LADY ROSAMUND: (*writing*) 'Twelve.'

LADY JESSICA: (*dictating*) 'I will give you a full explanation. You will then see how very simple the whole affair was, and how little cause you had for your suspicions of her.' That will do, won't it?

LADY ROSAMUND: Yes, I think. 'Yours sincerely' — no, 'Yours affectionately, Rosy.'

LADY JESSICA: '*PS* — You had perhaps better say nothing about this to Gilbert until after we have met. When you see how trifling the matter is, you can tell Gilbert or not, as you please.'

LADY ROSAMUND: (*writing*) 'As you please. George Nepean, Esquire.' What's his number?

LADY JESSICA: Two-twenty.

LADY ROSAMUND: (*writing*) 'Two-twenty, Sloane Street.'

LADY JESSICA: What about Freddie? Shall we tell him?

LADY ROSAMUND: Oh, no! I wouldn't trust my Freddie in a matter of this kind. He'd put a wrong construction on it — men always do. (*Puts letter in envelope, seals it.*)

LADY JESSICA: But if George asks him?

LADY ROSAMUND: Freddie won't come up to town tomorrow. We'll see how George takes it, and we'll keep Freddie out of it, if we can. (*She has risen, leaving stylograph on writing-table, where it remains. She seals letter.*) Stamp?

LADY JESSICA: I've got one in my purse. (*Takes letter.*)

LADY ROSAMUND: (*Has caught sight of the menu, has taken it up.*) Jess, you'll go straight to the station now?

LADY JESSICA: Yes. I'm awfully hungry —

LADY ROSAMUND: Yes, but I don't think this dinner would agree with you. (*Puts the menu down significantly.*)

LADY JESSICA: Very well. But I am hungry.

LADY ROSAMUND: And Jess, if I get you out of this — you won't take the wrong turning again?

LADY JESSICA: No! no!

LADY ROSAMUND: Honour?

LADY JESSICA: Honour! Really, really honour! Rosy, you know this is only a silly freak — nothing more.

LADY ROSAMUND: I may be sure of that, Jess? Honour?

LADY JESSICA: Honour! Really, really honour!

LADY ROSAMUND: (*Kisses her.*) I must be going. Tomorrow!

LADY JESSICA: Tomorrow at Cadogan Gardens, ten minutes to twelve. (*Rings bell.*)

LADY ROSAMUND: (*at window*) Those men are in the boat. My Freddie is look-ing for me. What shall I tell him? (*Exit at window.*)

>(LADY JESSICA *goes up to window, keeping well behind curtains. Looks off for a few seconds, then comes down. Enter* WAITER.)

LADY JESSICA: (*giving letter*) Please get that posted at once.

WAITER: (*taking letter*) *Bien, madame.* (*Exit with letter.*)

>(*Re-enter* FALKNER *at window.*)

LADY JESSICA: They've gone?

FALKNER: Yes. What have you done?

LADY JESSICA: Rosy has written to George to come and see her tomorrow morning at Cadogan Gardens. You had better come too.

FALKNER: At what time?

LADY JESSICA: Say a quarter to one. George will have gone by then and we can tell you if he accepts our explanation.

FALKNER: What is the explanation to be?

LADY JESSICA: That Rosy and I were dining together here, that she hadn't arrived, that you happened to come into the room, and that George saw you and put a wrong construction on it. That will be all right, won't it?

FALKNER: Yes — I daresay. I wish it had been possible to tell the truth.

LADY JESSICA: The truth? What truth? Rosy was actually here, and she *might* have stayed and dined with me — only she didn't — and — well, if it isn't the truth, it's only a little one.

FALKNER: I think those things are all the same size.

LADY JESSICA: Oh, please don't be disagreeable, just at our last moment too.

FALKNER: Our last moment? Ah, no, no, no! (*approaching her*)

LADY JESSICA: Ah, yes, yes, yes! I promised Rosy I'd go straight to the station—

FALKNER: There's no train till eight fifty. What harm can there be in your staying to dinner now?

LADY JESSICA: I promised Rosy I wouldn't. I'm fearfully hungry —
        (*Enter* WAITER *with letter on salver.*)

WAITER: (*advancing with letter on salver to* LADY JESSICA) *Pardon*, is this letter for *madame*?

LADY JESSICA: (*Takes letter, shows fright.*) Yes. Excuse me. Who brought it?
        (*Opens letter, takes out telegram.*)

WAITER: She is here in the passage.

LADY JESSICA: (*Opens telegram; shows great alarm. Goes to door.*) Ferris.

FERRIS: (*coming to door*) Yes, my lady.

LADY JESSICA: Come in.

WAITER: *Bien, madame.* (*Exit.*)

LADY JESSICA: When did this telegram come?

FERRIS: This afternoon, my lady. The moment I got in, Mr Rawlins said to me, 'Mr Nepean is coming back tonight; I've just had a telegram from him to get his room ready. And I expect this telegram is for her ladyship', he said, and he gave me that telegram. 'What time will her ladyship be back tonight?' he said. 'I don't know', I said. 'Where is her ladyship now?' he said. 'I don't know', I said.

LADY JESSICA: You didn't know?

FERRIS: No, my lady.

LADY JESSICA: Then why did you come here?

FERRIS: The other night when I was bringing your ladyship's shawl to the tent, I happened to hear you mention this hotel. I didn't think anything of it, your ladyship, and I didn't in the least expect to find you here, I assure your ladyship. But I thought your ladyship would like to be apprised that Mr Nepean is coming home tonight, and so I came, as I may say by pure chance, my lady; just as you might have come yourself, my lady.

LADY JESSICA: Quite right, Ferris. (*to* FALKNER) Mr Nepean is coming home tonight. He reaches Paddington at ten.

FERRIS: I've got a cab outside, my lady, and I've looked out the trains. If we make haste, we can drive over to Walton and just catch a train there. But we haven't a moment to spare.

LADY JESSICA: Come then.

FERRIS: I hope I've done right, my lady?

LADY JESSICA: Quite right, Ferris. (*to* FALKNER) No. Please don't trouble to come out. I'd rather you didn't. Rosy and I will dine with you some other night. Goodnight. (*Exit* FERRIS.)

FALKNER: (*seizing* LADY JESSICA's *hand*) And tomorrow?

LADY JESSICA: Tomorrow? (*grimace*) Petits rows conjugals – sauce tartare. (*Exit at door.* FALKNER *enraged, sulky, disappointed, takes several turns about the room, kicks a hassock savagely. Enter* WAITER *with two little morsels of caviare.*)

FALKNER: What's that?

WAITER: Caviare on toast.

FALKNER: Hang the caviare. Bring in the soup.

WAITER: Ah, it is not yet ready, two, three minutes. I am very sorry, but the cook say the *sauce Marguerite* –

FALKNER: What about it?

WAITER: It will not be made.

FALKNER: Very well.

WAITER: And the *salade*?

FALKNER: What about the salad?

WAITER: Will *m'sieu* mix it?

FALKNER: No, mix it yourself.

WAITER: *Bien, m'sieu* (*going off*).

FALKNER: Waiter!

WAITER: Sir!

FALKNER: (*pointing to cover laid for* LADY JESSICA) Take those confounded things away.

WAITER: Sir!

FALKNER: Take those confounded things away; I'm going to dine alone.

WAITER: *Bien, m'sieu.* (*Takes up the second cover, and the one plate of caviare, leaving the other on the table in* FALKNER's *place. Is going off with them.*)

FALKNER: Bring in the soup.

WAITER: *Bien, m'sieu.* (*Exit with things, leaving door open.* SIR CHRISTOPHER's *voice heard outside.*)

SIR CHRISTOPHER: Mr Falkner?

WAITER: Yes, sir. In number ten, sir.

SIR CHRISTOPHER: Has he dined?

WAITER: Not yet, sir. What name, sir?

SIR CHRISTOPHER: Oh, never mind my name. Show me in.

WAITER: (*at door, announcing*) The friend of the dinner.

                (*Enter* SIR CHRISTOPHER *in morning dress. Exit* WAITER.)

SIR CHRISTOPHER: (*very cordially*) Ah, dear old boy, here you are. (*shaking hands cordially*) All alone?

FALKNER: (*very sulkily*) Yes.

SIR CHRISTOPHER: (*looking at table*) You haven't dined?

FALKNER: No.

SIR CHRISTOPHER: That's all right. I'll join you. What's the matter?

FALKNER: Nothing.

SIR CHRISTOPHER: Nothing?

FALKNER: (*very sulky throughout*) No. What should be?

SIR CHRISTOPHER: You look upset.

FALKNER: Not at all.

SIR CHRISTOPHER: That's all right. (*going up to table very ravenously*) I say, old chap, dinner won't be long, eh?

FALKNER: No, why?

SIR CHRISTOPHER: I'm famished. I was over at Hounslow, I had no end of work to get through, so I stuck to it. I've had nothing but a biscuit and a glass of sherry since breakfast. I was going up to town for dinner, then I remembered you wrote to me from here; so I thought I'd run over on the chance of finding you. And here you are. (*cordially*) Well, how are you?

FALKNER: I'm very well.

SIR CHRISTOPHER: That's all right. And, and about the lady?

FALKNER: What about her?

SIR CHRISTOPHER: You're going to behave like a good true fellow and give her up, eh?

FALKNER: Yes, I suppose.

SIR CHRISTOPHER: That's all right. Love 'em, worship 'em, make the most of 'em! Go down on your knees every day and thank God for having sent them into this dreary world for our good and comfort. But, don't break your heart over 'em! Don't ruin your career for 'em! Don't lose a night's rest for 'em! They aren't worth it — except one! (*very softly*)

FALKNER: (*same sulky mood*) You're full of good advice.

SIR CHRISTOPHER: It's the only thing I am full of. I say, old fellow, could you hurry them up with the dinner? (FALKNER *goes and rings bell.* SIR CHRISTOPHER *casually takes up menu.*) No, Ned, they're not worth it, bless their hearts. And the man who — (*Suddenly stops, his face illuminated with delighted surprise.*) Ned!

FALKNER: What?

SIR CHRISTOPHER: This isn't the menu for tonight?

FALKNER: Yes.

SIR CHRISTOPHER: (*incredulously*) No! Dear old fellow! (*looking at him with*

---

morning dress: the grey trousers and dark jacket appropriate for business and social calls during the day: it later turns out that Sir Christopher has been on business.
Hounslow: 11 miles from Charing Cross, to the south-west.

great admiration) Dear old fellow! I say, Ned, you do yourself very well when
you're all alone.
FALKNER: Why shouldn't I?
SIR CHRISTOPHER: Why shouldn't you? Why shouldn't you? (*reading menu*)
FALKNER: Why shouldn't I? Excuse me a moment. (*Exit at door.*)

> (SIR CHRISTOPHER, *left alone, reads over the menu, showing great
> satisfaction, then goes up to sideboard, takes up bottles of wine,
> looks at them, shows great satisfaction, rubs his hands, comes up to
> writing-table, happens to catch sight of the stylograph pen, picks it
> up, is arrested by something inscribed on it, shows astonishment,
> comes down stage looking at it intently, puzzled and surprised. As
> WAITER re-enters with soup, SIR CHRISTOPHER puts stylograph
> in pocket.*)

WAITER: (*putting soup on table*) Mr Falkner say will you please excuse him? He
has gone to London just now, this minute.
SIR CHRISTOPHER: Gone to London!
WAITER: On very important business. He say will you please make yourself at
home with the dinner?
SIR CHRISTOPHER: (*puzzled*) Gone to London! What on earth — (*resolutely and
instantly takes seat at head of table.*) Serve up the dinner! Sharp!
WAITER: Caviare on toast?
SIR CHRISTOPHER: Oh, damn the caviare! Open the champagne! (*Takes the
morsel of caviare and throws it down his throat; helps himself to soup,
peppers it vigorously. Meantime WAITER opens champagne and pours out a
glass.*) The fish! Quick! (SIR CHRISTOPHER *throws spoonful after spoonful
of soup down his throat. The organ outside strikes up in the middle of the
bar at which it left off, a very rowdy street tune.*)
>   *Curtain*

(*One night passes between acts II and III.*)

ACT III

SCENE.   LADY ROSAMUND's *drawing-room, Cadogan Gardens, a
very elegant modern apartment, furnished in good taste. Door at back. Door right.
Large bow window forming an alcove up stage right. Fireplace left. LADY ROSA-
MUND discovered in outdoor morning dress. FOOTMAN showing in LADY
JESSICA at back.*
FOOTMAN: (*Announces.*) Lady Jessica Nepean. (*Exit FOOTMAN.*)
LADY ROSAMUND: Well, dear?
LADY JESSICA: (*Kisses her very affectionately.*) Oh, Rosy —
LADY ROSAMUND: What's the matter?
LADY JESSICA: Directly you had gone Ferris came in with a telegram from

---

The fish! Quick!: French's adds 'and the entrées — bring them both up at the same time — bring
up the whole bag of tricks!' The presence of a similar addition in the promptbooks and in
captions to illustrations in contemporary reviews suggests that Wyndham spoke this version of
the curtain-line.

Gilbert, saying he was coming home last night. Of course I flew back to town. When I got there I found a later telegram saying he hadn't been able to finish his business, and that he would come back today.

LADY ROSAMUND: (*taking letter from pocket*) He reaches Paddington at twelve.

LADY JESSICA: How do you know?

LADY ROSAMUND: (*giving letter*) Read that.

LADY JESSICA: (*looking at handwriting*) From George Nepean.

LADY ROSAMUND: Yes. He came here an hour ago to see me, and left that note. I'm afraid George means to be very horrid.

LADY JESSICA: (*reading*) 'Dear Lady Rosamund, I shall, of course, be quite ready to listen to any explanation you may have to offer. I will come back to Cadogan Gardens on my return from Paddington. I am now on my way there to meet Gilbert, who arrives from Devon at twelve. It is only fair to tell you that on leaving Lady Jessica last evening I telegraphed him I had a most serious communication to make to him, and that on his arrival I shall tell him exactly what I saw.' George does mean to be horrid (*retaining letter*).

LADY ROSAMUND: I cannot imagine how you —

LADY JESSICA: Oh, do not preach. I tell you it was the sign-post. It is most deceptive.

LADY ROSAMUND: It must be. The next time you come to that sign-post —

LADY JESSICA: I shall know which turning to take! You needn't fear.

LADY ROSAMUND: My Freddie's in a small fever.

LADY JESSICA: What about?

LADY ROSAMUND: My coming up to town this morning.

LADY JESSICA: You're sure he'll stay down there? He won't come up and — interfere?

LADY ROSAMUND: Oh, no, poor old dear! I snubbed him thoroughly and left him grizzling in his tent, like Achilles. He'll stay there all day, fuming and trying to screw up his courage to have a tremendous row with me when I get back to dinner this evening. I know my Freddie so well!

 (FREDDIE *saunters in at back, half timid, half defiant.*)

LADY ROSAMUND: (*looking at him with amused surprise.*) Hillo, my friend! Hillo!

FREDDIE: (*Very severe and dignified, takes no notice of her.*) How do, Jess?

 (LADY JESSICA *alternately reads* GEORGE's *letter and looks at* FREDDIE.)

LADY ROSAMUND: What has brought you to town?

FREDDIE: I came up with a purpose.

LADY ROSAMUND: Oh, don't say that. People are always so horrid who do things with a purpose.

FREDDIE: I came up with Mrs Crespin. She has lost the address of the cook that you gave her last evening. I told her you were in town. She will call here for it.

LADY ROSAMUND: (*sweetly*) Very well.

Achilles: during the siege of Troy Achilles quarrelled with the Greek commander Agamemnon, and remained sulking in his tent until the killing of his friend Patroclus roused him to fight again.

FREDDIE: Do you intend to stay in, or go out this morning?

LADY ROSAMUND: That depends. I may stay in − or I may go out. What are you going to do?

FREDDIE: That depends. I may stay in − or − I may go out.

LADY ROSAMUND: Very well, dear, do as you please. I'll take the alternative. (*to* LADY JESSICA) Come and take your things off in my room.

LADY JESSICA: (*glancing at* FREDDIE) But don't you think −

FREDDIE: (*rising with great dignity, placing himself in front of them*) I have come up to town this morning, because for the future I intend to place everything in this house on a new basis, an entirely opposite basis from that on which it now stands.

LADY ROSAMUND: You're going to turn all the furniture upside down! Oh, I wouldn't!

FREDDIE: Hitherto I have been content to be a cipher in this establishment. I will be a cipher no longer.

LADY ROSAMUND: No, I wouldn't. Come along, Jess!

LADY JESSICA: But − (*showing* GEORGE'*s letter*)

LADY ROSAMUND: We'll talk it over upstairs. Run away to your club, Freddie, and think over what figure you would like to be. I daresay we can arrange it. (*Exit* LADY ROSAMUND, *taking off* LADY JESSICA, *and closing the door rather sharply behind her.*)

FREDDIE: (*Left alone, marches up to the door, calls out in a forcible-feeble scream.*) I will not be a cipher! I will not be a cipher! (*Comes to centre of stage, gesticulates, his lips moving, sits down very resolutely, and then says in a tone of solemn conviction −*) I will *not* be a cipher!

(*Enter* FOOTMAN *at back, announcing.*)

FOOTMAN: Sir Christopher Deering!

(*Enter* SIR CHRISTOPHER. *Exit* FOOTMAN.)

SIR CHRISTOPHER: (*shaking hands*) I've just come on from Lady Jessica's. They told me I should find her here.

FREDDIE: She's upstairs with my wife.

SIR CHRISTOPHER: Can I see her for a few minutes?

FREDDIE: I don't know. Deering old fellow, we're tiled in, aren't we? If I ask your advice −

SIR CHRISTOPHER: Certainly, Freddie. What is it?

FREDDIE: I've been married for seven years −

SIR CHRISTOPHER: Seven years is it? It doesn't seem so long.

FREDDIE: Oh, doesn't it? Yes it does. Rosy and I have never quite hit it off from the first.

SIR CHRISTOPHER: No? How's that?

FREDDIE: I don't know. When I want to do anything, she doesn't. When I want to go anywhere, she won't. When I like anybody, she hates them. And when I hate anybody, she likes them. And − well − there it is in a nutshell.

SIR CHRISTOPHER: Hum! I should humour her a little, Freddie − let her have her own way. Try kindness.

FREDDIE: Kindness? I tell you this, Deering, kindness is a grand mistake. And I made that grand mistake at starting. I began with riding her on the snaffle. I ought to have started her on the curb, eh?

SIR CHRISTOPHER: Well, there's something to be said for that method in some cases. Kindness won't do, you say? Why not try firmness?

FREDDIE: I have.

SIR CHRISTOPHER: Well?

FREDDIE: Well, firmness is all very well, but there's one great objection to firmness.

SIR CHRISTOPHER: What's that?

FREDDIE: It leads to such awful rows, and chronic rowing does upset me so. After about two days of it, I feel so seedy and shaky and nervous, I don't know what to do. (*Has a sudden wrathful outburst.*) And she comes up as smiling as ever!

SIR CHRISTOPHER: Poor old fellow!

FREDDIE: I say, Deering, what would you advise me to do?

SIR CHRISTOPHER: Well, it requires some consideration —

FREDDIE: (*with deep conviction*) You know, Deering, there must be some way of managing them.

SIR CHRISTOPHER: One would think so. There must be some way of managing them!

FREDDIE: (*Has another wrathful outburst.*) And I used to go and wait outside her window, night after night, for hours! What do you think of that?

SIR CHRISTOPHER: I should say it was time very badly laid out.

FREDDIE: (*pursuing his reminiscences*) Yes, and caught a chill on my liver and was laid up for six weeks.

SIR CHRISTOPHER: Poor old fellow!

FREDDIE: I say, Deering, what would you do?

SIR CHRISTOPHER: Well — well — it requires some consideration.

FREDDIE: (*walking about*) You know, Deering, I may be an ass —

SIR CHRISTOPHER: Oh!

FREDDIE: (*firmly*) Yes, I may be an ass, but I'm not a *silly* ass. I may be a fool, but I'm not a *d-ee-d* fool! Now there's something going on this morning between Rosamund and Jess. They're hob-nobbing and whispering, and when two of 'em get together —

SIR CHRISTOPHER: Oh, my dear fellow, when two women get together, do you think it can ever be worth a man's while to ask what nonsense or mischief they're chattering? By the way, did you say that I could see Lady Jessica?

FREDDIE: She's upstairs with Rosy. I'll send her to you. Deering, if you were married, would you be a cipher in your own house?

SIR CHRISTOPHER: Not if I could help it.

FREDDIE: (*very determinedly*) Neither will I. (*Exit.*)

(SIR CHRISTOPHER, *left alone, takes out the stylograph and looks*

---

snaffle: 'Bridle consisting of snaffle-bit, or plain slender jointed bit without curb, and single rein' (*OED*). The *curb* is a 'chain or strap passing under the lower jaw of the horse', and allows tighter control of the mount by its rider.

> *at it carefully. In a few seconds enter* LADY JESSICA. *As she enters he drops his left hand, which holds the stylograph.*)

SIR CHRISTOPHER: How d'ye do?

LADY JESSICA: How d'ye do? You wish to see me?

> (SIR CHRISTOPHER *presents the stylograph. She shows alarm.*)

SIR CHRISTOPHER: I see from the inscription that this belongs to you.

LADY JESSICA: (*taking stylograph*) Where did you find it?

SIR CHRISTOPHER: In a private sitting-room at the Star and Garter at Shepperford.

LADY JESSICA: I must have left it there some time ago. I could not imagine where I had lost it. Thank you so much.

SIR CHRISTOPHER: Pray don't mention it. Good morning. (*Is going.*)

LADY JESSICA: Good morning. (SIR CHRISTOPHER *has got to door at back.*) Sir Christopher — (*He stops.*) You were at Shepperford — ?

SIR CHRISTOPHER: Last evening.

LADY JESSICA: Pretty little spot.

SIR CHRISTOPHER: Charming.

LADY JESSICA: And a very good hotel?

SIR CHRISTOPHER: First-class. Such splendid cooking!

LADY JESSICA: The cooking's good, is it? — Oh, yes, I dined there once, some time ago.

SIR CHRISTOPHER: I dined there last night.

LADY JESSICA: Did you? At the *table d'hôte*?

SIR CHRISTOPHER: No, in a private sitting-room. Number ten.

LADY JESSICA: With a friend, I suppose?

SIR CHRISTOPHER: No. All alone.

LADY JESSICA: All alone? In number ten?

SIR CHRISTOPHER: All alone. In number ten.

LADY JESSICA: I suppose you — I suppose —

SIR CHRISTOPHER: Suppose nothing except that I had a remarkably good dinner, that I picked up that stylograph and brought it up to town with me last night. And there is an end of the whole matter, I assure you. Good morning (*going*).

LADY JESSICA: Good morning. Sir Christopher — you (*He is again arrested at door.*) — you — a — (*He comes down to her.*)

LADY JESSICA: May I trust you?

SIR CHRISTOPHER: If I can help you — yes.

LADY JESSICA: Nothing — nothing is known about my being there?

SIR CHRISTOPHER: Your being there?

LADY JESSICA: (*after a pause — embarrassed*) I was to have dined in number ten.

SIR CHRISTOPHER: All alone?

LADY JESSICA: (*same embarrassed manner*) No — with Mr Falkner. I was coming up to town from my cousin's. I started to walk to the station. I must have taken the wrong turning, for instead of finding myself at the station, I found myself at the Star and Garter. I was very hungry and I asked Mr Falkner to give me a mere mouthful of dinner.

SIR CHRISTOPHER: A mere mouthful.

LADY JESSICA: And then George Nepean caught sight of me, came in, saw Mr

Falkner, and telegraphed my husband that I — of course Gilbert will believe the worst and I — oh, I don't know what to do!

SIR CHRISTOPHER: Can I be of any service?

LADY JESSICA: How would you advise me to — to get out of it?

SIR CHRISTOPHER: Let us go over the various possibilities of the case. There are only two.

LADY JESSICA: What are they?

SIR CHRISTOPHER: Possibility number one — get out of it by telling fibs. Possibility number two — get out of it by telling the truth. Why not possibility number two?

LADY JESSICA: Oh, I couldn't!

SIR CHRISTOPHER: Couldn't what?

LADY JESSICA: Tell my husband that I was going to dine with Mr Falkner.

SIR CHRISTOPHER: But was it quite by accident?

LADY JESSICA: Oh, quite! Quite!

SIR CHRISTOPHER: Well — ?

LADY JESSICA: But if Gilbert made inquiries —

SIR CHRISTOPHER: Well?

LADY JESSICA: It was such a good dinner that Mr Falkner ordered.

SIR CHRISTOPHER: It was! It was! If he didn't expect you, why did he order that very excellent dinner?

LADY JESSICA: I'm sure you ought to be the last person to ask that, for it seems you ate it.

SIR CHRISTOPHER: I did.

LADY JESSICA: It's an ill wind that blows nobody good!

SIR CHRISTOPHER: I'm not grumbling at the wind, or at the dinner, but if I'm to help you out of this, you had better tell me all the truth. Especially as I'm not your husband. Now frankly, is this a mere indiscretion, or — (*looking at her*)

LADY JESSICA: A mere indiscretion, nothing more. Honour — really, really honour.

SIR CHRISTOPHER: A mere indiscretion that will never be repeated.

LADY JESSICA: A mere indiscretion that will never be repeated. You believe me?

SIR CHRISTOPHER: Yes, I believe you, and I'll help you.

LADY JESSICA: Thank you! Thank you!

SIR CHRISTOPHER: Now did Falkner expect you?

LADY JESSICA: He ought not.

SIR CHRISTOPHER: He ought not. But he did.

LADY JESSICA: I told him I shouldn't come.

SIR CHRISTOPHER: Which was exactly the same as telling him you would.

LADY JESSICA: Have you seen Mr Falkner?

SIR CHRISTOPHER: Only for a minute just before dinner. He came up to town.

LADY JESSICA: Without any dinner?

SIR CHRISTOPHER: Without any dinner. To come back to these two possibilities.

LADY JESSICA: Yes, Rosy and I have decided on — on —

SIR CHRISTOPHER: On possibility number one, tell a fib. I put that possibility first out of a natural deference and chivalry towards ladies. The only objection I have to telling fibs is that you get found out.

LADY JESSICA: Oh, not always! I mean, if you arrange things not perhaps exactly as they were, but as they ought to have been.

SIR CHRISTOPHER: I see. In that way a lie becomes a sort of idealised and essential truth —

LADY JESSICA: Yes. Yes —

SIR CHRISTOPHER: I'm not a good hand at — idealising.

LADY JESSICA: Ah, but then you're a man! No, I can't tell the truth. Gilbert would never believe me. Would you — after that dinner?

SIR CHRISTOPHER: The dinner would be some tax on my digestion.

(LADY ROSAMUND *enters, followed by* FREDDIE, *with a self-important and self-assertive air.*)

LADY ROSAMUND: Good morning. Sir Christopher.

SIR CHRISTOPHER: (*shaking hands*) Good morning, Lady Rosamund.

LADY ROSAMUND: Jess, I've had to tell Freddie.

LADY JESSICA: And I've had to tell Sir Christopher. He was at Shepperford last evening, and he has promised to help us.

FREDDIE: I must say, Jess, that I think you have behaved — well — in a — confounded silly way.

LADY JESSICA: That is perfectly understood.

FREDDIE: (*solemnly*) When a woman once forgets what is due —

LADY JESSICA: Oh, don't moralise! Rosy, Sir Christopher, do ask him not to improve the occasion.

SIR CHRISTOPHER: The question is, Freddie, whether you will help us in getting Lady Jessica out of this little difficulty.

FREDDIE: Well, I suppose I must join in.

LADY JESSICA: Now, Rosy, do you fully understand —

SIR CHRISTOPHER: I don't think I do. What is the exact shape which possibility number one has taken — or is going to take?

LADY ROSAMUND: Jess and I had arranged to have a little *tête-à-tête* dinner at Shepperford. Jess got there first. I hadn't arrived. George saw Jess at the window, and came in. At that moment Mr Falkner happened to come into the room, and Jess knowing that appearances were against her, was confused, and couldn't on the spur of the moment give the right explanation.

SIR CHRISTOPHER: I suppose the waiter will confirm that right explanation?

LADY JESSICA: The waiter? I hadn't thought of that. Waiters will confirm anything, won't they? Couldn't you settle with the waiter?

SIR CHRISTOPHER: Well, I —

LADY JESSICA: You did have the dinner, you know!

SIR CHRISTOPHER: Very well, I'll settle with the waiter.

(*Enter* FOOTMAN.)

FOOTMAN: (*at back announcing*) Mrs Crespin.

(*Enter* MRS CRESPIN. *Exit* FOOTMAN.)

MRS CRESPIN: (*Shows a little surprise at seeing them all, then goes very affection-*

(s.d.) Enter MRS CRESPIN: French's adds an s.d.: 'SIR CHRISTOPHER *cautions* LADY JESSICA *by putting his fingers to his lips.*'

ately to LADY ROSAMUND.) Good morning, dear. Good morning, Sir
Christopher. (SIR CHRISTOPHER *bows. To* FREDDIE) I've seen you. (*Goes
to* LADY JESSICA.) Good morning, dearest. (*Kisses her.*)

LADY JESSICA: Good morning, dearest. (*Kisses her.*)

MRS CRESPIN: (*to* LADY JESSICA, *looking anxiously at her*) You're looking pale
and worried.

LADY JESSICA: Me? Oh no, I'm sure I don't, do I?

SIR CHRISTOPHER: Not to masculine eyes.

MRS CRESPIN: (*to* LADY ROSAMUND) Dear, I've lost the address of that cook.
Would you mind writing it out again?

LADY ROSAMUND: Certainly. (*Goes to writing-table and writes.*)

MRS CRESPIN: (*to* LADY JESSICA) What's the matter with our dear friend
George Nepean?

LADY JESSICA: Matter?

MRS CRESPIN: I ran into him in a post office on my way from Paddington just
now.

LADY JESSICA: Yes?

MRS CRESPIN: Your husband is quite well, I hope?

LADY JESSICA: My husband? Oh, quite! He always is quite well. Why?

MRS CRESPIN: George Nepean seemed so strange.

LADY JESSICA: How?

MRS CRESPIN: He said he was going to Paddington to meet your husband — and
he made so much of it.

LADY JESSICA: Ah! You see, my husband is a big man, so naturally George would
make much of it.

MRS CRESPIN: I always used to go to the station to meet my husband — when I
had one.

LADY JESSICA: (*a little triumphantly*) Ah! Rosy and I know better than to kill
our husbands with too much kindness.

MRS CRESPIN: Still, I think husbands need a little pampering —

SIR CHRISTOPHER: Not at all. The brutes are so easily spoilt. A little overdose of
sweetness, a little extra attention from a wife to her husband, and life is never
the same again!

FREDDIE: (*who has been waiting eagerly to get a word in*) I suppose you didn't
mention anything to George Nepean about our dining with you last evening?

MRS CRESPIN: (*alert*) Did I? Let me see! Yes! Yes! I did mention that you were
over. Why?

(*They all look at each other.*)

FREDDIE: Oh, nothing, nothing!

MRS CRESPIN: I'm so sorry. Does it matter much?

LADY JESSICA: Not in the least.

LADY ROSAMUND: Oh, not in the least.

FREDDIE: Not in the least.

SIR CHRISTOPHER: Not at all.

MRS CRESPIN: I'm afraid I made a mistake.

LADY ROSAMUND: How?

MRS CRESPIN: Your husband —

LADY ROSAMUND: Oh, my dear, what does it matter what my Freddie says or does or thinks, eh, Freddie? (*frowning angrily at* FREDDIE) There's the address of the cook (*giving the paper on which she had been writing*).
MRS CRESPIN: Thank you so much. Good morning, dearest. (*kiss*)
LADY ROSAMUND: Good morning, dearest. (*kiss*)
MRS CRESPIN: (*going to* LADY JESSICA) Goodbye, dearest. (*kiss*)
LADY JESSICA: Goodbye, dearest. (*kiss*)
MRS CRESPIN: (*very sweetly, shaking hands*) Goodbye, Sir Christopher.
SIR CHRISTOPHER: Goodbye.
        (LADY ROSAMUND *rings bell.*)
MRS CRESPIN: You are quite sure that I didn't make a mistake in telling George Nepean that Lady Rosy and Mr Tatton dined with me last evening?
SIR CHRISTOPHER: It was the truth, wasn't it?
MRS CRESPIN: Of course it was.
SIR CHRISTOPHER: One never makes a mistake in telling the truth.
MRS CRESPIN: Really? That's a very sweeping assertion to make.
SIR CHRISTOPHER: I base it on my constant experience – and practice.
        (FOOTMAN *appears at door at back.*)
MRS CRESPIN: You find it always answers to tell the truth?
SIR CHRISTOPHER: Invariably.
MRS CRESPIN: I hope it will in this case. Goodbye! Goodbye! Goodbye! (*Exit* MRS CRESPIN. *Exit* FOOTMAN. *They all stand looking at each other, nonplussed.* SIR CHRISTOPHER *slightly touching his head with perplexed gesture.*)
SIR CHRISTOPHER: Our fib won't do.
LADY ROSAMUND: Freddie, you incomparable nincompoop!
FREDDIE: I like that! If I hadn't asked her, what would have happened? George Nepean would have come in, you'd have plumped down on him with your lie, and what then? Don't you think it's jolly lucky I said what I did?
SIR CHRISTOPHER: It's lucky in this instance. But if I am to embark any further in these imaginative enterprises, I must ask you, Freddie, to keep a silent tongue.
FREDDIE: What for?
SIR CHRISTOPHER: Well, old fellow, it may be an unpalatable truth to you, but you'll never make a good liar.
FREDDIE: Very likely not. But if this sort of thing is going on in my house, I think I ought to.
LADY ROSAMUND: Oh, do subside, Freddie, do subside!
LADY JESSICA: Yes, George – and perhaps Gilbert – will be here directly. Oh, will somebody tell me what to do?
SIR CHRISTOPHER: We have tried possibility number one. It has signally failed. Why not possibility number two?
LADY JESSICA: Tell the truth? My husband would never believe it! Besides, he threatened that he wouldn't spare me. And he won't. No! No! No! Somebody dined with me last night, or was going to dine with me, and that somebody was a woman.
        (*Enter* FOOTMAN *at back.*)

FOOTMAN: (*announcing*) Mrs Coke!
>   (*Enter* DOLLY. *Exit* FOOTMAN.)

LADY JESSICA: (*Goes affectionately and a little hysterically to her.*) Dolly! How good of you! (*kissing her*)

DOLLY: What's the matter?

LADY JESSICA: Dolly, you dined with me, or were going to dine with me at the Star and Garter at Shepperford last evening. Don't say you can't, and didn't, for you must and did!

DOLLY: Of course I'll say anything that's — necessary.

LADY JESSICA: Oh, you treasure!

DOLLY: But I don't understand —
>   (LADY JESSICA *takes her aside and whispers eagerly.*)

SIR CHRISTOPHER: (*glancing at* LADY JESSICA *and* DOLLY) Possibility number one — with variations. I'm not required any further. (*Takes up his hat and is about to bolt.*)

LADY ROSAMUND: Oh, Sir Christopher, you won't desert us?

SIR CHRISTOPHER: Certainly not, if I can be of any use. But if this is to be a going concern, don't you think the fewer partners the better?

LADY ROSAMUND: Oh, don't go. You can help us so much.

SIR CHRISTOPHER: How?

LADY ROSAMUND: Your mere presence will be an immense moral support to us.

SIR CHRISTOPHER: (*uncomfortable*) Thank you! Thank you!

LADY ROSAMUND: You can come to our assistance whenever we are in the lurch, and corroborate us whenever we need corroboration — and —

SIR CHRISTOPHER: Bolster up generally.

LADY ROSAMUND: Yes. Besides, everybody knows you are such an honourable man. I feel they won't suspect you.

SIR CHRISTOPHER: (*uncomfortable*) Thank you! Thank you!

DOLLY: (*to* LADY JESSICA) Very well, dear. I quite understand. After George went away, you were so upset at his suspicions that you came back to town without any dinner. Did I stay and have the dinner?

SIR CHRISTOPHER: No, no. I wouldn't go so far as that.

DOLLY: But what did I do? I must have dined somewhere, didn't I? Not that I mind if I didn't dine anywhere. But won't it seem funny if I didn't dine somewhere?

LADY JESSICA: I suppose it will.

DOLLY: Very well then, where did I dine? Do tell me. I know I shall get into an awful muddle if I don't know. Where did I dine?
>   (*Enter* FOOTMAN *at back.*)

FOOTMAN: (*announcing*) Mr George Nepean.
>   (*Enter* GEORGE NEPEAN. *Exit* FOOTMAN.)

GEORGE: (*Enters very frigidly, bows very coldly. Very stiffly*) Good morning, Lady Rosamund! (*to the others — bowing*) Good morning.

LADY ROSAMUND: (*very cordially*) My dear George, don't take that tragic tone. (*Insists on shaking hands.*) Anyone would suppose that something dreadful was the matter. I've just explained to Sir Christopher your mistake of last night.

GEORGE: My mistake?

LADY JESSICA: You shouldn't have left so hurriedly, George. I sent Mr Falkner after you to explain. Dolly, tell him.

DOLLY: Jess and I had arranged to have a little dinner all by our two selves —

GEORGE: Indeed!

DOLLY: There's nothing strange in that, Sir Christopher?

SIR CHRISTOPHER: Not at all. I'm sure any person of either sex would be only too delighted to dine *tête-à-tête* with you.

DOLLY: And when I got there, I found poor Jess in an awful state. She said you had come into the room and had made the most horrid accusations against her, poor thing!

GEORGE: I made no accusation.

LADY JESSICA: What did you mean by saying that Gilbert must know?

GEORGE: Merely that I should tell him what I saw.

LADY JESSICA: And have you told him?

GEORGE: Yes, on his arrival an hour ago.

LADY JESSICA: Where is he?

GEORGE: Round at Sloane Street waiting till I have heard Lady Rosamund's explanation.

LADY ROSAMUND: Well, you have heard it. Or, rather, it's Dolly's explanation. The whole thing is so ridiculously simple. I think you ought to beg Jess's pardon.

GEORGE: I will when I am sure that I have wronged her.

FREDDIE: Oh, come, I say, George! you don't refuse to take a lady's word —

LADY ROSAMUND: Freddie, subside!

DOLLY: (*to* GEORGE) Poor Jess was so much upset by what you said that she couldn't eat any dinner, she nearly had hysterics, and when she got a little better, she came straight up to town, poor thing!

GEORGE: What was Mr Falkner doing there?

LADY JESSICA: He was staying in the hotel and happened to come into the room at that moment.

      (*a little pause*)

LADY ROSAMUND: Is there anything else you would like to ask?

GEORGE: No.

LADY ROSAMUND: And you're quite satisfied?

GEORGE: The question is not whether I'm satisfied, but whether Gilbert will be. I'll go and fetch him. Will you excuse me? (*going*)

SIR CHRISTOPHER: (*Stops him.*) Nepean, I'm sure you don't wish to embitter your brother and Lady Jessica's whole future life by sowing jealousy and suspicion between them. Come now, like a good fellow, you'll smooth things over as much as you can.

GEORGE: I shall not influence my brother one way or the other. He must judge for himself. (*Exit at back.* SIR CHRISTOPHER *shrugs his shoulders.*)

DOLLY: I got through very well, didn't I? (*to* LADY JESSICA)

LADY JESSICA: Yes, dear. Thank you so much. But George didn't seem to believe it, eh?

FREDDIE: It's so jolly thin. A couple of women dining together! Why should a couple of women dine together? Oh, it's too thin, you know!

LADY JESSICA: And you don't think Gilbert will believe it? He must! He must! Oh, I begin to wish that we had tried –

SIR CHRISTOPHER: Possibility number two. I'm afraid it's too late now.

LADY JESSICA: Oh, what shall I do? Do you think Gilbert will believe Dolly?

LADY ROSAMUND: He must if Dolly only sticks to it.

DOLLY: Oh, I'll stick to it. Only I should like to know where I dined. Where did I dine?

(*Enter* FOOTMAN *at back, comes up to* DOLLY.)

FOOTMAN: If you please, ma'am, Mr Coke is waiting for you below.

DOLLY: (*with a scream*) Oh, dear! Oh, dear! I'd quite forgotten!

LADY ROSAMUND: What?

DOLLY: I arranged to meet Archie here and take him on to the dentist's. (*to* FOOTMAN) Tell Mr Coke I'll come in a moment. (*Exit* FOOTMAN. *To* LADY JESSICA) Dear, I must go –

LADY JESSICA: You can't! You must stay now and tell Gilbert – mustn't she, Sir Christopher?

SIR CHRISTOPHER: I'm afraid you must, Mrs Coke. You are our sheet-anchor.

DOLLY: But what can I tell Archie?

LADY ROSAMUND: Can't you put him off, send him away?

DOLLY: What excuse can I make? He is so fidgetty and inquisitive. He'll insist on knowing something. No, I must go.

LADY JESSICA: (*desperate*) You can't! You can't! You must stay! Couldn't we tell Archie and ask him to help us?

DOLLY: Oh, I wouldn't tell Archie for the world. He wouldn't understand.

(*Enter by door at back* ARCHIBALD COKE, *in very correct frock-coat, very prim and starchy.*)

COKE: Good morning, Rosy! Freddie! Sir Christopher! (*nodding all round*) Now, Dolly, are you ready?

DOLLY: I – I –

LADY JESSICA: She can't go, Archie.

COKE: Can't go?

LADY JESSICA: She – she isn't well.

COKE: Not well? (*alarmed*) Not influenza again?

DOLLY: No, not influenza. But I'd rather not go.

COKE: Oh, nonsense, nonsense! I cannot take the gas alone. (*to* SIR CHRISTOPHER) I've a terrible dread of the gas. I'm sure they'll give me too much some day. Now, Dolly.

LADY ROSAMUND: (*to* SIR CHRISTOPHER) Gilbert will be here directly. Can't you get him away?

SIR CHRISTOPHER: Coke, your wife isn't just the thing, as you can see. I'll go to the dentist's with you. Come along! (*linking his arm with* COKE'*s*) I'll see they give you the right dose.

COKE: (*resisting*) No. My wife is the proper person to go to the dentist with me, and see that the gas is rightly administered. Come, Dolly!

LADY JESSICA: (*Comes desperately to* COKE.) Dolly can't go!

COKE: Why not?

LADY JESSICA: She must stay here and tell Gilbert that she dined with me last evening.

COKE: Tell Gilbert that she dined with you last evening! What for?

SIR CHRISTOPHER: (*aside to* LADY ROSAMUND) We're taking too many partners into this concern.

COKE: She dined with me. Why should she tell Gilbert she dined with you?

LADY JESSICA: If you must know, I was coming to the station from Barbara's and I must have taken the wrong turning —

COKE: (*very suspicious*) The wrong turning?

LADY JESSICA: Yes, for instead of finding myself at the station, I found myself at the Star and Garter.

COKE: The Star and Garter?

LADY JESSICA: And as I was frightfully hungry I asked Mr Falkner to give me a little dinner.

COKE: A little dinner?

LADY JESSICA: George Nepean happened to come in, and seeing the dinner things laid, actually suspected me of dining with Mr Falkner! And he has told Gilbert, and don't you see — if Dolly will only say that it was she who was dining with me — don't you see?

COKE: No, I don't. I cannot lend myself to anything of the sort. And I expressly forbid Dolly to say that she dined with you.

LADY JESSICA: But she has said so. She has just told George Nepean.

COKE: Told George Nepean!

DOLLY: I couldn't leave poor Jess in a scrape. And now I have said so, I must stick to it, mustn't I? You wouldn't have me tell another one now.

COKE: Well, I'm surprised! Really, I consider it quite disgraceful.

FREDDIE: Look here, Coke, we can't let Gilbert think that Jess was dining with Falkner, can we? He'd only make a howling scandal, and drag us all into it. We've got to say something. I know it's jolly thin, but can you think of a better one?

COKE: No, and I decline to have anything to do with this! I should have thought my character was too well known for me to be asked to a — a — It is too disgraceful! I will not lend my countenance to anything of the kind!

LADY ROSAMUND: Very well then, will you please take yourself off and leave us to manage the affair ourselves?

COKE: No, I will not forfeit my self-respect, I will not permit my wife to forfeit her self-respect by taking part in these proceedings. Really, it is — it is — it is too disgraceful!

(LADY JESSICA *suddenly bursts into tears, sobs violently.*)

SIR CHRISTOPHER: (*Comes up to him very calm, touches him on the shoulder.*) Coke, I assure you that theoretically I have as great an objection to lying as you or any man living. But Lady Jessica has acted a little foolishly. No more. Of that I am sure. If you consent to hold your tongue, I think Gilbert Nepean will accept your wife's explanation and the affair will blow over. If, however, you insist on the truth coming out, what will happen? You will very likely bring about a rupture between them, you may possibly place Lady Jessica in a position where she will have no alternative but to take a fatal plunge, and you will drag yourself and your wife into a very unpleasant family scandal. That's the situation.

COKE: But it places me in a very awkward position. No, really, I cannot consent — I'm an honourable man.

SIR CHRISTOPHER: So are we all, all honourable men. The curious thing is that ever since the days of the Garden of Eden, women have had a knack of impaling us honourable men on dilemmas of this kind, where the only alternative is to be false to the truth or false to them. In this instance I think we may very well keep our mouths shut without suffering any violent pangs of conscience about the matter. Come now!

COKE: (*Sits down overwhelmed.*) Well, understand me, if I consent to keep my mouth shut, I must not be supposed to countenance what is going on. That is quite understood?

SIR CHRISTOPHER: Oh, quite! Quite! We'll consider you as strictly neutral. Then you will?

COKE: (*rising up violently*) No! On second thoughts, I really cannot. I cannot!

LADY ROSAMUND: Very well! Then will you go away and leave us to manage it as we can?

COKE: And I had arranged to take the gas so comfortably this morning. It's most unfair to place me in a position of this kind. I must protest — I really —
(*Enter* FOOTMAN.)

FOOTMAN: (*at back, announcing*) Mr Gilbert Nepean. Mr George Nepean.
(*Enter* GILBERT *and* GEORGE NEPEAN. *Exit* FOOTMAN.)

LADY ROSAMUND: (*Advances very cordially to* GILBERT *who does not respond.*) Good morning, Gilbert.

GILBERT: Good morning. Good morning, Coke.

COKE: (*very uncomfortable*) Good morning.

GILBERT: (*nodding*) Freddie! Deering! (*Looks at* LADY JESSICA, *who looks at him. They do not speak. Pause. Looking round*) I thought I was coming here for a private explanation.
(SIR CHRISTOPHER *takes up his hat quickly. Is going to bolt.*)

LADY ROSAMUND: No, Sir Christopher. If Gilbert is determined to carry this any further we shall need the unbiassed testimony of an impartial friend, so that people may know exactly what did occur. Please stay.

SIR CHRISTOPHER: (*Puts down hat.*) Whew! (*to himself*)

LADY ROSAMUND: Gilbert, don't be foolish. Everybody here knows all about the stupid affair of last evening.

GILBERT: Everybody here knows? Well, I don't. I shall be glad to be informed.
(*Looks round.*)
(COKE *shows symptoms of great discomfort.*)

SIR CHRISTOPHER: Nepean, I'm sure you don't wish to make any more than is necessary of Lady Jessica's trifling indiscretion —

GILBERT: I wish to make no more of it than the truth, and I'll take care that nobody makes less of it. Now — (*to* LADY JESSICA, *very furiously*) — you were dining with this fellow, Falkner, last evening?

LADY JESSICA: No.

GILBERT: No? Then whom did you dine with?

LADY JESSICA: If you speak like that I shan't answer you.

GILBERT: Will you tell me what I ask?

LADY JESSICA: No.

GILBERT: I can't get the truth from you. Perhaps, as you all know, somebody else will oblige me. Coke —

COKE: (*most uncomfortable*) Really, I — I don't know all the particulars, and I would prefer not to be mixed up in your private affairs.

GILBERT: Deering — you?

SIR CHRISTOPHER: My dear fellow, I only know what I've heard, and hearsay evidence is proverbially untrustworthy. Now, if I may offer you a little advice, if I were you I should gently take Lady Jessica by the hand, I should gently lead her home, I should gently use all those endearing little arts of persuasion and entreaty which a husband may legitimately use to his wife, and I should gently beguile her into telling me the whole truth. I should believe everything she told me, I shouldn't listen to what anybody else said, and I should never mention the matter again. Now, do as I tell you, and you'll be a happy man tomorrow, and for the rest of your life.
     (*pause*)

GILBERT: (*Looks at* LADY JESSICA.) No. (SIR CHRISTOPHER *shrugs his shoulders, and retires.*) I came here for an explanation, and I won't go till I've got it.

LADY ROSAMUND: My dear Gilbert, we're patiently waiting to give you an explanation, if you'll only listen to it. Dolly, do tell him how it all happened, and let him see what a donkey he is making of himself.

DOLLY: Yes, Gilbert, I wish you wouldn't get in these awful tempers. You frighten us so that in a very little while we shan't know whether we're speaking the truth or whether we're not.

GILBERT: Go on! Go on!

DOLLY: Jess and I had arranged to have a little *tête-à-tête* dinner at Shepperford and talk over old times, all by our two selves (COKE *gets very uncomfortable.*) — hadn't we, Jess? Rosy, you heard us arranging it all?

LADY ROSAMUND: Yes, on the last night you were at our place.

DOLLY: Yes. Well, Jess got there first and then Mr Falkner happened to come into the room, and then George happened to come into the room, and wouldn't wait to listen to Jess's explanation, would he, Jess? Well, when I got there, I found Jess in strong hysterics, poor old dear! I couldn't get her round for ever so long. And as soon as she was better she came straight up to town. And that's all.
     (*pause*)

GILBERT: And what did you do?

DOLLY: I came up to town too.

GILBERT: Without any dinner?

DOLLY: Eh?

GILBERT: Where did you dine?

DOLLY: I didn't really dine anywhere — not to say dine. I had some cold chicken and a little tongue when I got home. (*pause*) And a tomato salad.

GILBERT: Coke, what do you know of this?

COKE: Well – I know what Dolly has just told you.

GILBERT: You allow your wife to dine out alone?

COKE: Yes – yes – on certain occasions.

GILBERT: And you knew of this arrangement?

COKE: Yes – at least, no – not before she told me of it. But after she told me, I did know.

GEORGE: But Jessica said that she expected a small party.

DOLLY: I was the small party.

GILBERT: (*to* COKE) What time did Dolly get home last evening?

COKE: Eh? Well, about –

DOLLY: A little before nine.

GEORGE: Impossible! I was at Shepperford after half-past seven. If Lady Jessica had hysterics, and you stayed with her, you could scarcely have reached Kensington before nine.

DOLLY: Well, perhaps it was ten. Yes, it was ten.

GILBERT: Coke, were you at home last evening when your wife got back?

COKE: I? No – yes, yes – no – not precisely.

GILBERT: (*growing more indignant*) Surely you must know whether you were at home or not when your wife returned?

COKE: No, I don't. And I very much object to be cross-questioned in this manner. I've told you all I know, and – I – I withdraw from the whole business. Now, Dolly, are you ready?

GILBERT: No, stop! I want to get at the bottom of this and I will. (*coming furiously to* LADY JESSICA) Once more, will you give me your version of this cock-and-bull story?

(*Enter* FOOTMAN *at back.*)

FOOTMAN: (*announcing*) Mr Falkner!

GILBERT: Ah!

SIR CHRISTOPHER: Nepean! Nepean! Control yourself!

(*Enter* FALKNER. *Exit* FOOTMAN.)

GILBERT: Let me be, Deering. (*going to* FALKNER) You were at Shepperford last evening. My wife was there with you?

FALKNER: I was at Shepperford last evening. Lady Jessica was there. She was dining with Lady Rosamund –

LADY ROSAMUND: No! No!

GILBERT: Lady Jessica was dining with Lady Rosamund?

FALKNER: I understood her to say so, did I not, Lady Rosamund?

LADY ROSAMUND: No! No! It was Mrs Coke who was dining with Lady Jessica.

FALKNER: Then I misunderstood you. Does it matter?

GILBERT: Yes. (*going to him*) I want to know what the devil you were doing there?

No! No!: French's adds business which seems to have been used by Wyndham, but which surely distracts the audience at an important moment: 'SIR CHRISTOPHER *turns to* LADY ROSA-MUND, *gesticulating, turns, sees* GILBERT *watching him* – *picks up vase of flowers from table, R.C., smells them, offers them to* LADY ROSAMUND, *who smells ad. lib.*'

SIR CHRISTOPHER: Nepean! Nepean!

GILBERT: Do you hear? What the devil were you doing there. Will you tell me, or
— (*Trying to get at* FALKNER. SIR CHRISTOPHER *holds him back.*)

LADY JESSICA: (*Rises very quietly.*) Mr Falkner, tell my husband the truth.

FALKNER: But, Lady Jessica —

LADY JESSICA: Yes, if you please — the truth, the whole truth, and nothing but
the truth. Tell him all. I wish it.

GILBERT: You hear what she says. Now then, the truth — and be damned to you!

FALKNER: (*Looks round, then after a pause, with great triumph.*) I love Lady
Jessica with all my heart and soul! I asked her to come to me at Shepperford
last evening. She came. Your brother saw us and left us. The next moment
Lady Rosamund came, and she had scarcely gone when the maid came with
your telegram and took Lady Jessica back to town. If you think there was
anything more on your wife's side than a passing folly and amusement at my
expense, you will wrong her. If you think there is anything less on my side
than the deepest, deepest, deepest love and worship, you will wrong me.
Understand this. She is guiltless. Be sure of that. And now you've got the
truth, and be damned to *you.* (*Goes to door at back — turns.*) If you want
me you know where to find me. (*to* LADY JESSICA) Lady Jessica, I am at
your service — always! (*Exit at back. They all look at each other.*)

SIR CHRISTOPHER: (*very softly to himself*) Possibility number two — with a
vengeance!

> *Curtain*

(*A few hours, from morning till evening, pass between acts III and IV.*)

ACT IV

SCENE.   *Drawing-room in* SIR CHRISTOPHER'*s flat in Victoria
Street. At back left a large recess, taking up half the stage. The right half is taken up
by an inner room furnished as library and smoking-room. Curtains dividing library
from drawing-room. Door up stage, left. A table down stage, right. The room is in
great confusion, with portmanteau open, clothes, etc., scattered over the floor;
articles which an officer going to Central Africa might want are lying about. Time:
night, about half-past nine o'clock.* SIR CHRISTOPHER *and* TAPLIN *are busy
packing. Ring at door.*

SIR CHRISTOPHER: See who it is, Taplin; and come back and finish packing the
moment I am disengaged.

> (*Exit* TAPLIN. *He re-enters in a few moments, showing in*
> BEATRICE *in evening dress.* SIR CHRISTOPHER *goes to her, and
> shakes hands cordially. Exit* TAPLIN.)

BEATRICE: I was dining out when you called. But I got your message and I came
on at once.

---

with all my heart and soul: according to French's s.d., 'GILBERT *makes a movement to get at*
FALKNER, SIR CHRISTOPHER *restrains him.*'

SIR CHRISTOPHER: I couldn't wait. I had to come back and pack. (*going on with his packing*) I haven't one half-moment to spare.

BEATRICE: When do you start?

SIR CHRISTOPHER: Tomorrow morning. It's very urgent. I've been at the War Office all the afternoon. You'll excuse my going on with this. I've three most important duties to fulfil tonight.

BEATRICE: What are they?

SIR CHRISTOPHER: (*packing*) I've got to pack. I've got to persuade Ned to come out there with me — if I can. And I've got (*looking straight at her*) to make you promise to be my wife when I come home again.

BEATRICE: Oh, Kit, you know what I've told you so often!

SIR CHRISTOPHER: (*packing always*) Yes, and you're telling it me again, and wasting my time when every moment is gold. Ah, dear, forgive me, you know I think you're worth the wooing. And you know I'm the man to woo you. And you know I'm ready to spend three, five, seven, fourteen, or twenty-one years in winning you. But if you'd only say 'Yes' this minute, and let me pack and see Ned, you'd save me such a lot of trouble. And I'll do all the love-making when I come back.

BEATRICE: Where is Ned?

SIR CHRISTOPHER: Playing the fool for Lady Jessica. Poor fellow! There never was but one woman in this world that was worth playing the fool for, and I'm playing the fool for her. I've sent for Ned to come here. That's a digression. Come back to brass tacks. You'll be my wife when I come home?

BEATRICE: Let me think it over, Kit.

SIR CHRISTOPHER: No. You've had plenty of time for that. I can't allow you to think it over any longer.

BEATRICE: But it means so much to me. Let me write to you out there.

SIR CHRISTOPHER: (*very determinedly*) No. (*Leaves his packing, takes out his watch.*) It's a little too bad of you when I'm so pressed. (*Comes to her.*) Now, I can only give you five minutes, and it must absolutely be fixed up in that time. (*coming to her with great tenderness and passion*) Come, my dear, dear chum, what makes you hesitate to give yourself to me? You want me to come well out of this, don't you?

BEATRICE: You know I do!

SIR CHRISTOPHER: Then you don't love your country if you won't have me. Once give me your promise, and it will give me the pluck of fifty men! Don't you know if I'm sure of you I shall carry everything before me?

BEATRICE: Will you? Will you? But if you were to die —

SIR CHRISTOPHER: I won't die if you're waiting to be my wife when I come home. And you will? You will? I won't hear anything but 'Yes'. You shan't move one inch until you've said 'Yes'. Now! say it! Say 'Yes!' Say 'Yes!' — do you hear?

BEATRICE: (*throwing herself into his arms*) Yes! Yes! Yes! Take me! Take me!

SIR CHRISTOPHER: (*kissing her very reverently*) My wife when I come home again.

   (*a pause*)

BEATRICE: You know, Kit, I can love very deeply.

SIR CHRISTOPHER: And so you shall, when I come home again. And so will I when I come home again. (*looking at his watch*) A minute and a quarter! I must get on with my packing. Play something to me while I pack.

BEATRICE: (*Going to piano. Stops.*) Kit, there will be some nursing and other woman's work out there?

SIR CHRISTOPHER: Yes, I suppose —

BEATRICE: I'll come with you.

SIR CHRISTOPHER: Very well. How long will it take you to pack?

BEATRICE: Half an hour.

SIR CHRISTOPHER: All right! I must wait here for Ned. Come back and have some supper by and by?

BEATRICE: Yes — in half an hour.

SIR CHRISTOPHER: We might be married at Cairo — on our way out?

BEATRICE: Just as you please.

SIR CHRISTOPHER: Or before we start tomorrow morning?

BEATRICE: Will there be time?

SIR CHRISTOPHER: Oh, I'll find time for that! What do you say?

BEATRICE: Just as you please.

SIR CHRISTOPHER: Very well, I'll fix that up.

     (*Enter* TAPLIN.)

TAPLIN: Mr Gilbert Nepean is below, Sir Christopher.

SIR CHRISTOPHER: (*glancing at his packing*) Show him up, Taplin.

     (*Exit* TAPLIN.)

SIR CHRISTOPHER: (*holding* BEATRICE*'s hand*) Tomorrow morning, then?

BEATRICE: Yes, I've given you some trouble to win me, Kit?

SIR CHRISTOPHER: No more than you're worth.

BEATRICE: I'll give you none now you have won me.

     (*Enter* TAPLIN.)

TAPLIN: (*announcing*) Mr Gilbert Nepean.

     (*Enter* GILBERT NEPEAN. *Exit* TAPLIN.)

BEATRICE: How d'ye do?

GILBERT: How d'ye do? (*shaking hands*)

BEATRICE: And goodbye. (*to* SIR CHRISTOPHER) No, I won't have you come down all those stairs, indeed I won't. *Au revoir.* (*Exit.*)

GILBERT: Excuse my coming at this hour.

SIR CHRISTOPHER: I'm rather pressed. What can I do for you?

GILBERT: I've been down to Shepperford this afternoon. It seems you dined there last evening.

SIR CHRISTOPHER: I did.

GILBERT: I want to get all the evidence.

SIR CHRISTOPHER: What for?

GILBERT: To guide me in my future action. Deering, I trust you. Can I take that fellow's word that my wife is guiltless?

SIR CHRISTOPHER: I'm sure you can.

GILBERT: How do you know?

SIR CHRISTOPHER: Because he'd give his head to tell you that she is not.

GILBERT: Why?

SIR CHRISTOPHER: It would give him the chance he is waiting for – to take her off your hands.

GILBERT: Take her off my hands – he's waiting for that?

SIR CHRISTOPHER: Don't you see he is? And don't you see that you're doing your best to make him successful?

GILBERT: How?

SIR CHRISTOPHER: Don't think when you've married a woman that you can sit down and neglect her. You can't. You've married one of the most charming women in London, and when a man has married a charming woman, if he doesn't continue to make love to her, some other man will. Such are the sad ways of humankind! How have you treated Lady Jessica?

GILBERT: But do you suppose I will allow my wife to go out dining with other men?

SIR CHRISTOPHER: The best way to avoid that is to take her out to dinner yourself – and to give her a good one. Have you dined tonight?

GILBERT: Dined? No! I can't dine till I know what to believe.

SIR CHRISTOPHER: The question is, what do you want to believe? If you want to believe her innocent, take the facts as they stand. If you want to believe her guilty, continue to treat her as you are doing, and you'll soon have plenty of proof. And let me tell you, nobody will pity you. Do you want to believe her innocent?

GILBERT: Of course I do.

SIR CHRISTOPHER: Where is she?

GILBERT: I don't know – at home, I suppose.

SIR CHRISTOPHER: Go home to her – don't say one word about what has happened, and invite her out to the very best dinner that London can provide.

GILBERT: But after she has acted as she has done?

SIR CHRISTOPHER: My dear fellow, she's only a woman. I never met but one woman that was worth taking seriously. What are they? A kind of children, you know. Humour them, play with them, buy them the toys they cry for, but don't get angry with them. They aren't worth it! Now I must get on with my packing. (SIR CHRISTOPHER *sets to work packing.* GILBERT *walks up and down the room, biting his nails, deliberating.* GILBERT, *after a moment or two, speaks.*)

GILBERT: Perhaps you're right, Deering.

SIR CHRISTOPHER: Oh, I know I am!

GILBERT: I'll go to her.

SIR CHRISTOPHER: (*busy packing*) Make haste, or you may be too late.

    (GILBERT *goes to door. At that moment enter* TAPLIN.)

TAPLIN: (*announcing*) Mr Falkner!

    (*Enter* FALKNER. *Exit* TAPLIN. GILBERT *and* FALKNER *stand for a moment looking at each other. Exit* GILBERT; FALKNER *looks after him.*)

They aren't worth it!: In French's this is amplified to refer to Beatrice: 'They're not worth it! Except one!'

SIR CHRISTOPHER: Well?

FALKNER: (*very elated*) You want to see me?

SIR CHRISTOPHER: Yes. You seem excited.

FALKNER: I've had some good news.

SIR CHRISTOPHER: What?

FALKNER: The best. She loves me.

SIR CHRISTOPHER: You've seen her?

FALKNER: No.

SIR CHRISTOPHER: Written to her?

FALKNER: Yes. I've just had this answer (*taking out letter*).

SIR CHRISTOPHER: Where is she?

FALKNER: Still at her sister's. (*reading*) 'I shall never forget the words you spoke this morning. You were right in saying that your love would not be wasted. I have learned at last what it is worth. You said you would be at my service always. Do not write again. Wait till you hear from me, and the moment I send for you, come to me.' I knew I should win her at last, and I shall!

SIR CHRISTOPHER: *Après*?

FALKNER: What does it matter? If I can persuade her I shall take her out to Africa with me.

SIR CHRISTOPHER: Africa? Nonsense! There's only one woman in the world that's any use in that part of the globe, and I'm taking her out myself.

FALKNER: Beatrice?

SIR CHRISTOPHER: We are to be married tomorrow morning.

FALKNER: I congratulate you — with all my heart (*shaking hands warmly*).

SIR CHRISTOPHER: Thank you. (*pause*) You'll come with me, Ned?

FALKNER: If she will come too.

SIR CHRISTOPHER: Oh, we can't have her.

FALKNER: Why not?

SIR CHRISTOPHER: In the first place, she'd be very much in the way. In the second place — it's best to be frank — Lady Deering will not recognise Lady Jessica.

FALKNER: Very well. (*Turns on heel.*) Goodnight, Kit! (*very curtly*)

SIR CHRISTOPHER: No. (*Takes out watch. Glances at packing.*) Now, my dear old Ned, you're still up that everlasting *cul-de-sac* — playing the lover to a married woman, and I've got to drag you out of it.

FALKNER: It's no use, Kit. My mind is made up. Let me go.

SIR CHRISTOPHER: To the devil with Lady Jessica? No, I'm going to stop you.

FALKNER: Ah, you'll stop me! How?

SIR CHRISTOPHER: There was a time when one whisper would have done it. (*Whispers.*) Duty. (FALKNER *moves uneasily away.* SIR CHRISTOPHER *follows him up.*) You know that you're the only man who can treat peaceably with the chiefs. You know that your going out may save hundreds, perhaps thousands of lives.

FALKNER: I'm not sure of that.

SIR CHRISTOPHER: You're not sure? Well then, for heaven's sake, try it — put it to the test. But you know there's every chance. You know the whole country is waiting for you to declare yourself. You know that you have a splendid chance of putting the crown on your life's work, and you know that if you don't seize it, it will be because you stay skulking here after her!

FALKNER: Skulking!

SIR CHRISTOPHER: What do you call it? What will everybody call it? Ned, you've faced the most horrible death day after day for months. You've done some of the bravest things out there that have been done by any Englishman in this generation; but if you turn tail now there's only one word will fit you to the end of your days, and that word is 'Coward!'

FALKNER: Coward!

SIR CHRISTOPHER: Coward! And there's only one epitaph to be written on you by and by — 'Sold his honour, his fame, his country, his duty, his conscience, his all, for a petticoat!'

FALKNER: Very well, then, when I die write that over me. I tell you this, Kit, if I can only win her — and I shall, I shall, I feel it — she'll leave that man and come to me; and then! — I don't care one snap of the fingers if Africa is swept bare of humanity from Cairo to Cape Town, and from Teneriffe to Zanzibar! Now argue with me after that!

SIR CHRISTOPHER: Argue with you? Not I! But I wish to God there was some way of kidnapping fools into sense and reason and locking them up there for the rest of their lives.

(Enter TAPLIN.)

TAPLIN: *(announcing)* Lady Jessica Nepean, Lady Rosamund Tatton.

(Enter LADY JESSICA *and* LADY ROSAMUND. *Exit* TAPLIN.
LADY JESSICA *shows delighted surprise at seeing* FALKNER, *goes to him cordially.* LADY ROSAMUND *tries to stop* LADY JESSICA *from going to* FALKNER.)

LADY JESSICA: *(to* FALKNER) I didn't expect to find you here.

FALKNER: I am waiting for you.

LADY ROSAMUND: *(interposing)* No, Jess, no. Sir Christopher! *(aside to him)* Help me to get her away from him.

(LADY JESSICA *and* FALKNER *are talking vigorously together.*)

SIR CHRISTOPHER: One moment. Perhaps we may as well get this little matter fixed up here and now. *(Takes out watch, looking ruefully at his packing.)* Lady Jessica, may I ask what has happened since I left you this morning?

LADY JESSICA: Nothing. My husband went away in a rage. I've stayed with Rosy all day.

LADY ROSAMUND: We've been talking it all over.

LADY JESSICA: Oh, we've been talking it all over — *(gesture)* — and over and over, till I'm thoroughly — *sea-sick* of it!

LADY ROSAMUND: And so I persuaded her to come and talk it over with you.

SIR CHRISTOPHER: *(glancing at his packing, to* LADY JESSICA) You can't arrive at a decision?

LADY JESSICA: Oh, yes, I can; only Rosy won't let me act on it.

LADY ROSAMUND: I should think not.

SIR CHRISTOPHER: What is your decision?

LADY JESSICA: I don't mind for myself. I feel that everything is in a glorious muddle and I don't care how I get out of it, or whether I get out of it at all.

SIR CHRISTOPHER: But on the whole the best way of getting out of it is to run away with Mr Falkner?

LADY JESSICA: Mr Falkner has behaved splendidly to me.

SIR CHRISTOPHER: He has! Dear old fellow! He's a brick! (*giving* FALKNER *an affectionate little hug around the shoulders*) And I'm quite sure that in proposing to ruin your reputation, and make you miserable for life, he is actuated by the very best intentions.

LADY JESSICA: I don't care whether I'm happy or miserable for the rest of my life.

SIR CHRISTOPHER: You don't care now, but you will tomorrow morning, and next week, and next year, and all the years after.

LADY JESSICA: No, I shan't! I won't!   .

FALKNER: I'll take care, Lady Jessica, that you never regret this step. Your mind is quite made up?

LADY JESSICA: Yes, quite.

FALKNER: Then no more need be said. (*Offering arm. Gesture of despair from* LADY ROSAMUND. SIR CHRISTOPHER *soothes her.*)

SIR CHRISTOPHER: One moment, Ned! (*Takes out his watch, looks ruefully at his packing. Half aside*) Good Lord! When shall I get on with my packing? (*Puts watch in pocket, faces* FALKNER *and* LADY JESSICA *very resolutely.*) Now! I've nothing to say in the abstract against running away with another man's wife! There may be planets where it is not only the highest ideal morality, but where it has the further advantage of being a practical way of carrying on society. But it has this one fatal defect in our country today — it won't work! You know what we English are, Ned. We're not a bit better than our neighbours, but, thank God! we do pretend we are, and we do make it hot for anybody who disturbs that holy pretence. And take my word for it, my dear Lady Jessica, my dear Ned, it won't work. You know it's not an original experiment you're making. It has been tried before. Have you ever known it to be successful? Lady Jessica, think of the brave pioneers who have gone before you in this enterprise. They've all perished, and their bones whiten the anti-matrimonial shore. Think of them! Charley Gray and Lady Rideout — flitting shabbily about the Continent at cheap *table d'hôtes* and gambling clubs, rubbing shoulders with all the blackguards and demi-mondaines of Europe. Poor old Fitz and his beauty — moping down at Farnhurst, cut by the county, with no single occupation except to nag and rag each other to pieces from morning to night. Billy Dover and Polly Atchison — cut in for fresh partners in three weeks. That old idiot, Sir Bonham Dancer — paid five thousand pounds damages for being saddled with the professional strong man's wife. George Nuneham and Mrs Sandys — George is conducting a tramcar in New York, and Mrs Sandys — Lady Jessica, you knew Mrs Sandys, a delicate, sweet little creature, I've met her at your receptions — she drank herself to death, and died in a hospital. (LADY

---

table d'hôtes: cf. *The Case of Rebellious Susan*, p. 127 above.
demi-mondaines: high-class prostitutes, supported by one or more wealthy 'protectors'.
cut in for fresh partners: as in a card game.

JESSICA *moves a little away from* FALKNER, *who pursues her.*) Not
encouraging, is it? Marriage may be disagreeable, it may be unprofitable, it
may be ridiculous; but it isn't as bad as that! And do you think the experiment is going to be successful in *your* case? Not a bit of it! (FALKNER *is
going to speak.*) No, Ned, hear me out. (*Turns to* LADY JESSICA.) First of
all there will be the shabby scandal and dirty business of the divorce court.
You won't like that. It isn't nice! You won't like it. After the divorce court,
what is Ned to do with you? Take you to Africa? I do implore you, if you
hope for any happiness in that state to which it is pleasing Falkner and
Providence to call you, I do implore you, don't go out to Africa with him.
You'd never stand the climate and the hardships, and you'd bore each other
to death in a week. But if you don't go out to Africa, what are you to do?
Stay in England, in society? Everybody will cut you. Take a place in the
country? Think of poor old Fitz down at Farnhurst! Go abroad? Think of
Charley Gray and Lady Rideout. Take any of the other dozen alternatives
and find yourself stranded in some shady hole or corner, with the one solitary
hope and ambition of somehow wriggling back into respectability. That's
your side of it, Lady Jessica. As for Ned here, what is to become of him?
(*angry gesture from* FALKNER) Yes, Ned, I know you don't want to hear,
but I'm going to finish. Turn away your head. This is for Lady Jessica. He's at
the height of his career, with a great and honourable task in front of him. If
you turn him aside you'll not only wreck and ruin your own life and reputation, but you'll wreck and ruin his. You won't! You won't! His interests,
his duty, his honour all lie out there. If you care for him, don't keep him
shuffling and malingering here. Send him out with me to finish his work like
the good, splendid fellow he is. Set him free, Lady Jessica, and go back to
your home. Your husband has been here. He's sorry for what is past, and he
has promised to treat you more kindly in the future. He's waiting at home to
take you out. You missed a very good dinner last night. Don't miss another
tonight. I never saw a man in a better temper than your husband. Go to him,
and do, once for all, have done with this other folly. Do believe me, my dear
Ned, my dear Lady Jessica, before it is too late, do believe me, it won't work,
it won't work, it won't work!
      (*a little pause*)
LADY JESSICA: I think you're the most horrid man I ever met.
SIR CHRISTOPHER: Because I've told you the truth.
LADY JESSICA: Yes, that's the worst of it! It is the truth.
LADY ROSAMUND: It's exactly what I've been telling her all the afternoon.
FALKNER: Lady Jessica, I want to speak to you alone.
LADY JESSICA: What's the use? We've got to part.
FALKNER: No! No!
LADY JESSICA: Yes, my friend. I won't ruin your career. We've got to part: and
    the fewer words the better.
FALKNER: I can't give you up.
LADY JESSICA: You must! Perhaps it's best. You can always cherish your fancy
    portrait of me, and you'll never find out how very unlike me it is. And I shall

read about you in the newspapers and be very proud – and – come along, Rosy! (*Going off,* FALKNER *is going after her.*)

SIR CHRISTOPHER: (*stopping him*) It can answer no purpose, Ned.

FALKNER: What the devil has it got to do with you? You've taken her from me. Leave her to me for a few minutes. Lady Jessica, I claim to speak to you alone.

LADY JESSICA: It can only be to say 'Goodbye'.

FALKNER: I'll never say it.

LADY JESSICA: Then I must. Goodbye!

FALKNER: No – say it to me alone.

LADY JESSICA: It can only be that – no more –

FALKNER: Say it to me alone (*pointing to curtains*).

LADY JESSICA: Rosy, wait for me. I won't be a minute. (*Going to* FALKNER. LADY ROSAMUND *makes a little movement to stop her.* SIR CHRISTOPHER *by a gesture silences* LADY ROSAMUND *and allows* LADY JESSICA *to pass through the curtains where* FALKNER *has preceded her.*)

SIR CHRISTOPHER: (*to* LADY JESSICA) Remember his future is at stake as well as yours. Only the one word.

LADY JESSICA: (*as she passes through the curtains*) Only the one word.

SIR CHRISTOPHER: (*to* LADY ROSAMUND) You'll excuse my packing. I've not a moment to waste.

(*Enter* TAPLIN.)

TAPLIN: Mr Gilbert Nepean, Sir Christopher; he says he must see you.

SIR CHRISTOPHER: You didn't say Lady Jessica was here?

TAPLIN: No, Sir Christopher.

SIR CHRISTOPHER: I'll come to him.

(*Exit* TAPLIN. LADY ROSAMUND *passes between the curtains.* SIR CHRISTOPHER *is going to door, meets* GILBERT NEPEAN *who enters very excitedly.*)

GILBERT: Deering, she's not at home! She's not at her sister's. You don't think she has gone to that fellow?

SIR CHRISTOPHER: Make yourself easy. She is coming back to you.

GILBERT: Where is she?

SIR CHRISTOPHER: Will you let me take a message to her? May I tell her that for the future you will treat her with every kindness and consideration?

GILBERT: Yes – yes. Say – oh – tell her what you please. Say I know I've behaved like a bear. Tell her I'm sorry, and if she'll come home I'll do my best to make her happy in future.

SIR CHRISTOPHER: And (*taking out watch*) it's rather too late for dinner, may I suggest an invitation to supper?

GILBERT: Yes – yes.

SIR CHRISTOPHER: Lady Rosamund – (*peeping through curtains*)

Yes – yes. Say – oh – tell her what you please . . . : only the first two words of this speech appear in the private edition: Jones evidently decided that Nepean's admission needed to be made more sympathetic.

(LADY ROSAMUND *enters.*)

GILBERT: You — (*Going towards curtains,* SIR CHRISTOPHER *intercepts him.*)

LADY ROSAMUND: We stepped over to ask Sir Christopher's advice.

SIR CHRISTOPHER: And, strange to say, they've taken it.

GILBERT: (*trying to get to curtains*) Where is Jessica?

SIR CHRISTOPHER: (*stopping him*) No, I'm to take the message. Lady Jessica,
    your husband is waiting to take you to supper. (*to* GILBERT) At the Savoy?

GILBERT: Anywhere — I don't mind.

SIR CHRISTOPHER: At the Savoy. You've only just time to go home and dress.
        (LADY JESSICA *draws curtains aside, turns and throws a last
        agonised adieu to* FALKNER *who stands speechless and helpless.*
        LADY JESSICA *then controls her features and comes out to*
        GILBERT. *The curtains close.*)

GILBERT: Will you come home and dress and go to the Savoy to supper? (*offering
    arm*)

LADY JESSICA: Delighted (*taking his arm*).

GILBERT: And you, Rosy?

LADY ROSAMUND: I can't. (*looking at watch*) It's nearly ten o'clock! Good
    night, Sir Christopher. Good night, dearest (*kissing* LADY JESSICA). Good
    night, Gilbert. Take care of her, or you'll lose her. Excuse my running away,
    I must get back to my poor old Freddie. (*Exit* LADY ROSAMUND.
    FALKNER'*s face appears through the curtains.* LADY JESSICA *sees it.*)

SIR CHRISTOPHER: Good night, Lady Jessica, and goodbye!

LADY JESSICA: Good night, Sir Christopher, and — (*at* FALKNER) one last
    'Goodbye'. (*She looks towards curtains as if about to break away from*
    GILBERT *and go to* FALKNER.)

SIR CHRISTOPHER: Good night, Nepean!

GILBERT: Good night, Deering.

SIR CHRISTOPHER: Try and keep her. She's worth the keeping.

GILBERT: I'll try. What would you like for supper, Jess?

LADY JESSICA: (*looking at* FALKNER) Could they give me some *sauce
    Arcadienne*? (*Exeunt* LADY JESSICA *and* GILBERT. SIR CHRISTOPHER
    goes towards door with them;* FALKNER *comes forward in great despair
    from curtains, throws himself into chair against table, buries his face in his
    hands.*)

SIR CHRISTOPHER: (*Goes to him very affectionately.*) Come! Come! My dear old
    Ned! This will never do! And all for a woman! They aren't worth it. (*softly*)
    Except one! They aren't worth it. Come, buckle on your courage! There's
    work in front of you, and fame and honour! And I must take you out and
    bring you back with flying colours! Come! Come! My dear old fellow!

FALKNER: Let me be for a minute, Kit. Let me be!
        (*Enter* BEATRICE. SIR CHRISTOPHER *goes to her.*)

Savoy: hotel and restaurant on the Strand, adjacent to the Savoy Theatre, opened by the
impresario Richard D'Oyly Carte in 1889.
Could they . . . Arcadienne: Gilbert's question, Lady Jessica's final line and her backward
glance omitted in French's edition: cf. introduction, p. 20 above.

BEATRICE: What's the matter?

SIR CHRISTOPHER: Hush! Poor old chap! He's hard hit! Everybody else seems to be making a great mess of their love affairs. We won't make a mess of ours?

BEATRICE: No. (*Goes to* FALKNER.) You'll get over this, Ned? We'll help you. You'll get over it?

FALKNER: (*rising with great determination*) Yes, I shall pull round. I'll try! I'll try! Tomorrow, Kit? We start tomorrow?

SIR CHRISTOPHER: (*putting one arm around each affectionately*) Tomorrow! My wife! My friend! My two comrades!

    Curtain

APPENDIX: The text of *The Silver King*

The Silver King was written by Jones in collaboration with Henry Herman and Wilson Barrett. In the autumn of 1885 Herman put around the story that Jones had robbed him of his rightful share in the credit for the play's success. Jones responded with a letter to the editor of *The Era*, setting out his version of the play's composition. This was published on 12 September 1885. Jones recalled that work on the melodrama had begun in the winter and spring of 1881–2: 'The understanding was that if we could get a satisfactory plot between us, I was to do the whole of the writing and the fees were to be shared.' He was frank about the origins of the play, admitting that it contained 'not one single new or original situation . . . in the sense that nothing like it had been done before', and instanced a short story in *Good Words*, an unpublished novel of his own and *East Lynne* as contributing to the plot. Barrett had made suggestions (including the omission of Nelly's parents from the play and the business of Denver hearing the children sing in act III). Herman had written one line only: 'An angel from heaven has sent it!' at the end of act III. The play's 'thoroughly English' tone showed that it could have been written only by a native, whereas Herman had 'not a drop of English blood in him' and could hardly speak English properly.

On 19 September *The Era* printed Herman's reply. He quoted a letter which he claimed Jones had written to him on 6 June 1882: 'Am getting on famously; am knee-deep in the snow, and starvation. It is coming out immensely strong. The more I write, the more I am filled with admiration for the man who conceived it . . . ' Herman insisted that he was responsible for substantial portions of the dialogue, including the recognition scene between Jaikes and Denver in act III and the 'dream' speech in act IV, which he had 'dictated' to Jones. Moreover, the central idea of an innocent man supposing himself guilty was his invention (he set a date and place to it) and Jones had devised 'no single scene, part or portion of the plot (except of the most trifling and incidental kind) in the play'. Barrett had called on him (as an experienced hand) to make 'an alteration in the sketch of Deaf Dicky' because 'the character of Denver in act four required more strength'. Jones's claim to sole credit for another play on which Herman had worked had been made during the latter's illness and W.G. Wills was playing the same game with *Claudian*, which had been written along lines laid down by Herman. Jones's arguments in the letter of 12 September showed that 'as a commercial traveller of experience, he knew extremely well how to protect his financial interests'.

In its context this remark was an ineffectual sneer at Jones's background, but it contained a good deal of truth. Jones was adept and energetic in defending his interests, as his correspondence with managers (particularly that with Palmer and Wallack in Harvard Theatre Collection) amply demonstrates. He seems to have had the support of the paper's editor, for Herman's letter was accompanied by an editorial regretting the controversy and offering no judgement beyond the reflection that collaboration breeds such disputes; a repudiation of the claims respecting *Claudian* by Wills; and Jones's reply, which took the form of a letter from Charles

Cathcart, a stage manager at the Princess's during the period in question. Although no editorial verdict was offered, the scale obviously tipped in Jones's favour. Cathcart's letter (dated 15 September) offered decisive evidence, and furnished a picture of the author's role during rehearsals:

> ... It has been my duty to hold the manuscripts of the plays at rehearsals, and to note down any alterations [Barrett] made or wished to have made in the construction and dialogue thereof. The alterations made in my presence and in Mr Herman's absence by Mr Barrett in *The Silver King*, and, indeed, in *Claudian*, were so numerous that I can only wonder at Mr Herman's assertion that 'The story and whole scheme of *The Silver King*, *the working out of the details*, and the construction of the same are mine.'
>
> I have repeatedly heard Mr Barrett give you [Jones] instructions to alter scenes and rewrite dialogue in *The Silver King*, and have been witness to the fact that you have accepted Mr Barrett's suggestions and adopted them; indeed, I have received some in your handwriting ...

The scope of the alterations made to *The Silver King* in its progress from Jones's desk to the stage of the Princess's and, later, into print can be gauged from three bodies of evidence. A volume of manuscript drafts was given to the Bodleian Library in 1929 by Jones's daughter; a manuscript of the play, deposited with the Lord Chamberlain for licensing purposes, is now in the British Library (MS Add. 53282 (D)); a manuscript used in New York as a promptbook by Osmond Tearle is now in the Theatre Research Collection of New York Public Library at the Lincoln Center. When Jones prepared the play for publication in 1903 he cut two entire scenes which had appeared in both the licensing copy and the promptbook and made numerous alterations in the dialogue, the general tendency of which was to tone down the more rhetorical and pious passages. The intention seems to have been to maintain the play's vigour and integrity as a melodrama while conceding that audiences in the two decades since it first appeared had grown less tolerant of some aspects of melodramatic style. These alterations were part of a process that had its beginnings in the winter and spring of 1881—2.

Among the major revisions requested by Barrett after reading the first draft (Jones recalled in his letter to *The Era*) was the rearrangement of the first act, which originally contained too much information, incidental character-sketching and local colour. One of the drafts in the Bodleian volume suggests why such changes were called for. In this early version Denver's parents-in-law are waiting, together with Jaikes and Florence (i.e. Nelly) for the hero to return from Epsom. The scene is the exterior of their home in Clapham. Nelly affirms that, whatever her parents say about him, she would rather live in a hovel with Claud (i.e. Wilfred) Denver than in a palace with Geoffrey Ware, the eligible but unprepossessing suitor whom she rejected in favour of her childhood sweetheart. Her mother is particularly unhappy about the falling-off in the family's status that Denver's fecklessness has brought about ('To think that ever I should have come to live in Clapham!'). Ware arrives, taunts Florence with her poor choice of husbands and reveals to the audience that Denver owes him a thousand pounds. When Denver at last arrives home after his unsuccessful day at the Derby he makes the first of a series of public threats to kill Ware. He has been drinking and has acquired a gun to shoot himself with, but he is prepared to use it on Ware. Denver goes inside, and Ware takes the opportunity to make another attempt on Florence's constancy. Denver overhears this, rushes on and reiterates his threat to Ware. In the second scene, the exterior of the Wheatsheaf public house, Jones brings on a number of low-life characters, including a precociously debauched potboy whose sideline is running a book on horse-racing. The plot involving Coombe, Corkett and Baxter gets under way and the action shifts to the interior of the Wheatsheaf, where Corkett is throwing around his Derby winnings. Denver once again announces in public his homicidal intentions. The act then proceeds to incidents which appear in the same order and similar form in subsequent versions: Corkett suborned as an accomplice, Ware's death, the chloroforming and awakening of Denver, the hero's flight.

In the process of revision the material originally spread over three scenes was concentrated in one, set in the skittle-alley of the Wheatsheaf. The message that Denver has come down in the world was conveyed in Jaikes's narration (pp. 39—40 above) and most of the moralising references to drink and gambling were cut. It is typical of the draft's crude distribution of these references that Ware, about to leave his office, announces that he will 'just have time to pop round to the Duke's Head for an hour and collar my sweepstakes'. Like Corkett and the potboy, Ware is made a victim of the gambling fever.

The religious tone of certain passages was modified. In one manuscript draft of the first scene of act II the fugitive Denver is assured by his wife, 'I have faith in you yet — yes, darling, you repent, and you will be pardoned.' Denver swears to this effect: ' . . . and hear me, witness, heaven, — listen to my oath — if once I shake myself free of this crime, all my future shall show the deepest and bitterest repentance of my soul. I have sworn it.' When in act IV Denver learns that he is in fact innocent he announces that he has 'come to life again to a new life, a life of hope, a life of retribution'. In a draft of the final scene he exclaims: 'Nell it was your faith that gave me faith in myself; it was your love that supported me in all my wanderings — it was your prayers that kept me true to heaven and home — and the same dear faith and love will be with me to the end.'

In the licensing copy the play has arrived at the overall design common to the New York promptcopy and (except for the omitted scenes) the printed text. Changes in the dialogue make piety less dominant than it is in the manuscript drafts, although the role played by drink in Denver's fall is still insisted on. Much is made of the sentimental associations of the countryside around the Grange. When she is reunited with Denver Nelly becomes hysterical, unable to believe her eyes, but she eventually cries out: 'Yes, this is my sweetheart, my brown-headed mischievous boy, that I steal out to meet down by the brook: and I shall be there tonight, they shall never make me marry anybody but you.' The stages of Denver's climb back to grace are still firmly marked. At the end of act III, after Nelly's defiance of Coombe, Denver has a jubilant aside: 'The first step towards my atonement!' In act IV he surreptitiously cuts a lock of his daughter's hair, which he kisses fondly as he leaves the stage, murmuring 'The second step towards my atonement.' His response to the discovery of his innocence is more vengeful and less sanctimonious than it had been in manuscript, but the pieties of the final scene are couched in language that is more figurative and scriptural than Jones had formerly allowed himself:

NELLY: Oh, Will, God has been very kind to me.

DENVER: Was ever man led and protected as I have been? Goodness and mercy have followed me all the days of my life — my mistakes, my follies, aye even all my sins have all worked together for my good — my tears have brought a harvest of peace and joy. Oh, Nell! my heart is too full.

In Tearle's promptbook most of the sententious passages have been further abbreviated and the 'sign-posting' of Denver's redemption is omitted. The exclamations at the end of act III, the business with the lock of hair and the references to being 'led and protected' have gone. In addition to the differences between the manuscript copy on which the promptbook is based and the licensing copy, there are marks which indicate a number of alterations made during the use of the book.

As well as the loss of two scenes and the changes in some of the play's language, the published edition of *The Silver King* differs in a number of particulars from the three manuscript versions discussed above. The scene (act II, scene 2) at Euston station has been simplified: the promptbook begins with the tipsy passenger and the entrance of a Lord and Lady (with the Inspector's deferential behaviour to them) before Denver arrives and has his exchange with the newsboy. A comic episode involving a lady passenger, her luggage and a cabman precedes Baxter's arrival and his discovery that Denver has escaped. In French's edition the omission of the 'country lane' scene (p. 224 below) produces a minor inconsistency in that the audience is not told that Denver shaves off his beard. A fanciful passage in which Jaikes advocates the imaginary division of the shilling into forty-eight parts has been cut from act III, scene 2. Several speeches are abbreviated in French's edition, notably Denver's frustrated outburst on p. 89 ('Shut out . . . !'), Denver's revelation of his identity on p. 94, Olive's speech on p. 95, Denver's speech beginning 'There stands the murderer of Geoffrey Ware!' (p. 101) and Nelly's reply. In a number of places French's stage directions need clarification with reference to the promptbook. This has been done silently in the present edition.

One of the two scenes which appeared in earlier texts but which were omitted from French's edition — that in which Denver describes his escape from the train — is printed below as it appears in Tearle's promptbook. It is accompanied by the text of an alteration necessary on p. 000 of the present edition if the scene is to be restored in performance. The other full scene also absent from French's edition, but not included here, is a preparation for the assembly of all the characters to be involved in the dénouement. Denver, still in his disguise as Deaf Dicky, returns to an 'elegant room' in his London house and instructs the astonished Selwyn to make preparations for his journey to the Grange. Jaikes arrives and tells him that Nelly now knows the identity of her benefactor. They leave together, and Skinner appears. He is looking for 'Franklin' and elicits his whereabouts from Selwyn. The villain leaves in pursuit of Denver. The final visitor is Baxter, who emerges from behind the window-curtain and sets off to follow everyone else. The scene holds back the action considerably and contains nothing that could not be supplied by slight alterations (in French's edition) to the final act, or left to the audience's imagination. The picture of 'Deaf Dicky' amid the elegant surroundings of 'John Franklin's' house may have been of some value, but the manner in which Jones accounted for the subsequent meeting up of his characters was laboured and added nothing to the play's interest.

(*a*) *Additional scene from Tearle's promptbook*
[To follow p. 57 of the present edition.]
Scene Third. 1st Grooves. A country lane — Fallen tree set centre to fly off.
DENVER *limps on.*
DENVER: I could bear it no longer! Another minute of that horror and I should
have gone mad. I kept on hearing voices. 'Stop the train.' 'Stop the train.'
And the wheels kept on rattle-rattle. Murder — murder — murder! Thank
heaven I'm out of it — and alive! What a fearful jump! What a mercy I was
not dashed to pieces! I've hurt this foot though! I must rest a moment. Did
anybody see me jump from the train, I wonder? The guard — perhaps — he
may have stopped the train, or if not they will be sure to search it when it
gets to Rugby. It will be found out that I have escaped, and then the hue and
cry will be raised for me all along the line — I mustn't stay here — I must get
away as fast as I can. — Oh! this foot! I've sprained it — I wonder what time
it is — it must be past eight o'clock — past eight o'clock! And yesterday at
this time I was innocent — Yesterday, he was alive, and I could laugh and play
the fool, and now. — Oh God! put back thy Universe and give me yesterday —
I must be at least thirty miles away from London. If I could reach some large
town there might be some chance for me. The disguise! I must shave, and
change these clothes and drown them! My angel wife — how thoughtful she
was — shall I never see her again — and the children?
    If I could but get to another line of rail — The Great Western branches out
somewhere near here — Which path shall I take? If I dared to ask the way —
    If there is a Providence that watches over wretched men — surely never
man needed it more than I do now. Oh, heaven! give me strength, give me
courage. Direct my steps — work out some way of escape for me — Not for
my own sake — not to shield me from the just punishment of my crime — but
for the sake of my dear wife and innocent children, who have never done
harm. Spare me to make atonement for the evil I have done. Which path shall
I take? (*looking off.*) Ah! this seems the quietest, I'll take this. (*bus. with leg*)
You must — you shall carry me — I must walk — I must drag on somehow —
Courage! Courage! (*Exit.*)
        Change scene.

(*b*) [For substitution on p. 61 of the present edition.]
DENVER: (*alone*) How long will it last? How long shall I hold out? They are looking for me now! There's a description of me in every police station in England
tonight — perhaps they have found out where I left the train and have put
bloodhounds on my track — Hark! What's that? (*Goes to door.*) Have they
traced me here? Where am I? How far from a station? I must have dragged
twenty miles today. (*Sees timetable on wall.*) Ah! Great Western timetables!
There must be a station somewhere near. (*Gets to table.*)

THE PLAYS OF
HENRY ARTHUR JONES

This list includes only the performed plays. An account of Jones's unpublished and unperformed work will be found in appendix A of Doris Arthur Jones's *Life and Letters of Henry Arthur Jones* (1930).

It's Only Round the Corner, produced Theatre Royal, Exeter, 11 December 1878; revived Grand Theatre, Leeds, as *Harmony Restored*, 13 August 1879; Strand Theatre, London, as *Harmony*, 14 January 1884; Lyceum, New York, as *The Organist*, May 1892.

Hearts of Oak, or, a Chip of the Old Block, produced Exeter, 29 May 1879 (revised and published as *Honour Bright*, Ilfracombe, 1879).

Elopement, produced Oxford, 19 August 1879.

A Clerical Error, produced Court Theatre, London, 13 October 1879.

An Old Master, produced Princess's Theatre, London, 6 November 1880.

His Wife, produced Sadler's Wells Theatre, London, 16 April 1881.

Home Again, produced Oxford, 7 September 1881.

A Bed of Roses, produced Globe Theatre, London, 26 January 1882.

The Silver King, produced Princess's Theatre, London, 16 November 1882, written in collaboration with Henry Herman.

Breaking a Butterfly, adapted from Ibsen's *A Doll's House*, in collaboration with Henry Herman. Produced Prince's Theatre, London, 3 March 1884.

Chatterton, written in collaboration with Henry Herman. Produced Princess's Theatre, London, 22 May 1884.

Saints and Sinners, produced Prince of Wales's Theatre, Greenwich, 17 September 1884; Margate, 22 September 1884; and Vaudeville Theatre, London, 25 September 1884.

Hoodman Blind, written in collaboration with Wilson Barrett. Produced Princess's Theatre, London, 18 August 1885.

The Lord Harry, written in collaboration with Wilson Barrett. Produced Princess's Theatre, London, 18 February 1886.

The Noble Vagabond, produced Princess's Theatre, London, 22 December 1886.

Hard Hit, produced Haymarket Theatre, London, 17 January 1887.

Heart of Hearts, produced Vaudeville Theatre, London, matinée 3 November 1887.

Wealth, produced Haymarket Theatre, London, 27 April 1889.

The Middleman, produced Shaftesbury Theatre, London, 27 August 1889.

Judah, produced Shaftesbury Theatre, London, 21 May 1890.

Sweet Will, produced New Club, Covent Garden, London, 5 March 1887; Shaftesbury Theatre, London, matinée 25 July 1890.

The Deacon, produced Shaftesbury Theatre, London, matinée 27 August 1890.

The Dancing Girl, produced Haymarket Theatre, London, 15 January 1891.

The Crusaders, produced Avenue Theatre, London, 2 November 1891.

The Bauble Shop, produced Criterion Theatre, London, 26 January 1893.

The Tempter, produced Haymarket Theatre, London, 20 September 1893.

The Masqueraders, produced St James's Theatre, London, 28 April 1894.

The Case of Rebellious Susan, produced Criterion Theatre, London, 3 October 1894.

The Triumph of the Philistines, and how Mr Jorgan preserved the Morals of Market Pewbury under Very Trying Circumstances, produced St James's Theatre, London, 11 May 1895.

Michael and his Lost Angel, produced Lyceum Theatre, London, 15 January 1896.

The Rogue's Comedy, produced Garrick Theatre, London, 21 April 1896.

The Physician, produced Criterion Theatre, London, 25 March 1897.

The Liars, produced Criterion Theatre, London, 6 October 1897.

The Manoeuvres of Jane, produced Haymarket Theatre, London, 29 October 1898.

Carnac Sahib, produced Her Majesty's Theatre, London, 12 April 1899.

The Lackey's Carnival, produced Duke of York's Theatre, London, 26 September 1900.

Mrs Dane's Defence, produced Wyndham's Theatre, London, 9 October 1900.

The Princess's Nose, produced Duke of York's Theatre, London, 11 March 1902.

Chance, the Idol, produced Wyndham's Theatre, London, 9 September 1902.

Whitewashing Julia, produced Garrick Theatre, London, 2 March 1903.

Joseph Entangled, produced Haymarket Theatre, London, 19 January 1904.

The Chevaleer, produced Garrick Theatre, London, 27 August 1904.

The Heroic Stubbs, produced Terry's Theatre, London, 24 January 1906.

The Hypocrites, copyright performance Grand Theatre, Hull, and first American performance Hudson Theatre, New York, 30 August 1906; Hicks's Theatre, London, 27 August 1907.

The Goal, produced Chicago, 1907; Palace Theatre, London, matinée 20 May 1919.

The Galilean's Victory, copyright performance Stockport, 25 September 1907; Knickerbocker Theatre, New York (as *The Evangelist*), 30 September 1907.

Dolly Reforming Herself, produced Haymarket Theatre, London, 3 November 1908; one-act version (*Dolly's Little Bills*) Hippodrome Theatre, London, 8 July 1912.

The Knife, produced Palace Theatre, London, 20 December 1909.

Fall in, Rookies!, produced Alhambra Theatre, London, 24 October 1910.

We Can't be as Bad as All That, produced Nazimova Theatre, New York, 30 December 1910; Hippodrome, Croydon, 4 September 1916.

The Ogre, produced St James's Theatre, London, 11 September 1911.

Lydia Gilmore, produced Lyceum Theatre, New York, 1 February 1912.

Mary Goes First, produced Playhouse Theatre, London, 18 September 1913.

The Lie, produced Harris's Theatre, New York, 24 December 1914; New Theatre, London, 13 October 1923.

Cock o' the Walk, produced Cohan Theatre, New York, 27 December 1915.

The Pacifists, produced Opera House, Southport, 27 August 1917; St James's Theatre, London, 4 September 1917.

Grace Mary, published in *The Theatre of Ideas*, 1915; produced Liverpool Playhouse, 10 October 1930.

BIBLIOGRAPHY

The two most useful published sources of information on Jones's life and works are Doris Arthur Jones's *Life and Letters* and the annotated bibliography of writings about Jones compiled by J.P. Wearing. Goodenough's thesis and Archer's *Play-Making* include the dramatist's responses to questions on his work. The chapter entitled 'The Drawing-Room' in Trewin's study of Edwardian theatre and Wallis's article on *Michael and his Lost Angel* are the most substantial recent discussions of Jones's plays in their theatrical and literary context, and a similar view of his position in the history of Victorian and Edwardian drama is offered by Booth's *Prefaces* and Rowell's *The Victorian Theatre*. The reprinted criticism of Beerbohm and Shaw offers the most accessible source of contemporary opinion on the plays.

Biographical

Jones, Doris Arthur. *The Life and Letters of Henry Arthur Jones* (1930)
    What a Life! (1932)
Laurence, Dan H., ed. *Collected Letters of Bernard Shaw, 1874–1897* (1965) and
    1897–1910 (1972)
Thompson, Marjorie. 'Henry Arthur Jones and Wilson Barrett: Some Correspondence, 1879–1904', *Theatre Notebook*, 11 (1957) 42–50
Wearing, J.P., ed. *The Collected Letters of Sir Arthur Wing Pinero* (Minneapolis, 1974)

Bibliographical

Jones, Doris Arthur. *Life and Letters*, appendices A and B
Nicoll, Allardyce. *English Drama 1900–1930: The Beginnings of the Modern Period* (Cambridge, 1973)
    A History of English Drama, 1660–1900, Volume V: Late Nineteenth Century Drama, 1850–1900, 2nd edn (Cambridge, 1967)
Wearing, J.P. 'Henry Arthur Jones: An Annotated Bibliography of Writings about him', *English Literature in Transition*, 22 (1979) 160–228

Criticism

Archer, William. *About the Theatre: Essays and Studies* (1886)
    English Dramatists of Today (1882)
    The Old Drama and the New: An Essay in Re-valuation (1923)
    Play-Making: A Manual of Craftsmanship (1912)
    The Theatrical 'World' for 1893 (1894; subsequent volumes 'of' 1894, 1895, 1896 and 1897 were published in 1895, 1896, 1897 and 1898 respectively)
Bailey, James Osler. 'Science in the Drama of Henry Arthur Jones', in Hill Shine, ed., *Brooker Memorial Studies: Eight Essays on Victorian Literature in Memory of John Manning Brooker, 1881–1949* (1950)
Beerbohm, Max. *Around Theatres* (1953)
    Last Theatres (1970)

More Theatres (1969)

Booth, Michael. *Prefaces to Nineteenth Century English Theatre* (Manchester, 1981)

Cordell, Richard A. *Henry Arthur Jones and the Modern Drama* (New York, 1932)

Filon, Augustin. *The English Stage, Being an Account of the Victorian Drama*, translated by Frederick Whyte, with an introduction by Henry Arthur Jones (1897)

Goodenough, Aubrey Ward. 'Henry Arthur Jones: A Study in Dramatic Compromise', unpublished PhD dissertation, Iowa State University, 1920

Northend, Marjorie. 'Henry Arthur Jones and the Development of the Modern English Drama', *Review of English Studies* 18 (1942) 448–63

Rowell, George. *The Victorian Theatre: A Survey*, 2nd edn (Cambridge, 1980)

Theatre in the Age of Irving (Oxford, 1981)

'Wyndham of Wyndham's', in Joseph W. Donohue, ed., *The Theatrical Manager in England and America: Player of a Dangerous Game* (Princeton, 1970)

Sawyer, Newell S. *The Comedy of Manners from Sheridan to Maugham* (Philadelphia, 1931)

Shaw, G.B. *Our Theatres in the Nineties* (3 vols, 1932)

Taylor, John Russell. *The Rise and Fall of the Well-Made Play* (1967)

Trewin, J.C. *The Edwardian Theatre* (Oxford, 1976)

Trewin, Wendy. *All on Stage: Charles Wyndham and the Alberys* (1980)

Wallis, Bruce. '*Michael and his Lost Angel*: Archetypal Conflict and Victorian Life', *The Victorian Newsletter*, no. 56 (Fall, 1979) 20–6

Wauchope, George Armstrong. 'Henry Arthur Jones and the Social Drama', *Sewanee Review*, 29 (1921) 147–52

Weales, Gerald. *Religion in the Modern English Drama* (Philadelphia, 1961)